# SPATIAL COMPUTING: ISSUES IN VISION, MULTIMEDIA AND VISUALIZATION TECHNOLOGIES

**SERIES IN MACHINE PERCEPTION AND ARTIFICIAL INTELLIGENCE***

*Editors:* **H. Bunke** (Univ. Bern, Switzerland)
**P. S. P. Wang** (Northeastern Univ., USA)

---

Vol. 17: Applications of AI, Machine Vision and Robotics
(Eds. *K. L. Boyer, L. Stark and H. Bunke*)

Vol. 18: VLSI and Parallel Computing for Pattern Recognition and AI
(Ed. *N. Ranganathan*)

Vol. 19: Parallel Image Analysis: Theory and Applications
(Eds. *L. S. Davis, K. Inoue, M. Nivat, A. Rosenfeld and P. S. P. Wang*)

Vol. 20: Picture Interpretation: A Symbolic Approach
(Eds. *S. Dance, T. Caelli and Z.-Q. Lin*)

Vol. 21: Modelling and Planning for Sensor Based Intelligent Robot Systems
(Eds. *H. Bunke, T. Kanade and H. Noltemeier*)

Vol. 22: Machine Vision for Advanced Production
(Eds. *M. Pietikainen and L. F. Pau*)

Vol. 23: Machine Learning and Perception
(Eds. *G. Tasini, F. Esposito, V. Roberto and P. Zingaretti*)

Vol. 24: Spatial Computing: Issues in Vision, Multimedia and Visualization Technologies
(Eds. *T. Caelli, Peng Lam and H. Bunke*)

Vol. 25: Studies in Pattern Recognition Memorial Volume in Honor of K S Fu
(Eds. *H. Freeman*)

Vol. 26: Neural Network Training Using Genetic Algorithms
(Eds. *L. C. Jain, R. P. Johnson and A. F. J. van Rooij*)

*Forthcoming*

Vol. 27: Intelligent Robots — Sensing, Modelling & Planning
(Eds. *B. Bolles, H. Noltemeier and H. Bunke*)

Document Analysis II
(Eds. *J. J. Hull and S. Taylor*)

Pattern Recognition
(*A. Kandel and M. Friedman*)

Bankcheck Processing
(*Eds. S. Impedovo, P. S. P. Wang and H. Bunke*)

*For the complete list of titles in this series, please write to the Publisher.

Series in Machine Perception and Artificial Intelligence - Vol. 24

# SPATIAL COMPUTING: ISSUES IN VISION, MULTIMEDIA AND VISUALIZATION TECHNOLOGIES

Editors

**T Caelli & Peng Lam**

*Department of Computer Science*
*Curtin University of Technology*
*1987 Perth, WA, Australia*

**Horst Bunke**

*Institut für Informatik und Angewandte Mathematik*
*Universität Bern*
*Neubrückstrasse 10, CH-3012*
*Bern, Switzerland*

*Published by*

World Scientific Publishing Co. Pte. Ltd.
P O Box 128, Farrer Road, Singapore 912805
*USA office:* Suite 1B, 1060 Main Street, River Edge, NJ 07661
*UK office:* 57 Shelton Street, Covent Garden, London WC2H 9HE

**British Library Cataloguing-in-Publication Data**
A catalogue record for this book is available from the British Library.

**SPATIAL COMPUTING: ISSUES IN VISION, MULTIMEDIA AND VISUALIZATION TECHNOLOGIES**



ISBN 981-02-2924-0



Printed in Singapore by Uto-Print

# CONTENTS

# FOREWORD

TERRY CAELLI and PENG LAM

*Department of Computer Science*
*Curtin University of Technology*
*1987 Perth, WA, Australia*

HORST BUNKE

*Institut für Informatik und Angewandte Mathematik*
*Universität Bern, Neubrückstrasse 10*
*CH-3012, Bern, Switzerland*

The book is a collection of papers that were presented at the Spatial Computing Workshop held at Curtin University, Perth from the 2nd to the 3rd December, 1995. The chapters represent the bringing together of experts from computer vision, visualization, multi-media and geographic information systems (GIS) to share common interests, problems and technologies. Problems common to all these areas include the encoding of synthetic and natural structures, the efficient detection, recognition, display, interpretation and retrieval of features and patterns. It is our hope that the reader will see these common problems emerging from the selected papers and form a general view of spatial computing.

The chapters essentially fall into two groups. The first deals with computer vision and interpretation systems. The second covers representative papers in visualization, multi-media and GIS. In the first section, topics vary from recent Bayesian formulations for image processing (Liu), feature extraction (West), recognition/matching techniques (Bunke, Caelli, Dickinson) and spatial reasoning (Matsuyama). One of the emerging themes in this domain is the need to consider domain knowledge or constraints in both high- and low-level vision processes. Such knowledge can be approached and modeled by Bayesian methods, machine learning or computer-aided design (CAD)/graphical models.

The same theme is evident in the second group of papers. Whether it be with visualization in general (Maeder, Robertson) or GIS in particular (Gahegan) — domain knowledge plays a critical role in determining what to display and how to display it or even if it can be displayed. Equally in multi-media the representation of image data and its relation to domain knowledge play critical roles in the development of efficient and robust image database query techniques (Shearer, Smith).

In all, then, this collection of papers clearly points to the need for communication between researchers in these different areas of spatial computing and it is the hope that this volume will help this dialogue come to fruition. This collection of papers has also been published as a special issue of the *International Journal of Pattern Recognition and Artificial Intelligence* (Volume 11, Numbers 1 & 2, 1997).

Finally, we want to thank all authors for a very friendly and stimulating atmosphere during the Workshop and for their co-operation in the preparation of these manuscripts.



Spatial Computing: Issues in Vision, Multimedia and Visualization Technologies (1997) 1

# BAYESIAN PARADIGMS IN IMAGE PROCESSING

ZHI-QIANG LIU

*Computer Vision and Machine Intelligence Lab. (CVMIL)*
*Department of Computer Science, The University of Melbourne*
*Parkville, Victoria 3052, Australia*
*E-mail: zliu@cs.mu.OZ.AU*

A large number of image and spatial information processing problems involves the estimation of the intrinsic image information from observed images, for instance, image restoration, image registration, image partition, depth estimation, shape reconstruction and motion estimation. These are *inverse* problems and generally ill-posed. Such estimation problems can be readily formulated by Bayesian models which infer the desired image information from the measured data. Bayesian paradigms have played a very important role in spatial data analysis for over three decades and have found many successful applications. In this paper, we discuss several aspects of Bayesian paradigms: uncertainty present in the observed image, prior distribution modeling, Bayesian-based estimation techniques in image processing, particularly, the maximum *a posteriori* estimator and the Kalman filtering theory, robustness, and Markov random fields and applications.

*Keywords*: Bayesian models, Markov random fields, image processing, Gaussian distribution, robustness, Kalman filter.

## 1. INTRODUCTION

In low-level vision tasks there are basically two types of processes: *image processing* such as image restoration, partition, and registration; *intrinsic image formation*[2] which includes estimation of depth, surface, motion, and stereo. All these processes require to extract or to recover certain properties given the observed image data. For instance, in image restoration, we are required to remove degradations due to noise and blurring introduced by the imaging sensor; whereas in image partition our task is to partition the image field into patches based on some homogeneity criteria (e.g. textures, surfaces in the image). In motion estimation, we need to infer qualitative and/or quantitative object motion information from observed image sequences. As low-level vision is the basic and integral part of any vision system, it has great impact on the usefulness of the entire system and deserves considerable attention and efforts in designing vision systems.

Due mainly to the physical limitations present in the imaging device and imaging conditions, the observed image is usually the result of mixed and distorted sources of information such as illumination, reflectivity, surface shape, and projective geometry. The low-level vision process produces an improved version of the observed image in terms of reduced noise, good contrast, or less distortion; and useful intrinsic image information in terms of depth, surface shape, or object motion. These in turn make higher-level vision tasks possible.

The problems associated with the low-level vision are to a large extent of an *inverse* nature.[42] The inverse problem arising in low-level vision is generally ill-posed[81] and difficult to solve due to lack of constraint and incomplete information — sometimes very little knowledge is available about what is being viewed. There



Spatial Computing: Issues in Vision, Multimedia and Visualization Technologies (1997) 3–33

are basically two approaches to this problem: regularization[93] which imposes additional weak smoothness constraints in the form of stabilizers. In order to solve such problems certain assumptions are necessary based on experience or previous data. For example, in 3D surface reconstruction from depth maps, surface smoothness is usually assumed. Another approach is based on the Bayesian theorem, which assumes a prior statistical distribution for the data being estimated, and models the image formation and sensing phenomena as stochastic or noisy processes. For example, when solving the image restoration problem it is assumed that the probability distribution of the contaminating noise is known and that the blurring effects can be modeled by some transfer functions. It is interesting to also notice that regularization is in fact a special case of the more general Bayesian approach to the formulation of inverse problems.

As mentioned before, the physical limitations in the imaging process often result in uncertainties in the image data. Imaging sensory induced uncertainties are (a) noise, (b) blurring, (c) incomplete data to sufficiently obtain a unique solution or it may require additional measurements (data-fusion). From the modeling point of view, we may have the following uncertainties:

(a) inaccurate prior models and unknown parameters due to insufficient knowledge about the nature of the process,
(b) space and time variables in many image processing problems.

In order to develop highly robust vision systems it is imperative that these uncertainties be handled and quantified at the early stages. Estimation techniques should be able to recover as much as possible the intrinsic nature or features in the image. Bayesian paradigms allow us to handle these uncertainties and provide a natural framework for developing powerful statistical estimation methods. As the Bayesian approach uses explicit probability models to incorporate our prior knowledge about the world and sensor in image processing, it combines effects of both prior probabilities and likelihood. This enables us to use the Bayesian formula to integrate our belief in (or intuition or knowledge about) the world. Such a framework allows us to consider image processing tasks as statistical inference problems. One important aspect of the Bayesian framework is its ability to assign confidence interval estimates through probability measures. This provides estimation algorithms with additional flexibility and control.[7] Further, the Bayesian theory provides us with a unified framework for developing a variety of algorithms for image analysis. Many recursive estimation algorithms have been developed in the Bayesian framework. These methods have been successfully applied to image processing problems such as image enhancement, feature extraction, image sequence processing, depth map generation, and real-time tracking of moving objects.

In this paper we will discuss some general aspects of Bayesian paradigms in low-level vision, or more specifically, in image processing tasks. These include image restoration, texture analysis, edge and boundary description, depth estimation, surface reconstruction, stereo, object motion, and shape, etc. We will describe the modeling process, some major estimation algorithms, the problems and dilemma, and recent developments and applications.

## 2. MODELS IN IMAGE PROCESSING

As shown in Fig. 1, in the imaging process we generally have two planes, namely, the object plane where the object being viewed is present and the image plane which is the image sensing media such as film. The object is perceived by an intensity distribution of some radiated energy, for instance, light illumination in normal photography, laser light in range finders, and positron emission energy in PET. The energy is then collected through the imaging system (e.g. lenses) to form the image of the object.

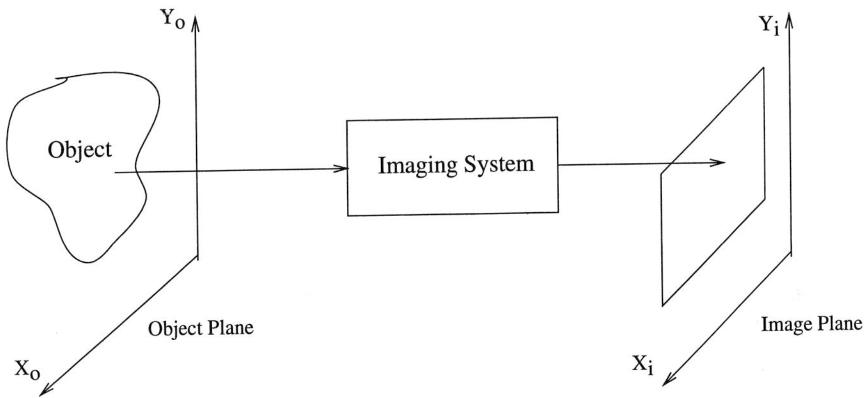


Fig. 1. Image formation.

Such a system can be depicted in terms of functional block diagrams shown in Fig. 2. The original image in fact represents the *ideal* distribution of the radiated energy (signal) $f$ from the object. The imaging system (which may include the imaging environment, e.g. under water, atmosphere) is considered as a filter with a particular transfer (point-spread) function $H$ which passes $f$. This results in blurring and geometrical distortions. For example, long term exposure of atmospheric turbulence can be modeled as

$$H_a(w_x, w_y) = \exp\left\{-\frac{w_x^2 + w_y^2}{\sigma^2}\right\}, \tag{1}$$

which is also called the Gaussian blur, whereas, horizontal camera motion blur of length $2d$ is modeled as follows,

$$h_b(i,j) = \begin{cases} 0 & j \neq 0 \ -\infty \leq i \leq \infty, \\ \dfrac{1}{2d} & j = 0 \ -d \leq i \leq d. \end{cases} \tag{2}$$

For defocused lens system with circular aperture, the blur can be approximated by a cylinder where the radius $r$ depends on the focus defect extent:

$$h_b(i,j) = \begin{cases} 0 & \sqrt{i^2 + j^2} > r, \\ \dfrac{1}{\pi r^2} & \sqrt{i^2 + j^2} \leq r. \end{cases} \tag{3}$$

It is very difficult to identify blurring models and parameters in practice. In addition, as the image sensors (e.g. film, CCD cameras) are not ideal devices, they will introduce noise $n$ into the final observed image $g$. It is often assumed that the noise is white Gaussian. However, in many imaging systems the image is formed based on counts of photon emissions (e.g. PET, SPECT). In such systems, the noise can be assumed to follow a Poisson distribution. Finally, the entire system is in general nonlinear $\phi$.

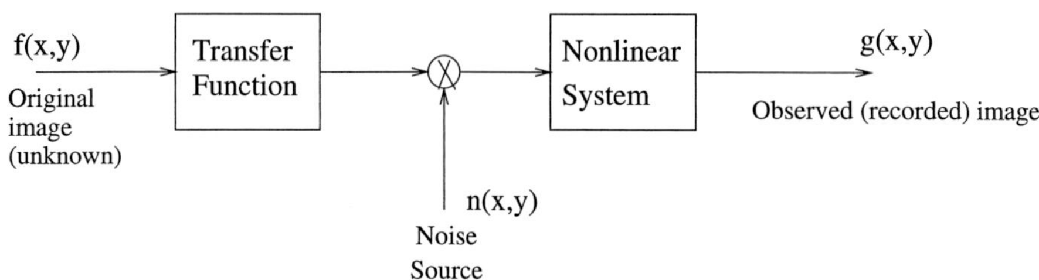


Fig. 2. Block diagram of a general imaging system.

In summary, an observed image can be generally represented by (see Fig. 2)

$$g(x,y) = \phi(Hf(x,y), n(x,y)), \tag{4}$$

where $H$ represents the point-spread function of the imaging environment, $f$ the original (ideal but unknown) image, and $n$ is the noise with some assumed properties.

In many applications, it is both natural and simple to assume additive noise. Under such an assumption, (4) can be written as follows

$$g(x,y) = \phi(Hf(x,y)) + n(x,y). \tag{5}$$

The additive noise assumption in (5) is justified on the basis of the nature of image sensors. In photoelectronic systems, the output current of the sensor is usually subject to the usual sources of thermal noise, amplifier electronic noise, etc. Such noise is to a large extent additive.[86] Although film-grain noise is signal dependent and very complex, studies have shown that assuming the signal-dependent nature of the noise does not gain much in terms of processed results.[97]

Further, if we assume that the system is linear and stationary with an additive noise as shown in Fig. 3, the general model (4) takes a much simpler form

$$g(v) = H(\theta)f(v) + n(v). \tag{6}$$

where $\theta$ is the parameter vector to be estimated, and $v$ is the variable vector: for 2D image processing problems $v = (x,y)$; for spatial-temporal image sequences, $v = (x,y,t)$, where $t$ is time; for 3D surfaces, $v = (x,y,u(x,y))$, and $(x,y)$ represents the coordinate of the pixel being computed.

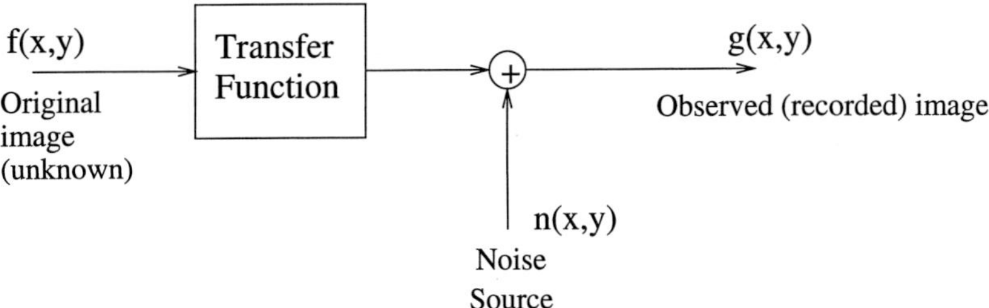


Fig. 3. Block diagram of a simplified imaging system.

## 3. BAYESIAN ESTIMATION

In image processing, there are different approaches to the model in (4). We will in this section first describe the classic least squares estimation method and discuss its problems and modifications. This leads naturally to the Bayesian approach which take both the prior model and the sensor model into account.

### 3.1. Least Squares Estimation

If (6) is to be considered as a deterministic problem, it is only a matter of finding the solution for the system. For instance, we may consider solving the following equation

$$e = g - Hf\,, \tag{7}$$

where we have dropped the variables for convenience of discussion. Letting the derivative of $\|e\|^2$ equal zero gives

$$H^T H f = H^T g\,, \tag{8}$$

which leads to the well-known result of least-squares estimator (LSE):

$$\hat{f} = (H^T H)^{-1} H^T g\,, \tag{9}$$

where $T$ denotes transpose of a vector or a matrix, and $\hat{f}$ indicates that the solution is indeed an estimate of $f$.

It is known from the Gauss–Markov theorem that LSE is optimal in all linear estimators.[36] In addition, it does not require to know or to assume the probability models for the parameter and data. However, the least-squares solution has two critical problems:

- It requires that $H$ must be of full rank. Otherwise, (9) cannot be solved without additional constraints, which happens very often in many applications. Furthermore, even if $H$ is of full rank, $H^T H$ will often be ill-conditioned resulting in numerical instability.
- It does not take into account of the prior knowledge about the process and the error distribution, which is frequently available in our practice. The use of prior knowledge will in many cases simplify the computation and obtain better estimation results.

Nevertheless, LSE has been widely used in many statistical analysis ever since its introduction by Legendre in 1805. It also found some applications[46,61] in the early days of image processing. However, Sondhi[88] reported that it is difficult to solve the image restoration problem due to the ill-conditioned nature. In order to solve the numerical instability problem present in the least squares estimator, Phillips[79] proposed the *constrained* least squares estimation method. Phillips argued that instability in the numerical solutions due to the inherent ill-conditioning is in fact contrary to our prior experience that the solution should be *smooth*. Phillips proposed to use a smoothness constraint in the original criterion for LSE solutions. This smoothness constraint is sensitive to the relative smoothness of the solution vector, and as a result, improves the numerical stability of LSE.

Hunt[46] extended the constrained LSE (CLSE) to 2D systems and applied it to image restoration with some success. In the following we briefly discuss this method.

Given the estimate $\hat{f}$ from (9), we reformulate the original problem to solve the following problem. Find $\hat{f}$, such that the following cost function is minimized

$$J(\hat{f}, C) = \hat{f}^T C^T C \hat{f}\,, \tag{10}$$

subject to

$$(g - H\hat{f})^T (g - H\hat{f}) = e^T e\,. \tag{11}$$

A simple Lagrangian minimization gives the following solution

$$\hat{f} = (H^T H + \lambda C^T C)^{-1} H^T g\,, \tag{12}$$

where $\lambda = \frac{1}{\gamma}$ and $\gamma$ is a Lagrange multiplier. As the constraint matrix $C$ was defined for 1D problems[79] which cannot be used directly for 2D estimation problems, Hunt used two different approaches, namely, the Laplacian operator and radial symmetry, to generate $C$.[46] Their experiments show that the proposed CLSE is effective for Gaussian and Dirac impulse point-spread functions and uniformly distributed white noise.

### 3.2. Bayesian Approach

If we consider that the image processing problem is of a stochastic nature and nonlinear (as shown in Eq. (5)) which requires us to estimate $f$ given observation $g$ and based on the prior knowledge about the noise. This leads naturally to the Bayesian approach:

$$p(f|g) = \frac{p(g|f)p(f)}{p(g)}\,, \tag{13}$$

where $p(g) = \sum_f p(g|f)$.

The Bayesian model (13) describes the problem of estimation of $f$ given the observation $g$ in terms of conditional probabilities with two major components:

- the prior model $p(f)$,
- the sensor model $p(g|f)$.

In other words, the *a posteriori* probability $p(f|g)$ is an expression relating to what we have learned (the prior knowledge) and what we have measured (observation) as shown in Fig. 4.

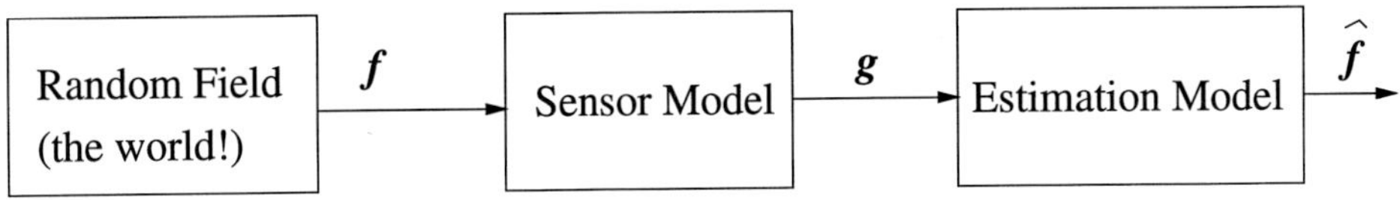


Fig. 4. The Bayesian estimation structure.

The use of Bayesian modeling for estimation in both signal processing and system identification has been well-known. Given such a model, a minimum error estimator indicates that an instance $\hat{f}$ of $f$ is present in $g$ if $p(\hat{f}|g)$ is maximum over all possible models. Such an estimator is called a *maximum a posteriori* (MAP) estimator. Given that the probability density of $g$ is independent of the hypothesis about $f$, our task is then to find $\hat{f}$ based on the minimum error criterion such that $p(g|\hat{f})p(\hat{f})$ is maximized. It is obvious that the *a posteriori* probability density function plays a central role in the general nonlinear estimation problem in the Bayesian framework.

If $p(f|g)$ is *available*, an estimate of $f$ can be determined from the posterior distribution in several ways. For instance, a common choice is the mean of the posterior distribution, i.e. the conditional expectation

$$\hat{f}_k = E(f_k|g_0, g_1, ..., g_{k-1}), \tag{14}$$

where the subscript denotes discrete time sequence. Particularly, for symmetric posterior distributions, such as Gaussian, the estimate coincides with that given in (14). Interestingly, $\hat{f}_k$ is also the value that minimizes the parameter error variance $E|f - \hat{f}_k|^2$ under very general conditions.

In practice, if the model for the prior model $p(f)$ is not known precisely, we may assume that all models are *equally* likely. This assumption results in a uniform prior distribution (which is also called *non-informative* prior) for the *a priori* probability. Consequently, we will obtain the maximum likelihood (ML) estimation which in this case is equivalent to MAP. Furthermore, it can be easily shown that for the special case of additive white Gaussian noise, MLE is equivalent to LSE.[75,90]

To summarize, the Bayesian estimation approach requires us to specify the following information:

- the world model (or the random field) parameter vector:
  - image fields for grey-level, color, or multi-spectrum images,
  - spatial-temporal random fields for dynamic image sequences,
  - different modality models.
- the sensory system parameter vector: camera, laser range finder, tomographic imaging devices (CT, MRI, PET, SPECT, etc.), remote sensing devices, etc.

Proper assumptions about the prior model are essential for the Bayesian approach, which will help the estimator to perform efficiently with good accuracy. Under the Bayesian estimation structure, the estimation paradigm is to

- construct a cost function $J(\hat{f}, f)$,
- find the estimate value $\hat{f}$ of $f$,
- the objective is to minimize (or maximize) the averaged or expected value $E[J(\hat{f}, f)]$.

If the posterior distribution function $p(f|g)$ is available, if at all, the task in the Bayesian framework is then to find the value (estimate) $\hat{f}$ of $f$, such that the *a posteriori* $p(f|g)$ is maximized (MAP):

$$max_f p(f|g) = max_f\{\log p(g|f) + \log p(f)\}\,. \tag{15}$$

It is very important to realize, however, that in most applications, the posterior $p(f|g)$ is very difficult to obtain without considering specific random fields. As mentioned above, if our assumption is too simple and unrealistic it is likely that the MAP algorithm we developed for a particular image processing problem will be equivalent to LSE which has been shown[36,44,90] to be non-robust — a small aberration in data will tip over the scale resulting in the wrong estimate.

## 4. IMAGE PROCESSING USING MAP

As discussed in the previous section, given observation $g$ in (5) and the *a posteriori* model $p(f|g)$ we can develop estimation algorithms based on the Bayes theory, namely,

$$p(f|g) = \frac{p(g|f)p(f)}{p(g)}\,. \tag{16}$$

Obviously, in such a framework, the estimate depends primarily on two models, namely, the prior probability density function $p(f)$ and the likelihood function $p(g|f)$ which according to (5) is governed by $p(n)$ the density function for the additive noise $n$. In choosing particular forms of density functions we often have to base our judgments on the following criteria,

(a) the underlying physics that govern the imaging process,
(b) tractable mathematical representation,
(c) computational feasibility,
(d) our knowledge and experience about the nature of the object being viewed.

For instance, it is possible to model the noise as a white Gaussian process for both film and photoelectronic imaging media,[8,72] whereas in many imaging systems based on counts of photon emission, for example, X-ray, PET (Positron Emission Tomography) and SPECT (Single-Photon Emission Computerized Tomography), the process can be modeled by a Poisson distribution.[34,52] However, the Gaussian assumption applies to MRI (Magnetic Resonance Imaging) where the major source of noise is the thermal noise associated with the resistive loading of the collecting coil.[26,43] Most statistical image processing, or for that matter, signal processing methods have used the Gaussian model for noise. Although Hunt and Cannon[48] have pointed out that Gaussian assumption for modeling images is not evident, the Gaussian modeling is nevertheless justified by the need for a *workable* mathematical formulation.

The Gaussian or normal model occupies a unique position in both mathematics and engineering. In image processing it is not an exception. It is due to the following reasons that the Gaussian distribution is considered as a suitable model: the central-limit theorem states that the density function $p(s)$ for the sum of the independent random variable $s_i$

$$s = \sum_{i=0}^{M} s_i \,, \tag{17}$$

approaches a bell-shaped curve referred to as the Gaussian distribution as $M \to \infty$. However, as this condition cannot be reached in reality, we may have to settle for a *sufficiently* large $M$ in practice. It can be shown that passing a Gaussian random signal through a linear filter results in a new signal that is also a Gaussian process. It is possible to generate non-Gaussian signals by passing a Gaussian random signal through a nonlinear system. Computationally, the Gaussian model is most efficient as it is completely determined by the statistic mean $\mu$ and covariance $\sigma^2$. Furthermore, it is known that in information theory terms, Gaussian noise is the *noisest* waveform, as this is the only noise that reaches the theoretical limit where its entropy power equals its variance.[9] We have to stress at this point that Gaussian modeling is an approximation based in many ways on our belief about how the signal *ought* to behave in the natural world.

Hunt in his pioneering work[47] proposed to model the noise process $n$ by a multivariate normal probability density: $n \sim G(0, R_n)$:

$$p(n) = \frac{1}{(2\pi)^{M/2}|R_n|^{1/2}} \exp\left( -\frac{1}{2} n^T R_n^{-1} n \right), \tag{18}$$

and to model the prior distribution for the image as $f \sim G(\mu_f, R_f)$:

$$p(f) = \frac{1}{(2\pi)^{M/2}|R_f|^{1/2}} \exp\left\{ -\frac{1}{2}(f - \mu_f)^T R_f^{-1}(f - \mu_f) \right\}, \tag{19}$$

where $\mu_f$ is the mean vector for the original image $f$. More recently, MAP has been used in 3D surface estimation from image sequences.[45] In this case they assumed joint distribution $p(g_i|f_i)$ similar to (18) (or equivalently, $p(n_i)$) for the observed image sequence $g_i$:

$$p(g_i(u)|f_i(u)) = \frac{1}{(2\pi\sigma^2)^{d_i/2}} \exp \sum_{u \in D_i} \left\{ -\frac{1}{2\sigma^2} [g_i(u) - f_i(u)]^2 \right\}, \tag{20}$$

where $d_i$ represents the number of pixels in the selected region $D_i$ of the $i$th image, and $u \in D_i$.

Given that for a particular image $f$, the variation in $g$ is in fact caused solely by the noise $n$ (refer to (5)), according to (18), the *a priori* model for $p(g|f)$ can be represented as follows

$$p(g|f) = \frac{1}{(2\pi)^{M/2}|R_n|^{1/2}} \exp\left\{-\frac{1}{2}(g - \phi(Hf))^T R_n^{-1}(g - \phi(Hf))\right\}. \tag{21}$$

The necessary condition for MAP estimate is

$$\frac{\partial \ln p(f|g)}{\partial f} = \frac{\partial \ln p(g|f)}{\partial f} + \frac{\partial \ln p(f)}{\partial f} = 0. \tag{22}$$

From (21) and (19), we may solve (22) for the MAP estimate:

$$\hat{f} = \mu_f + R_f H^T \Phi R_n^{-1}[g - \phi(H\hat{f})], \tag{23}$$

where $\Phi$ is a diagonal matrix consisting of derivatives of the form $\frac{\partial\phi(x)}{\partial x}$.

Hunt *et al.* has studied the effectiveness of MAP algorithms for image restoration with Gaussian noise models and various prior means $\mu_f$ under different blurring degradations.[48,94,95] Bresler *et al.*[13] applied the MAP algorithm to 3D reconstruction problems from noisy and incomplete projections. They were able to obtain satisfactory results from only four views in a 135° sector with an SNR as low as 1.5.

Hunt *et al.* argued that in the Bayesian framework it is possible to use the image prior model (19) and to produce reasonable results with a stationary variance about the mean $\mu_f$ which is not necessarily constant. The non-uniform image mean assumption is interesting in that it maintains the *structural* information about the image ensemble, which is related to visible characteristics of the image. For instance, instead of giving an averaged (constant) value of a scene, the nonstationary mean provides *general* shapes and shadings to represent objects present in the scene. Incidentally, the solution in (23) is in fact a discrete version of the Wiener filter with the *a priori* mean $\mu_f$, which can be easily carried out by FFT for computational efficiency. This coincidence is the result of the Gaussian distribution assumption in developing the MAP estimator.[96] It is also of interest to notice that MAP estimates in many situations are the same as minimum mean squares error (MMSE) estimates which are the mean of the *a posteriori* density (the conditional mean), and particularly, for linear image models (6) under the Gaussian assumption, MAP and MMSE are equivalent.

## 5. KALMAN FILTER

The Kalman filter[54] is an estimation technique developed in the Bayesian framework, which is able to solve the estimation problem for nonstationary random processes. It uses conditional expectation and state transfer to solve estimation problems. Due to its high computational feasibility and efficiency, the Kalman filter theory has long been applied to control systems and signal processing. Extending Kalman filter to multi-dimensional signals (e.g. images, spatial-temporal signals) gained considerable popularity in the early 70s. Nahi[76] and Habibi[35] probably were among the first to use the Kalman filter for image estimation problems. Further work on the development of two-dimensional Kalman filters has been carried out by many others, such as Powell and Silverman,[82] Murphy and Silverman,[74] and Liu *et al.*[63,64] Willsky[98] has done a thorough survey of the related research. Woods and his colleagues[57,100–103] have done probably the most extensive study of two-dimensional Kalman-type filter theory and techniques for image estimation.

In dynamic image sequence processing, motion compensated spatial-temporal filters have been developed based on the Kalman filtering theory,[12] and more recently in dynamic object tracking.[18,104] The Kalman filter also found applications in edge tracking.[3,4,69] Matthies *et al.*[70] used the Kalman for computing depth-from-motion. In 3D reconstruction using image sequences, many systems have been developed based on Kalman filtering theory.[1,14,29,30]

In this section we present a Kalman-type filter for image estimation. The image is modeled by an autoregressive model.

### 5.1. Image Modeling

We model the image based on a finite nonsymmetric half plane (NSHP)[27] which is illustrated in Fig. 5. For any spatial position of the scanner, all the previous processed pixels are considered "past" states, while the pixel which is presently being processed is called the "present" state, and all the pixels to be processed are referred to as the "future" states. Obviously, this definition is rather artificial, as the scanning operation can take any order.

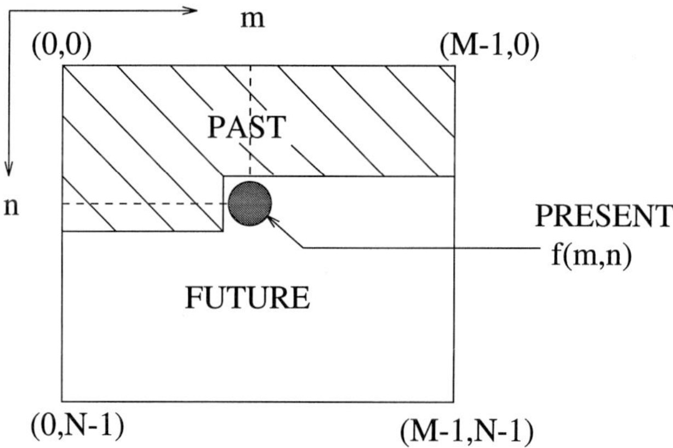


Fig. 5. Non-symmetric half plane (NSHP).

Let $(m, n)$ be the present position of the scanner, we define $P(m, n)$ as past region with respect to $(m, n)$,

$$P(m,n) = [(i,j) : \{1 < i < M, 1 < j < n-1\} \bigcup \{1 < i < m-1, j = n\}] , \quad (24)$$

where $\bigcup$ is union. The image signal at $(m, n)$ can be modeled by an autoregressive model, namely,

$$f(m,n) = \sum_{(i,j)\in P(m,n)} a(i,j)f(m-i,n-j) + w_s(m,n)\,, \tag{25}$$

where $w_s$ is the modeling error and is assumed to be Gaussian and white,[a] and $a(i, j)$ are the modeling coefficients.

Let $g(m, n)$ represent the observed image which is corrupted by an additive noise $v(m, n)$. We have

$$g(m,n) = f(m,n) + v(m,n)\,, \tag{26}$$

where $v(m, n)$ is assumed to be a Gaussian, white noise array with zero mean and variance $\sigma_v^2(m, n)$, and is independent of $f(m, n)$ and $w_s(m, n)$.

Usually the dimension of the image is very large, the simple use of (25) as the image model in (26) will lead to high dimensionality problem, and result in excessive computation. However, it is assumed[83,100] that only those pixels in a small neighborhood of the present pixel contribute significantly to the modeling of $f(m, n)$, we may reduce (25) to

$$f(m,n) = \sum_{(i.j)\in\Re} a(i,j)f(m-i,n-j) + w_s(m,n)\,, \tag{27}$$

where $\Re \triangleq (k, l)$ is the sub-region of the NSHP shown in Fig. 6, and $w_s$ is the modeling error with zero mean and variance $\sigma_{ws}^2$. Without loss of generality, we assume $E[f(m, n)] = 0$.

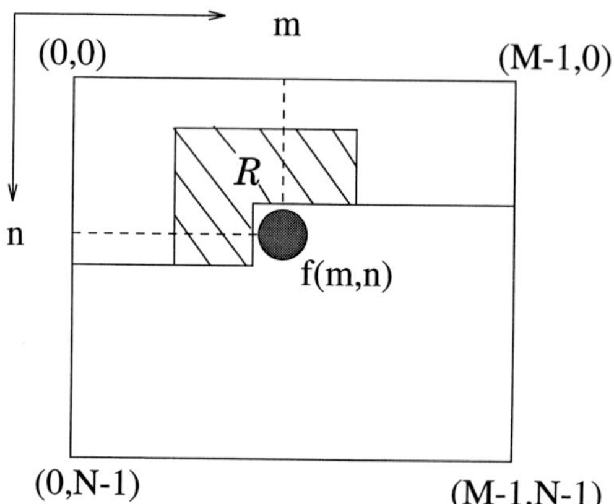


Fig. 6. Subregion of the NSHP for modeling the image.

We have used a spiral scanning operation which runs continuously along a square-shaped spiral line (see Fig. 7) and ends at the geometrical center of the image. Referring to Fig. 8, for simplicity of notation we denote $P$ as the "past",

[a]Valid for the autoregressive model only, otherwise $w_s(m, n)$ will not be white.[76]

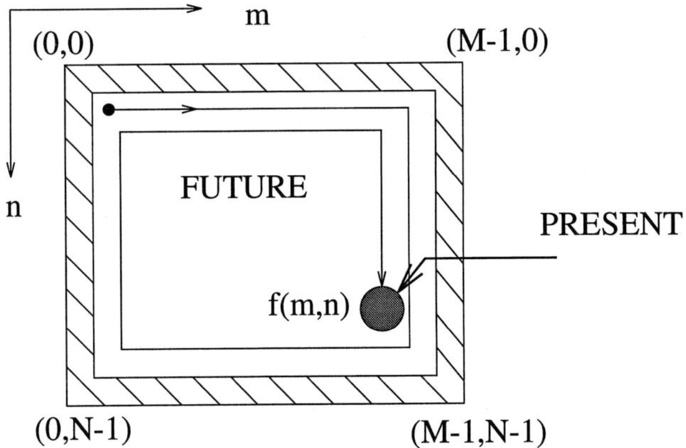


Fig. 7. Scanning process.

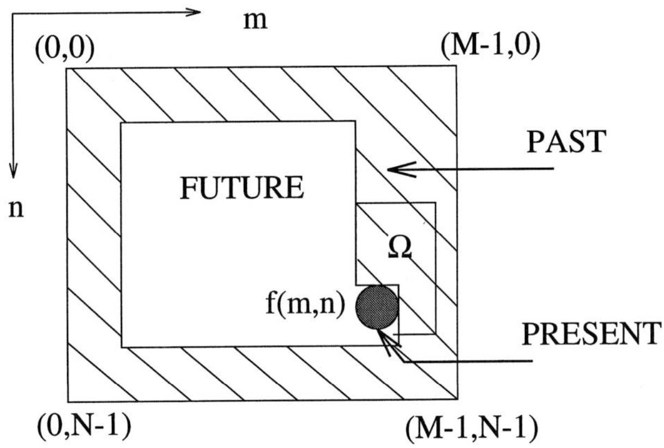


Fig. 8. Causal image field.

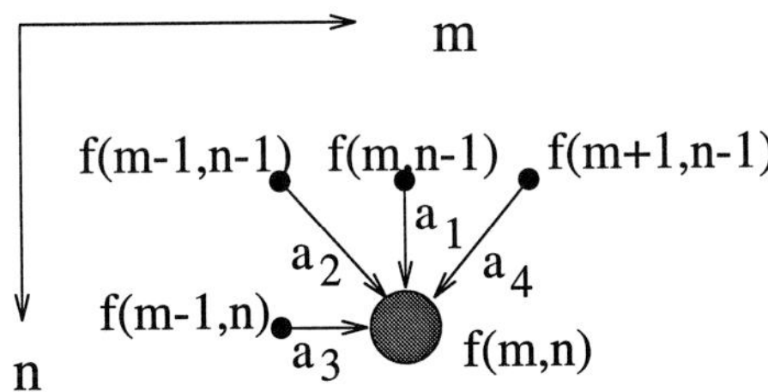


Fig. 9. Neighborhood of $f(m,n)$.

and $F$ as the "future". For the particular spiral scanning configuration, the entire image can be considered as a long string of pixels. The image model (27) can be rewritten for the subregion $\Omega$ of $P$ (see Fig. 8) as follows,

$$f(m,n) = \sum_{(i,j)\in\Omega} a(i,j)f(m-i,n-j) + w_s(m,n)\,. \tag{28}$$

Figure 9 shows a possible neighborhood of pixels that can be used in (28).

## 5.2. The Two-Dimensional Adaptive Kalman Filter

The Kalman filtering technique is based on the linear minimum variance (or, sometimes, minimum mean squares error) estimate of $f(m,n)$, given an observation $g(m,n)$.

This estimate is obtained by using the orthogonal projection principle[54,78], which states that the linear minimum variance estimate $\hat{y} = Ax + B$ of $y$ is such that the estimate error $(y - \hat{y})$ is orthogonal to the data $x$, or $\hat{y}$ is the orthogonal projection of $y$ onto $X$, in the sense that $E[y - \hat{y}] = 0$, where $X = x$. In the present context, we require an estimate $\hat{f}$ of $f$ given the observation $g$, such that $\hat{f}$ is the orthogonal projection of $f$ onto $P$. That is, $\hat{f} = \hat{E}\{f|P\}$. Here we have used $\hat{E}$ rather than $E$ to indicate that the linear minimum variance estimate is in general not the true conditional mean in the sense that the linear minimum variance estimate is a weighted linear combination of the observations.

The image models defined by Eqs. (26) and (28) over the causally partitioned image field provide the basis for all our succeeding development.

### Problem Statement

Given the models (26) and (28), determine an estimate $\hat{f}$ (of $f$) which is a linear combination of the observation $g$ and estimates $\hat{f}$. The estimate is optimal subject to the criterion that the expected value of the sum of the variance between $\hat{f}$ and $f$ is a minimum. That is, $\hat{f}$ is to be chosen so that

$$\hat{E}[f - \hat{f}]^2 = minimum\,. \tag{29}$$

### *Signal Prediction and Update*

We may write the estimate $\hat{f}(m,n)$ as

$$\hat{f}(m,n) = \hat{f}^-(m,n) + K(m,n)e(m,n)\,, \tag{30}$$

where $K(m,n)$ is an unknown weighting function (or the gain in the Kalman filter theory), the term $\hat{f}^-(m,n)$ defines the predicted estimate at $(m,n)$, and is given by

$$\hat{f}^-(m,n) = \sum_{(i,j)\in\Omega} a(i,j)\hat{f}(m-i,n-j)\,, \tag{31}$$

and

$$e(m,n) = g(m,n) - \hat{f}^-(m,n) \tag{32}$$

which is called the Kalman innovation process.[65]

It is easy to show that, if the minimum variance estimator is *unbiased* (meaning that $E\{\hat{f}\} = f$), the innovation process is also white, with zero mean provided that the noise $v$ is white with zero mean. We may write (32) as follows

$$e(m,n) = \tilde{f}^-(m,n) + v(m,n)\,, \tag{33}$$

where

$$\tilde{f}(m,n) = f(m,n) - \hat{f}(m,n)\,.$$

By the orthogonality principle and from equations (30) and (33), we have

$$E\{e(m,n)e(k,l)\} = E\{v(m,n)v(k,l)\} = 0, \forall m \neq k, n \neq l \tag{34}$$

and obviously, since $E\{w_s\} = 0$,

$$E\{e(m,n)\} = 0\,. \tag{35}$$

Equation (34) implies that $e$ is a white process, which may be written, in general, as

$$\begin{aligned} E\{e(m,n)e(k,l)\} &= [V_{\tilde{f}}^{-}(m,n;m,n) + \sigma_v^2(m,n)]\delta_{mk}\delta_{nl} \\ &= R_e(m,n) + \delta_{mk}\delta_{nl}, \end{aligned} \tag{36}$$

where $R_e(m,n) \triangleq [V_{\tilde{f}}^{-}(m,n;m,n) + \delta_v^2(m,n)]$ and

$$V_{\tilde{f}}^{-}(m,n;k,l) \triangleq E\{\tilde{f}^{-}(m,n)\tilde{f}^{-}(k,l)\} \tag{37}$$

which is the *a priori* error variance, and $\delta_{rs}$ is the Kronecker delta function,

$$\delta_{rs} = \begin{cases} 1, & \text{if } r = s, \\ 0, & \text{otherwise.} \end{cases}$$

*Gain Equation*

From Eq. (30) we have

$$E\{[f(m,n) - \hat{f}(m,n)]e(k,l)\} = E\{[\tilde{f}^{-}(m,n) - K(m,n)e(m,n)]e(k,l)\} = 0\,, \tag{38}$$

thus

$$E\{[\tilde{f}^{-}(m,n)e(k,l)\} = E\{K(m,n)e(m,n)e(k,l)\} = K(m,n)R_e(m,n)\delta_{mk}\delta_{nl}\,. \tag{39}$$

If $m = k, n = l$, we have

$$K(m,n) = E\{\tilde{f}^{-}(m,n)e(m,n)\}R_e^{-1}(m,n)\,, \tag{40}$$

where

$$E\{\tilde{f}^{-}(m,n)v(m,n)\} = 0\,, \tag{41}$$

and

$$e(m,n) = \tilde{f}^{-}(m,n) + v(m,n)\,.$$

The Kalman gain can now be written as

$$K(m,n) = V_{\tilde{f}}^{-}(m,n;m,n)R_e^{-1}(m,n)\,. \tag{42}$$

*A Priori Variance Algorithm*

In Eq. (37) we have defined the *a priori* variance, in the following we express the *a priori* variance in terms of estimate error $\tilde{f}$.

Recall that $\tilde{f}^{-} = f - \hat{f}^{-}$, and from the image model (28) we have

$$f(m,n) = \sum_{(i,j)\in\Omega} a(i,j)f(m-i,n-j) + w_s(m,n)\,. \tag{43}$$

Remember that $w_s$ is a white random process with the variance $\sigma^2_{ws}$, thus

$$\begin{aligned} V_{\tilde{f}}^{-}(m,n;m,n) &= \sum_{(k.l)\in\Omega}\sum_{(i,j)\in\Omega} a(i,j)E[\tilde{f}(m-i,n-j)\tilde{f}(m-k,n-l)]a(k,l) + \sigma^2_{ws} \\ &= \sum_{(k,l)\in\Omega}\sum_{(i,j)\in\Omega} a(i,j)V_{\tilde{f}}(r,s,t,u)a(k,l) + \sigma^2_{ws}\,, \end{aligned} \tag{44}$$

where $r = m-i$, $s = n-j$, $t = m-k$, $u = n-l$; and $V$ is called the *a posteriori variance* which is readily available.

We define

$$\tilde{f}(m,n) = f(m,n) - \hat{f}(m,n)\,. \tag{45}$$

Substituting (33) into (28) yields

$$\tilde{f}(m,n) = [f(m,n) - \hat{f}^{-}(m,n)] - K(m,n)e(m,n)\,,$$

or

$$\tilde{f}(m,n) = \tilde{f}^{-}(m,n) - K(m,n)e(m,n)\,. \tag{46}$$

Thus

$$E\{\tilde{f}^2(m,n)\} = E\{[\tilde{f}^{-}(m,n) - K(m,n)e(m,n)]^2\}\,. \tag{47}$$

It is known that $v$ is white noise, and from Eqs. (37), (41) and (44), we obtain

$$V_{\tilde{f}}(m,n;m,n) = E\{\tilde{f}^2(m,n)\} = [1 - K(m,n)]V_{\tilde{f}}^{-}(m,n;m,n)\,. \tag{48}$$

The equations (30), (42), (44) and (48) are the sequential Kalman filter for the image model (28) and the observation (26).

## 5.3. Identification of the Modeling Coefficients

In the image model (28), the modeling coefficients are normally not known, and must be estimated. We may write Eq. (28) in vector form, as,

$$f(m,n) = \mathbf{A}^{\top}(m,n)\mathbf{F}(m,n) + w_s(m,n)\,, \tag{49}$$

where $\mathbf{A}$ is the vector composed of the modeling coefficients, and $\mathbf{F}$ the signal vector. The structures of $\mathbf{A}$ and $\mathbf{F}$ depends on the specific scanning operation and the neighborhood configuration. The Eq. (28) is causal, and the original image is also assumed to be an ergodic random field. We may use the identification algorithm[65] to estimate $\{a(i,j)\}$. In order to make the notations simple, we define $k \triangleq (m,n)$ and use $k+j$ to represent moving $j$ steps further from $(m,n)$ or $k$. With this definition, equation (49) can be written as

$$f(k) = \mathbf{A}(k)\mathbf{F}(k) + w_s(k)\,. \tag{50}$$

From (50), a general parameter identification algorithm is readily available as follows, assuming that the modeling coefficients $\{a(i,j)\}$ are constants,

$$\left.\begin{aligned}
&\hat{\mathbf{A}}(k+1 \mid k+1) = \hat{\mathbf{A}}(k \mid k) + \Phi(k+1)[f(k) - \mathbf{F}(k)\hat{\mathbf{A}}(k)]\,,\\
&\Phi(k+1) = \mathbf{R}(k+1 \mid k)\mathbf{F}^\top(k)[\mathbf{F}(k)\mathbf{R}(k+1 \mid k)\mathbf{F}^\top(k) + \sigma_{ws}^2(k+1)\mathbf{I}]^{-1}\,,\\
&\mathbf{R}(k+1 \mid k) = \mathbf{R}(k \mid k) + \sigma_{ws}^2(k)\mathbf{I}\,,\\
&\mathbf{R}(k+1 \mid k+1) = [\mathbf{I} - \Phi(k+1)\mathbf{F}(k)]\mathbf{R}(k+1 \mid k)\,,
\end{aligned}\right\} \tag{51}$$

where

$$\mathbf{R}(k \mid k) = E\{[\mathbf{A}(k) - \hat{\mathbf{A}}(k \mid k)][\mathbf{A}(k) - \hat{\mathbf{A}}(k \mid k)]^\top\}\,, \tag{52}$$

and $\sigma_{ws}^2$ is constant for stationary white process.

From Eq. (51) we can see that this algorithm actually uses the original image to estimate $\mathbf{A}(k)$. Unfortunately, in restoration problems, the original image is not available at all, the direct use of (51) is seemingly meaningless. However, in many practical applications the gross structure of the original image may be observed, and we may apply (51) over images with similar structure to obtain $\{a(i,j)\}$.

In most cases we may have or assume some prior knowledge about the original image, e.g. the statistical characteristics of the image. Experiments have shown that many images can be regarded as wide-sense stationary random fields with the following autocorrelation function,[31]

$$R(i,j) = \sigma_s^2 exp[-\alpha|i| - \beta|j|]\,, \tag{53}$$

where $\sigma_s^2$ is the global image variance, $i$ and $j$ are the horizontal and vertical displacements, respectively, and $\alpha$ and $\beta$ are constants.

With (53) given we are now in a position to introduce another parameter estimation method which is more realistic than (51). From (49) we have

$$w_s(m,n) = f(m,n) - \mathbf{A}(m,n)\mathbf{F}(m,n)\,, \tag{54}$$

we seek $\mathbf{A}$ such that

$$J(w_s(m,n)) = E\{w_s^2(m,n)\}\,, \tag{55}$$

is minimized. This gives

$$\mathbf{A}(m,n) = [\sum_{\Omega} \mathbf{F}(m,n)\mathbf{F}^\top(m,n)]^{-1}[\sum_{\Omega} f(m,n)\mathbf{F}(m,n)]. \tag{56}$$

The right side of Eq. (56) is, in fact, composed of the autocorrelation $\{R(i,j); (i,j) \in \Omega(m,n)\}$. Since (53) is known (56) can be solved.

However, the Kalman filter in general has high computational complexity and — being a type of recursive least squares (RLS) algorithm — is very sensitive to round off errors which means that it can become unstable in fixed-point implementations.

## 6. MARKOV RANDOM FIELDS

In the previous section we discussed that under the Bayesian framework, the estimation problem is essentially to find $\hat{f}$ given observation such that $p(f|g)$ is maximized. This results in a very simple and straightforward maximum *a posteriori* (MAP) estimation method. However, in order to solve the MAP estimation problem we have to know the distribution functions involved in the model. This is a very difficult problem in most applications. Although the Bayesian framework is natural and philosophically correct for dealing with image estimation problems, choosing correct probability functions is rather *ad hoc* and of a heuristic nature as it primarily relies on our intuition. As a result, the distribution functions we assume may not reflect the true reality and represent our *ignorance*. It is therefore more desirable to find a sound modeling structure such that the problem can be modeled properly. Markov random fields (MRFs) have been shown to be suitable for the problem of spatial statistical modeling. MRF has the following properties that make it most suitable for probabilistic modeling of spatial information[32,68]:

1. The interaction in Markov random fields between pixel elements is local which satisfies the piecewise smoothness requirement.
2. The local interaction characteristic makes it possible to be implemented parallely for computational efficiency.[17,32]. More importantly though, this also ensures the existence of priors rich enough for modeling different spatial behaviors.
3. In MRF the prior distribution function is proven to be Gibbsian[5] under a very mild condition. This makes the modeling process in the Bayes theorem straightforward.
4. With a sound distribution model it is possible to carry out optimization procedures (e.g. stochastic relaxation, simulated annealing) and to systematically verify the consistency between the model and our prior knowledge.

In recent years, Markov random field has gained considerable popularity as a method for modeling images in a variety of applications, for instance, image restoration,[32,40,50,51,85,106] texture segmentation and modeling,[16,20,28,55,56,67,77] edge detection,[21,33,49,91,105] medical image analysis,[34,37,39,62,87] motion estimation,[41,59,66,84,107] document processing,[92] and even in image interpretation,[73] just to mention a few.

### 6.1. Neighborhood System

The theory of Markov random fields has been around for about thirty years due to Dorushin.[24,58] MRF is defined on a neighborhood system.[6,32] In time sequence we have a causal ordering of states: $\Omega = \{\omega_1, \omega_2, ..., \omega_L\}$, the neighborhood for this sequence in terms of first order homogeneous Markov chain is given by $\aleph_i =$

$\{i-1, i+1, 2 \leq i \leq L-1\}$ with two boundary neighborhoods: $\aleph_1 = \{2\}$ and $\aleph_L = \{L-1\}$,

$$p(\omega_i|\omega_j, j < L) = p(\omega_i|\omega_{i-1}) .$$

It can be shown that

$$p(\omega) = p(\omega_1) \prod_{i=2}^{L} p(\omega_i|\omega_{i-1}).$$

However, in a two-sided neighborhood system $\aleph = \{\aleph_1, \aleph_i, \aleph_L\}$ (see Fig. 10), the Markov chain in general is also dependent on $\omega_{i+1}$[15]:

$$p(\omega) = p(\omega_1) \prod_{i=2}^{L} p(\omega_i|\omega_{i-1}, \omega_{i+1}) .$$

This can be applied to $k$-nearest neighbors[32].

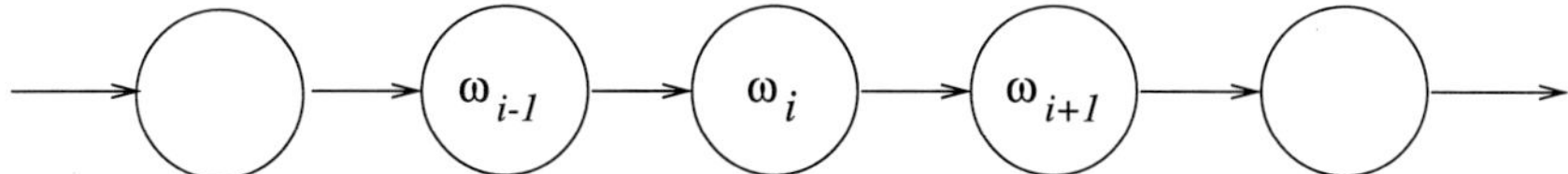


Fig. 10. Two-sided neighborhood of $\omega_i$.

In most spatial computing tasks we are dealing with two-dimensional information, it is necessary to extend the usual Markov chains to 2D cases. In fact in the previous section, Fig. 9 shows a typical nearest neighborhood system for the 2D Markov chain. However, in such a *nonsymmetric* neighborhood system[99] it is difficult to verify the Markovian property and does not provide a natural description of the image (spatial) field.

Let $S = \{s_1, s_2, \ldots, s_L\}$ be a set of lattice points (e.g. pixel locations $(i,j)$ in images) and $f_{s_i} \in \Re$ is the value at point $s_i$, for instance, in grey-level images $f_{s_i} \in [0, 255]$. Define a neighborhood system $\aleph = \{\aleph_s, s \in S\}$. We require that the neighborhood system $\aleph$ be symmetric:

$$\forall t \in \aleph_s \Rightarrow s \in \aleph_t \text{ and } s \notin \aleph_s . \tag{57}$$

In addition we define clique $C \subseteq S$ as a set of points, $c \in C$ with the following property,

$$\forall s, c \in C, c \in \aleph_s . \tag{58}$$

That is, from (57), they are neighbors to each other.

Figure 11 shows some typical nearest-neighborhood configurations used in many image processing applications. Besag[7] suggested a neighborhood system defined on a hexagonal lattice, which offers one more orientation for line (edge) sites and removes the problem of four or more lines converging at a point.

Figure 12 shows some clique types. It is apparent that for the configuration in Fig. 11(a) the possible cliques are {(a), (b), (c)} in Fig. 12. The 8-connected configuration in Fig. 11(b) has the clique set $C_8$ = {(a), (b),(c),(d),(e),(f),(g),(h),(i), (j)} in Fig. 12.

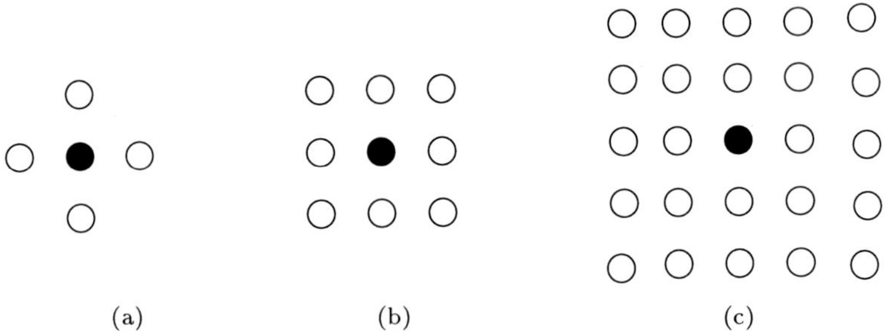


Fig. 11. Some typical nearest-neighborhood configurations.

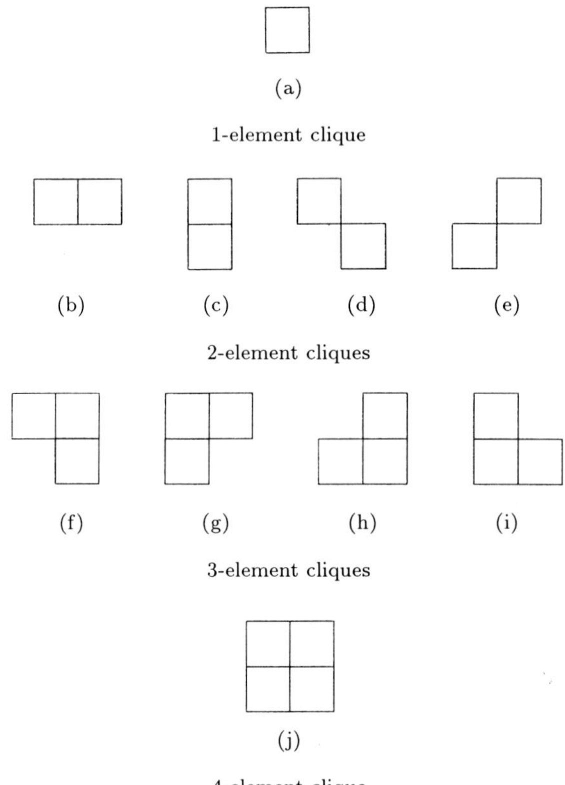


Fig. 12. Examples of cliques.

In such a neighborhood system, it is possible to model different image processes in addition to intensity at a pixel site. For instance, between each pair of pixel sites we can assign line (edge) sites (Fig. 13), orientation discontinuities, and depth discontinuities in 3D surface reconstruction. Combining these fields we obtain a Markov random field.

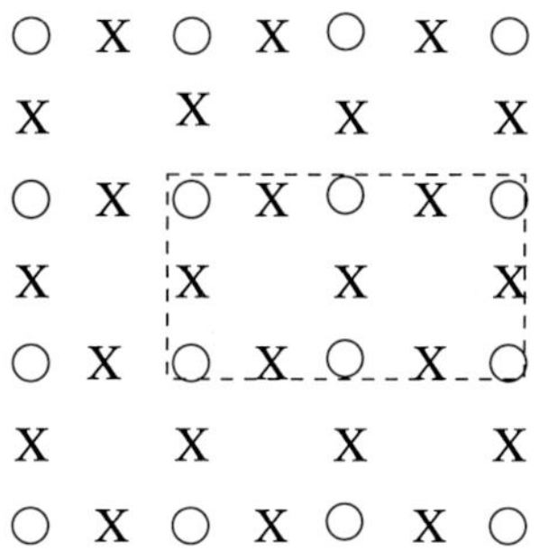

```
O X O X O X O
X   X   X   X
O X O X O X O
X   X   X   X
O X O X O X O
X   X   X   X
O X O X O X O
```

Fig. 13. Line (edge) sites are indicated by Xs. Each line site has six line sites as its neighbors.

## 6.2. Gibbs Distribution

The Markov random field is defined under the neighborhood system described above if $p(\omega) > 0$ and $p(\omega_s|\omega_r, r \neq s) = p(\omega_s|\omega_r, r \in \aleph_s)$, where $\omega = \{\omega_i \in \Re, i \in [1, L]\}$ is a realization of possible configurations (e.g. an image). The Hammersley–Clifford theorem[5] states that in the neighborhood system $\aleph = \{\aleph_s, s \in S\}$, MRFs can be modeled as by a Gibbs (Boltzmann) distribution[b]:

$$p(f) = \frac{1}{Z} \exp\{-\sum_{c \in C} V_c(f_c)\} = \frac{1}{Z} \exp\{-U(f)\}, \tag{59}$$

where $C$ is the set of all cliques, $Z$ is the normalizing constant for the density, also known as the partition function, and $U(f)$ the energy function:

$$U(f) = \sum_{c \in C} V_c(f_c),$$

where potentials $V_c$ are assigned certain values depending on the nature of the application. Figure 14 shows the potentials used in Geman and Geman's pioneering work[32] on the use of MRF in image segmentation and restoration. Obviously, smoothness of image regions and continuity of edges are the basis for assigning these potentials. However, the presence of an edge at an edge site has to be derived based on the pixel values *observed* (measured) in the neighborhood of the edge site. For instance, Jain and Nadabar[49] have discussed this problem in detail and defined two different statistics to measure the strength of jump edges and crease edges for their work on range image segmentation.

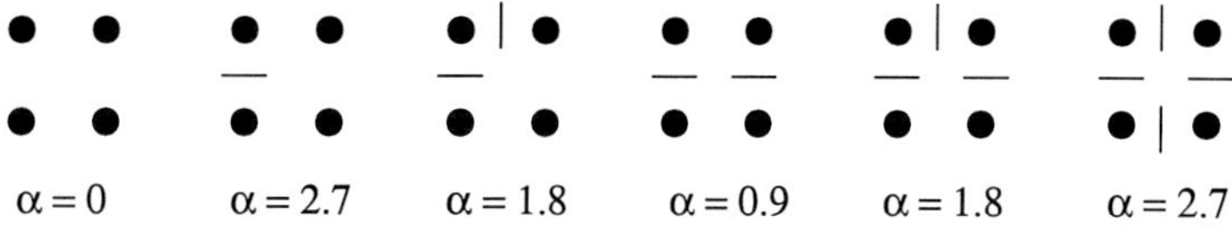


Fig. 14. Potential values assigned to different cliques.

[b]Spitzer[89] has shown that Gibbs random fields and Markov random fields are equivalent.

In Ref. 49 Jain and Nadabar used a second order neighborhood system (Fig. 15) to model edge sites for detecting jump and crease edges in range images. In this case, MRF is used to represent the prior knowledge about the nature of edges in range images and the specific consideration is given to continuity and smoothness of edges. For the second order neighborhood system they proposed a set of 14 cliques of edge and non-edge type as shown in Fig. 16 and assigned a specific value for each clique. The rationale here is to assign lower values to continuous line segments and higher values for *broken* line sites. This scheme reinforces our belief in continuity and smoothness of certain intrinsic features in the spatial data.

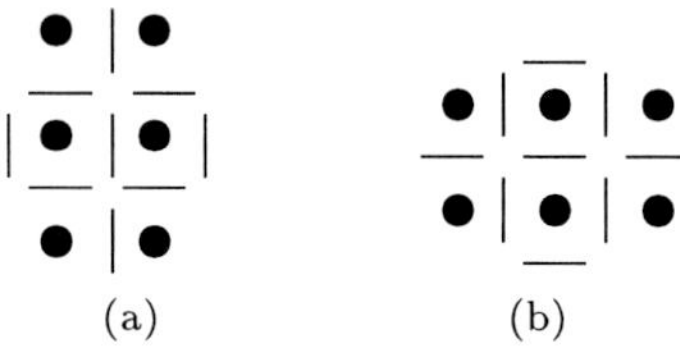


Fig. 15. Edge sites in the second-order neighborhood system (a) vertical edge site, (b) horizontal edge site.

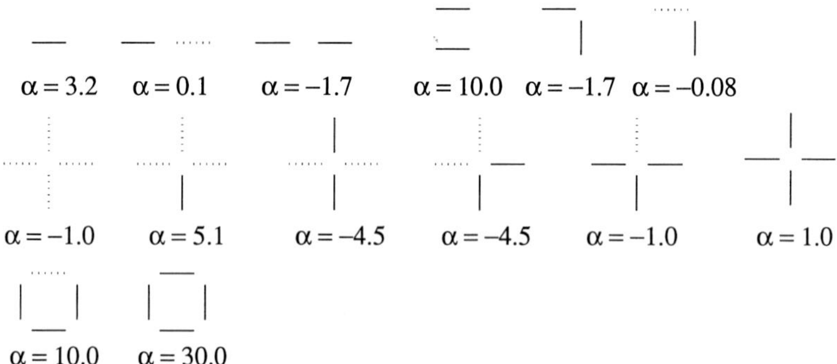


Fig. 16. Potential values assigned to different cliques of edge (solid lines) and non-edge (dotted lines) type.

## 6.3. Conditional Probabilities

The conditional probability of a pixel given neighbors is defined as:

$$p(f_s|f_t, s \neq r) = \frac{p(f)}{\sum_{f_s \in \Re} p(f)}, \tag{60}$$

where $p(f)$ is the prior Gibbs distribution (59), and $\Re$ may represent, for instance, the set of grey levels or edge orientations. For example, considering an 8-connected nearest neighborhood (as that shown in Fig. 11(b)) with the cliques formed by two pixels, there will be eight cliques that contain $f_s$, since by definition any pixel $f_t$ at site $t$ in a clique containing $f_s$ at site $s$ must be a neighbor of $f_s$. We can use (60) to calculate the conditional probability of the pixel $f_s$ as follows

$$p(f_s|f_t, s \neq t) = \frac{\exp\{-\sum_{t=1}^{8} \alpha_t \delta(f_s \neq f_t)\}}{\sum_{f_s=0}^{255} \exp\{-\sum_{t=1}^{8} \alpha_t \delta(f_s \neq f_t)\}}, \tag{61}$$

where $\alpha_t$ are the potential value assignments for the potential function $V(f_t)$, and $\delta(x)$ is defined as

$$\delta(x) = \begin{cases} 1 & \text{if } x \neq 0, \\ 0 & \text{otherwise.} \end{cases}$$

Potential assignment is difficult in most applications and requires careful analysis[32,49] of the problem at hand.

In the Bayesian estimation paradigm, most researchers use MAP as the optimality criterion. The *a posteriori* distribution function $p(f|g)$ is conditioned on observation. In Markov random fields, the prior $p(f)$ can be modeled as a Gibbs distribution. Furthermore, using Markov random fields it can be shown[32] that for the image model (5), the *a posteriori* distribution $p(f|g)$ is also Gibbsian:

$$p(f|g) = \frac{1}{Z_g} e^{-U(f|g)}, \tag{62}$$

with an energy function given as follows

$$U(f|g) = U(f) + \|\mu - \Phi(g, \phi(Hf))\|^2 / 2\sigma^2, \tag{63}$$

where $\mu$ is mean vector for the white Gaussian noise $n$, and $\Phi(g, \phi(Hf)) = g - \phi(Hf)$ for the model in (5) with an additional noise, and $\Phi$ represents an inverse operation. Although (63) is derived based on white Gaussian noise assumption, Geman and Geman[32] stressed that extension to other forms of noise is only notational.

This result enables us to formulate the MAP estimation problem in Markov random fields with a sound knowledge about specific distribution functions that can be used in the modeling process. The problem of maximizing the posterior distribution for a given $g$ is to minimize (63). However, this is a computationally very demanding operation even for images of moderate sizes. There are many algorithms[25] available for this minimization problem, for instance, simulated annealing, stochastic relaxation,[32] Monte Carlo approach to maximizer of *a posteriori* marginals (MPM),[68] iterated conditional modes (ICM),[6] and high-confidence first (HCF).[19]

## 7. CONCLUSIONS

As with most other signal processing and control problems, image processing is in general of an inverse nature. This type of problems is ill-posed due to lack of constraints, incomplete observed data, and limited knowledge about the process. To solve such problems we have to use our experience and prior knowledge in addition to measured signals. The Bayesian framework is a natural and unified environment for modeling uncertainties in image and spatial data processing tasks. It provides us with a structure for inference given observation.

In this paper we have discussed several important aspects of Bayesian methods in image and spatial information processing. The Bayesian paradigm is based on two probabilistic models, namely, the prior model $p(f)$ which describes the world where the original data $f$ is present and the sensor model $p(g|f)$ which represents the sensor behavior under the influence of $f$. According to the Bayes theorem, these two models determine the *a posteriori* probability $p(f|g)$ which expresses the relationship between the observed (measured) data and the original data $f$. As such, this framework allows us to consider the problem of estimation as a statistical inference that requires the incorporation of our intuition and knowledge for the solution. Although our knowledge in some cases is biased due to limited experience, judicious use of the prior knowledge will in many practical applications help us to constrain the ill-posed problem and to obtain satisfactory results efficiently.

In the Bayesian milieu, many estimation algorithms have been developed based on different optimality criteria. One of the most frequently used algorithm is the maximum *a posteriori* estimator (MAP), which attempts to find $\hat{f}$ such that

$$maxp(\hat{f}|g) = max\{\log p(g|\hat{f}) + \log p(\hat{f})\}.$$

However, in order to solve this maximization problem it is necessary to specify the probability distribution functions involved. This has been the most difficult problem in the Bayesian approach, and as stated above, requires considerable knowledge and experience. In the estimation theory it is customary to assume some simple distribution functions based primarily on the following factors: (i) our expectation of the underlying physics involved in the data collection process, (ii) tractable or workable mathematics, (iii) computational feasibility. For instance, a very popular assumption for $p(g|f)$ is the ubiquitous Gaussian distribution, and occasionally $p(f)$ is assumed to be uniformly distributed. Hunt *et al.*[47,48,94,95] were among the pioneers in using the Bayesian approach to image estimation problems. They developed MAP for 2D signals based on Gaussian priors. Apart from some other nice properties, the fundamental reason for using the Gaussian model is due to the central limit theorem.[78] While this is true (at least theoretically) for independent random variables over infinite observations, such an assumption often leads to least-squares (LS) type estimators which have been shown to be non-robust due to their sensitivity to minor deviations from the Gaussian model. As a consequence, many image processing algorithms, albeit theoretically elegant, are unfortunately very unreliable in real applications. This has been recognized as a major problem facing the computer vision community and has been addressed recently (inadequately though) by several researchers.[38,71,108]

Modeling the image field as a nonsymmetric half plane, Woods *et al.*[57,100–103] proposed a 2D Markov chain which imposes causality in the image field that is otherwise non-causal. Based on this causal Markov random field a number of 2D Kalman-type filters has been developed and applied to image estimation problems. In this paper we have derived such a filter in detail. Kalman-type filters have subsequently been used in many image processing problems that involve dynamics, for instance, dynamic feature tracking, image sequence filtering, edge and object tracking, and depth-from-motion applications. However, despite its computational flexibility and modeling capability, the Kalman filter is very difficult to use in real applications due mainly to its numerical instability and computational complexity. This is a pathological characteristic of recursive least squares (RLS) type filters.

Geman and Geman's work on using Markov random fields[32] in image processing and computer vision has provided a solid foundation for image modeling and inspired many new developments in recent years. We have in this paper discussed some major aspects of the Markov random field. Motivated by the intuition that pixels interact in a small local region, we define a neighborhood system in which cliques are formed according to specific requirements. The Markov random field is defined in such a neighborhood system. More significantly, the Hammersley–Clifford theorem, under a minor technical condition, *guarantees* that MRF can be modeled by a Gibbs distribution. Under the Bayesian framework, we are able to use Gibbs distribution to model both the prior $P(f)$ and the *a posteriori* $p(f|g)$. As Markov random fields combine both pixel sites and line sites, it is possible for us to integrate contextual information and our knowledge about the underlying process through specifying clique types and assigning potential values. The estimation problem in MRFs can be solved by a number of approaches, including simulated annealing, stochastic relaxation, maximizer of posterior marginals (MPM), iterative conditional modes (ICM), and high confidence first (HCF). The use of MRF in the Bayesian framework provides us with a better control of the modeling process and greater flexibility in algorithm design. As a result, Bayesian methods have gained considerable attention recently and have found applications in a variety of image processing problems.

An important consequence of applying the Bayesian paradigm to Markov random fields is the opportunity to gain better insights into the regularization theory and to handle the ill-posed problem with greater certainty. As we discussed before, image processing is ill-posed, solutions for such problems require that additional constraints be imposed by the system designer. The ill-posed problem normally solved by regularization methods which for the most part impose the smoothness constraint.[10,81,93] In the Markov random field, through the Bayesian modeling and the Gibbs distribution it can be shown that this type of regularization is in fact a special case of the Bayesian paradigm.[68] This is to be expected as in MRF we assign the potentials in the Gibbs distribution according to continuity and smoothness assumptions.[49]

Indeed, the Bayesian approach is a powerful tool for modeling and inference in many image processing problems, particularly, in Markov random fields, where we have a sound knowledge about the distribution function, namely, the Gibbs distribution. This significantly reduces the ignorance present in the Bayesian paradigms. However, we are still left with the task of determining *proper* cliques and assigning *reasonable* potentials for the energy function in the Gibbs distribution. This on one hand gives us the flexibility and control in the design process, on the other hand we are still left with uncertainties as to what constitutes the proper or reasonable choice. It would be better if we could develop some learning algorithms that can learn and decide on types of cliques and potentials for some *domain specific* applications. Recently, Devijer and Dekesel[22] have proposed a learning algorithm for hidden Markov random fields. Their approach is applicable to Pickard random fields that are both causal and non-causal. The learning process is similar to those in speech recognition. It is also desirable to investigate techniques for learning cliques and potentials based on known spatial information and our heuristics.

Another important issue which deserves urgent considerations is the robustness issue in MRF-based Bayesian approaches. As indicated by Geman and Geman,[32] their derivation of the Gibbs posterior is based on the more traditional white Gaussian noise assumption. Indeed, in many applications, most researchers followed the same assumption.[68] It is interesting to investigate the effects on the system's performance if the Gaussian model is modified as follows[44]:

$$G_f(\mu, \sigma^2, \epsilon) = (1 - \epsilon)G(\mu, \sigma^2) + \epsilon D, D \in P,$$

where $G(\mu, \sigma^2)$ is the Gaussian distribution and $D$ represents the set of unknown distributions. With this modeling function it is possible to study effects of Gaussian noise assumption on the Gibbs posterior and to develop techniques to handle modeling uncertainties.[108] Investigation of robustness in this context represents a significant challenge to researchers in the area of image processing, or more generally, in spatial computing.

## REFERENCES


1. N. Ayache and O. D. Faugeras, "Maintaining representations of the environment of mobile robot", *Int. Symp. Robotics Res.*, 1987, MIT Press, also INRIA Tech. Rep., France, 1987.
2. H. G. Barrow and J. M. Tenenbaum, "Recovering intrinsic scene characteristics from images", in *Computer Vision Systems*, eds. A. R. Hanson and E. M. Riseman, New York: Academic Press, 1978, pp. 3–26.
3. H. H. Baker, "Building surfaces of evolution: the weaving wall", *Int. J. of Computer Vision* **3**, 1 (1989).
4. H. H. Baker and R. C. Bolles, "Generalizing epipolar-plane image analysis on the spatiotemporal surface", *Int. J. of Computer Vision* **3**, 1 (1989).
5. J. Besag, "Spatial interaction and the statistical analysis of lattice systems", *J. Royal Statistical Society B* **36**, 2 (1974) 192–236.
6. J. Besag, "On the statistical analysis of dirty pictures", *J. Royal Statistical Society B* **48**, 3(1986) 259–302.
7. J. Besag, "Towards Bayesian image analysis", *J. Applied Statistics* **16**, 3 (1989) 395–407.
8. L. M. Biberman and S. Nudelman, *Photoelectronic Imaging Devices*, Vols. 1 and 2, Plenum, 1971.
9. R. Blahut, *Principles and Practice of Information Theory*, Addison-Wesley Publishing Company, 1988.
10. A. Blake and A. Zisserman, *Visual Reconstruction*, MIT Press, 1987.
11. G. E. P. Box, T. Leonard, and C.-F. Wu, eds., *Scientific Inference, Data Analysis, and Robustness*, Academic Press, 1983.

12. J. C. Brailean, R. P. Kleihorst, S. Efstratiadis, A. K. Katsaggelos, and R. L. Lagendijk, "Noise reduction filters for dynamic image sequences: A review", *Proc. IEEE* **83**, 9 (1995) 1272–1292.
13. Y. Bresler, J. A. Fessler, and A. Macovski, "A Bayesian approach to reconstruction from incomplete projections of a multiple object 3D domain", *IEEE Trans. Pattern Analysis and Machine Intelligence* **PAMI-11**, 8 (1989) 840–858.
14. T. J. Broida and R. Challappa, "Kinematics and structure of a rigid object from a sequence of noisy images", *Proc. IEEE Workshop on Motion: Representation and Analysis*, Charleston, May 1986, pp. 95–100.
15. D. Brook, "On the distinction between the conditional probability and the joint probability approaches in the specification of nearest-neighbour systems", *Biometrika* **51**, 3&4 (1964), pp. 481 483.
16. R. Chellappa and S. Chatterjee, "Classification of textures using Gaussian Markov random fields", *IEEE Trans. on Acoust. Speech and Signal Proc.* **ASSP-33**, 4 (1985) 959–963.
17. R. Chellappa and A. Jain, eds., *Markov Random Fields: Theory and Application*, Academic Press, 1993.
18. T. K. Cheng, L. Kitchen, and Z. Q. Liu, "Kalman filtering and clustering for 3D motion tracking using stereo", *Proc. Asian Conf. on Computer Vision*, **ACCV'95**, vol. I, Singapore, Dec. 1995, pp. 34–38.
19. P. Chou, C. Brown, and R. Raman, "A confidence-based approach to the labeling problem", *Proc. IEEE Workshop on Computer Vision*, Miami Beach, Florida, 1987, pp. 51–56.
20. F. S. Cohen, Z. Fan, and M.A. Patel, "Classification of rotated and scaled textured images using Gaussian Markov random field models", *IEEE Trans. Pattern Analysis and Machine intelligence* **PAMI-13**, 2 (1991) 192–202.
21. D. B. Cooper, H. Elliott, F. Cohen, L. Reiss, and P. Symosek, "Stochastic boundary estimation and object recognition", *Computer Vision Graphics and Image Process* **12** (1980) 326–356.
22. P. A. Devijer and M. Dekesel, "Learning the parameters of a hidden Markov random field image model: a simple example", *Pattern Recognition Theory and Applications*, Springer-Verlag, 1987, pp. 141–163.
23. P. A. Devijer and J. Kittler, eds., *Pattern Recognition Theory and Applications*, Springer-Verlag, 1987.
24. R. L. Dorushin, "Description of a random field by means of conditional probabilities and the conditions govern its regularity", *Theory of Probability and its Applications*, (English translation of *Teoriia Veriatn*) **13** (1968) 197–224.
25. R. Dubes, A. Jain, S. Nadabar, and C. Chen, "MRF model-based algorithms for image segmentation", *Proc. 10th Int. Conf. on Pattern Recognition*, Atlantic City, NJ, June 1990, pp. 808–814.
26. W. A. Edelstein *et al.*, "Signal, noise, and contrast in NMR imaging", *J. Comput. Assisted Tomography* **7** (1983) 391–401.
27. M. P. Ekstrom and J. W. Woods, "Two-dimensional spectral factorization with applications in recursive digital filtering", *IEEE Trans. Acoustics, Speech, and Signal Processing* **24**, 2 (1976) 115–128.
28. I. M. Elfadel and R. W. Picard, "Gibbs random fields, co-occurrences and texture modeling", *IEEE Trans. Pattern Analysis and Machine Intelligence* **PAMI-16**, 1 (1994) 24–37.
29. O. D. Faugeras, N. Ayache, and B. Faverjon, "Building visual maps by combining noisy stereo measurements", *Proc. IEEE Int. Conf. Robotics Automation*, San Francisco, April 1986, pp. 1433–1438.

30. O. D. Faugeras, F. Lustman, and G. Toscani, "Motion and structure from motion from point and line matches", *Proc. 1st Int. Conf. Computer Vision*, London, April 1987, pp. 1433–1438.
31. L. E. Franks, "A model for the random video process", *Bell Syst. Tech. J.* **45** (1966) 609–630.
32. S. Geman and D. Geman, "Stochastic relaxation, Gibbs distribution, and the Bayesian restoration of images", *IEEE Trans. Pattern Analysis and Machine Intelligence* **PAMI-6**, 6 (1984) 721–741.
33. D. Geman, S. Geman, C. Graffigne, and P. Dong, "Boundary detection by constrained optimization", *IEEE Trans. Pattern Analysis and Machine Intelligence* **PAMI-12**, 7 (1990) 609–628.
34. P. J. Green, "Bayesian reconstructions from emission tomography data using a modified EM algorithm", *IEEE Trans. Medical Imaging* **9**, 1 (1990).
35. A. Habibi, "Two-dimensional Bayesian estimation of images", *Proc. IEEE* **60** (1972) 878–883.
36. F. R. Hampel, E. M. Ronchetti, P. J. Rousseeuw, and W. A. Stahel, *Robust Statistics: The Approach Based on Influence Functions*, John Wiley & Sons, Inc., 1986.
37. K. Hanson and G. Wecksung, "Bayesian approach to limited-angle reconstruction computed tomography", *J. Opt. Soc. Am.* **73**, 11 (1983) 1501–1509.
38. R. M. Haralick, "Computer vision theory: the lack of it", *Computer Vision, Graph., and Image Processing* **36** (1986) 372–386.
39. T. Hebert and R. Leahy, "A generalized EM algorithm for 3-D Bayesian reconstruction from Poisson data using Gibbs priors", *IEEE Trans. Medical Imaging* **8**, 2 (1989) 194–202.
40. T. J. Hebert and K. Lu, "Expectation-maximization algorithms, null spaces, and MAP image restoration", *IEEE Trans. Image Processing* **4**, 8 (1995) 1084–1095.
41. F. Heitz and P. Bouthemy, "Multimodal estimation of discontinuous optical flow using Markov random fields", *IEEE Trans. Pattern Analysis and Machine Intelligence* **15**, 12 (1993) 1217–1232.
42. B. K. P. Horn, "Understanding image intensities", *Artificial Intelligence* **8** (1977) 201–231.
43. D. I. Hoult and R. E. Richards, "Signal-to-noise ratio of nuclear magnetic resonance experiment", *J. Magn. Reson.* **24** (1976) 71–85.
44. P. Huber, *Robust Statistics*, John Wiley & Sons, Inc., 1981.
45. Y. P. Hung, D. B. Cooper, and B. Cernuschi-frias, "Asymptotic Bayesian surface estimation using an image sequence", *Int. J. of Computer Vision* **6**, 2 (1991) 105–132.
46. B. R. Hunt, "The application of constrained least squares estimation to image restoration by digital computer", *IEEE Trans. Computers* **C-22**, 9 (1973) 805–812.
47. B. R. Hunt, "Bayesian methods in nonlinear digital image restoration", *IEEE Trans. Computers* **C-26**, 3 (1976) 219–229.
48. B. R. Hunt and T. M. Cannon, "Nonstationary assumptions for Gaussian models", *IEEE Trans. Systems, Man, and Cybernetics* **6**, 12 (1976) 876–882.
49. A. Jain and S. G. Nadabar, "Range image segmentation using MRF models", in *Markov Random Fields: Theory and Application*, eds. R. Chellappa and A. Jain, Academic Press, 1993, pp. 543–572.
50. B. D. Jeffs and M. Gunsay, "Restoration of blurred star field images by maximally sparse optimization", *IEEE Trans. Image Process.* **2**, 2 (1993) 202–211.
51. F.-C. Jeng and W. Woods, "Compound Gauss-Markov random fields for image estimation", *IEEE Trans. Signal Processing* **39**, 3 (1991) 683–697.

52. V. E. Johnson, W. H. Wong, X. Hu, and C.-T. Chen, "Image restoration using Gibbs priors: boundary modeling, treatment of blurring, and selection of hyperparameter", *IEEE Trans. Pattern Analysis and Machine Intelligence* **13**, 5 (1991) 413–425.
53. J. B. Kadane, ed., *Robustness of Bayesian Analysis*, Elsevier North-Holland, 1984.
54. R. E. Kalman, "A new approach to linear filtering and prediction problems", *J. Basic Engineering, (ASME Trans.)* (1960) 35–45.
55. R. Kashyap, R. Chellappa, and A. Khotanzad, "Texture classification using features derived from random field models", *Pattern Recogn. Lett.* **1**, 1 (1982) 43–50.
56. R. Kashyap and R. Chellappa, "Estimation and choice of neighbors in spatial-interaction models of images", *IEEE Trans. Information Theory* **IT-29**, 1 (1983) 60–72.
57. H. Kaufman, J. W. Woods, S. Dravida, and A. M. Tekalp, "Estimation and identification of two-dimensional images", *IEEE Trans. Automatic Control* **AC-28**, 7 (1983) 745–756.
58. R. Kindermann and J. Snell, *Markov Random Fields and Their Applications*, American Mathematical Society, 1980.
59. J. Konrad and E. Dubois, "Bayesian estimation of motion vector fields", *IEEE Trans. Pattern Analysis and Machine Intelligence* **PAMI-14**, 9 (1992) 910–927.
60. D. T. Kuan, A. A. Sawchuk, T. C. Strand, and P. Chavel, "Nonstationary 2-D recursive restoration of images with signal-dependent noise", *Int. Conf. on Acoustics, Speech, and Signal Processing*, San Diego, CA, April 1984, pp. 37.4.1–37.4.4.
61. M. J. Lahart, "Local image restoration by a least-squares method", *J. Opt. Soc. Am.* **69**, 10 (1979) 1333–1339.
62. K. Large, "Convergence of EM image reconstruction algorithms with Gibbs smoothing", *IEEE Trans. Medical Imaging* **9**, 4 (1990) 439–446.
63. Z. Q. Liu and T. M. Caelli, "A sequential recursive filter for image restoration", *Computer Vision, Graph., and Image Processing* **44**, 3 (1988) 332–349.
64. Z. Q. Liu, V. G. Gourishankar, and T. M. Caelli, "A new adaptive iterative algorithm for image restoration", *Image and Vision Computing* **6**, 3 (1988) 151–161.
65. L. Ljung and T. Söderström, *Theory and Practice of Recursive Identification*, MIT Press, 1983.
66. M. R. Luettgen, W. C. Karl, and A. S. Willsky, "Efficient multiscale regularization with applications to the computation of optical flow", *IEEE Trans. Image Processing* **3**, 1 (1994).
67. J. Mao and A. K. Jain, "Texture classification and segmentation using multiresolution simultaneous autoregressive models", *Pattern Recognition* **25**, 2 (1992) 173–188.
68. J. Marroquin, J. Mitter, and T. Poggio, "Probabilistic solution of ill-posed problems in computational vision", *J. American Statistical Association* **82**, 397 (1987) 76–89.
69. L. H. Matthies and S. A. Sharer, "Error modeling in stereo navigation", *IEEE J. Robotics and Automation* **RA-3**, 3 (1987) 239–248.
70. L. H. Matthies, R. Szeliski, and T. Kanade, "Kalman filter-based algorithms for estimating depth from image sequences", *Int. J. of Computer Vision* **3** (1989) 209–236.
71. P. Meer, D. Mintz, and A. Rosenfeld, "Robust-regression methods for computer vision: a review", *Int. J. of Computer Vision* **6**, 1 (1991) 59–70.
72. C. E. K. Mees, *The Theory of Photographic Process*, MacMillan, 1954.
73. J. W. Modestino and J. Zhang, "A Markov random field model-based approach to image interpretation", in *Markov Random Fields: Theory and Applications*, eds. R. Chellappa and A. Jain, Academic Press, Inc., Boston, 1993, pp. 369–408.
74. M. S. Murphy and L. M. Silverman, "Image model representation and line-by-line recursive restoration", *IEEE Trans. Automatic Control* **AC-23** (1978) 809–816.
75. N. E. Nahi, *Estimation Theory and Applications*, John Wiley & Sons, Inc., 1969.

76. N. E. Nahi, "Role of the recursive estimation in statistical image enhancement", *Proc. IEEE* **60** (1972) 872–877.
77. D. Panjwani and G. Healey, "Markov random field models for unsupervised segmentation of texured color images", *IEEE Trans. Pattern Analysis and Machine Intelligence* **PAMI-17**, 10 (1992) 939–954.
78. A. Papoulis, *Probability, Random Variables, and Stochastic Processes*, 2nd edn., McGraw-Hill Book Company, 1984.
79. D. L. Phillips, "A technique for numerical solution of certain integral equations of the first kind", *J. Assoc. Comput. Mach.* **9** (1962) 97–101.
80. J. Pliz, *Bayesian Estimation and Experimental Design in Linear Regression Models*, John Wiley & Sons, Inc., 1991.
81. T. Poggio and V. Torre, "Ill-posed problems and regularization analysis in early vision", *Proc. Image Understanding Workshop*, Science Applications International Corporation, New Orleans, Louisiana, 1984, pp. 257–263.
82. S. R. Powell and L. M. Silverman, "Modeling of two-dimensional covariance functions with application to image restoration", *IEEE Trans. Automatic Control*, **AC-19**, 1 (1974) 8–13.
83. A. Rosenfeld and A. C. Kak, *Digital Picture Processing*, Academic Press, 1982.
84. B. Rouchouze, P. Mathieu, T. Gaidon, and M. Bariand, "Motion estimation based on Markov random fields", *Proc. IEEE Int. Conf. on Image Proc.*, vol. 3, Austin, TX, Nov. 1994, pp. 270–274.
85. R. R. Schultz and R. L. Stevenson, "Stochastic modeling and estimation of multispectral image data", *IEEE Trans. Image Processing* **4**, 8 (1995) 1109–1119.
86. M. Schwartz, *Information Transmission, Modulation, and Noise*, McGraw-Hill, 1962.
87. K. Sauer and C. A. Bouman, "A local update strategy for iterative reconstruction from projections", *IEEE Trans. Signal Processing* **41**, 2 (1993).
88. M. M. Sondhi, "Image restoration: the removal of spatially invariant degradations", *Proc. IEEE* **60** (1972) 842–853.
89. F. Spitzer, "Markov random fields and Gibbs ensembles", *Amer. Math. Mon.* **78** (1971) 142–154.
90. R. G. Staudte and S. J. Sheather, *Robust Estimation and Testing*, John Wiley & Sons, Inc., 1990.
91. H. Tan, S. Gelfand, and E. Delp, "A comparative cost function approach to edge detection", *IEEE Trans. Systems, Man and Cybernetics* **SMC-19**, 6 (1989) 1337–1349.
92. T. Taxt, P. Flynn, and A. Jain, "Segmentation of document images", *IEEE Trans. Pattern Analysis and Machine Intelligence* **11**, 12 (1989) 1322–1329.
93. A. N. Tikhonov and V. Y. Arsenin, *Solutions of Ill-Posed Problems*, V. H. Winston, 1977.
94. H. J. Trussell and B. R. Hunt "Sectioned methods for image restoration", *IEEE Trans. Acoustics, Speech, and Signal Processing* **ASSP-26**, 2 (1978) 157–164.
95. H. J. Trussell, "Notes on linear image restoration by maximizing the *a posteriori* probability", *IEEE Trans. Acoustics, Speech, and Signal Processing* **ASSP-26**, 2 (1978) 174–176.
96. H. L. Van Trees, *Detection, Estimation, and Modulation Theory*, John Wiley & Sons, Inc., 1968.
97. J. F. Walkup and R. C. Choens, "Image processing in signal-dependent noise", *Opt. Eng.* **13** (1974) 258–266.
98. A. S. Willsky, "Relationships between digital signal processing and control and estimation theory", *Proc. IEEE* **66**, 9 (1979) 996–1917.

99. J. W. Woods, "Two-dimensional discrete Markovian fields", *IEEE Trans. Information Theory* **18** (1972) 232–240.
100. J. W. Woods and C. H. Radewan, "Kalman filtering in two dimensions", *IEEE Trans. Information Theory* **23**, 4 (1977) 473–482.
101. J. W. Woods, "Correction to 'Kalman filtering in two dimensions'", *IEEE Trans. Information Theory* **25**, 5 (1979) 628–629.
102. J. W. Woods, "Two-dimensional Kalman filtering", *Two-Dimensional Digital Signal Processing: I*, ed. S. T. Huang, Springer-Verlag, 1981, pp. 155–205.
103. J. W. Woods and V. K. Ingle, "Kalman filtering in two dimensions: further results", *IEEE Trans. Acoustics, Speech, and Signal Processing* **29**, 2 (1981) 188–197.
104. J. J. Wu, R. E. Rink, T. C. Caelli, and V. G. Gourishakar, "Recovery of the 3D location and motion of rigid object through camera image (an extended Kalman filter approach)", *Int. J. of Computer Vision* **3** (1988) 373–394.
105. J. Zerubia and R. Chellappa, "Mean field annealing using compound Gauss–Markov random fields for edge detection and image estimation", *IEEE Trans. Neural Networks* **4**, 4 (1993) 703–709.
106. J. Zhang, "The mean field theory in EM procedures for blind Markov random field image restoration", *IEEE Trans. Image Processing* **2**, 1 (1993) 27–40.
107. J. Zhang and G. G. Hanauer, "The application of mean field theory to image motion estimation", *IEEE Trans. Image Processing* **4**, 1 (1995) 19–33.
108. X. H. Zhuang, T. Wang, and P. Zhang, "A highly robust estimator through partially likelihood function modeling and its application in computer vision", *IEEE Trans. Pattern Analysis and Machine Intelligence* **PAMI-14**, 1 (1992) 19–35.

---

**Zhi-Qiang Liu** is an Associate Professor with the Department of Computer Science, The University of Melbourne. He received a M.A.Sc. degree in aerospace engineering from the Institute for Aerospace Studies, The University of Toronto, and a Ph.D. degree in electrical engineering from The University of Alberta, Canada.

Dr. Liu is the leader and the Principal Investigator of the Computer Vision and Machine Intelligence Laboratory (CVMIL) at the Department of Computer Science, The University of Melbourne.

His research interests include image processing, computer vision, neural networks, image information management, and intelligent and knowledge-based systems. Dr. Liu has over 100 refereed publications and one book in these areas.

# ROBOT NAVIGATION BY VISUAL DEAD-RECKONING: INSPIRATION FROM INSECTS

M. V. SRINIVASAN, J. S. CHAHL and S. W. ZHANG

*Centre for Visual Science, Research School of Biological Sciences*
*Australian National University, P.O. Box 475, Canberra, A.C.T. 2601, Australia*
*E-mail: M.Srinivasan@anu.edu.au*

Insects such as ants and bees are capable of surprisingly good navigation, despite the small size and relative simplicity of their brains. Recent experimental research in our laboratory, summarized in this chapter, indicates that honeybees estimate the distance travelled to a food site in terms of the image motion that they experience *en route*. This finding has inspired us to design and build a robot that navigates using a visually-driven odometer.

*Keywords*: Dead reckoning, path integration, honeybee navigation, insect vision, movement perception, image processing, optic flow, robotics.

## 1. INTRODUCTION

While certain animals, such as pigeons, are renowned for their extraordinary navigational abilities,[1,2] it is noteworthy that many arthropods, such as bees and ants, also exhibit a surprisingly good capacity to navigate by dead-reckoning, despite the smaller size and relative simplicity of their brains. In principle, a walking insect (or a ground-based vehicle) can keep track of the distance it has traveled by counting footsteps (or measuring wheel rotations). However, a flying insect (or airborne vehicle) cannot rely on analogous methods of odometry: counting wingbeats or measuring energy consumption, for example, can be confounded by errors due to the presence of head or tailwinds. How, then, do flying insects measure distance traveled, and can the principles be exploited for the design of navigational strategies for mobile robots? This chapter first describes experiments designed to unravel the basis by which flying honeybees measure distance traveled. Then it describes the design, construction and operation of an autonomous mobile robot that embodies this principle of dead-reckoning.

## 2. HONEYBEE NAVIGATION: A VISUALLY-DRIVEN ODOMETER

It is well known that honeybees can navigate accurately and repeatedly to a food source, as well as communicate to their nestmates the distance and direction in which to fly to reach it.[3] However, the cues by which bees gauge the distance flown to the goal remain controversial. Early studies suggested that this distance is measured in terms of the total energy expended during flight.[4] Recent studies, however, question this hypothesis and suggest instead that an important cue is the amount of image motion experienced by the bee's visual system *en route* to the target.[5] We investigated the ability of bees to gauge short distances flown under



Spatial Computing: Issues in Vision, Multimedia and Visualization Technologies (1997) 35–47

controlled laboratory conditions where a variety of potential cues were manipulated. Our findings indicate that bees measure short distances traveled solely through image motion.[6]

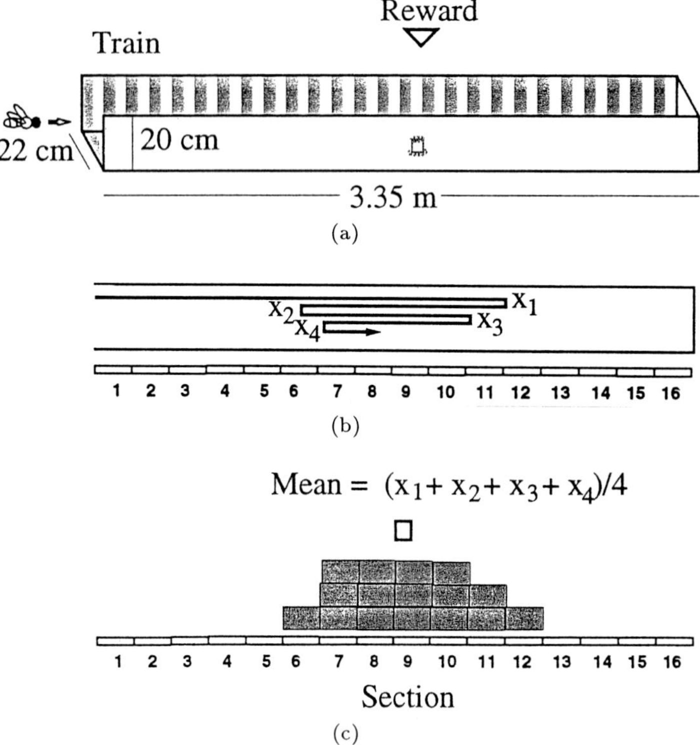


Fig. 1. (a) Bees are trained to fly into a tunnel 3.35 m long, 22 cm wide and 20 cm high, to find a reward of sugar water placed at a fixed location. They are subsequently tested in an identical, but fresh tunnel which carries no reward. Each tunnel is lined with black and white stripes of period 4 cm, is covered by a transparent sheet of perspex, and is subdivided into 16 sections for the purposes of analysis. (b) In the tests, the bees' behavior whilst searching for the reward is recorded by noting the locations of the first, second, third and fourth U-turns of the bee, $x_1, x_2, x_3$ and $x_4$, respectively. (c) The mean of the four values (square) provides an estimate of the mean searching location, and the spatial distribution of the search is estimated by measuring the number of times the bee enters each section during this period.

In the experiments, bees were trained to enter a 3.35 m long tunnel and collect a reward of sugar solution at a feeder placed in the tunnel, a fixed distance from the entrance (Fig. 1(a)). The walls and floor of the tunnel were lined with black-and-white stripes perpendicular to the tunnel's axis. During training, the position and orientation of the tunnel were changed frequently to prevent the bees from using external landmarks to gauge their position in the tunnel. The bees were then tested by recording their searching behavior in a fresh tunnel which carried no reward, and was devoid of any scent cues (Fig. 1(b)). Analysis of the test data is described in the legend to Fig. 1. Bees trained in this way showed a clear ability to search for the reward at the correct distance (Fig. 2(a)). The mean searching position is very

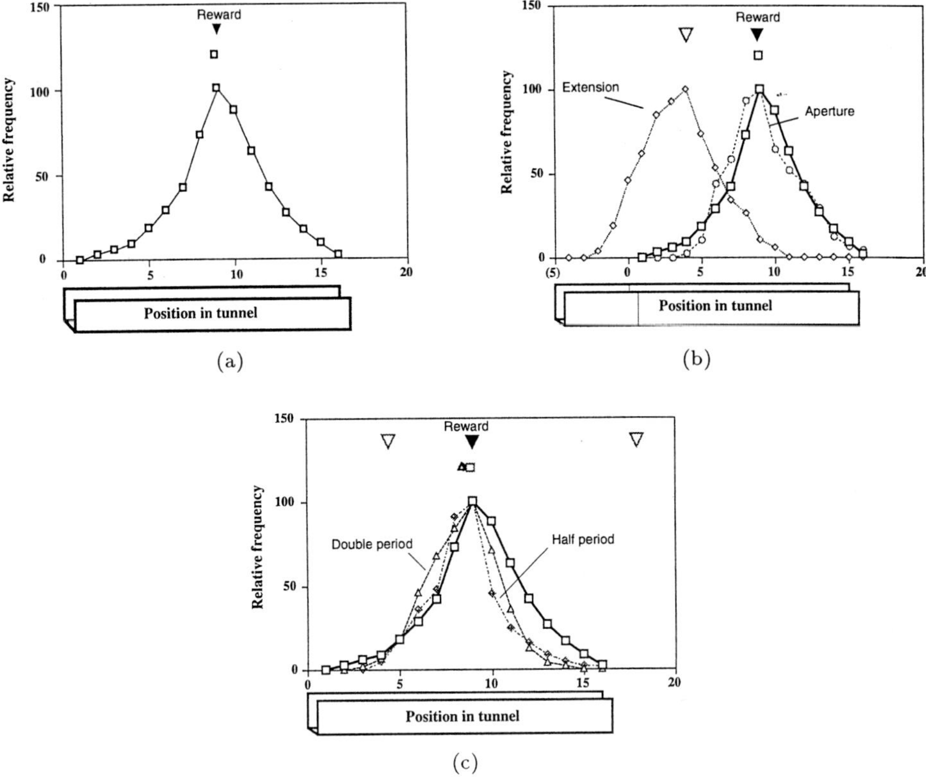


Fig. 2. Bees, trained to find a reward in section 9 of a training tunnel (see Fig. 1(a)), are subsequently tested in a variety of tunnels that carry no reward. In each case, the inverted arrow indicates the former position of the reward, the symbol below it indicates the mean searching location, and the curve shows the spatial distribution of the search. (a) Test in tunnel identical to training tunnel. (b) Tests in tunnels that carry a $4 \times 4$ cm aperture at the entrance or a 1.5 m extension at the front end. (c) Tests in tunnels that carry stripes of half (2 cm) or double (8 cm) the period of the stripes in the training tunnel. The inverted arrows on the left and right depict the mean searching locations that would be expected in the tests with the narrower and wider stripes, respectively, if the bees were estimating the distance to the reward by counting stripes.

close to the actual position of the reward. The search distribution typically exhibits a half-width of ca. 80 cm, but this figure is likely to be an overestimate of the bees' error in distance judgement because the distribution reflects the boundaries of the region that is searched by the bee when the reward is absent.

How were the bees gauging the distance flown? A number of experiments were carried out to investigate this question. We first investigated the possibility that the bees were using the visual angle subtended by the entrance or the end wall to gauge their position in the tunnel. Bees trained as in Fig. 1(a) were tested in situations in which the entrance aperture to the tunnel was made smaller, or where the length of the tunnel was extended. We found that the trained bees searched at the correct distance from the tunnel entrance regardless of these manipulations (Fig. 2(b)). This eliminates the possibility that the bees were using features of the tunnel as reference landmarks.

Were the bees gauging the location of the reward by counting the number of stripes or other features passed whilst flying through the tunnel? This is an intriguing possibility, especially in the light of recent evidence that bees exhibit a capacity for "counting" landmarks *en route* to a target.[7] We found, however, that trained bees searched at the correct distance from the tunnel entrance even when the spatial period of the stripes lining the tunnel was altered in tests (Fig. 2(c)). This eliminates stripe-counting as a means of estimating distance flown in our experiments.

Could the bees be gauging the location of the reward in the tunnel by measuring the energy consumed *en route*, the duration of flight, or other related parameters? To investigate this, bees were trained as in Fig. 1(a) and tested in a tunnel that presented a headwind or a tailwind, created by a fan at the far end of the tunnel. In a headwind, bees flew slower and took longer to reach the estimated location of the reward. The opposite was true in a tailwind. The average times elapsed between the entry into the tunnel and the first U-turn were $7.2 \pm 2.6$ sec in still air, $10.1 \pm 2.7$ sec in a headwind of 0.7 m/s and $5.9 \pm 1.8$ sec in a tailwind of 0.65 m/s. Since these times were significantly different from each other, we infer that distance traveled is not estimated in terms of time of flight, or other correlated parameters such as number of wingbeats. In a headwind, bees overshot the location of the reward slightly; in a tailwind, they undershot it (Fig. 3(a)). While the reasons for these misjudgments remain to be discovered, it is clear that distance flown is not measured in terms of energy consumption, because the errors made by the bees are in directions *opposite* to those expected on this basis.

Were the bees measuring distance flown by integrating the motion of the image of the surrounding panorama as they flew to the goal? To examine this possibility, we trained bees in a tunnel of a given width and then tested them in a tunnel that was narrower or wider. For a given distance traveled by the bee, the narrower tunnel induces a larger motion of the image on the eye, and the wider tunnel a smaller image motion. Thus, if bees integrate image motion to estimate distance traveled, they should search at a shorter distance from the entrance in a narrower tunnel, and at a farther distance in the wider tunnel. This is indeed what we found (Fig. 3(b)). These results suggest that one cue used by bees to gauge distance flown, is the total amount of image motion experienced whilst flying through the tunnel.

The image-motion hypothesis was tested further in an experiment in which bees were trained and tested in tunnels in which this cue was eliminated by using axially oriented stripes on the walls and floor. Bees flying along such a tunnel would experience very little image motion, since they fly in a direction parallel to the stripes. Strikingly, bees trained in the axial-striped tunnel displayed no ability to gauge distance traveled: they searched uniformly over the entire length of the tunnel (Fig. 3(c)). The behavior of these bees was very different from that in the other experiments. Here the bees, upon entering the tunnel flew directly to the other end, without turning or even pausing near the former location of the reward. After making a U-turn at the far end, they flew straight back to the entrance. They then exited the tunnel and re-entered it to repeat the above procedure over and over again. Clearly, removal of image motion cues completely disrupts the bees' ability to localize the position of the reward. This finding confirms the hypothesis that image motion, integrated over time, is an important cue for estimating distance flown.

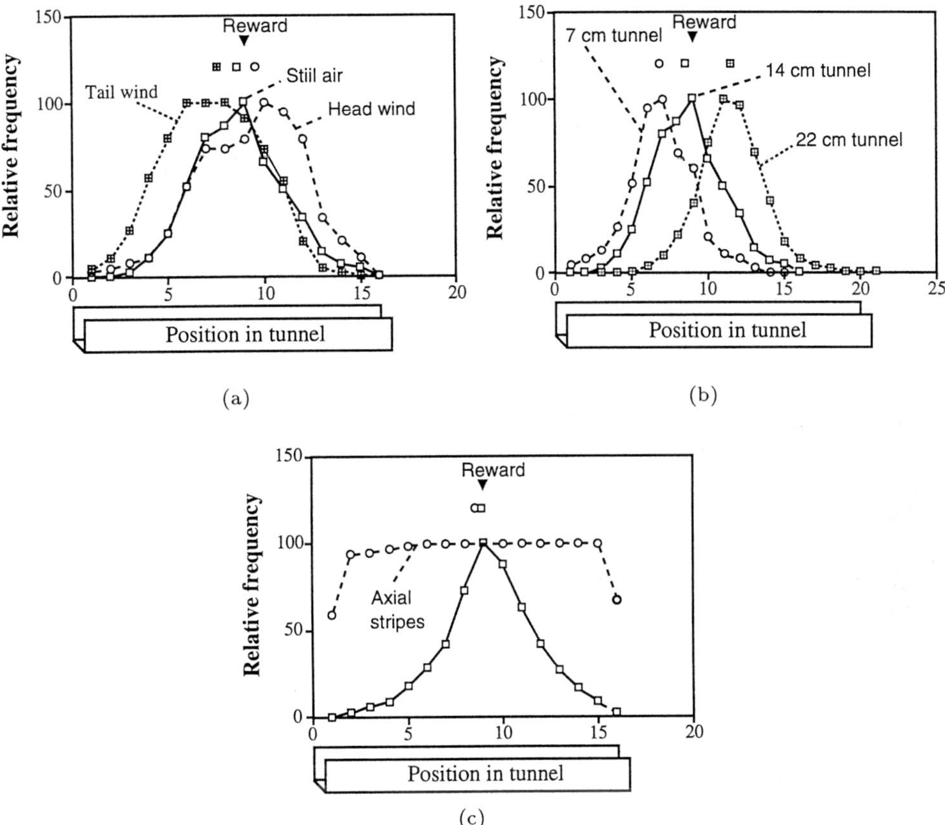


Fig. 3. (a) Bees, trained to find a reward in section 9 of a training tunnel (see Fig. 1(a)), are subsequently tested in an identical tunnel in still air, a headwind or a tailwind. (b) Bees, trained to find a reward in section 9 of a training tunnel of width 14 cm, are tested in tunnels whose widths are the same (14 cm), narrower (7 cm) or wider (22 cm). (c) Bees are trained to find a reward in section 9 of a training tunnel similar to that in Fig. 1(a) but lined with axial stripes of period 4 cm, and then tested in an identical tunnel.

Are there additional cues that bees use to measure their progress in the tunnel? For example, do they also use some form of inertial navigation? If bees possess an (as yet unknown) means of measuring translatory acceleration, they could, in principle, double-integrate this signal to estimate distance flown. To investigate this possibility, bees were trained as in the experiment of Fig. 2(a) and tested in a tunnel that was moved continuously and smoothly along its long axis as the bee flew through it. The total displacement of the tunnel was about 40% of its length and the duration of this displacement was such that the movement was completed before the bee made its first U-turn. Bees tested in the moving tunnel searched

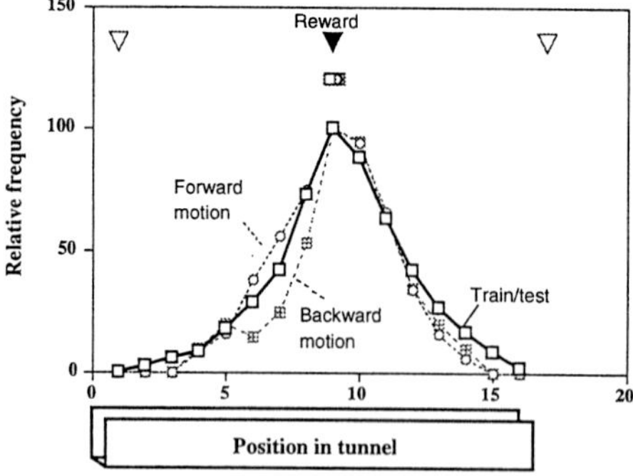


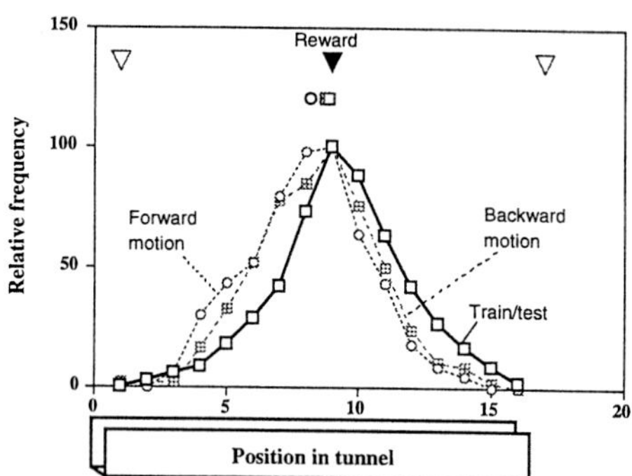


Fig. 4. (a) Bees, trained to find a reward in section 9 of a training tunnel (see Fig. 1(a)), are subsequently tested in an identical tunnel that is either stationary (Train/test), moved in the same direction as the bee's flight ("Forward motion") or moved against it ("Backward motion") at a mean rate of 0.36 metres/sec, for ca. 4.4 sec. This is done with the far end of the tunnel closed (as in the other experiments) to test the inertial navigation hypothesis (a), and with the far end open to test the airspeed integration hypothesis (b).

at the previous location of the reward *relative to the tunnel entrance*, regardless of whether the tunnel was moved with or against the bee. This means that, compared with the training situation, the bee flew a 40% *greater* absolute distance before making a U-turn when the tunnel was moved with the bee, and a 40% *smaller* absolute distance when the tunnel was moved against it. The arrows to the left and the right depict the expected searching locations if the bee were using inertial navigation to fly a fixed absolute distance, irrespective of tunnel motion. Thus, the bees were not measuring absolute distance flown, but the distance flown relative to the tunnel entrance. This finding rules out inertial navigation as a possible mechanism, but is consistent with integration of image motion.

Were the bees obtaining additional information on distance traveled by integrating airspeed? Most insects possess wind-sensitive hairs on the head that could, in principle, be used to provide an indication of airspeed (e.g. Ref. 8). If insects can measure airspeed and integrate it over time, they should be able to gauge the distance flown relative to the body of air in which they fly. (Such a mechanism, however, would indicate true distance flown only if the air is still.) To investigate this possibility, we tested bees in a moving tunnel as described above, but with the far end of the tunnel open. This ensured that the body of air in the tunnel did not move with the tunnel but was stationary in absolute space, as confirmed by an anemometer. Bees flying in the moving tunnel searched at the previous location of the reward *relative to the tunnel entrance*, irrespective of whether the tunnel was moved with or against the bee. This meant that, compared with the training situation, the bee flew through a 40% *longer* column of air before making a U-turn when the tunnel was moved with the bee, and a 40% *shorter* column of air when the tunnel was moved against it. The arrows to the left and the right depict the expected searching locations relative to the tunnel if the bee were to fly through a constant length of air column, irrespective of tunnel motion. Thus, the bees were not measuring distance flown relative to the air, but the distance flown relative to the tunnel entrance. This finding rules out integration of airspeed as a possible mechanism, a conclusion that is also supported by the results of Figs. 3(a) and 3(c).

In summary, our findings reveal that bees possess a visually-driven "odometer" that estimates distance flown by integrating the image motion that is experienced on the way to the goal. The tests with different stripe periods suggest that this mechanism measures the speed of the image largely independently of its structure. This mechanism seems to be different from the one that mediates the well-studied optomotor response, which is sensitive to the structure of the moving image and does not provide an unambiguous indication of its speed.[9] Our results also argue against the hypotheses that short distances flown are measured in terms of (a) time of flight, (b) energy consumption, (c) number of wingbeats, (d) integrated airspeed or (e) inertial navigation. The observation that feeder-locating performance deteriorates dramatically when image-motion cues are removed provides further evidence against participation of the other cues in our experiments.

Our conclusions are in agreement with those of a recent study by Esch and Burns,[5] who investigated distance measurement by honeybees through a different experimental approach. They examined how dancing bees signaled the distance to a food source that was a constant horizontal distance away (70 m), but whose elevation was systematically varied. They found that the bees signaled a *shorter* distance as the food was moved higher. From this, they inferred that distance flown is gauged in terms of the motion of the image of the ground below, and not through energy consumption. Evidently, visual odometry is used not only in short-range navigation (as in our experiments), but also in situations that typify foraging flights of moderate length.

Unlike energy-based cues, visual cues would not be affected by wind or by the load of nectar that the bee carries. However, a visual odometer, as described here, would work accurately only if the bee followed a fixed route each time it flew to its destination (or if a follower bee followed the same route as a dancing scout bee). This is because the total amount of image motion that is experienced during the trip would depend upon the distances to the various objects that are passed *en route*. The integrative nature of the mechanism implies that errors in the measurement of image speed accumulate with distance, so that larger distances would be estimated with greater error. We presume that such cumulative errors are reduced in flights along familiar routes, by re-commencing the integration of image motion whenever a known landmark is passed.

## 3. A ROBOT WITH A VISUALLY-DRIVEN ODOMETER

Inspired by the bee's visual odometer, we have designed and equipped a robot with an optical egomotion computer that gives the robot an indication of how far and in what direction it has traveled. The computation of egomotion is based on an *Image-Interpolation algorithm* developed in our laboratory.[10] The algorithm makes use of the fact that if a sensor captures images of the environment from two different reference positions, a known distance apart, the image corresponding to an unknown intermediate position can be approximated by a weighted linear combination of the images obtained from the two reference positions. The intermediate position of the sensor can then be determined from the coefficients of the interpolation. This technique is accurate provided that the reference images are captured at positions that are close enough to permit accurate linear interpolation of the intermediate image.[11]

This concept is applied in the following example to compute robot egomotion. Two panoramic views of the world are captured simultaneously, a fixed, known distance apart on the axis along which the robot translates (the fore-aft axis). Each view corresponds to a ringlike, horizontal slice of the environment, and is acquired by a separate video camera mounted under a cone-shaped mirror (see Fig. 5(a)). The separation of the two cameras is equal to the largest displacement that is expected. Let $f_0(\theta)$ and $f_1(\theta)$ denote the images captured by the rear and front cameras, respectively. Now assume that the robot translates forward by an unknown distance $\alpha$ expressed as a fraction of the separation between the two cameras. We capture a third image $f(\theta)$ at this location, using the rear camera. We wish to determine the translation of the robot by measuring how far the rear camera has moved. The rear camera is now located somewhere between the original locations of the front and rear cameras. We assume that the new image captured by the rear camera at this intermediate location can be approximated by $\hat{f}(\theta)$, a weighted linear combination of the reference images $f_0(\theta)$ and $f_1(\theta)$ as follows:

$$\hat{f}(\theta) \cong (1-\alpha) f_0(\theta) + \alpha f_1(\theta) \tag{1}$$

where $\alpha (0 \leq \alpha \leq 1)$ specifies the fractional displacement of the rear camera relative to the distance between the two cameras. This equation is valid provided the image $f_0$ deforms linearly to $f_1$ as $\alpha$ is varied, a condition which can be ensured by low-pass filtering the image adequately. From (1) we see that when $\alpha = 0$, $\hat{f}(\theta) = f_0(\theta)$ and when $\alpha = 1$, $\hat{f}(\theta) = f_1(\theta)$. Thus, the approximation $\hat{f}(\theta)$ satisfies the boundary conditions.

To determine the value of $\alpha$ that gives the best approximation to $f(\theta)$, we minimize the mean square error between $f(\theta)$ and $\hat{f}(\theta)$. That is, we minimize

$$\int_0^{2\pi} [(1-\alpha) f_0(\theta) + \alpha f_1(\theta) - f(\theta)]^2 d\theta \tag{2}$$

with respect to $\alpha$. This minimization yields

$$\alpha = \frac{\int_0^{2\pi} [f(\theta) - f_0(\theta)][f_1(\theta) - f_0(\theta)] d\theta}{\int_0^{2\pi} [f_0(\theta) - f_1(\theta)]^2 d\theta} \tag{3}$$

Since $f_0(\theta)$, $f(\theta)$ and $f_1(\theta)$ are known, $\alpha$ can be readily computed. Thus, the translatory displacement of the robot can be measured optically by capturing three images, and processing them as specified above.

(a)

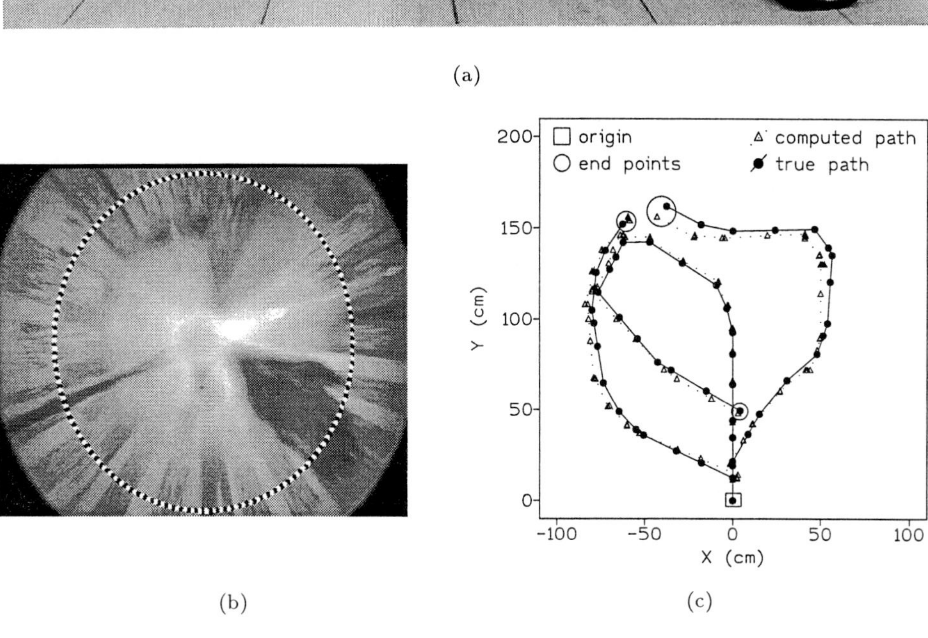


(b) (c)

Fig. 5. (a) Photograph of the robot in the laboratory in which all experiments were undertaken, showing the grid on the floor and some of the objects in the environment. (b) An image captured by one of the video cameras via the conical reflector which is used to obtain a horizontal, panoramic strip view of the environment. The black and white annulus represents the part of the image that was decoded to form the narrow strip. Individual visual units along the strip are indicated by the alternating black and white segments. (c) Comparisons between the path determined by the integration of motion calculated by the interpolation algorithm (dotted line), and the actual path followed by the robot (solid line). Three different trajectories are shown.

An analogous approach can be used to measure rotations of the robot about the optical axis of the rear camera. In this case, the reference images can be obtained by software-rotating the image captured by the rear camera, because rotation about the optical axis causes all points in the ring image to be displaced by the same amount, irrespective of the distances of the objects in the environment.

We have embodied this technique in a mobile robot, thereby enabling it to measure its egomotion in an unknown environment. A view of the robot and its environment is shown in Fig. 5(a). The robot is approximately 40 cm long and moves on three wheels, consisting of two drive wheels at the rear and a casting wheel at the front. The drive wheels are independently controllable, allowing the robot to either

(i) translate along the long axis,
(ii) turn about a point on the rear axle midway between the two rear wheels or
(iii) move along a curve, i.e. translate and rotate simultaneously.

Figure 5(a) also shows the two camera/cone assemblies. The image captured by each camera is $344 \times 288$ pixels of 128 grey levels (Fig. 5(b)). The egomotion algorithm uses a ring-shaped strip of this image, of radius 140 pixels and of thickness 5 pixels, centred on the axis of the cone, that is divided into an array of 250 units. These are shown as a ring of black and white circles superimposed on the grey level image in Fig. 5(b). This ring corresponds to a horizontal slice of the environment at a height of 15 cm above the floor, covering an elevational angle of $1^\circ$.

The performance of the egomotion algorithm in computing the motion of the robot is illustrated in Fig. 5(c). The robot moved along three different trajectories, each encompassing 30–40 individual steps. The figure compares the path determined by integrating the motions computed for the individual steps by the egomotion algorithm, with the actual path followed by the robot, as established from the grid marked out on the floor. Clearly, the algorithm performs well.

In each of the above tests there were objects around the edges of the test area, but no objects very close to the robot. Two further experiments were carried out (Figs. 6(a) and (b)) to investigate the performance of the algorithm as the robot translated through an aisle of columns and boxes that were placed at distances ranging from 30 to 80 cm from the robot. In these experiments, the relative proximity of the objects to the robot produced larger displacements of their images, therefore decreasing the accuracy with which interpolations could be carried out between the images captured by the two cameras. Furthermore, errors can arise due to occlusion of distant objects by nearer ones. Occlusions are not explicitly catered for by the image interpolation algorithm. Under these conditions the algorithm tends to underestimate egomotion slightly, as is evident from the trajectories shown in Fig. 6. Nevertheless, despite these unfavourable conditions, it is clear that the trajectories are computed with acceptable accuracy.

It is important to note that the egomotion algorithm requires absolutely no knowledge of the 3-d structure of the environment. For example, there is no need to assume that the world is locally planar. Nor is there need for any object recognition, feature matching, or even image velocity computation. The algorithm yields accurate results, provided the environment carries sufficient texture to provide the relevant visual information. Unlike the bee, the algorithm does not get "fooled" when corridor widths are changed: it measures absolute distance traveled regardless of the structure of the world. This is because the algorithm works on the basis of reference images captured from two locations that are a known distance apart. The Image-Interpolation algorithm, as applied here, uses the world "as its own model" to infer the motion of the robot.

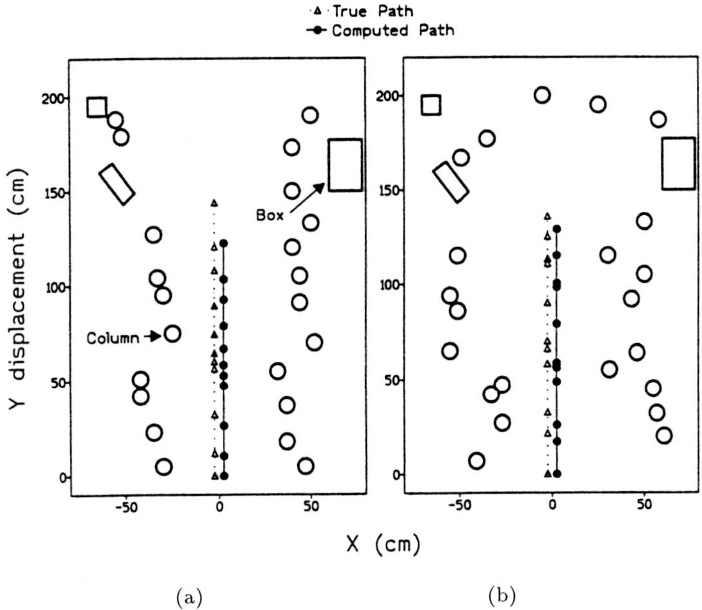


Fig. 6. Tests with robot in an environment that generates substantial occlusion and disocclusion. (a) and (b) show the path determined by the interpolation algorithm (solid line), compared to the actual path (dotted line). The paths are displaced laterally for ease of visualization. In these tests the environment was cluttered with columns and boxes that were very close to the robot.

## 4. CONCLUSIONS

Analysis of vision in simple natural systems, such as those found in insects, can often point to novel ways of tackling tenacious problems in autonomous navigation. This is probably because insects, with their "stripped down" nervous systems, have been forced to evolve ingenious strategies to cope with the visual challenges presented by their environment. This article has outlined one way in which observation of bees flying through tunnels has led to the design of a robot that uses vision to compute its egomotion. In constructing such machines, our aim is not to copy insect vision in the literal sense. The egomotion computing robot, with its forward and rear cameras, could hardly be described as an imitation insect. At present we do not know enough about the actual processing mechanisms that underlie insect vision to produce a carbon (or silicon) copy, anyway. Rather, our aim is to carry out behavioral experiments to reveal the *cues* that insects use to navigate, and to design machines that use such cues to advantage.

## REFERENCES


1. F. Papi, ed., *Animal Homing*, Chapman and Hall, London, 1992.
2. R. Wehner, M. Lehrer and W. Harvey, eds., *Navigation, J. Exp. Biol.* **199** (1996).
3. K. von Frisch, *The Dance Language and Orientation of Bees*, Harvard University Press, Cambridge, Mass. 1993.
4. H. Heran and L. Wanke, "Beobachtungen über die Entfernungsmeldung der Sammelbienen", *Z. vergl. Physiol.* **34** (1952) 383–393.
5. H. Esch and J. Burns, "Distance estimation by foraging honeybees", in *Navigation*, eds. R. Wehner, M. Lehrer and W. Harvey, *J. Exp. Biol.* **199** (1996) 155–162.
6. M. V. Srinivasan, S. W. Zhang, M. Lehrer, and T. S. Collett, "Honeybee navigation *en route* to the goal: visual flight control and odometry", in *Navigation*, R. Wehner, M. Lehrer and W. Harvey, *J. Exp. Biol.* **199** (1996) 155–162.
7. L. Chittka and K. Geiger, "Can honey bees count landmarks?", *Anim. Behav.* **49** (1996) 159–164.
8. C. H. F. Rowell, "Descending interneurones of the locust reporting deviation from flight course: What is their role in steering?", *J. Exp. Biol.* **146** (1989) 177–194.
9. W. Reichardt, "Movement perception in insects", in *Processing of Optical Data by Organisms and by Machines*, ed. W. Reichardt, Academic Press, New York, 1969, pp. 465–493.
10. M. V. Srinivasan, "An image-interpolation technique for the computation of optic flow and egomotion", *Biol. Cybernetics* **71** (1994) 401–416.
11. J. Chahl and M. V. Srinivasan, "Visual computation of egomotion using an image interpolation technique", *Biol. Cybernetics* **74** (1996) 405–411.

**Mandyam Srinivasan** holds an undergraduate degree in electrical engineering from Bangalore University, a Master's degree in electronics from the Indian Institute of Science, a Ph.D. in engineering and applied science from Yale University, and a D.Sc. in neuroethology from the Australian National University.

He was a Research Fellow in neurobiology and applied mathematics at the Australian National University, an Assistant Professor of zoology at the University of Zurich, and is presently Professor of Visual Sciences at the Australian National University's Research School of Biological Sciences and a Fellow of the Australian Academy of Science.

Dr. Srinivasan's research focuses on the principles of visual processing in simple natural systems, and on the application of these principles to machine vision and robotics.

**Javaan Chahl** received his Bachelor of computer engineering from the University of Newcastle, Australia, in 1991, his Graduate Diploma in neuroscience from the Australian National University in 1992, and completed his Ph.D. in 1996 at the Australian National University.

He is currently a Post Doctoral Fellow in the Research School of Biological Sciences at the Australian National University. His research interests include mobile robotics, machine vision, and arthropod behavior.

**Shao-Wu Zhang** studied applied mathematics at the Chinese University of Science and Technology and graduated in 1964. He was promoted to Assistant Professor in 1979, then Associate Professor in 1986 at the Institute of Biophysics, Chinese Academy of Sciences. As an Alexander von Humboldt Fellow he visited the Institute of Zoology at the Technical University of Darmstadt (Technische Hochschule) and the Max-Planck-Institute of Biological Cybernetics at Tuebingen in Germany from 1980 to 1983.

Since 1991, he has been at the Centre for Visual Science at the Australian National University. Dr. Zhang's research interests cover visual information processing in biological systems and engineering systems, biophysical aspects and modeling of visual systems, insect vision and behavioral analysis. Recently he is focusing on learning and memory in simple nervous systems.

# ASSESSING FEATURE IMPORTANCE IN THE CONTEXT OF OBJECT RECOGNITION

GEOFF A. W. WEST
*Department of Computer Science, Curtin University of Technology*
*Bentley, Perth, Western Australia*
*E-mail: geoff@cs.curtin.edu.au*

A popular paradigm in computer vision is based on dividing the vision problem into three stages namely segmentation, feature extraction and recognition. For example edge detection followed by line detection followed by planar object recognition. It can be argued that each of these stages needs to be thoroughly described to enable vision systems to be configured with predictable performance. However an alternative view is that the performance of each stage is not in itself important as long as the overall performance is acceptable.

This paper discusses feature performance concentrating on the assessment of edge-based feature detection and object recognition. Evaluation techniques are discussed for assessing arc and line detection algorithms and for features in the context of verification and pose refinement strategies. These techniques can then be used for the design and integration of indexing and verification stages of object recognition. A theme of the paper is the need to assess feature extraction in the context of the chosen task.

*Keywords*: Object recognition, performance assessment, verification, pose refinement.

## 1. INTRODUCTION

The history of computer vision has been characterized by the proposal and development of a very large number of different techniques for the different stages of object recognition systems. For example consider the number of edge detectors and object recognition techniques that have been produced. An unfortunate aspect of the research has been the lack of true scientific rigor when assessing the performance of such stages. However there are some notable exceptions. Edge detection performance quantification has been addressed,[5,38] feature salience[33] and object recognition.[11] In each case, some notion of ground truth has been used such as simulated images of edges and known objects in known orientations. A major reason for the lack of rigor has been the problem of how assessment should be performed and the initial need to see if such algorithms were feasible.[14] For example, there have been a number of algorithms proposed for the representation of edge pixels (edgels) by lines[22,25] and arcs and ellipses[33,39] which give different but perceptually good results. They each try to satisfy the same objective although different assessment criteria are used to guide the segmentation including accuracy of fit, correctness e.g., vertices in the correct place. In some situations, it is difficult to obtain ground truth because the accurate positions of edges and objects are difficult to determine except for simple images. This has lead to the use of simulation and computer generated images to investigate some aspects of vision.[30] In addition, there is the issue of how the edges were obtained. If edge detection was used, then



Spatial Computing: Issues in Vision, Multimedia and Visualization Technologies (1997) 49–77

there is the problem of scale of the edge detector and the local interaction of edges leading to poor edge localization and detection. There is also the problem of manually correctly defining the segmentation of curves as the interpretation is heavily dependent on the *context* or *task*. It has been reported that different segmentations of edges can be generated manually[8] depending on the task. For example segment the curve into five features using five points, or identify the five pieces of the curve generated by different processes.

This paper proposes a technique for assessing feature performance for a particular context, namely object recognition. Feature performance is assessed for different scales of edge detection, different salience factors and two different match metrics namely average error per point and the Hausdorff distance metric which computes the maximum error between the model and image.[17] Assessment is achieved by analyzing *extents* of error minima used for pose refinement but applicable to both indexing and verification stages of object recognition and is performed in the presence of noise and data distortions. Different parameter variations are considered namely three translations $(T_x, T_y, T_z)$ and three rotations $(\theta_x, \theta_y, \theta_z)$. Issues such as using four or eight connectivity for gradient descent are addressed and quantitative assessment of the results presented. The technique can be applied to the problem of viewsphere tesselation which is not simply dependent on the geometry of the objects but on how easy it is to discriminate the views given typical feature extraction processes. In addition the problems of assessing edge detection and feature extraction are addressed.

## 2. ASSESSMENT

Recently the issue of characterizing the performance of computer vision systems has been addressed[14,15] which has attracted much debate in the literature. This requires the following definitions: what the image processing or computer vision task is, how it is done, the error criterion and the performance with different random degradations. Haralick[14] proposes an engineering approach to address this. For a typical vision system, the stages are shown in Fig. 1 which shows envisaged feedback paths for assessment. In this system the scene is acquired and edges extracted. These are then segmented into lines which are used to index into 2D views of the objects to produce hypotheses of the likely matches. These are then confirmed/denied using the verifier. This is further discussed in Sec. 4.

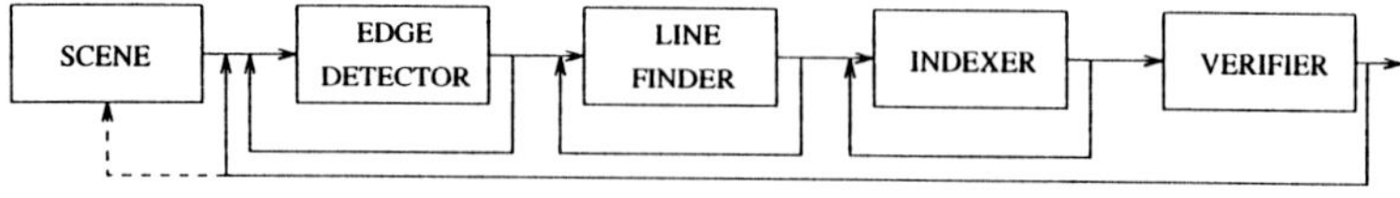


Fig. 1. Model 1 assessment architecture.

In this approach each stage of processing is analyzed independently using noise models, some notion of ground truth, etc. Hence to evaluate edge detection, the true positions of the real edges are required and edge detection assessed for different parameters and for criteria such as accuracy, false alarm rate and so on. This can be extended to evaluation of line detection (using polygonal approximation for example) again by having ground truth which defines the edgels forming the lines, the positions of vertices and the lines. In this case noise would be used to perturb the edgels. Hence, in this approach, each stage is assessed using the output of the previous stage as the ground truth. A problem with this approach is that line detection will almost always follow edge detection and the performance of one is closely coupled with the performance of the other. In fact perturbing a set of edgels with noise is a complex process involving, for each list, randomly moving edgels and then joining them together again in some way to form a connected set of edgels. Hence adding noise to edgels is not the same as adding noise to the image prior to edge detection. In addition it could be assumed that the resulting edgels will be passed to the line detector without further noise being added, the main source of error being any roundoff error from the edge detection. However the line detection can be assessed as a function of scale of the edge detector and in terms of the noise added before edge detection. A problem with this argument is that the edge and line detection are not local processes but are dependent on a variable number of pixels and edgels, respectively. A particular problem is the patterns of edges in the original image as edge detection can be affected by the proximity of edges to other edges. This is a well known problem for the Canny[5] and Marr–Hildreth[23] edge detectors because of the size of the masks or windows each uses. The extent of this problem is highly dependent on the expected image content. For example, planar objects will have sharp corners (actual angles are a function of object pose) and will give large errors in edge position whereas a curved object such as a toroid will produce small errors as there are less interacting edges (except in regions where occlusion occurs which can produce sharp corners).

A possible solution to the problem of assessment is to assess the performance of the complete system and not each individual stage as shown in Fig. 2. Now each stage is assessed with respect to the original image or ground truth available.

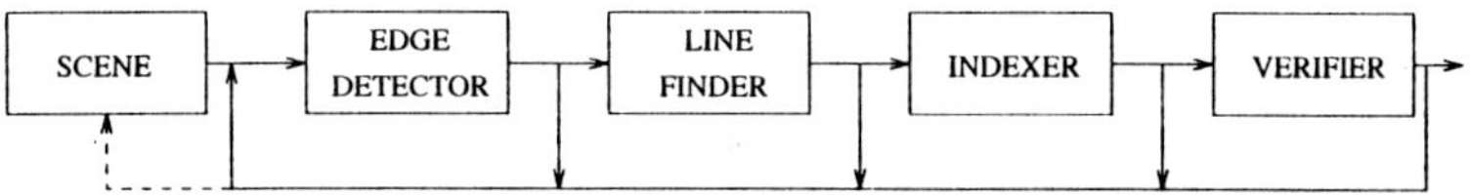


Fig. 2. Model 2 assessment architecture.

This is the approach taken for many pattern recognition situations in which the data is assumed to be noisy etc. and feature attributes clustered for classification. The errors are then taken as being combined with any true variation in the feature attribute because of size and shape variability in each class. Then errors in the edge detection, line detection and other subsystems will be accommodated by the object classification algorithm and modeled as simply errors in such feature attributes as position and angle. Grimson *et al.*[10] take this approach by processing images of real objects and perturbing the parameters for the resulting features in a controlled manner to test their system.

## 3. SALIENCE

Complicating the issue of feature extraction is the issue of salience. Salience is a way to define the *importance* of particular features such as edges, regions and lines. For example long edges may be defined as having a higher salience for object recognition — they are less likely to occur by accident in an image. The same can apply to the lines used in a polygonal description of a boundary. The definition of salience is usually in terms of the context. For example in object recognition where it can be used to define which are the most important features for matching. An obvious candidate for saliency is the number of degrees of freedom in the pose of an object in the image that can be constrained by the feature. For example a single ellipse in the image correctly matched to a circle on the model gives constraints on scale, position and rotation. There are only two degrees of freedom: the rotation of the object about the axis through the centre of the circle and the possible mappings of the circle onto the ellipse (four in the case of orthographic and perspective projection). Other features that give good localization are perceptual groups (parallel lines etc.),[21,41] vertex pairs[24] and pairs of ellipses.[31] There are many other features that can be found in the literature.

Salience is usually computed after feature extraction. For example, edges and then lines are extracted and the salience of each line is determined from its length and curvature[35] and orientation and curvature.[12] Recently the use of salience has been proposed for weighting the distances to features as encoded in a distance transform (DT) by edge strength, edge length, curvature and other properties producing salience distance transforms (salience DTs).[33] The important feature of salience is that it *weights* in some way the features such that the values do not have, for example, a geometric interpretation. The performance of such features cannot be solved analytically and requires the use of experimentation as proposed for pose refinement algorithms[16] and correlation-type registration algorithms.[2]

## 4. OBJECT RECOGNITION

2D and 3D object recognition can be regarded as consisting of the following two stages:

- obtain the estimate of the pose for the model (indexing), and
- confirm or deny the existence of the model (verification).

The process of recognition is complicated because there can be more than one object in the image, there can be more than one object to be recognized, and occlusion and variable segmentation means feature detection is unreliable producing false and missing features.[a]

[a]Note the issue of articulation of objects and deformable objects is not addressed, objects have to be rigid.

Currently there are two major paradigms for object recognition that are delineated by the modeling of the problem as either 2D or 3D. In the 2D paradigm, a 3D object is represented by a number of 2D views and recognition begins by detecting possible 2D views for models that fit the features extracted from the image. Notable examples of this approach are those based on geometric hashing[19] and conditional rule generation.[26] In the 3D paradigm, a full 3D model of each object is available. Features are chosen from the model that can be matched to projections of the same features in the image that have been detected. Then the model is projected onto the image and a measure of match determined. Notable examples of this approach are SCERPO[22] and alignment.[18,40] The latter[40] uses model circles matched to image ellipses to align the 3D model with the image features. A problem with such systems is the accuracy of feature detection with errors manifest as errors between the projected model and the image. This requires a pose refinement process to iteratively find the best match of the model with the image.

Both of the above described paradigms (hereon regarded as stages in recognition) are not, in themselves, adequate for object recognition. The first stage requires enough 2D views per object to disambiguate a 2D view of one model from a 2D view of another and requires reliable feature detection. The second stage can cope with unreliable feature detection but requires much computation. Using both stages, a number of 2D views can be used to build a fast indexing system which produces a number of *tentative* hypotheses of objects and *approximate* views. For each hypothesis a verification stage is invoked that tests each tentative pose against a large number of features in the image and determines the correct model and pose for the object in the scene. Essentially for a particular 3D model, the six pose parameters (three translations and three rotations) have to be determined.

The architecture of such a vision system is shown in Fig. 3.

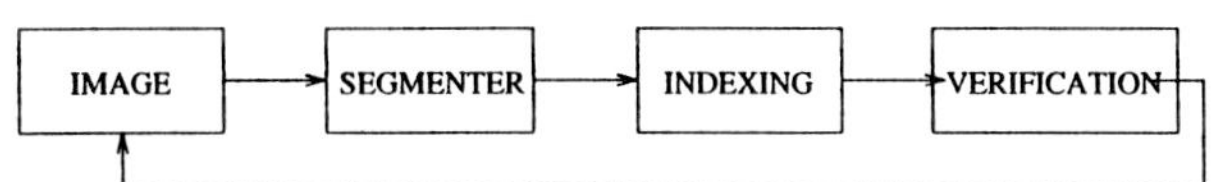


Fig. 3. A simple vision system architecture.

The indexing stage can be regarded as reducing the search space to a small number of interpretations which can then be confirmed/denied and refined in the second stage. An advantage of using the verification stage is that it improves the performance of recognition systems as it deals with the null set i.e. all objects and scenes that exist that do not contain the objects used to train the system. In other words it should produce a lower false alarm rate. This has been used by numerous researchers. In Ref. 20 geometric hashing was used to generate a number of hypotheses after which DTs were used to determine the best match.

A number of issues arise from the use of the two stages. Firstly, how accurate does the initial pose have to be to allow hypothesis confirmation and pose refinement to work? This is important as it affects the number of 2D views per object that need to be considered. The number of views is normally decided by the number of *unique* views required and is determined by analyzing a perfect 3D model of the object such as a CAD description and generating date structures of features that are visible from different viewpoints such as characteristic views,[6] aspect graphs[7] and viewspheres.[13] This process assumes that perfect or good feature extraction is possible as the features in each view are compared with those from the image. Note that a CAD object is a perfect model and will not reflect reality in terms of the position of edges and features. However the number of views is highly dependent on the segmentation performance because the features in the views required may not be detected, or not detected accurately. This issue has been addressed by the use of raytracing to generate perfect images from CAD descriptions and applying the same feature extraction processes as used for recognition.[30] An important issue is the number of views required as the greater the number of views the more processing is required. The minimum number of views is limited because the verification and pose refinement stage cannot determine the best and correct minimum if the initial pose is too far from the correct pose. For example pose refinement may lead to a local minimum which is not correct i.e. indicating the wrong view of the correct object or the wrong object. Of note is that the local minima problem can be overcome with a high degree of confidence using simulated annealing or a genetic algorithm. These have the ability to find the global minimum in the presence of many local minima. However they offer no advantage over gradient descent when the starting point is in the global minimum. There is also the issue of variability of objects. In the case of inspecting 3D objects for defects, a certain amount of dimensional variation is acceptable but not too much. Also many 3D objects have legal variability in dimensions e.g. cups which can take on a number of different shapes.

Secondly, there is the problem of reliable segmentation. For example the first stage of object recognition may have been trained on straight lines. All the lines or other features may not be detected in the images. This leads to attempts to generalize the first stage to accommodate variability in the features. This can be carried out by training on many images, perturbing the detected features or by assuming a particular statistical model for the feature parameters. However it is not always possible to obtain a good indexing scheme that will give firm results for recognition.

Given that some feature combination has been used to determine an initial pose, other features may have to be used for verification. Matching model vertices to image vertices, lines to lines etc. can be efficient but may be undesirable because of the reliance on low level segmentation. In addition features may have desirable qualities for indexing such as invariance and good noise immunity but not be adequate for recognition. Features such as lines and vertices when considered in isolation are not adequate for indexing as they have too many degrees of freedom. For example, a vertex just constrains one vertex of the model to match one vertex of the image. All other parameters are unconstrained. In the case of needing to solve for the six degrees of freedom (d.o.f.) (three rotations and three translations), this results in four d.o.f. to be determined. This is an important point as vertices and lines are regarded as important features for recognition. Ideally the indexing stage should require the minimum amount of processing of the image to generate enough features for a number of hypotheses to be constructed. Hence it is best to use easily derived features for indexing. The second stage of verification only considers a small number of hypotheses and regions of the image. Hence more complex features can be derived as only parts of the image have to be processed. These more complex features may be necessary to enable reliable object recognition to be carried out.

Other features that can be used for verification are simply the edge pixels (occluding boundary, internal edges, surface patterns), texture, color, etc. Ultimately the best features to use will be the actual pixel values in the image as features from the model can be directly compared with the image data as opposed to symbolic matching. Image data has been used successfully by Shirai[36] and more recently by Brisdon[4] and Mundy *et al.*[24] Using pixel data overcomes the problem of segmenting the image to find lines, regions and so on.

An important issue in object recognition is the scale at which features have to be determined. This is obvious given that an object can appear at a range of possible sizes in an image and different results for features will be obtained for the same object at different scales. The scale at which features for indexing or initial pose estimation and verification are used, may have to be different. For example, to get a good estimate of pose, accurate features such as edges are required leading to accurate estimation of feature positions. On the other hand, a fine scale may introduce noise producing fragmented features that would not be good for indexing. For verification, a coarser scale can be used to reduce noise and confusion to give a *cleaner* image. However for accuracy a fine scale may be better. Overall each stage may require a multiscale approach depending on the domain and context.

From the above discussion, it is concluded that the performance of the indexing and verification stages are highly dependent on feature extraction. The rest of this paper deals with the assessment of features. Initially the assessment of edge based features is tackled followed by methods for assessing features for verification and pose refinement.

## 5. EDGE DETECTION

There are a large number of edge detectors in the literature and consequently a number of methods have been proposed to assess their performance.[38,27] In Ref. 38, four criteria were proposed: false positives, false negatives, multiple edges and localization for assessment. There were combined using weights such that an overall measure for an edge detector was produced. Although the measure is comprehensive it cannot assess two properties of edge detectors that are important to many higher level feature extraction methods namely connectivity and vertex accuracy.

Connectivity is an important property when the edge information is used for higher order feature extraction such as line, arc and ellipse fitting. In this case it is crucial to have the edgels connected in a way that reflects reality i.e. a real edge should be represented by one list of connected edgels. Although connectivity was not considered the measures were determined along known edges (ground truth) to produce a measure of how well the edgels indicated this edge. To incorporate connectivity requires extra measures such as the number of edgels per list and the number of lists that fall on the ground truth edges.

The accuracy of the edgels can be important and is dependent on the algorithm used for linking edgels together. For example when fitting lines to edgels using the method of recursive division[21,25] the accurate position and representation of the vertices is an issue. The Marr–Hildreth and Canny edge detectors are good at representing linear edges but are poor at representing vertices because they assume only one edge is present under the mask used. This assumption is violated at corners. Hence they represent, for example, the edges of a cube accurately away from corners, and inaccurately at corners. To accommodate this factor, edge assessment must consider vertices separately from linear edges.

To illustrate these two points, the following images of a 3D object were generated: an image of an isolated cube (Fig. 4(a)), a cube on a cluttered background (Fig. 4(b)), and a cube on a cluttered background with Gaussian and 'salt and pepper' noise added (Fig. 4(c)).

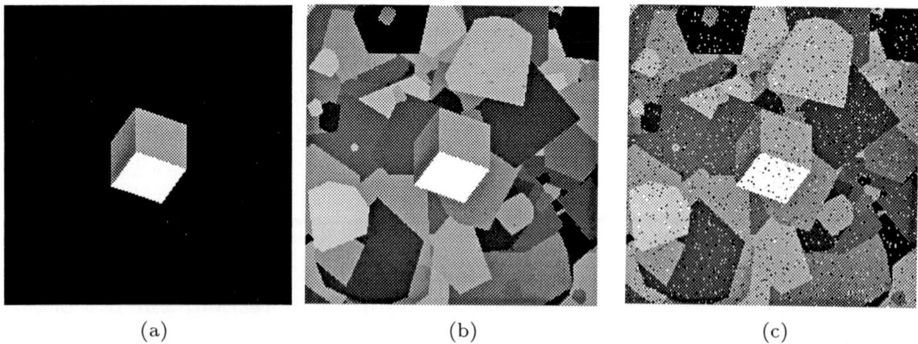

(a) (b) (c)

Fig. 4. Cube images, (a) isolated (cube1), (b) on a cluttered background (cube2), (c) added noise (cube3).

Only Fig. 4(b) is considered in this section. Figure 5 shows the edges for a scale of $\sigma = 2.0$ which clearly shows the way the edgels are connected and the poor representation of the vertices of the cube.

For different higher order feature detectors such as the Hough transform, connectivity and accuracy of the vertices is of less importance as the transform groups edgels that are on or nearly on the same line using a voting technique. Results are not dissimilar than those for least mean squares fitting or linear regression. The major lines will be extracted with reasonable accuracy and the errors at the vertices will be of less importance as vertices are defined as where pairs of lines intersect.

Ultimately the way to assess the performance of an edge detector is in the context of its application such as line finding, ellipse finding etc. where the sensitivity to errors in edge detection can be assessed.

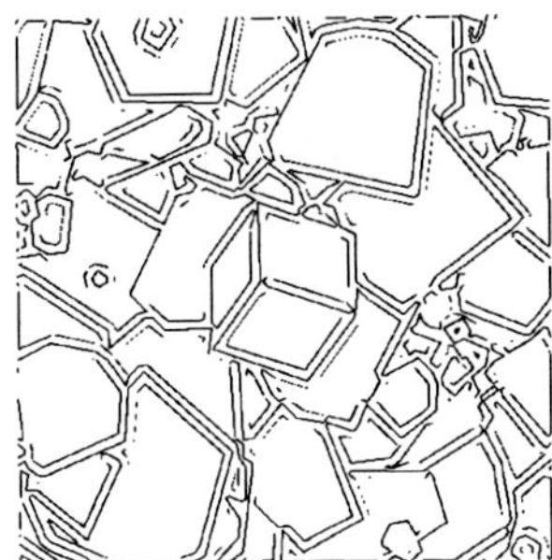

Fig. 5. Cube image after Marr–Hildreth edge detection for $\sigma = 2.0$.

## 6. FEATURE EXTRACTION

As with edge detection there have been numerous algorithms published for higher order feature extraction from lists of edgels. In this section we will concentrate on how to assess methods for line extraction. In practice it is difficult to quantify the performance of segmentation algorithms since they depend on a number of performance criteria such as geometric and topological distortions as well as accuracy and compactness.[1] As mentioned earlier it has been shown that manual segmentation produces different results depending on the context, task, and perceptual factors.[8,9] In addition to the problem in measuring the above criteria another problem is how to combine the criteria objectively. Note that in the context of object recognition, some of the factors are not of great importance e.g. compactness.

Consider one feature extraction algorithm based on recursive subdivision that uses the concept of significance to guide the segmentation. Recursive line fitting is used to produce the best set of lines to fit a curve based on minimizing significance which is defined as:

$$\frac{\text{maximum error between the data and the line}}{\text{length of the line}}. \tag{1}$$

Significance can be regarded as a normalized error such that long lines are allowed to fit with more error than short lines. The problem is assessing such an algorithm for performance. The algorithm has been assessed visually by observing the results and comparing them with the original image. For example, given the cube2 image, the detected lines are shown in Fig. 6.

The results are *visually pleasing* in that there are many situations where the algorithm has produced meaningful results. However there are other situations where the results are poor. For example some of the corners of the cube have more than one vertex and there are extra vertices on the edges of the cube.

The issue is how the performance of such an algorithm should be assessed. Rosin and West[32] have used several measures based on accuracy and compression to assess results of line fitting using the concept of significance which are

Fig. 6. Lines extracted for cube2 using the Marr–Hildreth edge detector with $\sigma = 2.0$.

repeated here. One measure for assessing this algorithm is the sum of the significance values which combines accuracy (the summed values of maximum deviation), and compression (number of items being summed). Two figures of merit similar to those proposed by Sarkar[34] for assessing polygonal approximations were also used.[32] Accuracy is calculated as the integral square error (ISE) between the original curve and the determined representation. If the perpendicular distance from the $i$th point of the curve to the approximation is $d_i$, then ISE $= \sum_{i=1}^{n} d_i^2$. Two alternative compression ratios are proposed. The first is the ratio of the number of features (i.e. curve primitives) in the approximation to the number of points on the original curve. The second draws on the concept from minimal length description encoding[29] in which the cost of encoding the parameters of each model are included in the overall measure. Note no attempt is made to model or quantify the noise term, or to specify different ranges (and therefore encoding costs) for the various values. The total number of curve primitive parameters is used for the measure of compression (four for each straight line (start and finish coordinates), and a minimum of five for each circular arc (centre, start coordinates and sweep angle)) divided by the number of curve points. The accuracy and compression terms are combined to produce the following figures of merit:

$$\text{FOM-1} = \text{ISE} \times \frac{\text{number of features}}{\text{number of points}} \tag{2}$$

and

$$\text{FOM-2} = \text{ISE} \times \frac{\text{number of parameters}}{\text{number of points}}. \tag{3}$$

The aim is to minimize the above figures of merit as well as the summed significance values. In general the figures of merit produced results that corroborated with the perceived performance of the algorithm for lines, lines and arcs, lines and ellipses etc.[32]

Note the above criteria use the edge detected curve as the ground truth. As such they ignore the effect of edge detection on the performance of the algorithm. By using the *actual* or ground truth edge positions from the cube model used to generate the images, then the true accuracy of the segmentation can be determined. Figure 7 shows the two situations.

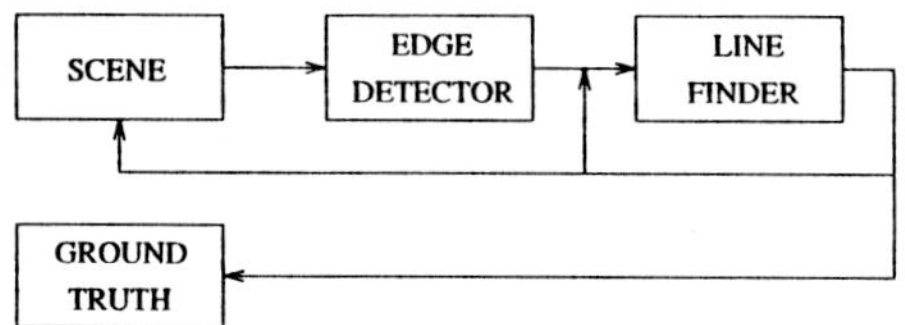


Fig. 7. Assessment paths for line fitting algorithms.

Using the DT the ground truth pixels can be used in the analysis instead of the edgels from the edge detector. The criteria of interest used are those related to the usefulness of the feature to object recognition. Suitable attributes include error in length, error in angle for lines and error in position for the vertices. These are typical attribute values used in object recognition systems such as Geometric Hashing (vertices) and Conditional Rule Generation (line length and angle between lines). Also of interest are the relationships between features e.g. two vertices joined by a single straight line. A pair of *connected* vertices is important for Geometric Hashing because they are used as a basis for indexing.[20]

A possible scenario for investigating the feature performance would process the cube images (see Fig. 4) at different scales of edge detection and use an algorithm such as the recursive technique[21] as implemented by Rosin and West[32] to extract features. The lines from the BRep of the cube can then be matched with the lines extracted from the images interactively and measures of error determined.

However the issue here is which feature best matches the ground truth as there will be a number of candidates. Which image feature matches which model feature will depend on the model as two poor matches may be better than one good match. That is the error is really determined by the model and not simply for each feature in isolation. Hence to fully assess feature extraction performance requires the context to be defined and cannot be meaningfully performed in isolation.

## 7. QUANTIFYING FEATURE PERFORMANCE ON VERIFICATION

The previous two sections have discussed the problems of assessing edge detection and higher order feature extraction. It has been shown that these are difficult to assess in isolation but must be assessed in the context of the required task. In this paper it is argued that they should be assessed in the context of the two stages of object recognition namely indexing and verification. The rest of this paper concentrates on the assessment in the context of verification. The verification is considered for two cases in which the correct pose is determined using three degrees of freedom namely three translations $(T_x, T_y, T_z)$ and three rotations $(\theta_x, \theta_y, \theta_z)$.

There has been little investigation into assessing verification techniques. Of significance is the research by Brisdon[4] and Sullivan[37] who analyzed pose refinement algorithms for matching essentially 3D wire frame models with 2D edge data. Four criteria were investigated namely different search algorithms, smoothness of the error surface, accuracy of the initial pose and the prominence of the maximum amongst the false local minima. In this paper edge detection scale, match metric and salience are examined in the context of matching model edge data to image pixel data.

For translation, images of a cluttered background with a 2D object superimposed at the centre are used i.e. a circle (Fig. 8(a)) and a noisy pear (Fig. 8(b)). For rotation, a 3D object is used with or without a cluttered/noisy background (Fig. 4).

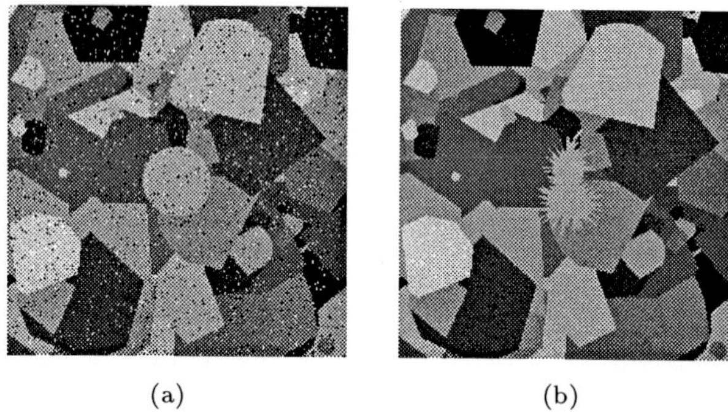

(a) (b)

Fig. 8. Images of the circle and noisy pear on a background of 200 polygons with noise added.

The background consists of 200 polygons of different sizes and numbers of sides to simulate randomly cluttered edges. A mixture of 'salt and pepper' and Gaussian noise was added to the final images to simulate real images. A circle is used because it is isotropic so rotation of the model is not a factor, and a noisy pear because it has boundary detail at a number of scales. A BRep of the cube is used to allow 3D rotations to be considered.

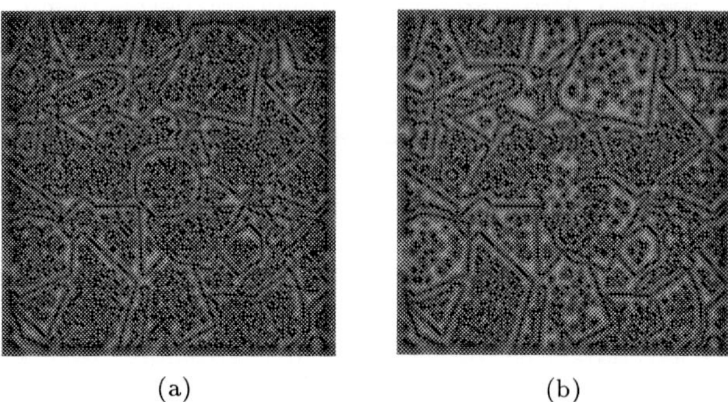

(a) (b)

Fig. 9. Distance transforms of Figs. 8 for $\sigma = 4.0$.

The features of interest are edges which are extracted using the Marr–Hildreth edge detector.[23] All the edges are thresholded out and the chamfer 3–4 DT[3] applied. Figure 9 shows the resulting DTs for $\sigma = 2.0$ for the circle and noisy pear.[b]

The DT can be defined as[33]:

$$d^i_{x,y} = \min_{a,b=-1\ldots 1} (d^{i-1}_{x+a,y+b} + w_{a,b}) \tag{4}$$

[b]These images have been non-linearly scaled to bring out the varying grey levels for the various distances.

where $d^i_{x,y}$ is the distance value at location $(x, y)$ calculated at iteration $i$, and $w_{a,b}$ is the value of the mask at location $(a, b)$ where the centre is $(0, 0)$ and $d^0$ is the initial binary edge map.

In addition to the DT, a salience measure was incorporated, namely edge strength. The DT was modified by weighting the distances using the edge strength obtained from the gradient of the zero crossings[33]:

$$\begin{aligned} a', b' &= \arg\left(\min_{a,b=-1\ldots1}(d^{i-1}_{x+a,y+b} + w_{a,b})\right) \\ d^i_{x,y} &= d^{i-1}_{x+a',y+b'} \\ m^i_{x,y} &= m^{i-1}_{x+a',y+b'} \end{aligned}$$

where $(a', b')$ is the location in the window producing the minimum distance, $m^i_{x,y}$ is the edge magnitude value propagated to $(x, y)$ at iteration $i$, $m^0_{x,y}$ is the initial edge map, and $d^i_{x,y}$ is the minimum distance which is propagated as in the standard DT algorithm. The strong edges have greater importance and hence are assigned lower distances. This is apparent in Fig. 10.

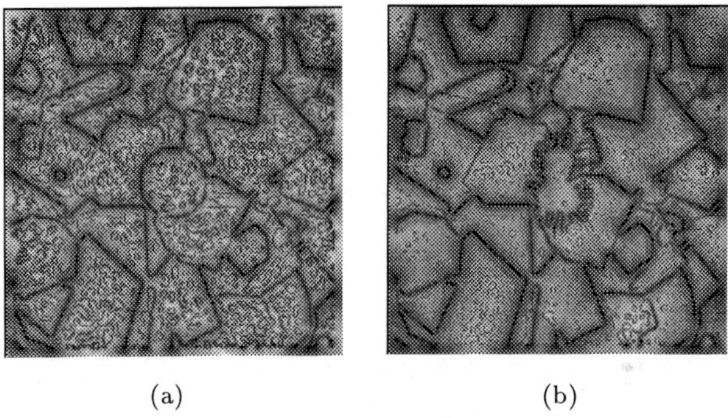

(a) (b)

Fig. 10. Salience DTs of Figs. 8 for $\sigma = 4.0$.

## 8. TECHNIQUES FOR SEARCHING AND QUANTIFYING MINIMA

To assess the performance of the feature extraction in the context of verification the error surface for each position of the model matched with the DT image is computed. The matching metrics used are a Euclidean metric and the Hausdorff metric. The Euclidean metric is:

$$M_{x,y} = \frac{1}{N}\sum_{i=1}^{N} D_{x+m_i,y+n_i} \tag{5}$$

where $D$ is the value of the pixel from the DT image, and $(m_i, n_i), i = 1 \ldots N$ indexes into the $N$ model coordinates i.e. the 2D coordinates of the data points. The match is computed at model position $(x, y)$ which are the translation parameters of interest. The DT is used to determine the distance to each edge point in the image and the average distance value determined.

The Hausdorff distance metric is defined as:

$$H_b(A,B) = \max(h(A,B), h(B,A)) \tag{6}$$

in which

$$h(A,B) = \max_{a\in A}\min_{b\in B} ||a-b|| \tag{7}$$

and $A$ and $B$ are finite point sets. $A$ is the set of model points and $B$ is the set of image points, and $||.||$ is the chosen norm e.g. Euclidean.[17] The model points $A$ are transformed to match with different parts of the image. This is the two directional version $H_b$ which matches model points to the image points and the image points to the model points allowing one to many mappings. In this paper the one directional Hausdorff distance metric $H_u$ is used in which the maximum distance of the model points to the image points is measured. This simply involves determining the maximum value of the DT of the image for the model data. That is:

$$H_u(A,B) = \max_{a\in A}\min_{b\in B} ||a-b|| \,. \tag{8}$$

The two-dimensional version $H_b(A,B)$ is required for situations where not all model points are present e.g. when matching a portion of one image to another. The one-dimensional version $H_u(A,B)$ is used in this paper as all the model points are available, for example from a CAD model.

The model is first transformed and projected onto the 2D plane to produce the 2D model points after which one of the metrics is applied. Considering just the Euclidean metric, for a perfect match of the model with the image $M_{x,y} = 0$. However the feature extraction process will, except for uncluttered simple images, result in $M_{x,y}$ being some small value. The important point is that $M_{x,y}$ is a minimum for a good match and should be the lowest minimum for correct recognition. This metric does not require correspondence and will match each point on the model with the *closest* edge point in the image.[c] This is automatic as the DT is used which, by definition, gives the distance to the closest edge point. Obviously when the model is close to the correct position, there is an approximately one-to-one match of model pixels and image pixels.[d] The above argument applies to the Hausdorff metric as well. To visualize what the error surfaces look like for the two different metrics, Fig. 11 shows the results of matching the circle using the DT of the circle on a noisy background (Fig. 8) for the Euclidean and Hausdorff metrics for two different scales of edge detection. For the Euclidean metric, the global minimum is in the centre of the images surrounded by many local minima. As expected, the higher scale results in a smoother error surface with fewer local minima and a larger global minimum. The Hausdorff error surfaces are more complex and reflect the fact that the metric simply finds

[c] Note the problem of many-to-one matches is not addressed in this paper.

[d] Note that no correspondence between the model points and the image points is used in this analysis.

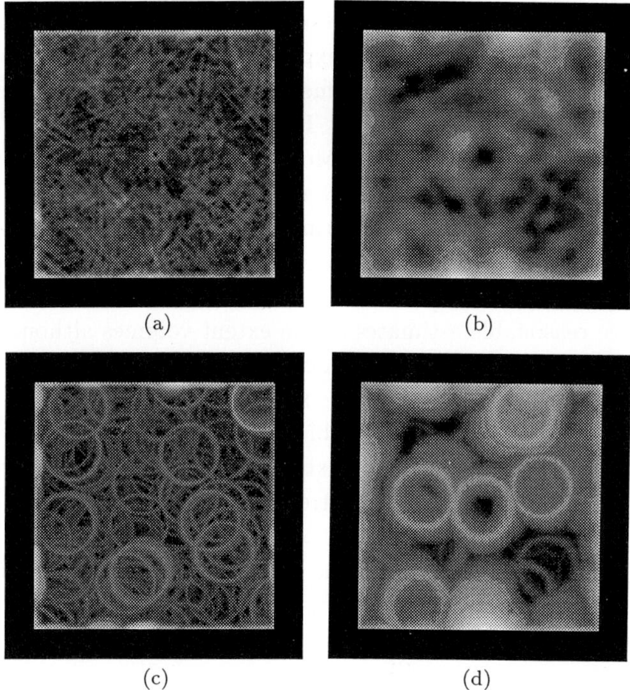


Fig. 11. Error images for translation for the Euclidean metric (a) $\sigma = 4.0$, (b) $\sigma = 16.0$, and the Hausdorff metric (c) $\sigma = 4.0$, (d) $\sigma = 16.0$. The model is the circle and the image processed is shown in Fig. 8.

the largest distance from the model to the image. Again the global minimum is at the centre of the image and there are many local minima present.

Once the error surface has been obtained, the extent of the minima around the point of correct match and the position of the global minimum are determined. The extent is computed by determining the parameter values from which, iteratively by strict gradient descent, the correct solution could be found. Strict gradient descent is defined as where the next point considered is the one with the steepest descent from the current point. For the 2D case this results in an image containing a 2D blob which surrounds the correct match of differing size and shape depending on the features used. These blobs are termed *extents*. The search for the extent can be over 2D (translation), 3D (translation and scale), 3D (Euler angles) and so on. As all parameter value combinations have to be examined, this results in much computation.

A number of algorithms have been investigated. The simplest is based on searching the space and labeling all points from which the correct pose can be reached and storing the extent in an array. The resulting extent array can then be analyzed. This is computationally feasible for translations up to 3D as the model can be transformed off-line w.r.t. scale and stored. Then translation is achieved by offsetting the model over the image. The exhaustive searching can be avoided by always searching outward from the known minimum error or current pose over the perimeter of a square in the 2D case, and over the surface of a cube in the 3D case. However this becomes computationally expensive in higher dimensions.

For 3D rotation and other higher dimensional searches the model pose has to be computed on-line during processing. To reduce the computation a number of stochastic methods were investigated. Monte Carlo estimation can be used[28] by sampling the search space in a random way for a number of points i.e. $N_t$. Each of these points can be processed to determine if it is in the extent (using gradient descent) i.e. $N_e$ are in the extent. An estimate of the volume of the extent is obtained from $(N_e/N_t)V$ where V is the total volume of the search space. Trials show this to give reasonable estimates of the extent volumes although the number of samples required to improve the confidence in the estimation gave computation times comparable with the exhaustive algorithm.

Instead an $n$-dimensional stochastic binary search algorithm was developed to find the points on the boundary of the extent. A number of points were randomly generated at a fixed distance from the correct pose. For each point, a binary search was made along the line to find the point on the line farthest from the correct pose that could, by gradient descent, get to the correct pose. Currently, for each extent, 100 points are used for the 3D search. This has proved to be the most efficient way to do the search.

The choice of connectivity affects the search time. Using 8-connectivity, eight directions are analyzed in 2D and 26 in 3D i.e. $3^n - 1$ directions where $n$ is the dimensionality. Using 4-connectivity this becomes four directions in 2D and six directions in 3D i.e. $2n$ directions. Experiments using the two different connectivities show that there are small differences between the results in both 2D and 3D cases so 4-connectivity was used for all experiments. An idea of the time required can be estimated from the fact that each run (for each scale) takes approximately an hour on a Silicon Graphics Challenge CPU when using 8-connectivity. From experiments the majority of the processing time was spent determining the metric value i.e. matching the model to image points.

The extents can be analyzed for performance assessment using a number of measures. The shape and size of the extents can be observed visually and qualitative assessment made e.g. the relative sizes and whether the shapes are convex or not. However quantitative measures are required and those that are useful for 2D and 3D translations include the area/volume, the bounding box, circularity/spheroidarity and the variance of each of the parameters. The area/volume of the extent gives a measure of the likelihood of getting close enough to the correct solution with little prior information. That is, given the bounds on the parameters assuming the object is in the image, the ratio of area/volume to that bounded by the parameters gives the probability of recognition. Note this is an unlikely scenario given that usually some idea of the position would have been determined i.e. by indexing. In this paper the area/volume of the extent and the bounding box are used. The bounding box of the extent gives the maximum and minimum allowable variation in parameters and can be used to aid in the tesselation of the viewsphere. Concavities and irregularity in the shape of the extent would reduce the confidence in the results leading to taking a conservative estimate of the size of the extent.

For 3D rotations, a more meaningful measure is the number of steps required to get to the minimum from a point on the boundary of the extent. Area/volume is meaningless because of the non-commutative nature of the transformations using angles and the problem of instability of the angles when two of the three combine to almost cancel each other out.

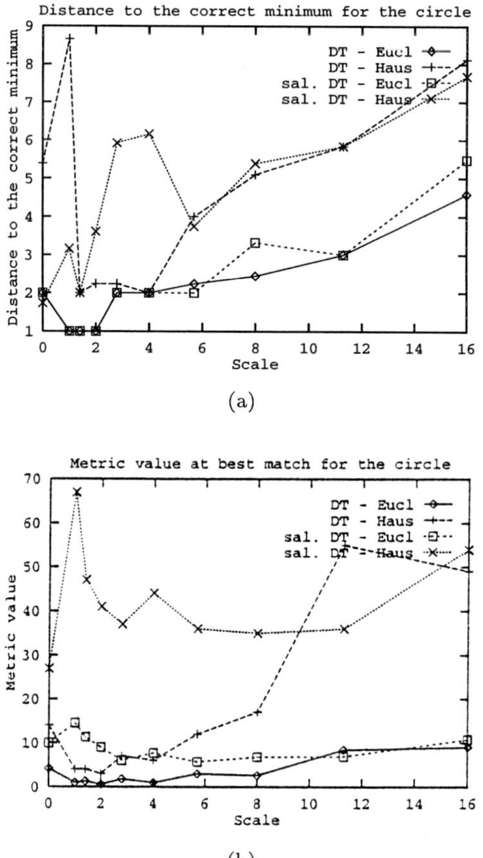


Fig. 12. For the circle model (a) error in match position, (b) metric value. Scale = 0 corresponds to "All" in the tables.

## 9. RESULTS

### 9.1. Three Translations

Results are presented for the circle and noisy pear models for 3D translation i.e. the parameters are translation of the model in $x$ and $y$ and the scale $z$ of the model is changed. In addition to each scale, results are also shown for a scale of "All". This is the multiscale DT which is formed by adding the DTs for all the scales

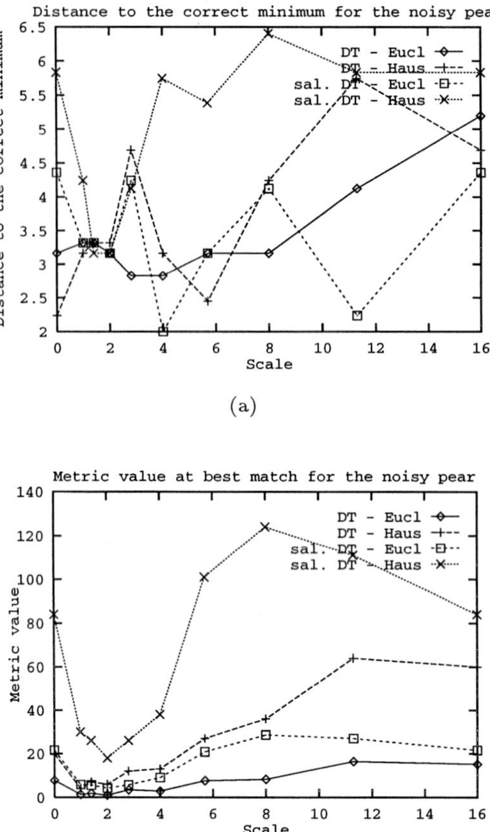


Fig. 13. For the noisy pear model (a) error in match position, (b) metric value. Scale = 0 corresponds to "All" in the tables.

together to form one distance image. The idea is that one image captures the important information for each scale. Results for 2D translation are a subset of the 3D analysis and are not presented here. First, Tables 1 and 2 show the results of searching in the region of the correct pose for the global minimum. Any differences between the two indicate the inaccuracy in pose estimation in the context of the particular model, the segmentation process, noise and other features. Figures 12 and 13 show these results graphically. For the circle model and the DT, the global minimum for each scale is close to the correct pose which is (256, 256, 50). The inaccuracy generally increases at larger scales. The salience DT does not improve the results so in this case its usefulness is not apparent. For the Hausdorff metric for both DTs, the results are worse which demonstrates that averaging the errors is better than taking the maximum error for determining the correct pose. The results for the noisy pear are similar to the circle which is good considering the complexity of the noisy pear model and the expected distortions due to edge detection etc.

Table 1. Position of the global minimum for the circle model for (a) Euclidean and (b) Hausdorff metrics. Correct pose at (256,256,50).

(a)

| | Distance transform | |
|---|---|---|
| Scale | Actual centre | Metric value |
| 1 | 256,256,51 | 0.983516 |
| 1.4 | 256,256,51 | 1.280220 |
| 2 | 256,256,51 | 0.565934 |
| 2.8 | 256,256,52 | 1.762274 |
| 4 | 256,256,52 | 0.930233 |
| 5.7 | 257,256,52 | 2.989664 |
| 8 | 257,255,52 | 2.602067 |
| 11.3 | 256,256,53 | 8.430025 |
| 16 | 258,255,54 | 9.014252 |
| All | 256,256,52 | 4.152455 |

| | Salience distance transform | |
|---|---|---|
| Scale | Actual centre | Metric value |
| 1 | 256,256,51 | 14.508242 |
| 1.4 | 256,256,51 | 11.313187 |
| 2 | 256,256,51 | 8.980769 |
| 2.8 | 256,256,52 | 6.025840 |
| 4 | 256,256,52 | 7.648579 |
| 5.7 | 256,256,52 | 5.710594 |
| 8 | 257,255,53 | 6.765903 |
| 11.3 | 256,256,53 | 6.916030 |
| 16 | 258,255,55 | 10.766170 |
| All | 256,256,52 | 9.976745 |

(b)

| | Distance transform | |
|---|---|---|
| Scale | Actual centre | Metric value |
| 1 | 251,251,55 | 4.000000 |
| 1.4 | 256,256,52 | 4.000000 |
| 2 | 256,255,52 | 3.000000 |
| 2.8 | 255,256,52 | 7.000000 |
| 4 | 256,256,52 | 6.000000 |
| 5.7 | 256,256,54 | 12.000000 |
| 8 | 256,255,55 | 17.000000 |
| 11.3 | 252,253,53 | 55.000000 |
| 16 | 260,251,55 | 49.000000 |
| All | 252,254,53 | 14.000000 |

| | Salience distance transform | |
|---|---|---|
| Scale | Actual centre | Metric value |
| 1 | 256,255,53 | 67.000000 |
| 1.4 | 256,256,52 | 47.000000 |
| 2 | 254,256,53 | 41.000000 |
| 2.8 | 253,255,55 | 37.000000 |
| 4 | 253,254,55 | 44.000000 |
| 5.7 | 257,259,52 | 36.000000 |
| 8 | 256,254,55 | 35.000000 |
| 11.3 | 252,259,53 | 36.000000 |
| 16 | 259,261,55 | 54.000000 |
| All | 257,257,51 | 27.000000 |

For both sets of results note the metric value. For the Euclidean metric, this is the average distance from each model point to the nearest edge pixel. For the Hausdorff metric the error signifies the largest distance from a model point to an edge pixel. For both metrics the error increases generally with scale reflecting the increase in distortion of the edges of the circle because of background clutter. Note the Hausdorff metric produces more variability across scale than the Euclidean metric.

Tables 3 and 4 detail the extents and bounding volumes for various scales of edge detection for 3D model matching for the circle using the Euclidean and Hausdorff metrics for both the DT and the salience DT. Figures 14 and 15 show the results graphically.

Table 2. Position of the global minimum for the noisy pear model for (a) Euclidean and (b) Hausdorff metrics. Correct pose at (256,256,50).

| Distance transform | | |
|---|---|---|
| Scale | Actual centre | Metric value |
| 1 | 255,259,51 | 1.337984 |
| 1.4 | 255,259,51 | 1.844961 |
| 2 | 255,259,50 | 1.057515 |
| 2.8 | 256,258,52 | 3.382946 |
| 4 | 256,258,52 | 2.885271 |
| 5.7 | 255,259,50 | 7.623466 |
| 8 | 257,259,50 | 8.281442 |
| 11.3 | 256,260,51 | 16.418604 |
| 16 | 259,259,53 | 15.192248 |
| All | 256,259,51 | 7.719380 |

| Salience distance transform | | |
|---|---|---|
| Scale | Actual centre | Metric value |
| 1 | 255,259,51 | 5.854264 |
| 1.4 | 255,259,51 | 5.603101 |
| 2 | 255,259,50 | 4.187883 |
| 2.8 | 255,260,49 | 5.694099 |
| 4 | 256,258,50 | 9.069785 |
| 5.7 | 256,259,49 | 20.812111 |
| 8 | 256,260,49 | 28.618011 |
| 11.3 | 256,258,51 | 26.982946 |
| 16 | 259,257,53 | 21.555038 |
| All | 259,257,53 | 21.555038 |

(a)

| Distance transform | | |
|---|---|---|
| Scale | Actual centre | Metric value |
| 1 | 255,259,50 | 4.000000 |
| 1.4 | 255,259,49 | 7.000000 |
| 2 | 255,259,49 | 6.000000 |
| 2.8 | 253,258,53 | 12.000000 |
| 4 | 256,259,49 | 13.000000 |
| 5.7 | 257,254,49 | 27.000000 |
| 8 | 257,260,51 | 36.000000 |
| 11.3 | 252,257,54 | 64.000000 |
| 16 | 259,254,53 | 60.000000 |
| All | 256,257,52 | 20.000000 |

| Salience distance transform | | |
|---|---|---|
| Scale | Actual centre | Metric value |
| 1 | 255,260,49 | 30.000000 |
| 1.4 | 256,259,49 | 26.000000 |
| 2 | 256,259,49 | 18.000000 |
| 2.8 | 254,259,48 | 26.000000 |
| 4 | 252,260,51 | 38.000000 |
| 5.7 | 256,251,52 | 101.000000 |
| 8 | 252,259,54 | 124.000000 |
| 11.3 | 251,256,53 | 111.000000 |
| 16 | 253,256,55 | 84.000000 |
| All | 253,256,55 | 84.000000 |

(b)

The results show that the Hausdorff metric is reasonably scale independent producing similar extent volumes and bounding boxes for each scale. The Euclidean metric produces bigger extents for large values of $\sigma$ for both DTs. For the multiscale DT and salience DT, row "All" in the tables, the size of the extents are a compromise between those for the small and large scales. Table 4 and Fig. 15 show the results for the same processing using the noisy pear model and images. Even though the noisy pear has much fine detail which can locally match with the image and is very different from the circle, the size of the extents and bounding boxes are similar in value and nature for both DTs and metrics.

Figure 16 shows some of the cross sections through the 3D extent for the noisy pear model, Euclidean metric and the DT. These show how the shape of the extent changes as the scale of the pear changes.

Table 3. Extent details for the circle model for (a) Euclidean and (b) Hausdorff metrics.

(a)

| Distance transform | | | |
|---|---|---|---|
| Scale | Extent vol. | Bounding vol. | |
| 1.0 | 1451 | 249,250,43 | 263,263,56 |
| 1.4 | 1469 | 249,248,43 | 263,263,57 |
| 2.0 | 1489 | 248,248,43 | 263,262,58 |
| 2.8 | 1640 | 248,247,41 | 265,263,58 |
| 4.0 | 1840 | 247,246,44 | 266,265,59 |
| 5.7 | 5492 | 240,237,40 | 274,272,65 |
| 8.0 | 16398 | 232,228,37 | 280,276,68 |
| 11.7 | 153639 | 193,211,25 | 315,308,75 |
| 16.0 | 267948 | 200,180,25 | 325,309,75 |
| All | 76818 | 209,214,25 | 303,297,74 |

| Salience distance transform | | | |
|---|---|---|---|
| Scale | Extent Vol. | Bounding vol. | |
| 1.0 | 1957 | 245,247,39 | 270,264,62 |
| 1.4 | 2054 | 247,245,39 | 266,267,62 |
| 2.0 | 3154 | 246,239,38 | 271,268,64 |
| 2.8 | 4737 | 239,240,35 | 273,267,63 |
| 4.0 | 7006 | 238,242,32 | 276,275,70 |
| 5.7 | 33919 | 221,225,25 | 286,286,75 |
| 8.0 | 62166 | 210,215,25 | 291,301,75 |
| 11.7 | 141549 | 206,217,25 | 311,310,75 |
| 16.0 | 124960 | 204,225,25 | 317,305,75 |
| All | 34128 | 221,230,25 | 286,287,75 |

(b)

| Distance transform | | | |
|---|---|---|---|
| Scale | Extent vol. | Bounding vol. | |
| 1.0 | 1403 | 249,250,44 | 263,262,56 |
| 1.4 | 1417 | 249,249,43 | 263,261,56 |
| 2.0 | 1421 | 250,250,43 | 264,262,57 |
| 2.8 | 1641 | 249,249,43 | 267,263,59 |
| 4.0 | 2068 | 247,248,43 | 267,267,61 |
| 5.7 | 2068 | 247,248,43 | 267,267,61 |
| 8.0 | 6965 | 234,241,33 | 271,273,67 |
| 11.3 | 1523 | 246,251,44 | 263,264,56 |
| 16.0 | 2305 | 213,251,44 | 262,270,56 |
| All | 1816 | 242,249,40 | 265,264,59 |

| Salience distance transform | | | |
|---|---|---|---|
| Scale | Extent Vol. | Bounding vol. | |
| 1.0 | 1606 | 247,249,43 | 266,263,58 |
| 1.4 | 1725 | 248,248,40 | 265,265,58 |
| 2.0 | 1889 | 248,247,41 | 267,264,59 |
| 2.8 | 1970 | 246,248,41 | 266,264,61 |
| 4.0 | 1878 | 246,249,41 | 265,265,60 |
| 5.7 | 4409 | 234,244,25 | 265,277,69 |
| 8.0 | 5539 | 238,249,26 | 267,279,75 |
| 11.3 | 3588 | 238,250,27 | 263,276,71 |
| 16.0 | 3550 | 230,250,27 | 261,261,55 |
| All | 2100 | 242,250,36 | 268,265,62 |

These are of a generally simple shape but with many concavities present and are typical of slices obtained for numerous objects. An interesting observation is Fig. 16(b) which shows two distinct regions demonstrating concavities in all three parameter dimensions. Generally the area of the extents for each slice are of maximal size for the correct value of $z$ and reduce in size as $z$ increases/decreases giving a single 3D blob.

In addition, the volume increases as the value of $\sigma$ for the edge detector increases which means the hypothesized initial pose of the object does not have to be that accurate. This demonstrates that the choice of $\sigma$ is crucial to the design of the object recognition system as the larger the value of $\sigma$ the less complex the model indexing has to be and vice versa. The sizes of the bounding boxes of Table 3 are a significant proportion of the area of the model indicating that the estimation of pose for the first stage of object recognition is not that crucial.

Table 4. Extent details for the noisy pear model for (a) Euclidean and (b) Hausdorff metrics.

| Distance transform | | | |
|---|---|---|---|
| Scale | Extent vol. | Bounding vol. | |
| 1 | 1422 | 250,249,43 | 262,263,57 |
| 1.4 | 1561 | 250,250,42 | 263,263,58 |
| 2 | 2577 | 243,248,37 | 266,268,60 |
| 2.8 | 4809 | 242,246,29 | 273,269,60 |
| 4 | 18840 | 233,242,25 | 283,286,73 |
| 5.7 | 61645 | 221,221,25 | 289,297,75 |
| 8 | 92954 | 210,224,25 | 296,297,75 |
| 11.3 | 107780 | 221,207,25 | 303,314,70 |
| 16 | 216656 | 213,186,25 | 322,314,75 |
| All | 106813 | 214,214,25 | 300,294,75 |

| Salience distance transform | | | |
|---|---|---|---|
| Scale | Extent Vol. | Bounding vol. | |
| 1 | 7195 | 234,244,25 | 273,272,65 |
| 1.4 | 16794 | 226,241,25 | 280,278,70 |
| 2 | 48631 | 221,234,25 | 286,294,75 |
| 2.8 | 59420 | 219,230,25 | 286,299,75 |
| 4 | 70542 | 220,223,25 | 288,303,75 |
| 5.7 | 80136 | 219,228,25 | 291,307,75 |
| 8 | 61414 | 216,230,25 | 283,303,75 |
| 11.3 | 68217 | 222,238,25 | 292,306,73 |
| 16 | 81541 | 221,234,25 | 302,313,72 |
| All | 80136 | 219,228,25 | 291,307,75 |

(a)

| Distance transform | | | |
|---|---|---|---|
| Scale | Extent vol. | Bounding vol. | |
| 1 | 1377 | 250,250,44 | 263,262,56 |
| 1.4 | 1424 | 250,250,43 | 262,262,56 |
| 2 | 1508 | 248,250,44 | 262,264,57 |
| 2.8 | 1636 | 245,249,43 | 264,263,58 |
| 4 | 2131 | 244,248,40 | 265,266,57 |
| 5.7 | 2632 | 236,243,38 | 276,265,58 |
| 8 | 2213 | 237,240,37 | 276,266,58 |
| 11.3 | 2081 | 250,236,45 | 265,263,58 |
| 16 | 4595 | 226,235,40 | 268,263,58 |
| All | 1842 | 247,244,41 | 264,266,58 |

| Salience distance transform | | | |
|---|---|---|---|
| Scale | Extent Vol. | Bounding vol. | |
| 1 | 1723 | 247,249,42 | 264,266,57 |
| 1.4 | 1961 | 246,249,40 | 264,269,60 |
| 2 | 2259 | 245,246,40 | 266,267,62 |
| 2.8 | 2323 | 243,242,40 | 267,264,60 |
| 4 | 2495 | 239,245,40 | 264,266,60 |
| 5.7 | 1939 | 245,248,40 | 263,264,57 |
| 8 | 2312 | 238,248,40 | 266,279,57 |
| 11.3 | 2212 | 245,249,43 | 264,265,65 |
| 16 | 2583 | 243,244,40 | 266,269,61 |
| All | 2583 | 243,244,40 | 266,269,61 |

(b)

## 9.2. Three Rotations

Table 5 and Fig. 17 show the detected global minimum for matching the cube to the edge data using the Euclidean and Hausdorff metrics and the DT and salience DT measures. The correct pose parameters for this experiment were (−45,19,162) in degrees. These illustrate that as the scale increases, the error in pose estimation also increases along with the minimum error. Table 6 and Fig. 18 shows the statistics for the number of steps required to get to the minimum error, that is the position as determined from Table 5. For both the Euclidean and Hausdorff metrics, the number of rotation steps to get to the correct pose is approximately scale independent although the Euclidean metric generally requires more steps. The results are similar for both the cube2 and cube3 images showing the noise in cube3 has little effect. The cube2 image is a clean image although there are background edges present. It may be that these are corrupting the edges of the cube which is nullified to a certain extent by the added noise in the cube3 image. The maximum number of rotation steps to get to the correct pose is high indicating that either a complex route for gradient descent is being used or in some cases, the model pose can be far from the correct pose and still get to the correct pose.

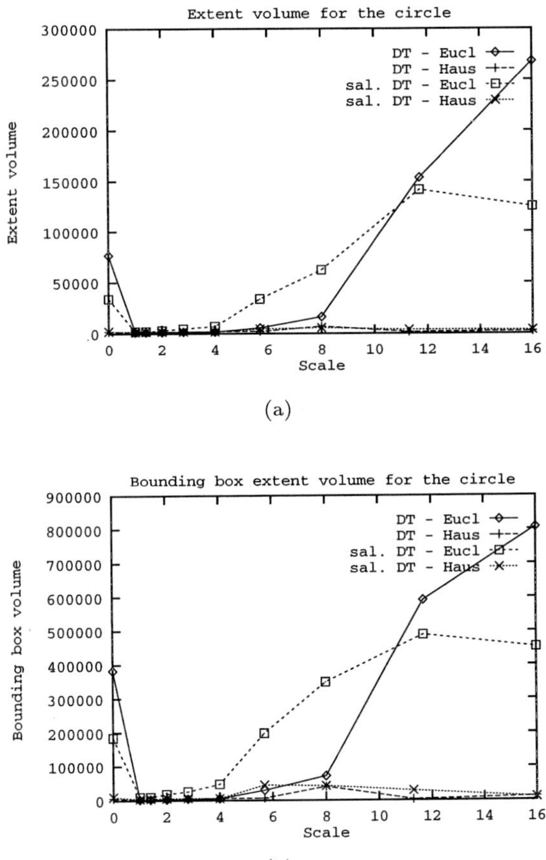


Fig. 14. For the circle model (a) volumes of the extents, (b) volumes of the bounding boxes. Scale = 0 corresponds to "All" in the tables.

## 10. CONCLUSION

This paper has discussed the problem of assessing the various stages in an object recognition system. From considering a number of well known processes for edge detection and line/arc/ellipse feature extraction it is concluded that the way to assess these processes is in the context of the task they are being used for. For learning indexing strategies this is already the case where features are extracted from images and then used to build an indexing system. Feature variability for different objects in the same class are combined with the variability in the various segmentation processes to form some cluster in attribute space.

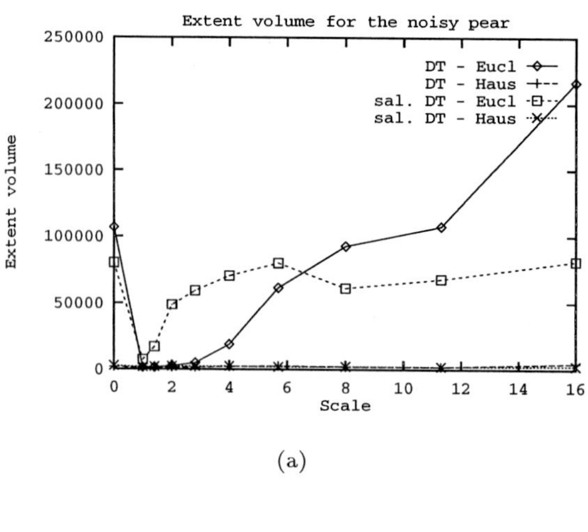


(a)

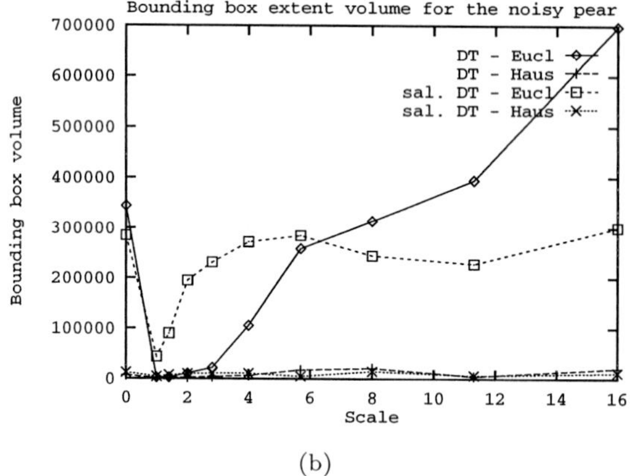


(b)

Fig. 15. For the noisy pear model (a) volumes of the extents, (b) volumes of the bounding boxes. Scale = 0 corresponds to "All" in the tables.

Fig. 16. Slices through 3D space for the noisy pear extent for scale=40 (0.8), 50 (normal size) and 60 (1.2).

Table 5. Accuracy of the estimation of the centre of the cube for different metrics for images cube2 and cube3. Correct pose at (−45,19,162).

| Euclidean for cube2 | | |
|---|---|---|
| Scale | Actual centre | Metric value |
| 1.0 | −43,20,161 | 0.968132 |
| 1.4 | −46,20,162 | 1.162252 |
| 2.0 | −46,20,162 | 1.246137 |
| 2.8 | −46,20,162 | 1.459161 |
| 4.0 | −46,20,162 | 1.905077 |
| 5.7 | −45,20,162 | 2.905391 |
| 8.0 | −45,20,162 | 5.320132 |
| 11.3 | −45,20,162 | 9.378438 |
| 16.0 | −42,16,164 | 21.264574 |

| Hausdorff for cube2 | | |
|---|---|---|
| Scale | Actual centre | Metric value |
| 1.0 | −45,19,162 | 4.000000 |
| 1.4 | −45,19,162 | 6.000000 |
| 2.0 | −47,20,162 | 7.000000 |
| 2.8 | −46,21,161 | 9.000000 |
| 4.0 | −47,21,163 | 13.000000 |
| 5.7 | −45,19,162 | 19.000000 |
| 8.0 | −50,23,165 | 35.000000 |
| 11.3 | −46,14,167 | 48.000000 |
| 16.0 | −50,14,158 | 107.000000 |

(a)

| Euclidean for cube3 | | |
|---|---|---|
| Scale | Actual centre | Metric value |
| 1.0 | −44,20,161 | 1.059341 |
| 1.4 | −43,20,161 | 1.361538 |
| 2.0 | −46,20,162 | 1.546358 |
| 2.8 | −46,20,162 | 1.854305 |
| 4.0 | −46,20,162 | 2.363135 |
| 5.7 | −46,20,162 | 3.447020 |
| 8.0 | −45,20,162 | 5.566556 |
| 11.3 | −45,20,162 | 9.514852 |
| 16.0 | −42,16,164 | 21.205156 |

| Hausdorff for cube3 | | |
|---|---|---|
| Scale | Actual centre | Metric value |
| 1.0 | −45,19,162 | 6.000000 |
| 1.4 | −46,20,163 | 7.000000 |
| 2.0 | −46,20,163 | 7.000000 |
| 2.8 | −45,19,162 | 9.000000 |
| 4.0 | −47,20,162 | 12.000000 |
| 5.7 | −50,18,161 | 23.000000 |
| 8.0 | −50,19,167 | 34.000000 |
| 11.3 | −46,14,167 | 47.000000 |
| 16.0 | −50,14,158 | 106.000000 |

(b)

For verification strategies, the same procedure is proposed in which the verification stage has a number of functions to fulfill and the issue is how well do various feature extraction methods and match metrics perform. Although the analysis is extendable to many types of feature e.g. texture, lines, arcs, regions, only edge pixels in the context of the boundary of an object have been considered.

The images generated for processing are complex in that they have a large number of extraneous edges and noise added that results in distorted, missing and extra edges i.e. inaccuracy and false alarms. The extents produced are a reasonable proportion of the sizes of the models and indicate that inaccurate pose estimation is allowable at the expense of extra computation in pose refinement and hence indexing is less critical.

Finally the analysis shows that the Hausdorff metric is useful in situations where the scale varies as it is relatively invariant to scale. On the other hand, the Euclidean

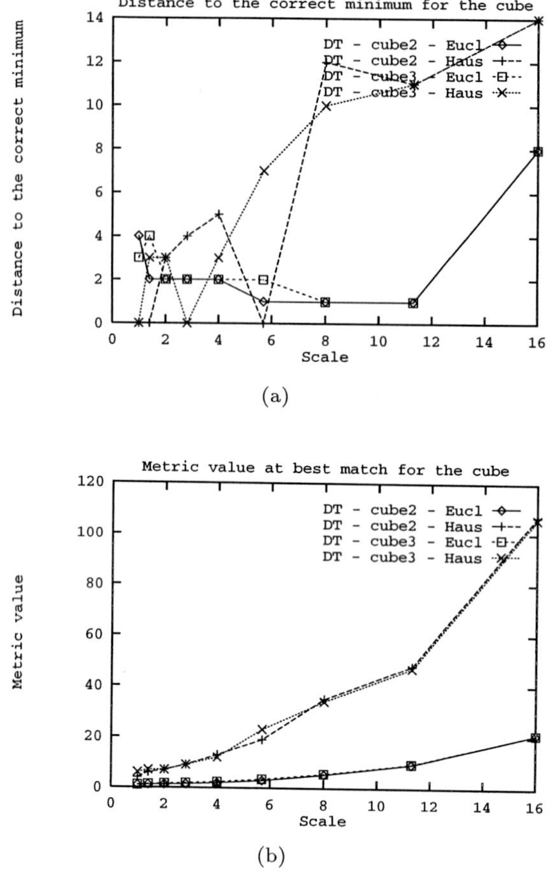


Fig. 17. For the two cube images, (a) accuracy of the estimation of the centre of the cube for different metrics, (b) metric values. Correct pose at (−45,19,162).

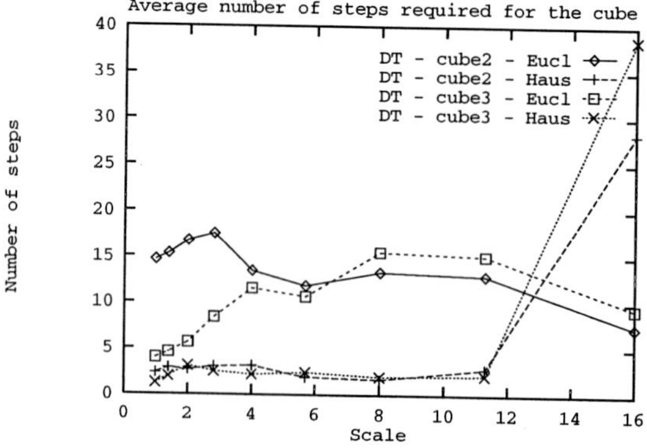


Fig. 18. Mean number of steps required to get to the correct pose for cube2 and cube3.

Table 6. Steps required to get to the correct pose for cube2 and cube3.

| Euclidean for cube2 | | | |
|---|---|---|---|
| Scale | Mean | Min | Max |
| 1.0 | 14.640000 | 1 | 58 |
| 1.4 | 15.300000 | 1 | 127 |
| 2.0 | 16.740000 | 1 | 69 |
| 2.8 | 17.490000 | 1 | 66 |
| 4.0 | 13.440000 | 1 | 44 |
| 5.7 | 11.830000 | 1 | 45 |
| 8.0 | 13.320000 | 1 | 44 |
| 11.3 | 12.950000 | 1 | 53 |
| 16.0 | 7.370000 | 1 | 75 |

| Hausdorff for cube2 | | | |
|---|---|---|---|
| Scale | Mean | Min | Max |
| 1.0 | 2.350000 | 1 | 6 |
| 1.4 | 2.890000 | 1 | 15 |
| 2.0 | 2.670000 | 1 | 31 |
| 2.8 | 3.020000 | 1 | 20 |
| 4.0 | 3.150000 | 1 | 52 |
| 5.7 | 1.890000 | 1 | 6 |
| 8.0 | 1.670000 | 1 | 3 |
| 11.3 | 2.830000 | 1 | 9 |
| 16.0 | 28.290001 | 1 | 168 |

(a)

| Euclidean for cube3 | | | |
|---|---|---|---|
| Scale | Mean | Min | Max |
| 1.0 | 3.980000 | 1 | 11 |
| 1.4 | 4.580000 | 1 | 12 |
| 2.0 | 5.640000 | 1 | 17 |
| 2.8 | 8.390000 | 1 | 24 |
| 4.0 | 11.540000 | 1 | 24 |
| 5.7 | 10.650000 | 1 | 29 |
| 8.0 | 15.520000 | 1 | 45 |
| 11.3 | 15.100000 | 1 | 52 |
| 16.0 | 9.400000 | 1 | 55 |

| Hausdorff for cube3 | | | |
|---|---|---|---|
| Scale | Mean | Min | Max |
| 1.0 | 1.240000 | 1 | 5 |
| 1.4 | 1.940000 | 1 | 10 |
| 2.0 | 3.090000 | 1 | 11 |
| 2.8 | 2.500000 | 1 | 7 |
| 4.0 | 2.170000 | 1 | 15 |
| 5.7 | 2.420000 | 1 | 15 |
| 8.0 | 1.960000 | 1 | 4 |
| 11.3 | 2.120000 | 1 | 9 |
| 16.0 | 38.540001 | 1 | 163 |

(b)

metric is shown to be suitable for a multi-scale pose refinement approach as the extents are large for coarse scales reducing for fine scales.

Future research will concentrate on analyzing extents for more than three dimensions such as three translations and 1/2/3 rotations for different applications, and incorporating the results into strategies for indexing and verification for object recognition.

## REFERENCES


1. H. Aoyama and M. Kawagoe, "A piecewise linear approximation method preserving visual feature points of original figures", *CVGIP: Graphical Models and Image Processing* **53**, 5 (1991) 435–446.
2. P. Aschwanden and W. Guggenbühl, "Experimental results from a comparative study on correlation-type registration algorithms", *Robust Computer Vision*, eds. W. Förstner and St. Ruwiedel, Wichmann, 1992, pp. 268–289.
3. G. Borgefors, "Distance transforms in digital images", *Computer Vision, Graphics and Image Processing* **34** (1986) 344–371.

4. K. Brisdon, "Evaluation and verification of model instances", in *Proc. 3rd Alvey Vision Conf.*, Cambridge, UK, Alvey Vision Club, 1987, pp. 33–37.
5. J. Canny, "A computational approach to edge detection", *IEEE Trans. Pattern Analysis and Machine Intelligence* **8** (1986) 679–698.
6. S. Chen and H. Freeman, "On the characteristic views of quadric-surfaced solids", in *First IEEE Workshop on Directions in CAD-based Vision*, Maui, USA, IEEE, 1991, pp. 34–43.
7. D. Eggert and K. Bowyer, "Perspective projection aspect graphs of solids of revolution: An implementation", in *First IEEE Workshop on Directions in CAD-based Vision*, Maui, USA, IEEE, 1991, pp. 44–63.
8. M. A. Fischler and R. C. Bolles, "Perceptual organization and curve partitioning", *IEEE Trans. on Pattern Analysis and Machine Intelligence* **8**, 1 (1986) 100–105.
9. M. A. Fischler and H. C. Wolf, "Locating perceptually salient points on planar curves", *IEEE Trans. on Pattern Analysis and Machine Intelligence* **16**, 2 (1994) 113–129.
10. W. E. L. Grimson and D. P. Huttenlocher, *Object Recognition by Computer*, MIT Press, 1990.
11. W. E. L. Grimson, D. P. Huttenlocher, and T. D. Alter, "Recognizing 3D objects from 2D images: An error analysis", *IEEE Conf. on Computer Vision and Pattern Recognition*, Ann Arbor, Michigan, USA, IEEE, 1992, pp. 316–321.
12. G. Guy and G. Medioni, "Perceptual grouping using global saliency-enhancing operators", in *11th Int. Conf. on Pattern Recognition*, The Hague, Netherlands, IEEE, 1992, pp. 99–103.
13. C. Hansen and T. C. Henderson, "CAGD-based computer vision", *IEEE Trans. on Pattern Analysis and Machine Intelligence*, **11**, 11 (1989) 1181–1193,
14. R. M. Haralick, "Performance characterization in computer vision", in *Proc. of the British Machine Vision Conf.*, Leeds, UK, BMVA, 1992, pp. 1–8.
15. R. M. Haralick, "DIALOGUE: Performance characterisation in computer vision", *CVGIP: Image Understanding* **60**, 2 (1994) pp. 245–249.
16. R. M. Haralick, H. Joo, and C.-N. Lee, "Pose estimation from corresponding point data", *Machine Vision for Inspection and Measurement*, ed. Herbert Freeman, Academic Press, 1989, pp. 1–84.
17. D. P. Huttenlocher, G. A. Klanderman, and W. J. Rucklidge, "Comparing images using the Hausdorff distance", *IEEE Trans. on Pattern Analysis and Machine Intelligence* **15** (1993) pp. 850–863.
18. D. P. Huttenlocher and S. Ullman, "Recognizing solid objects by alignment with an image", *Int. J. of Computer Vision* **5**, 2 (1990) 195–212.
19. Y. Lamdan and H. J. Wolfson, "Geometric hashing: A general and efficient model-based recognition scheme", in *2nd Int. Conf. on Computer Vision*, Florida, USA, IEEE, 1988, pp. 238–249.
20. M. Leishman, G. A. W. West, and S. Venkatesh, "Geometric hasing on SIMD architectures", in *Australasian Conf. on Parallel and Real-Time Systems*, 1995, pp. 279–286.
21. D. G. Lowe, "Three-dimensional object recognition from single two-dimensional images", *Artificial Intelligence* **31** (1987) 355–395.
22. D. G. Lowe, *Perceptual Organisation and Visual Recognition*, Kluwer, 1987.
23. D. Marr and E. Hildreth, "Theory of edge detection", in *Proc. of the Royal Society*, London **B207** (1980) 187–217.
24. J. L. Mundy and A. J. Heller, "The evaluation and testing of a model-based object recognition system", in *3rd Int. Conf. on Computer Vision*, Osaka, Japan, IEEE, 1990, pp. 268–282.
25. T. Pavlidis and S. L. Horowitz, "Segmentation of plane curves", *IEEE Trans. on Computers* **C-23**, 8 (1974) 860–870.

26. A. Pearce, T. Caelli, and W. F. Bischof, "Rulegraphs for graph matching in pattern recognition", *Pattern Recognition* **27**, 9 (1994) 1231–1247.
27. W. K. Pratt, *Digital Image Processing*, Wiley, 1991.
28. W. H. Press, B. P. Flannery, S. A. Teukolsky, and W. T. Vettering, *Numerical Recipes in C*, Cambridge University Press, Cambridge, UK, 1988.
29. J. Rissanen, *Stochastic Complexity in Statistical Inquiry*, World Scientific, 1989.
30. M. Robey, G. West, and S. Venkatesh, "An investigation into the use of physical modeling for the prediction of various feature types visible from different viewpoints", *CVGIP: Image Understanding* **61**, 3 (1995) 417–429.
31. P. L. Rosin and G. A. W. West, "Detection and verification of surfaces of revolution by perceptual grouping", *Pattern Recognition Lett.* **13** (1992) 453–461.
32. P. L. Rosin and G. A. W. West, "Non-parametric segmentation of curves", *IEEE Trans. Pattern Analysis and Machine Intelligence* **17**, 12 (1995).
33. P. L. Rosin and G. A. W. West, "Salience distance transforms", *CVGIP: Graphical Models and Image Processing* **58** (1995).
34. D. Sarkar, "A simple algorithm for detection of significant vertices for polygonal approximation of chain-coded curves", *Pattern Recognition Lett.* **14** (1993) 959–964.
35. A. Sha'ashua and S. Ullman, "Structural saliency: the detection of globally salient structures using a locally connected network", in *2nd Int. Conf. on Computer Vision*, Florida, USA, IEEE, 1988, pp. 321–327.
36. Y. Shirai, "Recognition of real-world objects using edge cues", *Computer Vision Systems*, eds. A. R. Hanson and E. M. Riseman, Academic Press, 1978.
37. G. D. Sullivan, "*A priori* knowledge in vision", *Computer Vision: Craft, Engineering and Science*, ed. D. Vernon, Basic Research Series, ESPRIT, Springer-Verlag, 1994, pp. 59–79.
38. S. Venkatesh and L. J. Kitchen, "Edge evaluation using necessary components", *CVGIP: Graphical Models and Image Processing* **54**, 1 (1992) 23–30.
39. G. A. W. West and P. L. Rosin, "Techniques for segmenting image curves into meaningful descriptions", *Pattern Recognition* **24**, 7 (1991) 643–652.
40. G. A. W. West and P. L. Rosin, "Using symmetry, ellipses and perceptual groups for detecting surfaces of revolution in 2D images", in *Conf. on Applications of Artificial Intelligence: Machine Vision and Robotics*, vol. 1964, SPIE, 1993.
41. S. Zhang, G. D. Sullivan, and K. D. Baker, "The automatic construction of a view-independent relational model for 3D object recognition", *IEEE Trans. on Pattern Analysis Machine Intelligence* **15**, 6 (1993) 531–544.

---

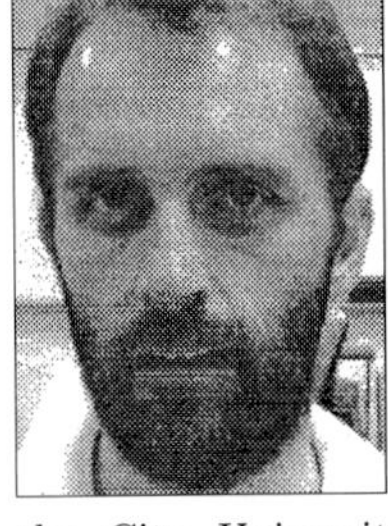

**Geoff A. W. West** received the B.Sc. (Honours) degree in 1978 and the Ph.D. degree in 1982 from the City University, London.

From 1982 to 1988 he was employed as a research fellow and from 1988 as a lecturer at the City University in the School of Engineering investigating techniques for automatic inspection. Since 1990, he has been on the staff of the School of Computing at Curtin University of Technology in Perth, Western Australia where is currently an Associate Professor and Deputy Head of School. His current research interests include 3D object recognition, active vision, visualization, computer graphics, automatic visual inspection and related applications.

# GEOMETRIC VARIATIONS: ANALYSIS, OPTIMIZATION AND CONTROL

BRETT T. DANIEL, GEOFF A. W. WEST
*Department of Computer Science, Curtin University of Technology*
*Bentley, Perth, Western Australia*
*E-mail: geoff@cs.curtin.edu.au*

MICHAEL CARDEW-HALL
*Department of Engineering, Faculty of Engineering and Information Technology*
*Australian National University, Canberra*
*Australian Capital Territory*
*E-mail: mch@faceng.anu.edu.au*

This paper is concerned with the design and manufacturing of 2D and 3D components in the context of process modeling and inspection. A methodology is proposed that models manufacturing processes and learns shape deformations that are the result of out-of-tolerance components. Then during inspection, a deformed shape is analyzed and the process parameter values determined. The key aspect of this approach is that the mapping between process parameters and shape is determined which is not possible using standard process modeling approaches such as finite element analysis. This is different to the traditional approach to tolerancing which is very much as additional procedure to design and doesn't consider process parameter variation, just shape variation. A review of tolerancing is presented as well as a description of techniques for process modeling.

*Keywords*: Automatic inspection, deformable models, process modeling.

## 1. INTRODUCTION

The inherent variability of manufacturing processes means it is impossible to produce a component that is exactly the nominal shape as specified by the designer. In order to constrain this variability in the component the designer will assign limits on the nominal shape. In assigning such limits due regard will have to be paid to the functionality of the part, performance, assembly and cost of manufacture. The limits of such variation are generally termed the tolerance variation and the process of assigning tolerances: tolerance synthesis, and determining their effect: tolerance analysis. Once the design has been completed and appropriate dimensions and tolerances assigned, this design specification needs to be communicated to other functional areas to be used for manufacture, costing, planning, inspection, etc. Traditional methods of design have made extensive use of engineering drawings to achieve this information definition and transfer process. The choice of limits on geometric variation, or tolerances, their format and meaning have been developed over the last 100 years and are laid down in national[44,45,26] and company[36] standards. These standards define the methods of specifying tolerances in a mathematically informal way and are broadly divided into two groups: dimensional size



Spatial Computing: Issues in Vision, Multimedia and Visualization Technologies (1997) 79–113

tolerances and geometric tolerances. Despite the fact that great efforts have been made to clarify the meaning and layout of tolerances it is still common for confusion to arise, especially with complicated components with many datum features and unusual freeform surfaces. Such tolerances are not covered by standards resulting in the definition of new tolerance schemes for these special cases.

CAD based solid and surface modeling systems are now widely used for design specification. The CAD based geometric design forms one component of a product database that holds a complete representation of the required component. Such a database must provide all the information that may be required by functional activities in the manufacturing process. Much work has been carried out over the last 15 years on the mathematical definition of geometric dimensions and tolerances. The impetus for this work has been the need for an explicit definition of such geometric attributes such that a complete definition of the acceptable variation in a part or component is specified. The rationale behind many of the methods put forward is to:

- provide a mathematical basis for specifying dimensions and tolerances for functional component definition and communication,
- provide a method that retains consistency with current standards, and
- provide a method that allows tolerance analysis and synthesis within the design process.

Such methods have largely been developed from a design specification and tolerance analysis point of view. They use a geometric solid model as a nominal shape and define limits to the allowable variation. However, applications in the area of inspection analysis and manufacturing process optimization require a much more flexible geometric model that can be deformed to the shape produced. The computational parameters that then control this deformation can be used as a basis for specifying limits to permissible variation. To set the context of the system proposed, a review of CAD based tolerancing, variational modeling, process optimization and process modeling is carried out in the following sections. This is followed by a description of a proposed method in which geometric variation in inspected components is controled by a set of eigenvectors that correspond to the principle error modes that are likely to occur in the component. These eigenvectors and eigenvalues can be directly related to known or predicted variation due to the manufacturing process. Limits can be placed on the component eigenvalues, effectively geometrically tolerancing the component. In addition, the variations can be fed into an optimization algorithm to predict desired changes to the manufacturing process control variables. The importance of this work is that the process modeling schemes can be used to generate components with various defects. The eigenvector analysis relates shape variations back to the process variables which ultimately enables the process variable that has caused the defect to be determined during inspection.

## 2. TOLERANCING REVIEW

Two basic types of geometric modeling have become common in CAD based solid modeling, boundary representation (BRep) and constructive solid geometry (CSG). For a full discussion on such modeling systems the reader is referred to Refs. 18 and 40.

Due to the way in which dimensioning and tolerancing standards evolved during the nineteenth and early twentieth century there was little formal underlying mathematical theory behind the national and company standards that were laid down. Requicha[39] and Hillyard[22] were the first to address this area in an attempt to give it a mathematical basis suitable for incorporating into a solid modeling system.

Requicha's work attempted to generalize the current design engineering standards whilst retaining consistency with them as much as possible. An object satisfies a tolerance specification if the boundary of the object lies within an appropriate region of space or tolerance zone. This defines a variational class of objects that are functionally equivalent. Geometric tolerances such as flatness, roundness, etc., are generalized and are referred to as *surface form* tolerances. This is a departure from the standard tolerance representation. It is also not clear how tolerances on freeform surfaces may be represented by such a scheme. Of note is that the theory put forward Requicha requires the definition of a *master datum system* for all dimensions. An experimental system based on this theory has been implemented in the PADL-2 CSG solid modeler by Requicha and Chan.[38]

Hillyard proposed a method of modeling an object, along with its dimensions and tolerances, based on *stiffness* and constraints. This scheme required the calculation of an inverse of a rigidity matrix to solve the scheme constraints and provide an indirect parametric modeling system. This scheme has a number of drawbacks. It is not easily extended to geometric standard tolerances or non-standard tolerance types. In addition, it is computationally intensive. Similar schemes have been proposed.[31,23] Variational modeling is discussed more fully in Sec. 3.

Roy and Liu[43] have proposed representing a CAD assembly model as a hierarchy of sub-assemblies based on a hybrid CSG/BRep structure. This proposal would seem to be quite powerful in terms of definition of tolerance information, although it appears no implementation has been carried out. Pennington *et al.*[16] have proposed a mathematical framework to allow worst case tolerance analysis for assemblies based on a CSG model. This builds up a unidirectional tolerance graph with tolerance represented by triplex numbers. However, this framework is restricted to linear (uni-directional) tolerance analysis. Turner[46] proposes a vector space approach to tolerance specification and has implemented the scheme within a system called GEOTOL. This scheme appears suitable for the inclusion of size and geometric tolerances, but appears unlikely to be extendable to tolerancing of freeform surfaces. Bernstein and Preiss[6] have proposed a *constraint propagation* approach which is based on a BRep modeling structure. The model of the object is decomposed into features, connected by a constraint network which represents spatial information. This approach lends itself to the representation of standard tolerance types and appears extendible to tolerancing of freeform surfaces. Cardew-Hall *et al.*[10] extended the work of Bernstein and Preiss to allow incorporation of tolerance control on freeform surfaces and also to allow specification of tolerances for non-standard geometric variations such as bow and twist. An implementation of this work using the CADDS4X CAD system as the geometric modeler showed that the approach is appropriate to the tolerance specification of turbine blade geometries. It should be noted that the main aim of this work was to provide a method of specifying allowable geometric variation for inspection analysis. Rivest *et al.*[41] have proposed a kinematic formulation for the definition of tolerances which has elements similar to that proposed by Cardew-Hall *et al.*[10] The work of Rivest *et al.* focussed on developing a method that allows tolerance analysis for manufacturing purposes, in particular calculation of manufacturing tolerances based on the process plan followed. This system has been implemented as an application husk to the ACIS geometric modeler.

There has been much interest in the use of high density sampling using video technology and computer tomography. This has led to new techniques for inspection which are not possible using standard low sampling densities that are available with coordinate measuring machines. Techniques have been developed to use these high densities for tolerancing tasks.[32] Recently there has been interest in using deformable models for inspection in situations where there is an inter-dependence of features on each other.[33–35] Examples are vent holes in turbine blades which have to be a certain distance apart but their absolute positions are not that critical.

## 3. MODELING GEOMETRIC VARIATION

Being able to define allowable limits on variation of a nominal geometry is a necessary tool for many tolerance analysis and synthesis activities. However, such activities do not require an ability to actually deform or change the nominal geometry. Rather it is used as a static reference. Developing new designs and manufacturing processes usually requires many iterations to reach an acceptable solution. Such a solution may not be optimal, but close enough. To produce an effective optimization tool, the ability to interactively vary the geometry is required.

### 3.1. Variational Modeling

As mentioned above a method put forward for interactive control of geometry by dimensions[22] and in a much more general way[31] is that of *variational modeling*. In this method geometry is determined from a set of dimensions where a dimension is described as a constraint on a characteristic point of the geometry. Each constraint is described by a nonlinear equation made up of the coordinates of the characteristic points of the geometry. A complete dimensioning scheme is represented by a set of such equations.

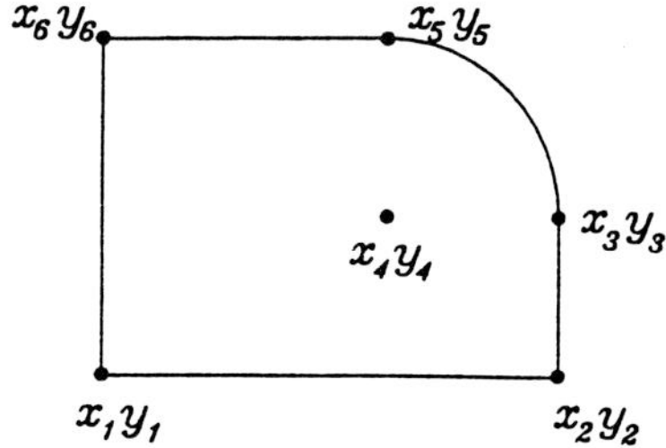


Fig. 1. Characteristic points.

As an example consider the 2D geometry in Fig. 1 which is described by $N$ characteristic points:

$$\mathbf{x} = \{x_1, y_1, z_1, x_2, y_2, z_2, \ldots, x_N, y_N, z_N\}^T$$

or more generally:

$$\mathbf{x} = \{x_1, x_2, x_3, x_4, x_5, x_6, \ldots, x_{n-1}, x_n\}^T$$

where $n = 3N$.

The general constraint equation can then be expressed analytically by equations of the form:

$$F_i(\mathbf{x}, \mathbf{d}) = 0 \qquad i = 1, 2, 3, 4, \cdots, m \tag{1}$$

where $\mathbf{d}$ is the dimension vector (i.e. distance between points), $\mathbf{x}$ is the geometry vector, and $m$ is the number of constraints. A typical constraint equation given in Ref. 31 is shown in Table 1.

Table 1. Typical set of geometric constraint equations.

| Constraint | Entities | Constraint equation |
|---|---|---|
| Horizontal distance | $p_1, p_2$ | $x_1 - x_2 - D_1 = 0$ |
| Vertical distance | $p_1, p_2$ | $y_1 - y_2 - D_2 = 0$ |
| Linear distance | $p_1, p_2$ | $(x_1 - x_2)^2 + (y_1 - y_2)^2 - D_3^2 = 0$ |

The set of constraint equations is not unique and will be arranged by the designer to suit the functionality of the design. Other constraints may be based on the area of the object or even on non-geometric characteristics such as maximum stress levels under given loads for a given geometric configuration.

Simultaneous solution of the equations (1) will result in the geometry corresponding to the dimensions specified. Solving the set of nonlinear equations by the Newton–Raphson scheme involves solving the following matrix equation for each iteration:

$$\mathbf{J}\Delta\mathbf{x} = \mathbf{r} \tag{2}$$

where $\boldsymbol{\Delta}\mathbf{x}$ are the vector displacements of the geometry vector $\{\Delta x_1, \Delta x_2, \ldots, \Delta x_n\}^T$, and $\mathbf{J}$ is the Jacobian containing the partial derivatives of each constraint equation with respect to each degree of freedom. That is:

$$\mathbf{J} = \begin{bmatrix} f_{11} & f_{12} & \cdots & f_{1n} \\ f_{21} & f_{22} & \cdots & f_{1n} \\ \vdots & \ddots & \ddots & \vdots \\ f_{m1} & \cdots & \cdots & f_{mn} \end{bmatrix},$$

$$f_{ij} = \frac{\partial F_i}{\partial x_j},$$

and

$$\mathbf{r} = \{-\mathbf{F}_1, -\mathbf{F}_2, \ldots, -\mathbf{F}_m\}^{\mathbf{T}}.$$

After each iteration $\mathbf{x}$ is updated using

$$\mathbf{x}_{i+1} = x_i + \Delta x_i .$$

The whole process is repeated until the residual $\mathbf{r}$ vanishes. Six constraint equations must be supplied to prevent rigid body motion, the remaining $m-6$ equations being the choice of the designer. If $m \neq n$, the Jacobian is structurally singular. If $m > n$, the shape is over constrained and if $m < n$ the shape is under constrained. For a valid scheme the Jacobian must be non-singular. However, the condition that $m = n$ is not sufficient as certain characteristic points may be over constrained and others under constrained leading to the matrix being numerically singular. Such a scheme provides a powerful variational modeling tool for design optimization. However, the solution of large sets of nonlinear equations can be numerically intensive.

## 4. MANUFACTURING PROCESS OPTIMIZATION

Once a component has been manufactured an inspection procedure will identify geometric variations of that part from its nominal design. This can then be compared to the allowable tolerance variation specified. However, if the component is *out of tolerance* the question that must be answered is *what needs to be done to the process to make it right?* Traditionally this would have been a process of trial and error with the number of iterations dependent on the experience of the process engineer. What is proposed here is that given a model of the process exists, the control variables of the process can be optimized to achieve a good part. This approach is perhaps best illustrated with an example.

Hot isothermal forging is a material deformation process under which billets of metal at elevated temperatures are squeezed between form dies. The variables which control this process include the rate of deformation (die velocity), the friction between the billet and the die, the initial position of the billet, material properties such as strain hardening coefficient and the geometry of the die and any pre-form dies. Optimization of the process requires iterative runs of the process changing the control variables appropriately as illustrated in Fig. 2.

If the process is now replaced by a Finite Element (FE) model the iteration can then be done off-line. Geometric deviations attained from the analysis of results

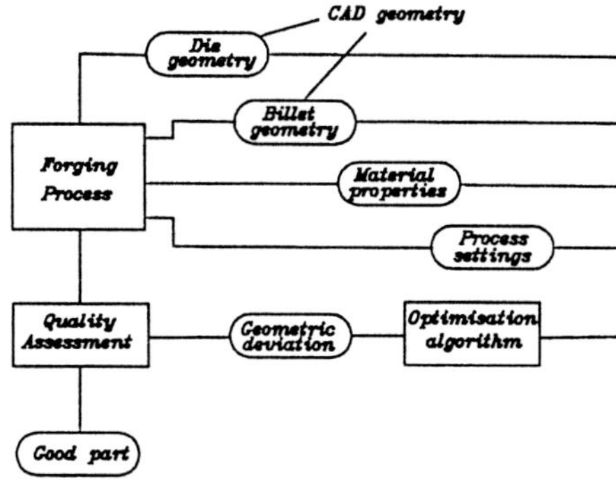


Fig. 2. Forging process optimization loop.

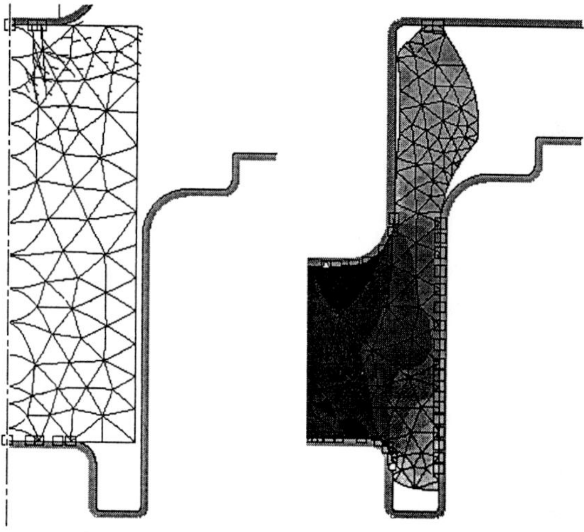

Fig. 3. Forging model: initial velocities and hydrostatic pressure.

is equivalent to "inspecting" the product and deviations from the nominal can be passed to an optimization algorithm so that the control variables can be updated.

## 5. FORGING MODEL

In metal forging the billet material behaves in a nonlinear way following some elasto-plastic or visco-plastic law. In addition the large scale deformations that occur lead to geometric nonlinearity. Thus, the discretization of the analysis domain of the billet yields a nonlinear set of equations that relate the force required for deformation $\{\mathbf{F}\}$ to the displacement at each node $\{\mathbf{a}\}$ of the discretized domain:

$$\{\mathbf{F}\} = [K(a)]\{a\} \tag{3}$$

where the stiffness matrix $[\mathbf{K}]$ is a function of the nodal displacements. Such a set of equations cannot be solved directly but require linearization and solution by iterative techniques. Thus we can break the analysis up into formulation of the nonlinear equations and their solution.

Forging is generally regarded as a velocity field problem where a velocity formulation is required. As with linear elastic analysis an application specific constitutive material law is required. In this case we will use a viscoplastic law for hot forming based on the general Levy–Mises equation as detailed by Evans.[19] (Others such as the Norton–Hoff law used by Chenot[11] are equally as valid). For hot deformation processes there is no change in volume and the material is incompressible. In such circumstances the mean pressure $p$ applies only a hydrostatic loading with the change in shape being due to the deviatoric stress component of the stress tensor. It is therefore convenient to split the stress tensor into two components. The deviatoric flow stress $\sigma'$ can then be related to the strain rate tensor by:

$$\dot{\varepsilon}_{ij} = \frac{3}{2}\frac{\dot{\bar{\varepsilon}}}{\bar{\sigma}}\sigma'_{ij}\,. \tag{4}$$

The deviatoric stress tensor, $\sigma'_{ij}$ is given by

$$\sigma'_{ij} = \sigma_{ij} - p \qquad (i = j)\,, \tag{5}$$

and

$$\sigma'_{ij} = \sigma_{ij} \qquad (i \neq j), \tag{6}$$

where $\sigma_{ij}$ is the Chaucy stress tensor at a point and $p$ is the mean stress defined as $\frac{1}{3}(\sigma_{11} + \sigma_{22} + \sigma_{33})$, $\bar{\varepsilon}$ and $\bar{\sigma}$ are the effective strain rate and effective stress, respectively and are defined by:

$$\bar{\sigma} = \sqrt{\frac{3}{2}\sigma'_{ij}\sigma'_{ij}} \qquad \text{and} \qquad \bar{\varepsilon} = \sqrt{\frac{3}{2}\dot{\varepsilon}_{ij}\dot{\varepsilon}_{ij}} \tag{7}$$

Now, the velocity at any point in the element can be given by:

$$u(x, y) = [\mathbf{N}]\{\mathbf{v}\} \tag{8}$$

where $[\mathbf{N}]$ is the interpolation function to be used for the element $\{\mathbf{v}\}$ are the nodal velocities of the element. We also have for the strain rate tensor:

$$\{\varepsilon\} = [B]\{v\} \tag{9}$$

where $[\mathbf{B}]$ contains the necessary spatial derivatives for the shape function.

Now the Principle of Virtual Work yields the following equilibrium statement

$$\int_V \sigma_{ij}\delta\dot{\varepsilon}_{ij}dV = \int_\Omega F_i\delta u_i d\Omega \tag{10}$$

where $dV$ is the incremental volume and $d\Omega$ is the incremental length on the boundary. Expressing in terms of the hydrostatic and deviatoric stress tensors yields for Eq. (10):

$$\int_V \sigma'_{ij}\delta\dot{\varepsilon}_{ij}dV + \int_V p\delta\dot{\varepsilon}_{ii}dV = \int_\Omega F_i\delta u_i d\Omega \tag{11}$$

with the condition that the sum of the strain rates in each principle direction equals zero for incompressibility:

$$\int_V \dot{\varepsilon_{ii}} dV = 0\,. \tag{12}$$

Substituting from Eqs. (4), (8) and (9) into Eq. (11) yields the elemental nonlinear stiffness equation

$$\int_V \bar{\sigma}\frac{1}{\bar{\varepsilon}}[\mathbf{P}]dV\{\mathbf{v}\} + \int_V \frac{\zeta}{2}\dot{\varepsilon_{ii}} dV = \int_\Omega [\mathbf{N}]\{\mathbf{F}\}d\Omega\,. \tag{13}$$

This is, again, our nonlinear stiffness term of Eq. (3), but with the second term being a penalty function to ensure the constant volume constraint applies.

These elemental equations can be assembled into an overall system of nonlinear equations for all elements. The solution procedure that is generally followed uses an iterative Newton–Raphson method where the equations are linearized through a Taylor expansion.[48]

### 5.1. Non-Steady State Deformation

The solution of the above system of equations results in the steady state velocity field being determined. Forging is a non-steady state process where the shape of the billet will change with time. The new position of the element nodes can be determined by a simple one step Euler scheme:

$$\{\mathbf{a}\}^{(t+1)} = \{\mathbf{a}\}^{(t)} + \{\mathbf{v}\}^t \Delta t$$

where $\Delta t$ is some appropriate time step. The value of $\Delta t$ is important for numerical stability and must be sufficiently small that the small strain approximations made in the Levy–Mises law are valid.

### 5.2. Contact

As the solution proceeds over time the billet will come into and out of contact with the dies. At each time step a contact algorithm will check to see if the displaced node has penetrated the die. If so it implies that the time step was too large and needs to be reduced and the computations repeated. Alternatively, if the penetration is small, the node could be projected onto the die surface negating the need for resolution of the system of equations.

If the node is deemed to be in contact with the die a constraint will be applied that, assuming it is experiencing compressive loads, it will remain in contact and be given a nodal velocity equal to the die velocity. The node will also experience a friction boundary condition due to the contact. This will be either stick, that is the node remains in the same position relative to the die, or slip, which is generally governed by a Coulombic friction law given by:

$$\tau = -\alpha k|\Delta v^{q-1}|\Delta v \tag{14}$$

where $\tau$ is the friction stress, $\Delta v$ is the velocity difference between die and billet, $\alpha$ is the friction coefficient, $q$ is the friction rate sensitivity index, and $k$ is the consistency value.

### 5.3. Remeshing

Most FE codes for forging modeling employ an updated Lagrangian formation. That is the nodes of the mesh follow the kinematic evolution of the billet. The calculation of equilibrium at a given time step is based upon a coordinate system of the previous step. Such a formulation may result in elements becoming grossly distorted which can lead to inaccuracies in the simulation. Thus, during a full analysis, regular re-meshing will be required when the element distortion reaches a critical limit. To provide a practical tool this re-meshing needs to be automatic and is usually based on a Delaunay triangulation algorithm.[2]

## 6. OPTIMIZATION

Finite element modeling methods have primarily been used for the analysis of complex mechanical and manufacturing problems. If a result obtained indicates a problem, the engineer is in a similar position as if he had carried out a physical experiment: What input variables need to be changed to achieve a desired change in the results? One focus of current research work is in how to use FE models of forging processes as an optimization and synthesis tool. Carrying out unstructured "what if" analysis may yield an improvement in the output results, but may not be the optimum procedure of produce optimum results.

Using the definitions put forward by Wilde[47] a forging process can be characterized by a system where the output can be expressed in terms of a number of inputs:

- Adjustable factors $x$. These are the independent controllable variable of the process such as die velocity, temperature, etc.
- Uncontroled but measured factors $p$. These are parameters that cannot be controled. They may be material properties, atmospheric conditions, etc.
- Unkown factors $r$. These are random variables.
- Results $y$. Dependent variables or objective function. These may be dimensions, surface condition, metallurgical condition, etc.

An important first stage in setting up a model of the system to be optimized is to ensure that all the independent variables and uncontroled parameters of interest are identified along with the objective optimization function. This will require analyzing the actual overall forging process as a system which includes the presses, furnaces, die geometry and the deformation process. Trying to optimize more than one objective function at a time is difficult and should thus be avoided. Given such a system, the aim is to then search the response surface (that is vary the independent variables) in order to achieve a maximum (or minimum) value of the objective function.

## 6.1. Optimization Search Strategy

The simplest search strategy is to hold all independent variables constant and vary one at a time and monitor the effect on the output function. This will give an indication of the sensitivity of the output function to that variable. However, such a search may only yield a partial improvement in the output as it may not find the optimum as shown in Fig. 4. In addition, it does not indicate the interdependence of the independent variables on the output function.

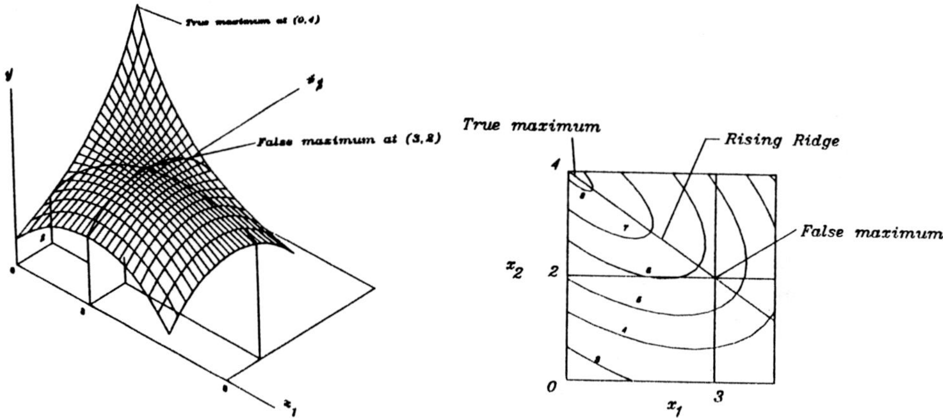


Fig. 4. False maxima.

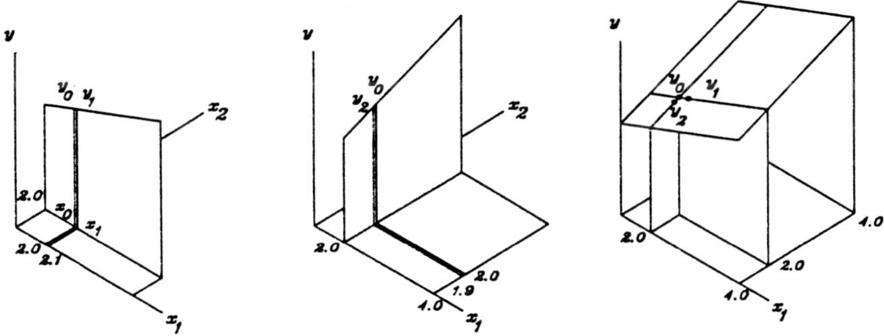


Fig. 5. Gradient search.

With this technique the first phase of the optimization consists of a series of small experiments, usually two level factorial of the independent variables, that yield discrete values of the response surface shown in Fig. 5. When analyzing the results of the experiments, the main effect of the change of variable is usually defined as the average change in the response as the variable is changed from the low to the high level. For two variable experiments the resulting points on the response surface can be used to generate a tangent plane to the surface showing the relative gradient. If the optimum variable settings are far from the initial conditions, the response surface is likely to have a steep gradient. In such cases, the main effects of the variables are usually relatively large and provide adequate information to determine the approximate direction of steepest ascent or descent. If large numbers of factors are being studied, hyperspace tangents can be calculated as detailed in Ref. 47.

The variable settings for the next experiment are determined based on the direction of maximal benefit established in the preceding experiment. When the experiment is run, a new direction is established, and the cycle is repeated until a point is reached where the change in experiment results are small and the gradient flat.

When near optimal conditions are reached, there is usually relatively more curvature in the response surface. The second order derivatives are more likely to be larger when compared to first order terms. This indicates the second phase of the optimization search. Whereas in the first stage a linear (planer) approximation to the response surface was used, the second stage uses a higher polynomial approximation to the response surface to predict where the next experiments are to be carried out. This will require more experiments to be carried out to establish the surface approximation.

This tangent or gradient ascent method provides a structured sequential optimum searching strategy that allows the next series of experiments to be based on an increased knowledge of the response surface. The technique can be used with $n$ independent variables to provide a hyperspace response function.[47] However, visualization of such a function is impossible and such a strategy needs to be computer generated.

The convergence rate of such a scheme will be dependent on the size of the interval between the independent variable values and the prediction of where to place the anchor point for the next set of experiments based on the calculated gradient. The simplest method is to add a position vector of standard length to the current point. If the subsequent response results are no better than the previous one, this vector can be reduced adaptively. A limitation of this approach is that it assumes a uni-modal response surface. Thus, if there are false maxima the strategy may find one of these instead of the optimum point.

### 6.2. Geometric Optimization of Forging Dies

A more formalized approach to geometric optimization of forming processes has been given by Balan *et al.*[20] which leads to similar results obtained by Doltsinis.[17] This is based on the analytical evaluation of the gradients of an objective function. In this example the aim is to find an optimum shape of a preform die (and hence initial billet shape) to produce a geometrically correct final component. The process parameters $p$ that can be varied are points ($x_i$) on the preform die which are interpolated with a cubic spline to define its shape.

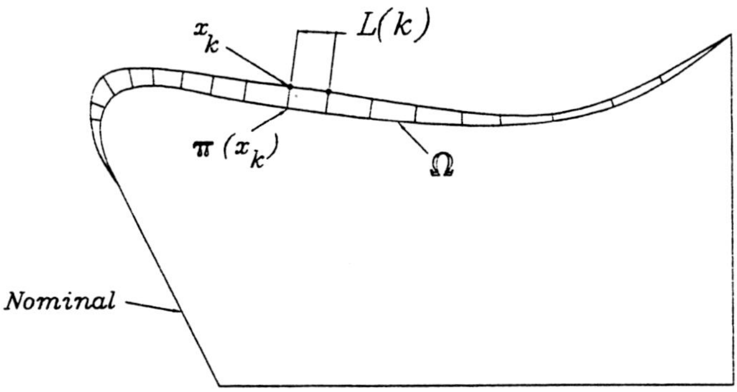


Fig. 6. Illustration of the error projection from the deformed to the nominal surface.

### 6.3. Optimization Algorithm

The key to effective optimization is in choosing an appropriate objective function. In this case the objective function needs to minimize the geometric distance between the predicted deformed shape and the nominal required shape, Fig. 6. This uses points on the boundary of the surface and can be expressed as:

$$\Phi = \int_{\partial\Omega} \|\pi(x(s)) - x(s)\|^2 ds \tag{15}$$

where $x(s)$ is the current point on the boundary of the deformed surface, $\pi(x(s))$ is a projection of that point onto the desired (nominal) surface $\Omega$ after a simulation iteration, and $ds$ is the incremental distance between points on the boundary of the surface. The projected errors between the deformed and nominal surfaces are shown in Fig. 6.

After the finite element discretization has taken place Eq. (15) becomes

$$\Phi(p) = \sum_{k \in \partial\Omega}^{n} \|\pi(x_k) - x_k\|^2 L(k) \tag{16}$$

where $L(k)$ is the segment length associated with the boundary node $x_k$, and $n$ is the total number of nodes and $p$ the current design parameter settings. Thanks to the simple expression of the objective function, the variation of the design parameters between two time iterations can be evaluated using the gradients of $\Phi(p)$. The following algorithm is taken from Ref. 20:

(a) Make an initial guess of the boundary point position for the first iteration $p^{(0)}$.
(b) $p^n$ being known, calculate $\Phi(p^{(n)})$ and $\frac{d\Omega_o}{dp}(p^{(n)})$.
(c) Calculate $\frac{d^2\Omega_o}{dp^2}(p^{(n)})$.

(d) Calculate the design parameter correction for iteration:

$$\Delta p^{(n)} = -\left(\frac{d^2\Omega}{dp^2}\right)^{-1} \frac{d\Omega_o}{dp}(p^{(n)}) .$$

(e) Carry out a line search to find a value of $\lambda$ which minimizes the function:

$$\Phi_o(p^{(n)} + \lambda\Delta p^{(n)}).$$

(f) Update the geometric design parameters $p^{(n)}$ using the minimized value of $\lambda$:

$$p^{(n+1)} = p^{(n)} + \lambda\Delta ap^{(n)} .$$

(g) Return to (b) until the convergence criteria has been reached.

The global efficiency of such an algorithm depends significantly on the way in which the gradients are calculated: numerically or analytically, which in turn is dependent on the optimization function chosen.

## 7. REGULARIZED PARAMETER SET

The example above is essentially a geometric optimization. However, the same results could have been obtained by optimizing other process control variables, or combinations of them. From this it can be seen that significant advantages in the design and efficiency of optimization algorithms for manufacturing processes can be obtained by having a regularized parameter set. That is, the input variables that control geometric variations required for optimization should be in a similar format to material properties, deformation rates, friction coefficients, etc. and that those parameters should be closely correlated with the output from inspection error analysis.

In the following analysis, a technique is described that enables shape variations to be modeled and related back to process parameter variations using deformable models. The system is trained on shapes derived from modeling systems using process parameters. Hence a regularized parameter set is obtained with different parameters controling different aspects of the shape variations.

## 8. DEFORMABLE MODELS

Deformable models are a relatively new technique finding many applications in computer vision, computer graphics and other areas. The concept of a deformable model is based on a parameterized model which is allowed to deform under certain constraints to fit or model some underlying, usually 2D or 3D, data. Deformable models can take many forms, some of which are related to, or based on, the finite element technique (FE). Finite elements are popular in mechanical and civil engineering to model processes such as forging, bridge dynamics and many others. In these examples the FE method is used to generate resulting instances of data such as the shape of a forged part as described above. In the field of inspection the model is manipulated to generate an instance that is as close to the actual data measured as possible.

### 8.1. Parametric Deformable Models

One of the earliest examples of a deformable model was described by Ballard and Brown[3] in which a shape was iteratively changed to reduce the error between the model and the data. In this case the parameters describing the model are used in a gradient descent approach. This is really an extension of the standard least squares algorithm for more simple models such as straight lines (two parameters), circles (three parameters) and ellipses (five parameters) and other curves. Work on fitting circles and ellipses can be found in Berman[5] (circles), Albano[1] and Rosin[42] (ellipses). For example, in Rosin[42] a Kalman filter was used and a binary search performed on the covariance values (by scaling them) to get the best fit ellipse to the data. Other better fits were hyperbolae which can be represented by the conic equation used. These were not wanted as the goal was ellipse fitting.

Kass[30] were the first to propose a deformable model based on some *physical* model and constraints. This model, known as the "Active Contour Model" (ACM) or "snakes", iteratively deforms geometry by minimizing the energy functional:

$$E^*_{snake} = \int_0^1 E_{data}(v(u)) + E_{int}(v(u)) + E_{con}(v(u))du \tag{17}$$

where $E_{int}$ represents the internal energy of the active contour, $E_{data}$ represents the data forces, and $E_{con}$ represents the external constraint forces such as limiting the closeness of the points on the curve. The internal energy is composed of the first and second order terms as follows:

$$E_{int}(v(u)) = \frac{\alpha(u)|v^{'}(u)|^2 + \beta(u)|v^{''}(u)|^2}{2} \tag{18}$$

where $\alpha(u)$ controls the elasticity of the contour that tries to pull the points on the contour together, and $\beta(u)$ controls the stiffness of the contour and tries to keep the contour smooth. The external energy $E_{data}$ is approximated by summing the energy under the contour:

$$E_{data}(v) = \gamma \sum_{i=0}^{n-1} E_{span} v(u)\,. \tag{19}$$

A minimum is found when the internal contour forces, data forces and constraint forces are in equilibrium. $E_{data}$ may be derived from data intensity, magnitude of data gradient or edge data using a distance transform.[8] The greater the value of $\gamma$, the greater the effect the data forces have. The external constraint forces $E_{con}$ allow interaction with the contour from outside sources such as a human operator or "physical barriers" within the local environment. They can be represented by *springs*, *volcanoes* or other force fields. A spring is an elastic energy potential with one end attached to the contour and the other end attached to the data. The *spring* applies a force to the contour pulling it toward an area of the data. *Volcanos* generate a repulsive potential pushing the contour away from a region of the data.

This method has been successfully used in a number of computer vision applications such as boundary fitting,[30] segmentation[30] and tracking of objects.[15] By choosing the constraints and curve parameterization for the model, *reasonable* fits of the model to the data can be obtained. Importantly, a smoothness constraint is usually applied to overcome noise and poor data capture. In fact, if the data is produced from a known model, then this method can successfully overcome the problem of much missing data. However if the data is subject to variation or contains much detail, then the snake may not *accurately* fit the data. An accurate fit is necessary for inspection, tolerancing and geometric differences due to process parameter variation. The objective in these applications is to accurately detect these perturbations and defects. The problem is the use of the parametric model which cannot fully describe the model of interest with enough detail. Finite Element Models (FEM)[12,27–29] were introduced to improve the numerical stability of the solution and make the representation more efficient. These FEMs act directly on the integral equation rather than transforming the integral into a set of differential equations to be solved numerically. The FEM converts the problem of optimizing the functional to approximating the minima of ordinary functions constructed from polynomial FE basis functions, commonly Lagrange, Hermite of quadratic functions, and the snake energy terms. Lower order basis functions such as these ensure that the boundary conditions between nodes are met. The FEM provides a far more efficient discretization of the contour than the finite difference method used in the ACM of Kass *et al.*[30] resulting in a greater accuracy of curve representation with a fewer number of points. It leads to a set of matrices that are symmetric and positive definite which can be efficiently solved using an existing numerical scheme.

There is also the problem of parameter choice. Most applications of snakes require the manual tuning of the parameters which is inevitably a compromise. An alternative method is to train the snake by iteratively adjusting the parameters until a best fit is achieved. However, this would require retraining the snake on every data set and some form of user interaction is required for the snake model to perform successfully. The parameters themselves do not uniquely characterize the snake deformation and hence the snake may arrive at minima using any one of a combination of different parameter settings. This limits the value of the snake for characterizing shape deformations and hence our applications.

### 8.2. Non-Parametric Deformable Models

A more recent technique has been proposed and investigated by Cootes and Taylor[14] which is based on eigenstructure analysis and learning. In this *non-parametric* technique, there is no requirement for a model of the curve or data as it can consider an arbitrary number of points and how they move under control of the model. Cootes and Taylor have analyzed this method for a number of applications, generally considering the boundary points of 2D binary objects.[14] However some 3D analysis has also been carried out.[21] Other curve descriptions have been looked at. For example the control points of a spline description of an object boundary have been used to track people moving through a scene.[4]

The Active Shape Model (ASM)[13] provides a direct mapping of points on the nominal model to the edge data through a combination of scale, rotation and translation transformations and residual shape adjustments. This model uses a Point Distribution Model (PDM)[14] to search for shapes, belonging to a shape set, within the data. The PDM is a way of representing a class of shapes using a flexible model of the position of labeled points placed on examples of the class. The labeled $(x, y)$ points can represent significant boundary locations on an object such as in Fig. 7 where the points are $P_i$ for $i = 0, \ldots, 48$.

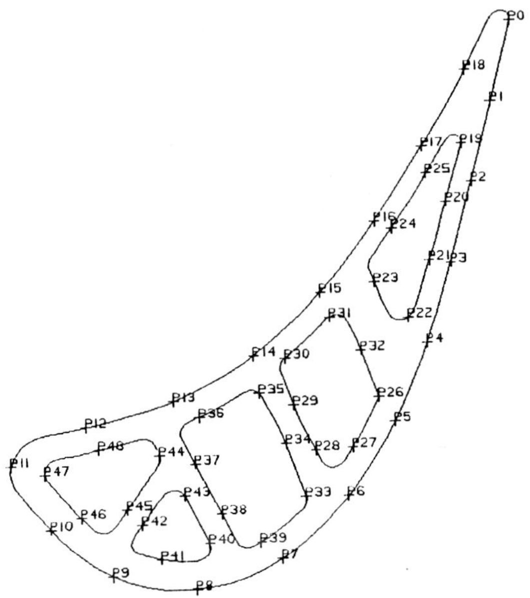


Fig. 7. Cross section of a blade showing the points for training the PDM. The points are positioned at equal arc lengths on the spline.

The model uses statistical information gathered from a set of aligned shapes to create new shapes within the class. The class constraints are enforced by a set of global constraints on the allowable variations to the nominal shape. A shape may be considered to be within a shape class if it conforms to these global constraints. The model consists of the mean positions of the labeled points and the main modes of variation of the points from their mean positions. These modes of variation correspond to the most significant eigenvectors in a principal component decomposition of the position variables. A new unique shape which belongs to the class of shapes can be created using the following equation:

$$\vec{x} = \vec{\bar{x}} + P\vec{b} \tag{20}$$

In 2D, $\vec{x}$ represents the $n$ points of the shapes:

$$\vec{x} = (x_0, y_0 \dots x_{n-1}, y_{n-1}) \tag{21}$$

and $(x_k, y_k)$ is the position of point $k$, $\bar{\vec{x}}$ is the mean position of all points on the shape, $P = (\vec{p_1}, \vec{p_2}, \dots, \vec{p_t})$ is a matrix of the $t$ most significant eigenvectors in a principal component decomposition of the position variables, and $\vec{b}$ is a vector of weights for each mode. This vector may be used to generate new examples from the class of shapes by varying it within suitable limits. These limits can be derived by examining the distributions of the points in the training set and can be adjusted to the required precision of the shape class definition. Smoothly varying $\vec{b}$ results in smooth changes to the shape.

An ASM combines a set of translation, rotation and scaling transformations with a PDM, in an iterative optimization process to fit the model to the data. Data points corresponding to model points can be selected by the criteria of maximum edge strength normal to the model points or alternatively, if the data points are known, then dynamic cooperation[9] between these points and the model points can be used to update the pose and shape of the model. This process involves updating the pose and shape parameters, to find the set of parameters that best fit the model onto the data at each iteration of the algorithm. This process is performed in a three step procedure:

1. Translate the centre of the model points to the centre of the data points.
2. Rotate the result of (1) by an angle $\theta$ which best maps the transformed model points onto the data points.
3. Adjust the weight vector $\vec{b}$ to optimize the form of the transformed model to fit the data points.

This procedure is repeated until the difference between the transformed model and the data has converged to an acceptable small error or the model has proceeded past a given number of iterations (in this case the process will be deemed to be out of control).

Rather than using a parametric curve, as used in the ACM,[30] the PDM consists of a set of labeled $(x, y)$ coordinates. This leads to the need to decide on the positions of the most appropriate places for the labeled points. Each labeled point has a number of degrees of freedom and the movement of each point is independent of the others. Hence it should be possible to capture all forms of component defects. Baumberg and Hogg[4] have implemented a PDM using the control points of the controling polygon of a B-spline as the labeled points. This enables the model to represent complex objects using a smaller number of labeled points reducing the size of the eigenvector space. This is not used in this application because there are constraints on splines that mean that each point is not independent of the others so preventing a wide range of defects and deformations to be modeled, i.e. a form of smoothness constraint has been applied.

For the analysis of 3D components, a 3D version of the above algorithm has been implemented using quaternions as described below. As rigid body alignment algorithms are inadequate for the alignment of 3D shapes, an accurate and efficient method for registering variable shapes using a 3D Deformable Shape Model (DSM) based on the PDM is proposed. The DSM expresses the difference in form between the model description and the sensed data as a vector of deformations of the nominal model.

The DSM matches the mean shape produced by the PDM to sensed data using six degrees of freedom, and the shape deformation restricted to the modes of variation defined by the PDM. The DSM uses dynamic cooperation between the model and data points to compute the model displacement at each iteration. This effectively pulls the model through local minima and resolves potential conflicts that may occur when using a nearest neighbor matching scheme.

## 9. GENERATING A 3D POINT DISTRIBUTION MODEL

In order to train the PDM on a set of example shapes, the shapes are first aligned using a set of rigid body transformations, so that the positions of corresponding labeled points represent the true shape variations of the training set. If there are $N$ shapes in the shape set then the $i$th shape can be described by a vector of $n$ points:

$$\vec{X_i} = (x_{i0}, y_{i0}, z_{i0}, x_{i1}, y_{i1}, z_{i1}, \ldots, x_{in-1}, y_{in-1}, z_{in-1})^T. \tag{22}$$

We use the quaternion-based algorithm of Horn[24] for the alignment of a pair of shapes. Using this method, a pair of shapes represented by the vectors $\vec{X_i}$ and $\vec{X_j}$, are aligned by minimizing the mean square objective function:

$$f(\vec{u}) = \frac{1}{n_i} \sum_{k=1}^{n_i} \|\vec{X_{ik}} - R(\vec{u_R})\vec{X_{jk}} - \vec{u_T}\|^2 \tag{23}$$

where $\vec{u}$ is the combined rigid motion quaternion vector, $\vec{u_T}$ is the translation quaternion vector, and $\vec{u_R}$ is the unit rotation quaternion vector.

This method utilises the cross-covariance matrix $\sum_{\vec{X_i}\vec{X_j}}$ of the two data sets and a good summary of this registration algorithm can be found in Ref. 7. All of the shapes in the set are aligned to a dynamically adjusted mean using an algorithm similiar to that described by Cootes and Taylor.[14]

Once the point sets are aligned, a principal components analysis is performed on the ordinates of the points (For a full discussion see Ref. 14). This produces a set of eigen-statistics which, combined with the mean shape, can describe any shape within the set using Eq. (20).

## 10. THE DEFORMABLE SHAPE MODEL (DSM)

The DSM performs an elastic registration of a nominal model with sensed data using the statistics recovered from the PDM described in the previous section. The basic algorithm is:

1. Using Point Displacement Vectors (PDV), find smoothed displacement vectors which will improve the position of the model points with respect to the data

points. An improvement is considered as a reduction in the Euclidean distance between the set of model points and the data points.

2. Compute the rotation quaternion $R$ and translation quaternion $T$ that will minimize the mean square objective function in Eq. (23), to update the current position of the model to a new position suggested by the PDVs.
3. Using Eq. (20), deform the shape of the current model to minimize the distance between the rotated and translated model and the points suggested by the PDVs. The values of the weight vector $\vec{b}$ are limited to prevent the shape deforming outside the class of allowable shapes (in our implementation we limit $\vec{b}$ to $\pm 3\sigma$).

The algorithm is repeated until a suitable convergence sentinel value is reached. The least mean square error, maximum residual and/or change in model points can be used as tests for convergence of the model and number of iterations.

### 10.1. Point Displacement Vectors

The nearest neighbor approach for finding the improved position of model points is inadequate for registration of variable shaped objects using a deformable model. If we simply find the closest point on the surface of the sensed data to each model point, as used in the Iterative Closest Point (ICP) algorithm,[7] it is possible that a misregistration could occur. In Fig. 8, a nominal tetrahedron is placed within a slightly enlarged example of the same shape.

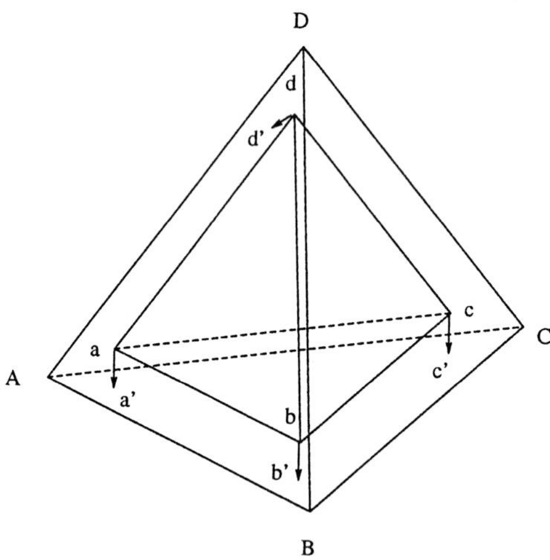


Fig. 8. A nominal tetrahedron model is placed within an enlarged object of a similar shape. Using the closest point criterion, vertices $a, b, c$ and $d$ are projected onto the surface $ABC$ and $ABD$, respectively with $a', b', c'$ and $d'$ being the projected points.

The model vertices $a$,$b$,$c$ and $d$ are projected onto the surfaces of the larger object, as shown by the vectors in Fig. 8. The model will deform to match the projected points and hence the misregistration illustrated in Fig. 9 occurs.

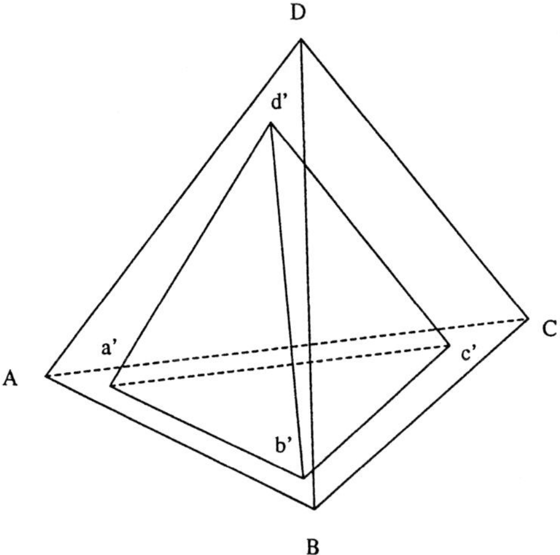


Fig. 9. Misregistration of a nominal tetrahedron with an enlarged tetrahedron.

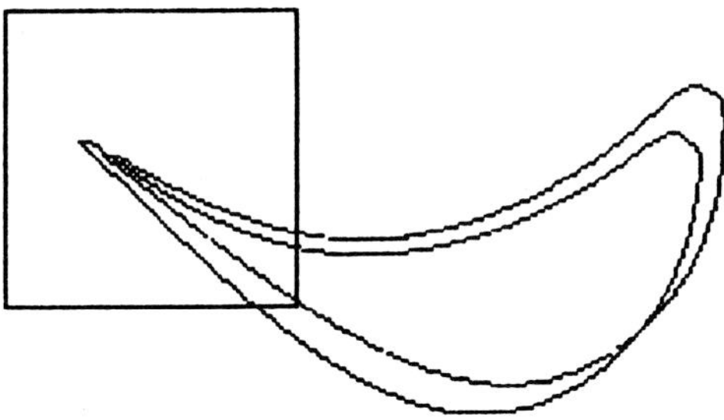

Fig. 10. Two turbine blade profiles are orientated slightly offset from one another.

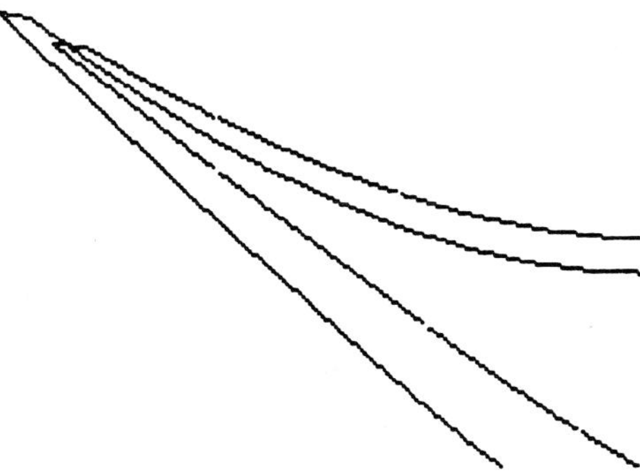

Fig. 11. The convex position of the tail on one profile is closer to the concave section on the other and hence it is possible that a misregistration could occur using a closest normal point correspondence criterion.

Unfortunately the above correspondence criteria is inappropriate when two surfaces of the model object are attracted to the same surface of the data object. Figures 10 and 11 illustrate how this erroneous matching could occur during the alignment of two turbine blade profiles. Another counter-example against using this correspondence criterion is when the tail of the model turbine blade profile is within the tail of the data blade. The model's tail may attempt to expand to fit the surface of the data, rather than attempting to match the cusp.

A better solution is to use dynamic cooperation between the model and data points as used for the automatic registration of deformed data.[9] This method allows the data points to pull, while forces push the model points toward them. Point Displacement Vectors (PDV) are constructed between the nearest neighbors of the model and the data points. If there are $n$ model points $l = 1 \ldots n$ on the $i$th shape, then for each model point $\vec{X}_{il}$ a PDV $\vec{D1}_l$ is computed by:

$$\vec{D}1_l = (\vec{X}_{jk'} - \vec{X}_{il}) \tag{24}$$

where $\vec{X}_{jk'}$ is the point on the data which has the minimum Euclidean distance to the point $\vec{X}_{il}$. Similiarly, for $K$ data points $\vec{X}_{jk}$ on the data, a PDV $\vec{D}2_k$ is computed by:

$$\vec{D}2_k = (\vec{X}_{il'} - \vec{X}_{jk})\,. \tag{25}$$

The new suggested model points $\vec{X}_i'$ are computed by combining $\vec{D}1_l$ and $\vec{D}2_k$ with a Gaussian smoothing function using:

$$\vec{X}_i' = \vec{X}_i + \left( \frac{\sum_{l=1}^{n} G1\vec{D}1_l}{\sum_{l=1}^{n} G1} - \frac{\sum_{k=1}^{K} G2\vec{D}2_k}{\sum_{k=1}^{K} G2} \right) * t \tag{26}$$

where $t$ is the step size and G1 and G2 are the Gaussian functions[9]:

$$G1 = \exp\left( \frac{-(X_{ix} - X_{ilx})^2 - (X_{iy} - X_{ily})^2}{\sigma^2} \right), \tag{27}$$

$$G2 = \exp\left( \frac{-(X_{ix} - X_{jkx} - D2_{kx})^2}{\sigma^2} - \frac{(X_{iy} - X_{jky} - D2_{ky})^2}{\sigma^2} \right). \tag{28}$$

The value of $\sigma$ is equivalent to the radius of the smoothing window. A large stepsize $t = 0.5$ and $\sigma$ (approximately the size of the data object) can be selected initially, to give a coarse initial registration. Both $\sigma$ and $t$ decay with each iteration, as the registration improves. Using a weighted average of all the PDVs enables the model to avoid the attraction conflict in Fig. 10.

## 11. ANALYSIS OF THE DEFORMABLE SHAPE MODEL

There are two main objectives that require the above analysis. These are:

1. Measure the accuracy of the registration of a deformable model to data that features global distortions such as bow and twist.

2. Compare the results of this algorithm with an ICP algorithm which uses only rigid body alignment.

To illustrate the performance of the above approach, a PDM training set consisting of 100 shapes, was created by twisting a nominal turbine blade model of 156 points by random amounts between $\pm\frac{\pi}{30}$. The initial PDV had a window size of $\sigma = 50.0$, with a decay rate of $\frac{\delta\sigma}{\delta T} = 0.85$. The step size $t$ was set at a constant of 0.2. Figure 12 shows the initial position of the nominal blade and a blade that has been twisted by $\frac{\pi}{45}$, rotated about the $x$,$y$ and $z$ axes by one, two and three degrees, respectively and translated in the $x$, $y$ and $z$ directions by 4 mm, 2 mm and 2 mm, respectively. Figure 13 shows the relative positions of the two blades after four iterations and Fig. 14 shows the blades after 39 iterations.

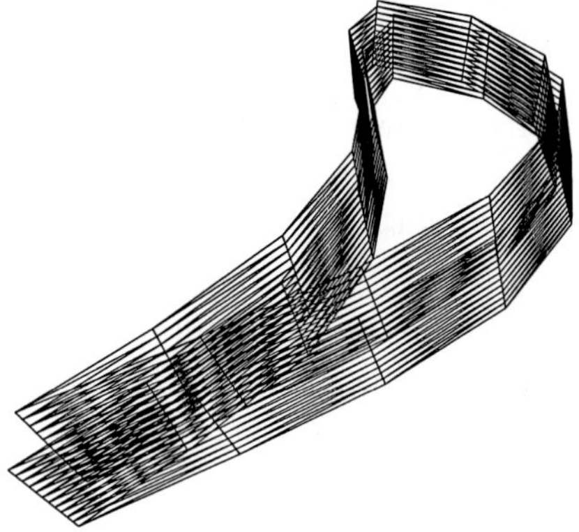

Fig. 12. Initial positions of nominal blade and twisted and transformed replica.

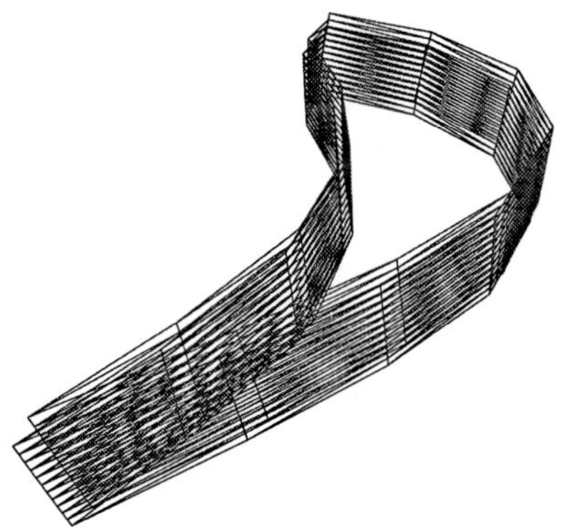

Fig. 13. Relative positions of blades after four iterations of the DSM.

The computation of the PDVs in this algorithm is more expensive than the closest point method. However for objects constructed from many points a parallel algorithm for computing the PDVs would improve efficiency. The number of PDVs could be reduced by matching corresponding features between model and data points, such as mean and Gaussian curvature to filter out those points that

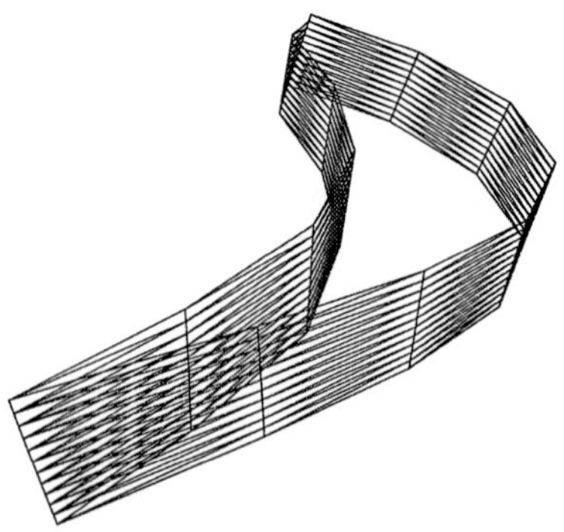

Fig. 14. Final positions of the blades after 39 iterations. The nominal blade has now matches the deformed blade.

are too dissimilar. Points on features such as the cusp on the tail of the turbine blade, could be weighted such that they have a higher matching priority, resulting in a reduction in the convergence time.

### 11.1. Use of the PDM for Analyzing Geometric Deformations

The output of the alignment of the DSM with measured data described in Sec. 11, gives a set of transformation parameters $(\theta, t)$ and the principal component weights $b$. We can ignore the transformation parameters and concentrate on the principal component weights which define the components shape because we are only concerned here with the shape, not its position.

The issue now is how the resulting values of $\mathbf{b}$ can be used for analyzing geometric distortions. The initial goal in this multivariate control procedure should be to discover if the component is within tolerance. A useful property of principal components analysis is that it allows us to easily compute an overall shape variability measure using Hotelling's[25] standard $T^2$ test:

$$T^2 = y^T y \tag{29}$$

where $y = \frac{b}{\sqrt{\lambda}}$. This enables us to detect significant departures from the mean shape and hence make an immediate accept/reject decision. If the part fails the initial test then the next most pressing questions are:

- what form does the defect take and
- how badly deformed is it?

By examining the combination of the principal component weights output from the DSM, we can elucidate:

- *which* defect is present, and
- the *amount* of each defect present.

In addition, there may be more than one defect present and there is a need to identify each defect and the amount. Note that various combinations of defect may produce the same shaped data. This is a factor that is ignored in this analysis.

The scheme currently being investigated consists of two stages for training:

- Determine the $P$ matrix using a training set of all combinations of defect i.e. shapes of all combinations generated or acquired.
- For each defect $i$ and defect amount $j$, determine the combination of weights: $b_{ij}$.

The first stage produces *one* matrix of eigenvectors encompassing all the defects such that varying $b$ will produce shapes containing combinations of one of more defects or different amounts. The second stage produces specific values for $b$, i.e. a value of $b_{ij}$ for a particular defect $i$ and amount of that defect $j$.

## 11.2. Robust Simultaneous Equation Solution

A simple approach to measuring defects is to take an unknown data set, determine $\vec{b}$ and see which $b_{ij}$ for each deformation $i$, and amount of deformation $j$, matches. Then the particular defect and amount are determined. This is not a satisfactory scheme as it assumes the defects are discrete. In real applications the amount of defect varies continuously and may have some uni-modal distribution, i.e. statistics of occurrence for each amount of each defect.

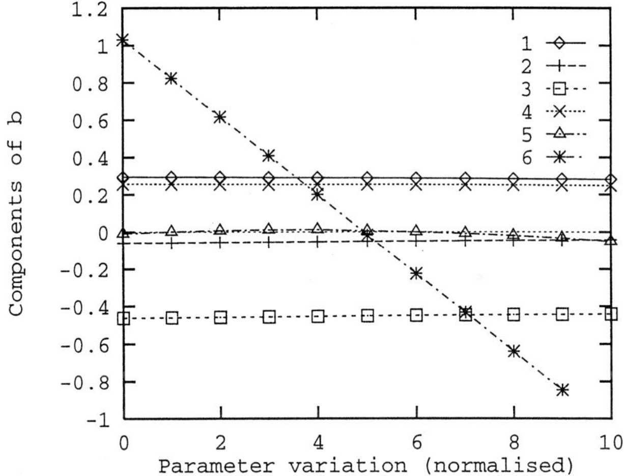


Fig. 15. $\vec{b}$ vectors for set of shapes bowed along the $z$ axis.

Figures 15 and 16 show examples of the graphs of the relationships between the values of the $\vec{b}$ resulting from the DSM registration of 152 shapes, consisting of 156 points each, representing turbine blades with continously varying defects. The PDM used to train the DSM was constructed using 400 shapes with pseudo-random combinations of defects. These defects were: bow along the $z$ axis; twist about the $x$, $y$ and $z$; skew in the $x$, $y$ and $z$ directions; and small distortions to the global scale of the turbine blade shapes. For each of these defects, 10 turbine blade shapes were generated using Eq. (20), with single defects that were known to be within the shape class ($\vec{b} \pm 3\sigma$). The size of the defect can be attained from the horizontal axis on each graph. The center of the horizontal axis of a graph represents the $\vec{b}$

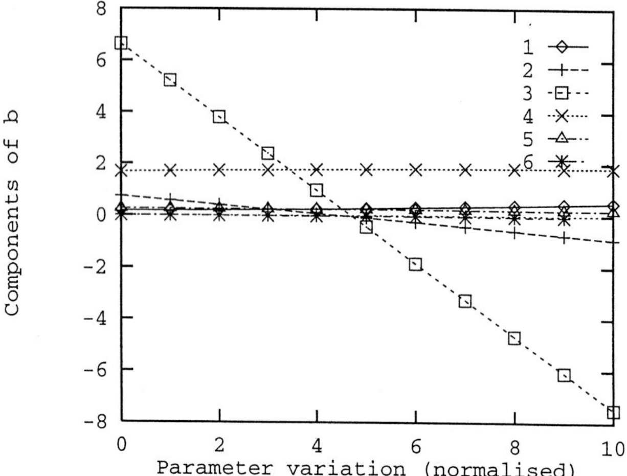


Fig. 16. $\vec{b}$ vectors for set of shapes twisted about the $z$ axis.

for a nominal shape. As can be seen the variation in each component $b_j$ is quasi-linear and the patterns of $\vec{b}$ are different for each defect. This is strong evidence that the combinations of $\vec{b}$ could be linearly separable for each defect.

A number of techniques can be used to analyze these curves. A simple technique is based on determining *all* the values of the amount of defect $d_j$ for each defect class $i$ and observing if they are similar. In other words, for each defect, determine the value for the defect amount for each component of $\vec{b}$. If these are consistent then the defect type is correct and the mean amount is the mean of the values. For all other classes the values of $\vec{b}$ will not be similar. Hence to decide the class of defect choose:

$$\sigma_i = \min_{j=1\ldots n} \sigma_j \tag{30}$$

where $n$ is the number of defect classes. Then the amount of the defect is $\bar{d}$. This analysis can be carried out whether the curves are linear or of some arbitrary shape. However interpolation is needed as computing constraints restrict the number of deformed shapes that can be used in training.

Examples of the preliminary results shown in Tables 4 and 5 show the classified defect, the actual defect, the mean defect size for an actual defect, standard deviation, actual defect size, residual error and mean absolute deviation. The technique correctly classified 80 except skew in the $z$ direction, which only classified 10. The results indicate that the accuracy of this technique generally decreased with the size of the actual defects.

### 11.3. Machine Learning Approach

The problem can also be stated as a pattern recognition problem in which $\vec{b}$ forms an $n$-dimensional feature space in which a point represents the amount of a particular defect. Hence a neural network, decision tree or linear classifier may be trained to recognize the defects. This may be better than the approach described above in that it can be trained for each task and analyzed to give confidence limits, classification performance, etc.

It is worth examining the shape of the feature space before selecting a learning algorithm to use as a classifier. As has been noted in Sec. 11.2 the sample $\vec{b}$ vectors vary in a quasi-linear fashion as the size of the defect changes. A decision tree classifier must discretize these continuously varying variables into a set of intervals possibly leading to a very large tree structure. There is also the danger of the tree over determining the solution, if only a small sample set of training data is available. To test the decision tree approach, experiments were conducted using C4.5[37] on the set of 152 sample shapes described in Sec. 11.2. Each shape is characterized by six principal components and the algorithm attempts to classify the shape into one of eight defects. We used an eight-fold cross-validation procedure removing 19 random shapes from the sample set without replacement and training the decision tree on the remaining 133. The result of classification of a single run is shown below.

```
Evaluation on training data (133 items):

     Before pruning               After pruning
    ----------------       -------------------------

    Size     Errors        Size    Errors     Estimate

     39    4( 3.0%)         37    4( 3.0%)     (20.5%)    <<

Evaluation on test data (19 items):

     Before pruning               After pruning
    ----------------       -------------------------

    Size     Errors        Size    Errors     Estimate

     39    5(26.3%)         37    5(26.3%)     (20.5%)    <<

     (a)   (b)   (c)    (d)   (e)   (f)   (g)   (h)      <- classified as
    ----  ----  ----   ----  ----  ----  ----  ----

      2                                                   (a): class bowz
            3                                             (b): class scale
                  2            1                          (c): class twistx
                          2    1                          (d): class twisty
            2                  2                          (e): class twistz
                               1                          (f): class skewx
                                           1              (g): class skewy
                                                 2        (h): class skewz
```

Tables 2 and 3 display the results of the nine test runs. The mean error for classification of training data was 4.04% and mean error for the test data was 22.4%. Better classification results could be obtained using a larger sample. Naturally, this leads to larger decision trees.

If we hypothesize that the classes of defect are linearly separable, a linear discriminant function is a simple method of distinguishing between them. However, if the data is not exclusively linearly separable then a multi-layer neural network with back-propagation could provide a superior discrimination between the classes.

Table 2. Evaluation on training data (133 items).

| *Before pruning* | | *After pruning* | | |
|---|---|---|---|---|
| Size | Errors | Size | Errors | Estimate |
| 39 | 4( 3.0%) | 37 | 4( 3.0%) | (20.5%) |
| 41 | 6( 4.5%) | 39 | 6( 4.5%) | (23.1%) |
| 41 | 6( 4.5%) | 41 | 6( 4.5%) | (23.6%) |
| 41 | 6( 4.5%) | 41 | 6( 4.5%) | (23.6%) |
| 37 | 4( 3.0%) | 37 | 4( 3.0%) | (20.5%) |
| 39 | 6( 4.5%) | 39 | 6( 4.5%) | (22.6%) |
| 35 | 8( 6.0%) | 33 | 8( 6.0%) | (22.4%) |
| 41 | 3( 2.3%) | 41 | 3( 2.3%) | (21.0%) |
| | | *Mean errors* | | |
| 39.25 | 5.375(4.04%) | 39.25 | 5.375(4.04%) | (22.16%) |

Table 3. Evaluation on test data (133 items).

| *Before pruning* | | *After pruning* | | |
|---|---|---|---|---|
| Size | Errors | Size | Errors | Estimate |
| 39 | 5(26.3%) | 37 | 5(26.3%) | (20.5%) |
| 41 | 3(15.8%) | 39 | 3(15.8%) | (23.1%) |
| 41 | 3(15.8%) | 41 | 3(15.8%) | (23.6%) |
| 41 | 3(15.8%) | 41 | 3(15.8%) | (23.6%) |
| 37 | 6(31.6%) | 37 | 6(31.6%) | (20.5%) |
| 39 | 6(31.6%) | 39 | 6(31.6%) | (22.6%) |
| 35 | 6(31.6%) | 33 | 5(26.3%) | (22.4%) |
| 41 | 3(15.8%) | 41 | 3(15.8%) | (21.0%) |
| | | *Mean errors* | | |
| 39.25 | 4.375(23.04%) | 39.25 | 4.25(22.4%) | (22.16%) |

It could also give us a confidence value for the discrimination. If the separation is close to linear then output weights of a linear discriminant function can provide a good initial starting point for the input weights of 3-layer back-propagation neural network. The maximum number of hyperplanes needed to separate classes can be used as an initial estimate for the number of required hidden nodes. Hidden nodes that have little influence on the final outcome and can be eliminated during training.

Finally we consider variations in shape for a forging process modeled using finite elements. Figures 17 and 18 show the variations in shape for two different parameters. In both of these figures, the shapes that are produced by the forging are overlaid to show where the variations occur. The billet used was rectangular in shape. The lower part of the die was a flat surface and the upper part of the die was partly conical in shape. The most serious deformations have occurred on the left side of the billet where the upper die has pushed the metal down approximately 30 units. Figure 17 shows the results where the only parameter varied was the coefficient of friction. For Fig. 18 the parameter varied was the $x$ position of the billet.

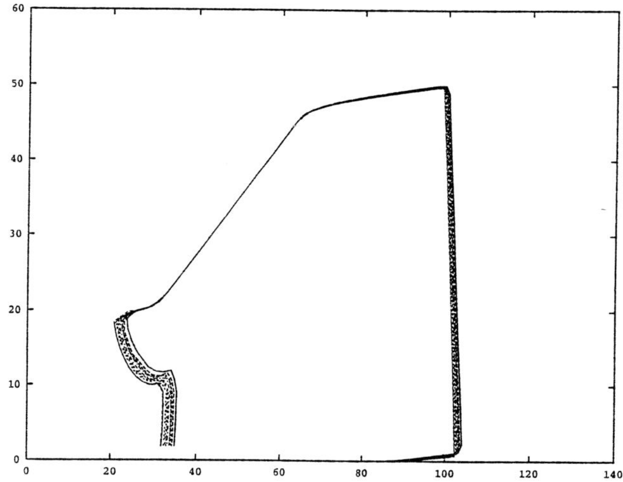


Fig. 17. Different final profiles of the billet for variation in friction.

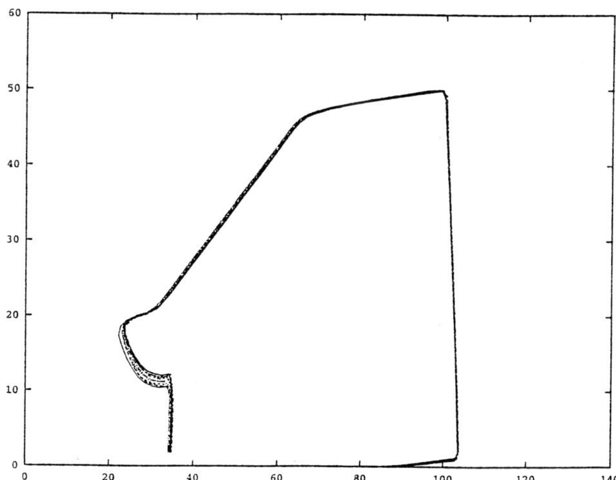


Fig. 18. Different final profiles of the billet for variation in $x$ position of the billet.

Table 4. Results for bowing about the $z$ axis.

| Dist | Actual Dist | Mean Dist | St. dev | Act Defsize | Resid err | Mean AbsDev |
|---|---|---|---|---|---|---|
| bowz | bowz | −0.209900 | 0.078704 | −0.208699 | −0.001201 | 0.053568 |
| bowz | bowz | −0.139772 | 0.029284 | −0.166915 | 0.027143 | 0.027036 |
| bowz | bowz | −0.114783 | 0.026950 | −0.125132 | 0.010348 | 0.018589 |
| bowz | bowz | −0.080655 | 0.043951 | −0.083348 | 0.002693 | 0.029678 |
| bowz | bowz | −0.048335 | 0.048220 | −0.041565 | −0.006771 | 0.033593 |
| bowz | bowz | −0.062865 | 0.085821 | 0.000219 | −0.063084 | 0.073521 |
| bowz | bowz | 0.034821 | 0.034831 | 0.042003 | −0.007182 | 0.024453 |
| bowz | bowz | 0.085907 | 0.017356 | 0.083786 | 0.002121 | 0.012265 |
| bowz | bowz | 0.134121 | 0.024988 | 0.125570 | 0.008551 | 0.019463 |
| bowz | bowz | 0.194731 | 0.060600 | 0.167353 | 0.027378 | 0.045081 |

Number of samples tested = 10
Percentage correctly classified = 100

Table 5. Results for twisting about the $z$ axis.

| Dist | Actual Dist | Mean Dist | St. dev | Act Defsize | Resid Err | Mean AbsDev |
|---|---|---|---|---|---|---|
| twistz | twistz | −0.072794 | 0.014072 | −0.069755 | −0.003039 | 0.009796 |
| twistz | twistz | −0.059302 | 0.013523 | −0.055825 | −0.003477 | 0.009882 |
| twistz | twistz | −0.041717 | 0.003942 | −0.041895 | 0.000178 | 0.003129 |
| twistz | twistz | −0.030785 | 0.011490 | −0.027966 | −0.002820 | 0.008378 |
| twistx | twistz | −0.006163 | 0.027100 | −0.014036 | 0.007873 | 0.019854 |
| twistx | twistz | 0.010979 | 0.057783 | −0.000106 | 0.011085 | 0.041385 |
| twistz | twistz | 0.012716 | 0.006520 | 0.013824 | −0.001107 | 0.005130 |
| twistz | twistz | 0.024068 | 0.015755 | 0.027754 | −0.003686 | 0.011024 |
| twistz | twistz | 0.039511 | 0.011739 | 0.041683 | −0.002173 | 0.008527 |
| twistz | twistz | 0.052779 | 0.013768 | 0.055613 | −0.002834 | 0.009547 |

Number of samples tested = 10
Percentage correctly classified = 80

Using a similar scheme to that described above for the turbine blades, the variation in the values of $\vec{b}$ were determined for the deformations. These are plotted in Figs. 19 and 20. The important characteristics for these cases are the nonlinear nature of the variations. These are to be expected because the change in shape of the billet is not linear with the parameter variations because of the nature of forging. To discover the mapping between $\vec{b}$ and the parameters is obviously more complex and requires more complex methods that those described above for the turbine blade.

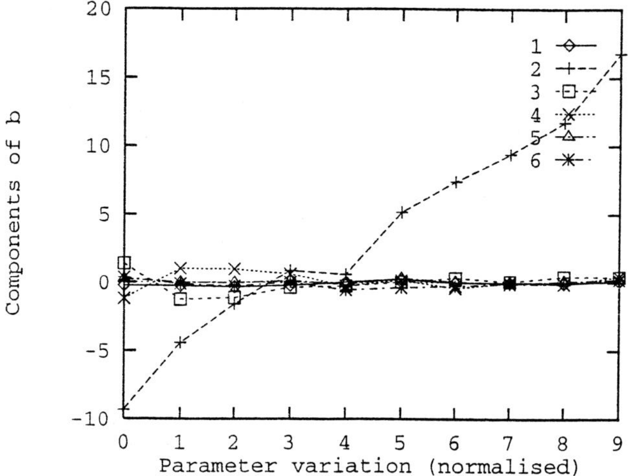


Fig. 19. Variation in $\vec{b}$ for variation in friction.

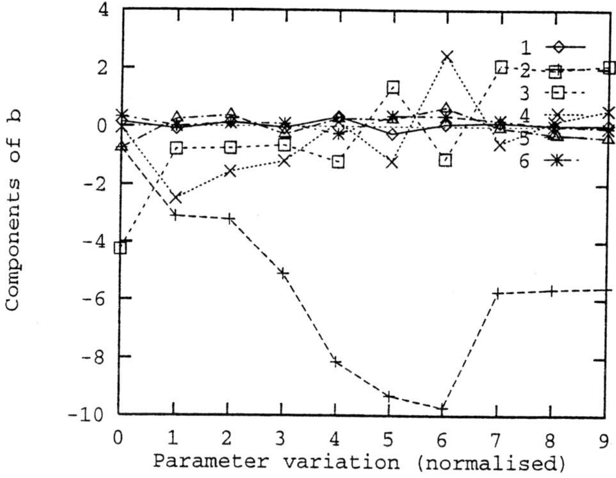


Fig. 20. Variation in $\vec{b}$ for variation in the $x$ position of the billet.

## 12. CONCLUSIONS

This paper has presented an approach to modeling a manufacturing process such that typical defective shapes can be generated and their variations in shape learnt and related to the process parameters. This approach then enables out-of-tolerance components to be detected which have complex shape deformations and allows these to control and modify the manufacturing process. An important aspect of this work is that it has closed the loop between the forward modeling of component manufacturing using finite element techniques where process parameters can be modified to cause shape variations, and the shape variations which point to which process parameters have changed. The results presented for the 2D forging example and 3D turbine blade demonstrate that this technique shows much promise although there is still much work that needs to be carried out to refine the technique. Associated with this technique is the use of the deformable modeling approach for inspecting components for fitness of purpose. Hence this is a new approach to tolerancing which does not require the use of set theoretic models or traditional tolerancing techniques that have numerous shortcomings.

## REFERENCES

1. A. Albano, "Representation of digitized contours in terms of conic arcs and stright-line segments", *Computer Graphics and Image Processing* **3** (1974) 23–33.
2. T. J. Baker, "Automatic mesh generation for complex three-dimensional regions using a contrained Delaunay triangulation", *Engineering with Computers* **5** (1989) 161–175.
3. D. H. Ballard and C. M. Brown, *Computer Vision*, Prentice-Hall, 1982.
4. A. Baumberg and D. Hogg, "Learning flexible models from image sequences", in *Proc. 3rd European Conf. on Computer Vision*, Springer-Verlag, 1994, pp. 299–308.
5. M. Berman, "Large sample bias in least squares estimators of a circular arc centre and its radius", *Computer Vision, Graphics and Image Processing* **45** (1989) 126–128.
6. N. S. Bernstein and K. Preiss, "Representation of tolerance information in solid models", in *Advances in Design Automation — 1989*, Montreal, Quebec, Canada, vol. 1, pp. 37–48.
7. P. J. Besl and N. D. McKay, "A method for registration of 3-D shapes", *IEEE Trans. on Pattern Analysis and Machine Intelligence* **14**, 2 (1992) 239–256.
8. G. Borgefors, "Distance transforms in arbitrary dimensions", *Computer Vision, Graphics and Image Processing* **27** (1984) 321–345.
9. D. J. Burr, "A dynamic model for image registration", *Computer Graphics and Image Processing* **15** (1981) 102–112.
10. M. J. Cardew-Hall, T. Labans, G. West, and P. Dench, "A method of representing dimensions and tolerances on solid based free form surfaces", *Robotics and Computer-Integrated Manufacturing* **10**, 3 (1993) 223–234.
11. J.-L. Chenot, "Finite element modeling of metal forming: From process simulation to physical identification", in *Conf. on Mathematical Models for Materials Processing*, Bristol, UK, 1991, pp. 43–65.
12. L. D. Cohen and I. Cohen, "A finite element method applied to new active contour models and 3D reconstruction from cross sections", in *3rd Int. Conf. on Computer Vision*, Osaka, Japan, 1990, pp. 587–591.
13. T. F. Cootes and C. J. Taylor, "Active shape models — 'smart snakes'", in *Proc. of the British Machine Vision Conf.*, Leeds, UK, 1992, pp. 266–274.
14. T. F. Cootes, C. J. Taylor, D. H. Cooper, and J. Graham, "Training models of shape from sets of examples", in *Proc. of the British Machine Vision Conf.*, Leeds, UK, 1992, pp. 8–18.
15. R. Curwen and A. Blake, "Dynamic contours: Real-time active splines", in *Active Vision*, eds., A. Blake and A. Yuille, MIT Press, 1992.
16. A. de Pennington, P. M. Dew, N. P. Juster, and L. P. Wickens, "A mathematical framework for unidirectional worst case tolerance analysis across assemblies", Technical Report, University of Leeds, UK.
17. I. Doltsinis, "Numerical analysis and design of industrial superplastic forming", *J. de Physique IV, Colloque C7* **3** (1989) 1187–1197.
18. C. M. Eastman and K. Preiss, "A review of solid shape modeling based on integrity verification", *Computer-Aided Design* **16**, 2 (1984).

19. R. W. Evans, "Modeling of metallurgical structural changes in forming", in *Conf. on Mathematical Models for Materials Processing*, Bristol, UK, 1991, pp. 21–42.
20. L. Fourment, T. Balan, and J.-L. Chenot, "Shape optimization for the forging process", in *Simulation of Materials Processing: Theory, Methods and Applications — Numiform95*, eds., S.-F. Shen and P. Dawson, Forming Processes, Ithaca, USA, 18–21 June 1995, pp. 557–562.
21. A. Hill, A. Thornham, and C. J. Taylor, "Model-based interpretation of 3D medical images", in *Proc. of the British Machine Vision Conf.*, Surrey, UK, 1993, pp. 339–348.
22. R. C. Hillyard and I. C. Braid, "Analysis of dimensions and tolerances in computer-aided mechanical design", *Computer Aided Design* **10**, 3 (1978) 161–166.
23. P. Hoffman, "Analysis of tolerances and process inaccuracies in discrete part manufacturing", *Computer Aided-Design* **14**, 2 (1982) 83–88.
24. B. K. P. Horn, "Closed form solution of absolute orientation using unit quaternions", *J. of Optical Society of America* **4**, 4 (1987) 629–642.
25. H. Hotelling, "The generalization of 'Student's' ratio", *Annals of Mathematical Statistics* **2** (1931) 360.
26. American National Standards Institute, "Dimensioning and tolerancing: ANSI Y14.5M", Technical Report, American Society of Mechanical Engineers, USA, 1982.
27. P. Karaolani, G. D. Sullivan, and K. D. Baker, "Parabolic and hermite cubic finite elements: A flexible technique for deformable models", in *Proc. of the British Machine Vision Conf.*, Oxford, UK, 1990, pages 325–330.
28. P. Karaolani, G. D. Sullivan, and K. D. Baker, "Active contours using finite elements to control local scale", in *Proc. of the British Machine Vision Conf.*, Leeds, UK, 1992, pp. 481–487.
29. P. Karaolani, G. D. Sullivan, K. D. Baker, and M. J. Baines, "A finite element method for deformable models", in *Proc. of the 5th Alvey Vision Conf.*, Reading, UK, 1989, pp. 73–78.
30. M. Kass, A. Witkin, and D. Terzopoulos, "Snakes: Active contour models", in *1st Int. Conf. on Computer Vision*, London, UK, 1987, pp. 259–268.
31. R. Light and D. C. Gossard, "Modification of geometric models through variational geometry", *Computer-Aided Design* **14**, 4 (1982) 209–214.
32. B. Modayur, L. G. Shapiro, and R. M. Haralick, "Visual inspection of machined parts", in *IEEE Conf. on Computer Vision and Pattern Recognition*, Champaign, Illinois, USA, 1992, pp. 393–398.
33. J. Mundy, A. Noble, C. Marinos, V. D. Nguyen, A. Heller, J. Farley, and A. T. Tran, "An object-oriented approach to template guided visual inspection", in *11th. Int. Conf. on Pattern Recognition*, The Hague, Netherlands, 1992, pp. 386–392.
34. A. Noble, V. D. Nguyen, C. Marinos, A. T. Tran, J. Farley, K. Hedegren, and J. L. Mundy, "Template guided visual inspection", in *Proc. 2nd European Conf. on Computer Vision*, Santa Margherita Ligure, Italy, 1992, pp. 893–901.
35. A. Noble and J. Mundy, "Toward template-based tolerancing from a Bayesian viewpoint", in *IEEE Conf. on Computer Vision and Pattern Recognition*, New York, USA, 1993, pp. 246–252.
36. Rolls-Royce plc. ES38: Compressor and turbine blades and vanes (company standard), Technical Report, Rolls-Royce plc, Derby, UK, 1987.
37. J. R. Quinlan, *C4.5 Programs for Machine Learning*, Morgan Kaufman, San Mateo, California, 1993.
38. A. A. G. Requicha and S. C. Chan, "Representation of geometric features, tolerances and attributes in solid modelers based on constructive solid geometry", *IEEE Trans. on Robotics and Automation* **2**, 3 (1986) 156–165.

39. A. A. G. Requicha, "Toward a theory of geometric tolerancing", *Int. J. of Robotics Research* **2**, 4 (1983) 45–60.
40. A. A. G. Requicha, "Representations for rigid solids: theory, methods and systems", *ACM Computing Surveys* **12**, 4 (1986) 437–464.
41. L. Rivest, C. Fortin, and C. Model, "Tolerancing a solid model with a kinematic formulation", *Computer-Aided Design* **26**, 6 (1994) 465–475.
42. P. L. Rosin and G. A. W. West, "Segmenting curves into elliptic arcs and straight lines", in *3rd Int. Conf. on Computer Vision*, Osaka, Japan, 1990, pp. 75–78.
43. U. Roy and C. R. Liu, "Feature-based representational scheme of a solid modeler for providing dimensioning and tolerancing information", *Robotics and Computer-Integrated Manufacturing* **4**, 3/4 (1988) 335–345.
44. British Standards, "Engineering drawing practice: Part 3 geometrical tolerancing", Technical Report, British Standards Institute, Milton Keynes, UK, 1972.
45. British Standards, "Engineering drawing practice: Part 2 recommendations for dimensioning and tolerancing of size", Technical Report, British Standards Institute, Milton Keynes, UK, 1985.
46. J. Turner, "Relative positioning of parts in assemblies using mathematical programming", *Computer Aided Design* **22**, 7 (1990) 394–400.
47. D. Wilde, *Optimum Seeking Methods*, Prentice-Hall, 1964.
48. O. C. Zienkiewicz, *The Finite Element Method*, McGraw-Hill, 1977.

**Brett Daniel** completed a Bachelor of Science Honours degree with a computing science major at Curtin University of Technology, Western Australia in 1992. He is currently developing vehicle tracking systems with Terra-Vision Pty. Ltd. while also completing a Ph.D. at Curtin University. His research interest include deformable models, dimensioning and tolerancing, computer graphics and geographical information systems.

**M. J. Cardew-Hall** graduated from Nottingham University in 1983 with a B.Sc.(Hons) in mechanical engineering. This was followed by a brief spell as a Design Engineer with GEC in the UK before joining the Rolls-Royce/Imperial College Teaching Company. This resulted of the awarding in 1988 of a Ph.D. in the area of computer-aided design, manufacture and inspection. After joining Rolls-Royce in 1986 he held the positions of Manufacturing Systems Engineer, Visiting Research Fellow at Curtin University in Perth WA, and Manager–Process Modeling. In 1993 he took up the position of Senior Lecturer in the Engineering Department at the Australian National University in Canberra, Australia.

His current research work is mainly industrially focused in the area of advanced manufacturing systems. In particular this includes variational representation in CAD modeling, modeling and simulation of forming processes, in particular sheet metal forming and process understanding and optimization. He is currently working closely with the Ford Motor Company in Australia in their stamping operations.

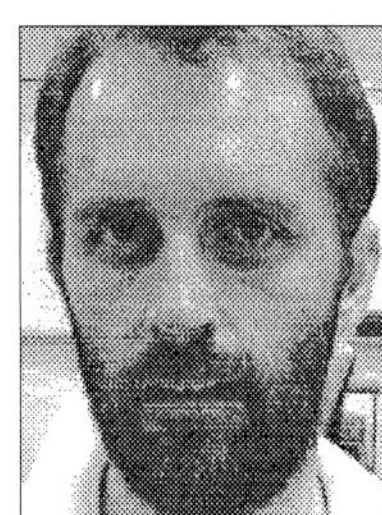

**Geoff A. W. West** received the B.Sc. (Honours) degree in 1978 and the Ph.D. degree in 1982 from the City University, London.

From 1982 to 1988 he was employed as a research fellow and from 1988 as a lecturer at the City University in the School of Engineering investigating techniques for automatic inspection. Since 1990, he has been on the staff of the School of Computing at Curtin University of Technology in Perth, Western Australia where is currently an Associate Professor and Deputy Head of School.

His current research interests include 3D object recognition, active vision, visualization, computer graphics, automatic visual inspection and related applications.

# USING ASPECT GRAPHS TO CONTROL THE RECOVERY AND TRACKING OF DEFORMABLE MODELS

SVEN J. DICKINSON
*Department of Computer Science and Rutgers Center for Cognitive Science (RuCCS)*
*Rutgers University, New Brunswick, NJ 08903, USA*

DIMITRI METAXAS
*Department of Computer and Information Science*
*University of Pennsylvania, Philadelphia, PA 19104-6389, USA*

Active or deformable models have emerged as a popular modeling paradigm in computer vision. These models have the flexibility to adapt themselves to the image data, offering the potential for both generic object recognition and non-rigid object tracking. Because these active models are underconstrained, however, deformable shape recovery often requires manual segmentation or good model initialization, while active contour trackers have been able to track only an object's translation in the image. In this paper, we report our current progress in using a part-based aspect graph representation of an object[14] to provide the missing constraints on data-driven deformable model recovery and tracking processes.

*Keywords*: Shape recovery, object tracking, deformable models, aspect graphs.

## 1. INTRODUCTION

In the computer vision community, active or deformable models have emerged as a popular modeling paradigm, and have been applied to both the problems of shape recovery and shape tracking. The approaches to shape recovery are exemplified by the class of deformable or active model recovery techniques, in which a model contour (in 2D) or surface (in 3D) adapts itself to the image data under the influence of "forces" exerted by the image data.[18,26,27,25] As shown in Fig. 1, points on the model are "pulled" towards corresponding (e.g., closest) data points in the image, with the integrity of the model often maintained by giving the model physical properties such as mass, stiffness, and damping. Having such flexible models is critical in an object recognition system, particularly when object models are more generic and do not specify exact geometry.

As powerful as these data-driven, deformable model recovery techniques are, they are not without their limitations. Their success relies on both the accuracy of initial image segmentation and initial placement of the model given the segmented data. For example, such techniques often assume that the bounding contour of a region belongs to the object, a problem when the object is occluded. Furthermore, focusing only on an object's silhouette assumes 3D models with rotational symmetry, i.e., no surface discontinuities, e.g., Ref. 25. In addition, such techniques often require a manual segmentation of an object into parts to which models are



Spatial Computing: Issues in Vision, Multimedia and Visualization Technologies (1997) 115–141

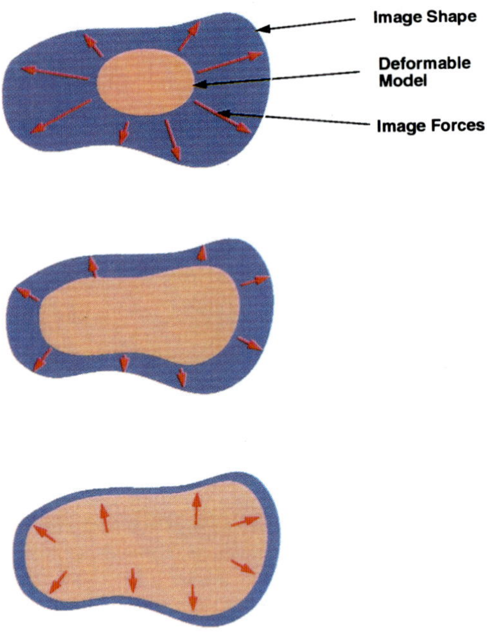


Fig. 1. Data-driven shape recovery.

fitted, e.g., Ref. 26. If the models are not properly initialized, a canonical fit may not be possible, e.g., Ref. 23. These limitations are a consequence of using such unconstrained models.

Data-driven, deformable models have also been applied to the problem of tracking both 2D and 3D shapes. As shown in Fig. 2, a properly initialized model in one frame is placed in a subsequent frame and, provided the motion is small between the two frames, will change its position and shape to align itself with the data in the new frame. These data-driven approaches to shape tracking track the silhouette of a blob in 2D (or surface of a blob in 3D), e.g., Refs. 6, 18 and 24. Although 2D translation can be recovered and, in some cases, translation in depth (e.g., Ref. 5), lack of any model information prevents the recovery of rotation in depth and the detection of occlusion.

In this paper, we show how an object representation integrating object-centered volumetric part models and viewer-centered part aspects, introduced in Ref. 14, can be used to provide strong constraints on the recovery and tracking of 3D shape using deformable models. We review our current progress in a number of areas, including the recovery of 3D deformable models from both 2D and 3D data, and both the qualitative and quantitative tracking of 3D shape from 2D data. An emerging theme thoughout the discussion will be the use of an aspect-based shape description to provide a number of powerful constraints whose absence limits current work in the recovery and tracking of deformable models. In the following sections, we review the object representation, and show how its application to both shape recovery and tracking can overcome the limitations of the deformable model shape recovery and tracking approaches described above.

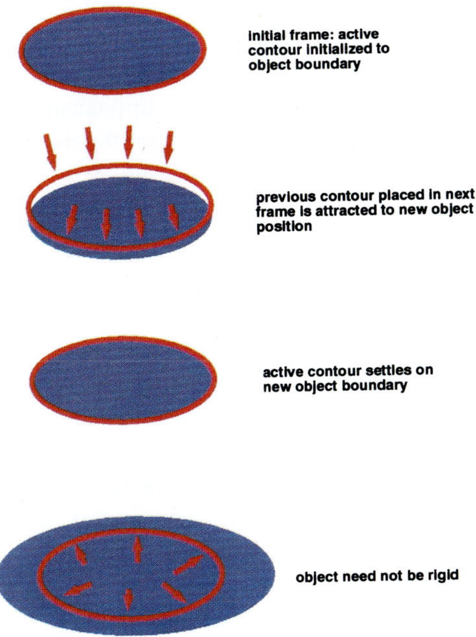


Fig. 2. Data-driven object tracking.

## 2. A PARTS-BASED ASPECT REPRESENTATION

In this section, we briefly review a representation which models an object's 3D shape in terms of a set of qualitatively-defined volumetric parts.[14] This representation, combining both object-centered and viewer-centered models, forms the backbone of our qualitative shape recovery and object recognition (both top-down and bottom-up) paradigms, reported in Refs. 9, 10, 15 and 16. In the following sections, we will see how this same representation can be used to constrain the recovery and tracking of deformable models from both 2D and 3D image data.

The hybrid representation we use to describe objects draws on two prevalent representation schools in the computer vision community. The first school is called object-centered modeling, whereby three-dimensional object descriptions are invariant to changes in their position and orientation with respect to the viewer. The second school is called viewer-centered modeling, whereby an object description consists of the set of all possible views of an object, often linked together to form an aspect graph. Object-centered models are compact, but their recognition from 2D images requires making 3D inferences from 2D features. Viewer-centered models, on the other hand, reduce the recognition problem from three dimensions down to two, but incur the cost of having to store many different views for each object.

In order to meet the goals of qualitative object modeling and matching, we first model objects as object-centered constructions of volumetric parts chosen from some arbitrary, finite set of part classes.[14] It is at the volumetric part modeling level, that we invoke the concept of viewer-centered modeling. Traditional aspect graph representations of 3D objects model an entire object with a set of aspects (or views), each defining a topologically distinct view of an object in terms of its visible surfaces.[19] Our approach differs in that we use aspects to represent a (typically small) set of volumetric parts from which objects appearing in our image database are constructed, rather than representing the entire object directly.

Our goal is to use aspects to recover the 3D volumetric parts that make up the object in order to carry out a recognition-by-parts procedure, rather than attempting to use aspects to recognize entire objects. The advantage of this approach is that since the number of qualitatively different volumes is generally small, the number of possible aspects is limited and, more important, *independent* of the number of objects in the database. By having a sufficiently large set of volumetric part building blocks, and by assuming that objects appearing in the image database can be composed from this set, our training phase, which computes the part views, is independent of the contents of the image database.

The disadvantage of our hybrid representation is that if a volumetric part is occluded from a given 3D viewpoint, its projected aspect in the image will also be occluded. We must therefore accommodate the matching of occluded aspects, which we accomplish by use of a hierarchical representation we call the *aspect hierarchy*. The aspect hierarchy consists of three levels, consisting of the set of *aspects* that model the chosen volumes, the set of component *faces* of the aspects, and the set of *boundary groups* representing all subsets of contours bounding the faces. The ambiguous mappings between the levels of the aspect hierarchy are captured in a set of upward and downward conditional probabilities, mapping boundary groups to faces, faces to aspects, and aspects to volumes.[8] The probabilities are estimated from a frequency analysis of features viewed over a sampled viewing sphere centered on each of the volumetric classes.

The representation for aspects has a tremendous impact on the coverage of the 3D part classes. If aspects encode a precise specification of angles between lines, curvature, etc., then even slightly stretching or bending a volumetric part, for example, would give rise to a new set of aspects. To ensure that our volumetric part classes are invariant to minor 3D shape deformations, we make our aspects invariant to minor 2D shape deformations. Thus, faces and boundary groups encode qualitative relationships (e.g., cotermination, parallelism, and symmetry) between qualitatively-defined contours (e.g., straight, convex, and concave), while aspects simply encode adjacencies between labeled faces.

For the experiments reported in this paper, we have selected a set of ten volumetric part classes, illustrated in Fig. 3, while Fig. 4 illustrates a portion of the corresponding aspect hierarchy. To construct objects, the primitives are attached to one another with the restriction that any junction of two primitives involves exactly one distinct surface from each primitive.

In an unexpected, or bottom-up, recognition framework, the aspect hierarchy is used to recover faces, aspects, and finally volumes from a region-segmented image, as shown in Fig. 5, while in an expected, or top-down recognition framework, the aspect hierarchy is used to direct a Bayesian search strategy mapping target objects to target faces in the image, as shown in Fig. 6. Details of these strategies will not be presented here, and can be found in Refs. 9, 10, 15 and 16.

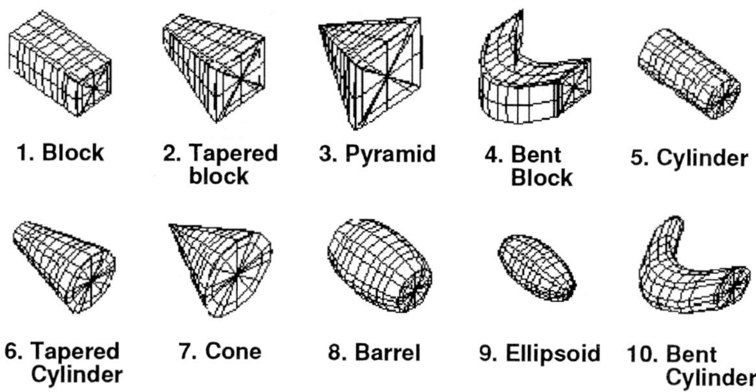


Fig. 3. The ten modeling primitives.

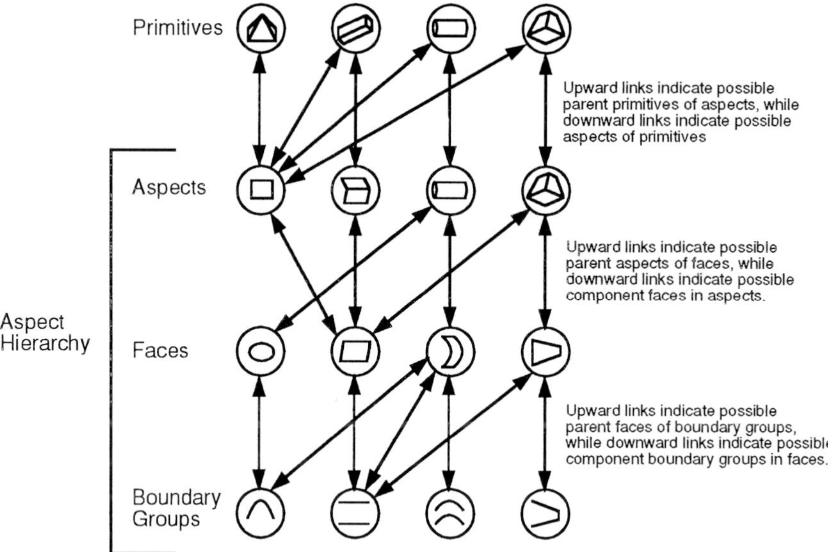


Fig. 4. The aspect hierarchy.

## 3. SHAPE RECOVERY FROM A 2D IMAGE

In Refs. 9, 10, 15 and 16, we outlined techniques for recovering and recognizing 3D objects from a single 2D image. Although the technique segments the scene into a set of qualitatively-defined parts, no metric information is recovered for the parts nor is the 3D position and orientation of the parts recovered. For problems such as subclass recognition, where finer shape distinctions are necessary, and grasping, where accurate localization is critical for gripper placement, these qualitative recognition strategies do not recover sufficient metric shape information.

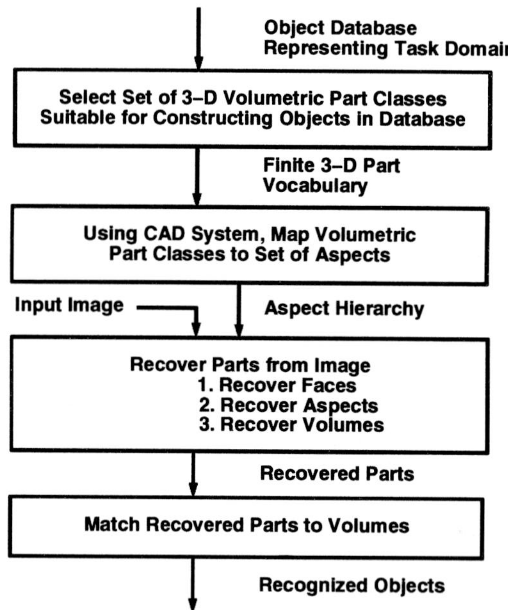


Fig. 5. Unexpected object recognition.

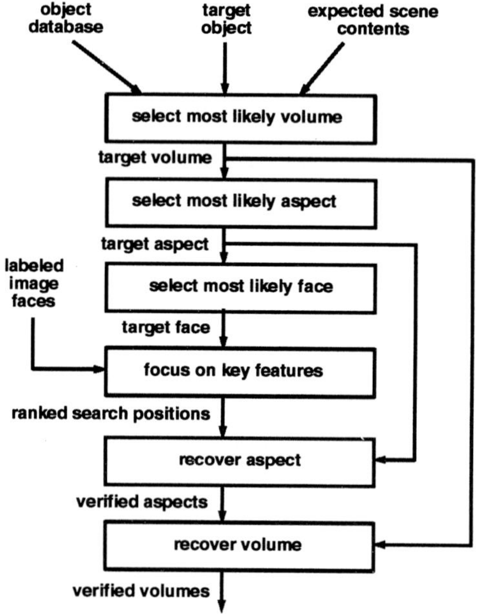


Fig. 6. Expected object recognition.

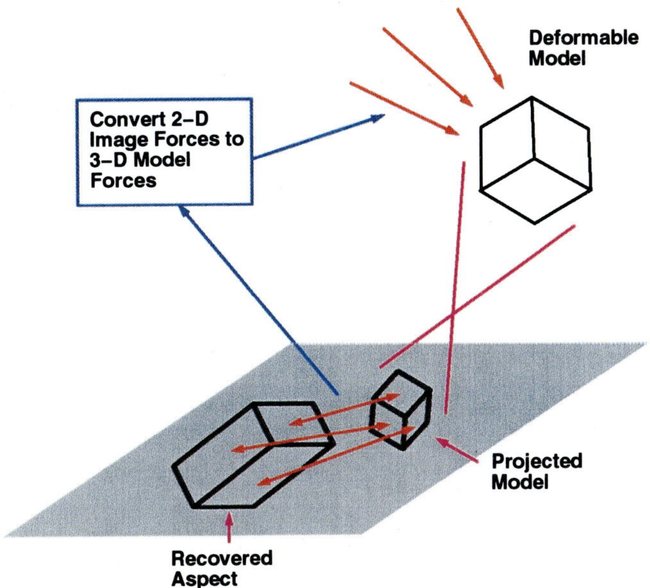


Fig. 7. Using qualitative shape to constrain physics-based deformable shape recovery.

In this section, we describe a technique whereby the recovered qualitative shape is used to constrain the physics-based recovery of a deformable quantitative model from the recovered image contours. As shown in Fig. 7, distances between a recovered aspect and a projected model aspect are converted to 2D image forces. These forces, in turn, are mapped to a set of generalized forces which deform the model and bring its projection into alignment with the recovered aspect. The technique:

(1) ensures that only data used to infer object shape will exert forces on the model;
(2) is not sensitive to model initialization;
(3) is able to recover shapes with surface discontinuities; and
(4) uses qualitative shape knowledge to constrain shape recovery.

Details of the algorithm can be found in Refs. 12 and 21.

### 3.1. The Geometry of the Deformable Model

Geometrically, the quantitative shape models that we recover are closed surfaces in space whose intrinsic (material) coordinates are $\mathrm{u} = (u, v)$, defined on a domain $\Omega$.[25,12] The positions of points on the model relative to an inertial frame of reference $\Phi$ in space are given by a vector-valued, time-varying function of u:

$$\mathbf{x}(\mathrm{u}, t) = (x_1(\mathrm{u}, t), x_2(\mathrm{u}, t), x_3(\mathrm{u}, t))^\top \tag{1}$$

where $\top$ is the transpose operator. We set up a noninertial, model-centered reference frame $\phi$,[20] and express these positions as:

$$\mathbf{x} = \mathbf{c} + \mathbf{R}\mathbf{p}\,, \tag{2}$$

where $\mathbf{c}(t)$ is the origin of $\phi$ at the center of the model, and the orientation of $\phi$ is given by the rotation matrix $\mathbf{R}(t)$. Thus, $\mathbf{p}(\mathrm{u}, t)$ denotes the canonical positions of points on the model relative to the model frame. We further express $\mathbf{p}$ as the sum of a reference shape $\mathrm{s}(\mathrm{u}, t)$ (global deformation) and a displacement function $\mathbf{d}(\mathrm{u}, t)$ (local deformation):

$$\mathrm{p} = \mathrm{s} + \mathbf{d}\,. \tag{3}$$

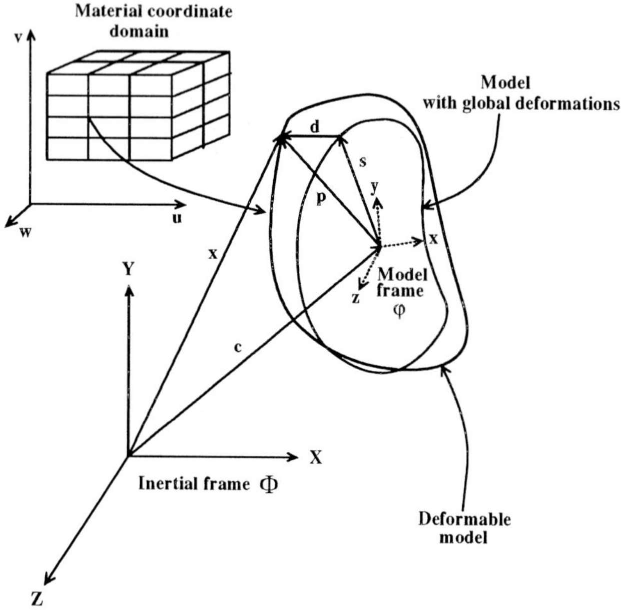


Fig. 8. Geometry of deformable models.

We define the global reference shape as

$$\mathrm{s} = \mathbf{T}(\mathbf{e}(\mathrm{u};\, a_0, a_1, \ldots);\, b_0, b_1, \ldots). \tag{4}$$

Here, a geometric primitive $\mathbf{e}$, defined parametrically in u and parameterized by the variables $a_i$, is subjected to the *global deformation* $\mathbf{T}$ which depends on the parameters $b_i$. Although generally nonlinear, $\mathbf{e}$ and $\mathbf{T}$ are assumed to be differentiable (so that we may compute the Jacobian of $s$) and $\mathbf{T}$ may be a composite sequence of primitive deformation functions $\mathbf{T}(\mathbf{e}) = \mathbf{T}_1(\mathbf{T}_2(\ldots \mathbf{T}_n(\mathbf{e})))$. We concatenate the global deformation parameters into the vector

$$\mathbf{q}_s = (a_0, a_1, \ldots, b_0, b_1, \ldots)^\top. \tag{5}$$

Even though our technique for defining $\mathbf{T}$ is independent of the primitive $\mathbf{e} = (e_1, e_2, e_3)^\top$ to which it is applied, we will use superquadric ellipsoid primitives due to their suitability in vision applications.

We first consider the case of superquadric ellipsoids,[1] which are given by the following formula:

$$\mathbf{e} = a \begin{pmatrix} a_1 C_u{}^{\epsilon_1} C_v{}^{\epsilon_2} \\ a_2 C_u{}^{\epsilon_1} S_v{}^{\epsilon_2} \\ a_3 S_u{}^{\epsilon_1} \end{pmatrix}, \tag{6}$$

where $-\pi/2 \leq u \leq \pi/2$ and $-\pi \leq v < \pi$, and where $S_w{}^{\epsilon} = \mathrm{sgn}(\sin w)|\sin w|^{\epsilon}$ and $C_w{}^{\epsilon} = \mathrm{sgn}(\cos w)|\cos w|^{\epsilon}$, respectively. Here, $a \geq 0$ is a scale parameter, $0 \leq a_1, a_2, a_3 \leq 1$ are aspect ratio parameters, and $\epsilon_1, \epsilon_2 \geq 0$ are "squareness" parameters.

We then combine linear tapering along principal axes 1 and 2, and bending along principal axis 3 of the superquadric $\mathbf{e}$[a] into a single parameterized deformation $\mathbf{T}$, and express the reference shape as:

$$\mathbf{s} = \mathbf{T}(\mathbf{e}, t_1, t_2, b_1, b_2, b_3) = \begin{pmatrix} \left(\dfrac{t_1 e_3}{a a_3 w} + 1\right) e_1 + b_1\ cos\left(\dfrac{e_3 + b_2}{a a_3 w} \pi b_3\right) \\ \left(\dfrac{t_2 e_3}{a a_3 w} + 1\right) e_2 \\ e_3 \end{pmatrix}, \tag{7}$$

where $-1 \leq t_1, t_2 \leq 1$ are the tapering parameters in principal axes 1 and 2, respectively; $b_1$ defines the magnitude of the bending and can be positive or negative; $-1 \leq b_2 \leq 1$ defines the location on axis 3 where bending is applied; and $0 < b_3 \leq 1$ defines the region of influence of bending. Our method for incorporating global deformations is not restricted to only tapering and bending deformations. Any other deformation that can be expressed as a continuous parameterized function can be incorporated in our global deformation in a similar way.

We collect the parameters in $\mathbf{s}$ into the parameter vector:

$$\mathbf{q}_s = (a, a_1, a_2, a_3, \epsilon_1, \epsilon_2, t_1, t_2, b_1, b_2, b_3)^{\top}. \tag{8}$$

The above global deformation parameters are adequate for quantitatively describing the ten modeling primitives shown in Fig. 3. In the following section, we describe how these global deformation parameters, describing a volume's quantitative shape, are recovered from an image. In cases where local deformations $\mathbf{d}$ are necessary to capture object shape details, we use the finite element theory and express the local deformations as

$$\mathbf{d} = \mathbf{S}\mathbf{q}_d, \tag{9}$$

where $\mathbf{S}$ is the shape matrix whose entries are the finite element shape functions, and $\mathbf{q}_d$ are the model's nodal local displacements.[20]

### 3.2. Simplified Numerical Simulation

When fitting the quantitative model to visual data, our goal is to recover $\mathbf{q} = (\mathbf{q}_c^{\top}, \mathbf{q}_\theta^{\top}, \mathbf{q}_s^{\top}, \mathbf{q}_d^{\top})^{\top}$, the vector of degrees of freedom of the model. The components

[a]These coincide with the model frame axes $x, y$ and $z$, respectively.

$\mathbf{q}_c$, $\mathbf{q}_\theta$, $\mathbf{q}_s$, and $\mathbf{q}_d$, are the translational, rotational, global deformation, and local deformation degrees of freedom, respectively. Our approach carries out the coordinate fitting procedure in a physics-based way. We make our model dynamic in $\mathbf{q}$ by introducing mass, damping, and a deformation strain energy. This allows us, through the apparatus of Lagrangian dynamics, to arrive at a set of equations of motion governing the behavior of our model under the action of externally applied forces.

The Lagrange equations of motion take the form[25]:

$$\mathbf{M}\ddot{\mathbf{q}} + \mathbf{D}\dot{\mathbf{q}} + \mathbf{K}\mathbf{q} = \mathbf{g}_q + \mathbf{f}_q, \tag{10}$$

where $\mathbf{M}$, $\mathbf{D}$, and $\mathbf{K}$ are the mass, damping, and stiffness matrices, respectively, where $\mathbf{g}_q$ are inertial (centrifugal and Coriolis) forces arising from the dynamic coupling between the local and global degrees of freedom, and where $\mathbf{f}_q(\mathrm{u}, t)$ are the generalized external forces associated with the degrees of freedom of the model. If it is necessary to estimate local deformations in (10), we tessellate the surface of the model into linear triangular elements.

For fast interactive response, we employ a first-order Euler method to integrate (10).[b] However, in fitting a model to static data, we simplify these equations by setting both $\mathbf{M}$ and $\mathbf{K}$ to zero, yielding a model which has no inertia and comes to rest as soon as all the applied forces vanish or equilibrate.

### 3.3. Applied Forces

In the dynamic model fitting process, the data are transformed into an externally applied force distribution $\mathbf{f}(\mathrm{u}, t)$. We convert the external forces to generalized forces $\mathbf{f}_q$ which act on the generalized coordinates of the model.[25] We apply forces to the model based on differences between the model's projected points and points on the recovered aspect's contours. Each of these forces is then converted to a generalized force $\mathbf{f}_q$ that, based on (10), modifies the appropriate generalized coordinate in the direction that brings the projected model closer to the data. The application of forces to the model proceeds in a face by face manner. Each recovered face in the aspect, in sequence, affects particular degrees of freedom of the model. In the case of occluded volumes, resulting in both occluded aspects and occluded faces, only those portions (boundary groups) of the regions used to infer the faces exert external global deformation forces on the model.

### 3.4. Model Initialization

One of the major limitations of previous deformable model fitting approaches is their dependence on model initialization and prior segmentation.[27,25,23] Using our qualitative shape recovery process as a front end, we first segment the data into parts, and for each part, we identify the relevant non-occluded data belonging to the part.[16,15,9,10] In addition, the extracted qualitative volumes explicitly define a

[b] In Sec. 6, we will see how Eq. (10) is also used in object tracking.

mapping between the image faces in their projected aspects and the 3D surfaces on the quantitative models. Moreover, the extracted volumes can be used to immediately constrain many of the global deformation parameters. For example, from the qualitative shape classes, we know if a volume is bent, tapered, or has an elliptical cross section.

Although the initial model can be specified at any position and orientation, the aspect that a volume encodes defines a qualitative orientation that can be exploited to speed up the model fitting process. Sensitivity of the fitting process to model initialization is also overcome by independently solving for the degrees of freedom of the model. By allowing each face in an aspect to exert forces on only one model degree of freedom at a time, we remove local minima from the fitting process and ensure correct convergence of the model.

### 3.5. Examples

To illustrate the fitting stage, consider the contours belonging to the recovered tapered cylinder, shown in Fig. 9. Having determined during the qualitative shape recovery stage that we are trying to fit a deformable superquadric to a tapered cylinder, we can immediately fix some of the parameters in the model. In addition, the qualitative shape recovery stage provides us with a mapping between faces in the image and physical surfaces on the model. For example, we know that the elliptical face maps to the top of the tapered cylinder, while the body face maps to the side of the tapered cylinder. For the case of the tapered cylinder, we will begin with a (superquadric) cylinder model and will compute the forces that will deform the cylinder into the tapered cylinder appearing in the image. Assuming that the $x$ and $y$ dimensions are equal, we compute the following forces:

1. The cylinder is initially oriented with its $z$ axis orthogonal to the image plane. The first step involves computing the centroid of the elliptical image face (known to correspond to the top of the cylinder). The distance between the centroid and the projected center of the cylinder top is converted to a force which translates the model cylinder. Figure 9(a) shows the image contours corresponding to the lamp shade and the cylinder following application of this force. Figure 9(b) shows a different view of the image plane, providing a better view of the model cylinder.
2. The distance between the two image points corresponding to the extrema of the principal axis of the elliptical image face and two points that lie on a diameter of the top of the cylinder is converted to a force affecting the $x$ and $y$ dimensions with respect to the model cylinder. Figures 9(c) and 9(d) show the image and the cylinder following application of this force.
3. The distance between the projected model contour corresponding to the top of the cylinder and the elliptical image face corresponds to a force affecting the orientation of the cylinder. Figures 9(e) and 9(f) show the image and the cylinder following application of this force. This concludes the application of forces arising from the elliptical image face, i.e., top of the tapered cylinder.

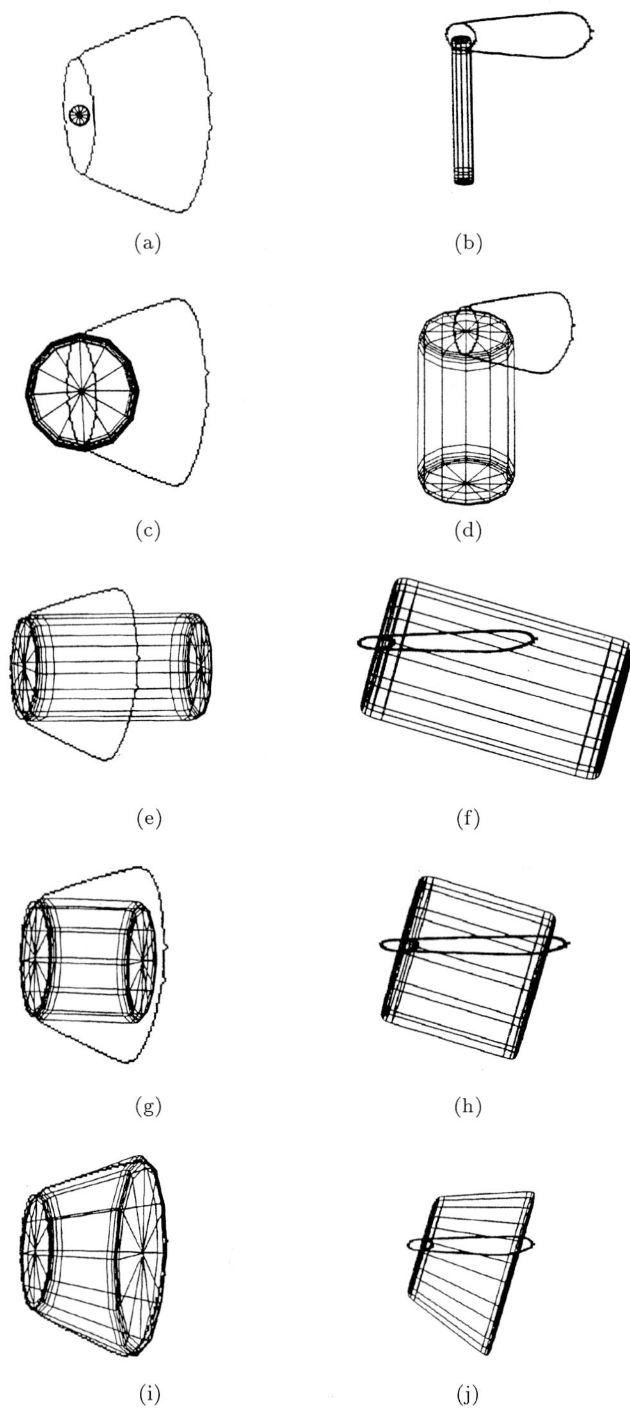


Fig. 9. Quantitative shape recovery for lamp shade.

4. Next, we focus on the image face corresponding to the body of the tapered cylinder to complete the fitting process. The distance between the points along the bottom rim of the body face and the projected bottom rim of the cylinder corresponds to a force affecting the length of the cylinder in the $z$ direction. Figures 9(g) and 9(h) show the image and the cylinder following application of this force.
5. Finally, the distance between points on the sides of the body face and the sides of the cylinder corresponds to a force which tapers the cylinder to complete the fit. Figures 9(i) and 9(j) show the image and the tapered cylinder following application of this force.

As shown in the above example, the recovered aspect plays a critical role in constraining the fitting process.

In Fig. 10, we show a set of snapshots extracted from the recovery of a block volume from a partial aspect recovered from an image of a block. Although one of the faces (top face) has been corrupted due to both shadow and occlusion, only those portions of its bounding contour that were used to match the recovered aspect's component face actually exert forces on the deformable model. Only by encoding qualitative shape information in the models (aspects) can we decide which contours belong to the object we are trying to recover.

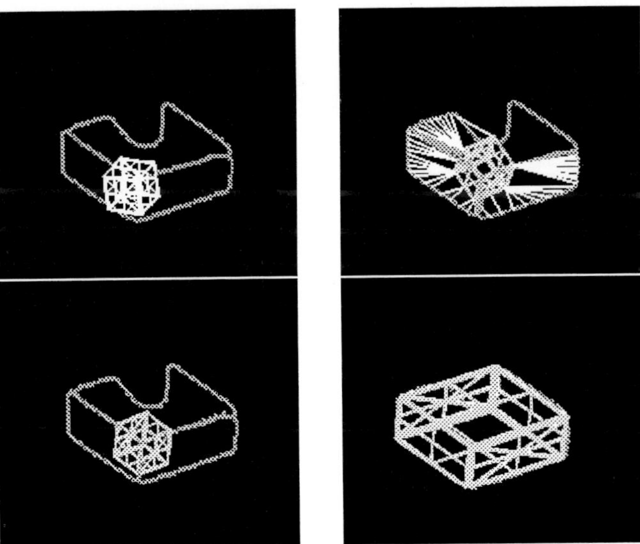

Fig. 10. Sequence of steps in the recovery of a deformable superquadric block from a recovered occluded aspect of a block.

## 4. SHAPE RECOVERY FROM A 3D IMAGE

The aspect hierarchy was originally introduced as a representation to support 3D object recognition from 2D images. By having faces in the aspect hierarchy represent 3D surfaces instead of 2D projections of 3D surfaces, the aspect hierarchy can now be used to constrain the recovery and recognition of 3D objects from range data. Furthermore, by adding face attributes such as mean and Gaussian curvature, we can effectively prune many of the mappings from boundary groups to faces, faces to aspects, and aspects to volumes. We call the new aspect hierarchy, the *range aspect hierarchy.*[13]

We demonstrate our approach by recovering the two parts in the range image shown in Fig. 11(a)[c]; the region segmented image is shown in Fig. 11(b). For this example, we invoked the expected object recognition mode to first search for the best instance of a block. Figure 11(c) shows the highlighted aspect recovered for the block; only those contours used to infer the block are highlighted in the image. Note that the most probable aspect for the block (containing three faces) was not recovered; however, the next most probable aspect (containing two faces) was recovered and used to locate the block. Figure 11(d) shows the highlighted aspect recovered for the cylinder.

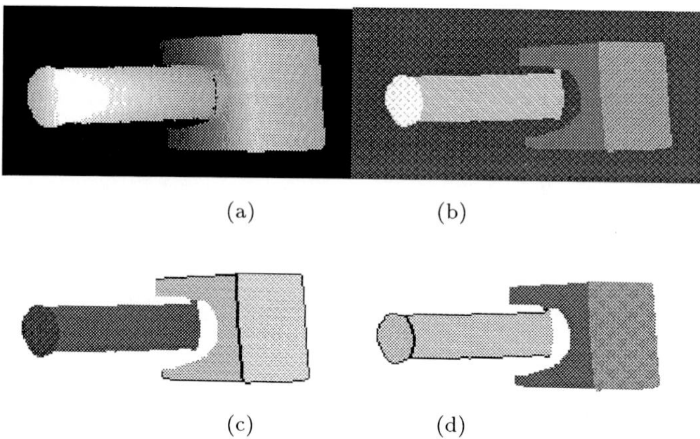

Fig. 11. Qualitative Shape Recovery: (a) range image, (b) region segmentation, (c) recovered qualitative block, and (d) recovered qualitative cylinder.

For each of the two recovered qualitative volumes, we now proceed to show the results of using the recovered qualitative shape to constrain the fitting of a deformable model to the original range data. In Figs. 12(a)–(c), we show the initial, an intermediate, and the final frame in the sequence of model deformations taking

[c]The image was captured using a Technical Arts Scanner at the Michigan State University's PRIP Laboratory.

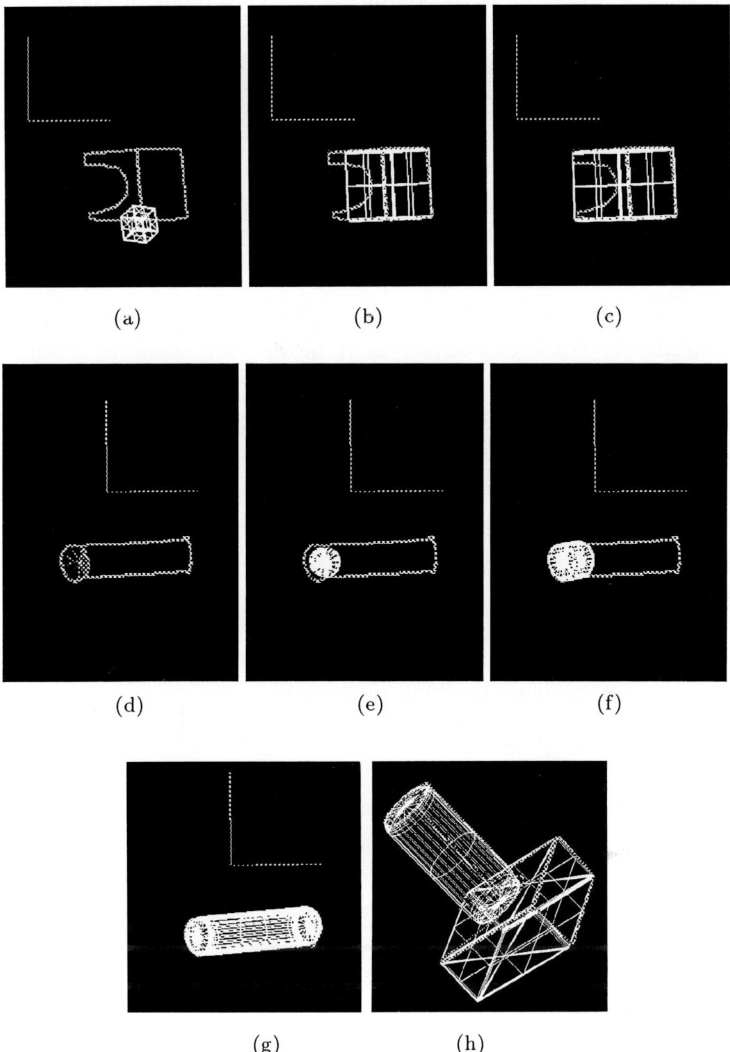

(a) (b) (c)

(d) (e) (f)

(g) (h)

Fig. 12. Selected frames from the part fitting sequence: (a) initial block frame; (b) intermediate block frame; (c) final block frame; (d) initial cylinder frame; (e) intermediate cylinder frame; (f) second intermediate cylinder frame; (g) final cylinder frame; (h) recovered object from a different viewpoint.

the initial model to its final shape describing the block. For clarity, only the recovered contours belonging to the block's recovered aspect are shown in the sequence. Next, in Figs. 12(d)–(g), we show the initial, two intermediate, and the final frame in the sequence of model deformations taking the initial model to its final shape describing the cylinder. Finally, in Fig. 12(h), we show the two fitted parts together from a different viewpoint.

The fitting constraints provided by the recovered qualitative shape allows the deformable model fitting process to be invariant to initial position, orientation, and shape of the model. Unfortunately, relying on the correspondence between recovered image faces and model surfaces means that the recovery process is sensitive to region segmentation errors. However, by only allowing high-scoring volumes to constrain the fitting process, the chances of letting any region segmentation problems affect the fitting process is low. In fact, low-scoring volumes can be used to guide the sensor to acquire a higher-scoring volume.[10]

## 5. QUALITATIVE SHAPE TRACKING

There are two ways in which an object can be tracked. If we have identified the object in the image from the qualitative shapes of its parts, we would like to be able to qualitatively track the object as it moves, for example, from "front" to "side" to "back" without knowing the exact geometry of the object. Alternatively, if we have used the recovered qualitative shape to recover the exact geometry of the object, then we would also like to be able to track the object's exact position and orientation, and possibly its shape if it is non-rigid.

In this section, we describe our approach to qualitative shape tracking, while in the next section, we address the problem of quantitative shape tracking. Our approach to qualitative object tracking, as shown in Fig. 13, combines a symbolic tracker and an image tracker.[11] Just as we used a qualitative shape model to govern a data-driven shape recovery process, we will use the same qualitative shape model to govern a data-driven shape tracking process.

### 5.1. Image Tracker

The image tracker employs a representation called an adaptive adjacency graph, or AAG. The AAG is initially created from the contours belonging to a recovered aspect, and consists of a network of active contours (snakes).[18] The active contours are controled by internal and external forces and change their shape and location so as to minimize their total energy defined as:

$$E_{contour} = \int_0^1 (E_{int}(v(s))ds + E_{image}(v(s))ds + E_{con}(v(s))ds) \tag{11}$$

$$v(s) = \text{a parametric representation of the contour}$$

$E_{int}$ represents internal energy corresponding to effects of contour bending or spanning discontinuities, and represents membrane and thin plate behaviors of the contour. External energy consists of two terms, $E_{image}$ and $E_{con}$. The first term represents forces exerted by the image, while the second represents external constraints. $E_{con}$ represents external energy imposed by a user in the form of repelling forces or constraints attaching a point of the snake to a particular location in the image or to a point on another snake. Desired effects of snake dynamics are achieved by selecting the relative weights of factors controlling the snake.

$E_{image}$, or the force image, is created by a sequence of morphological smoothing and gradient operators. The gradient image is thresholded and the result is blurred with a Gaussian. The standard deviation, $s$, of the Gaussian kernel determines the

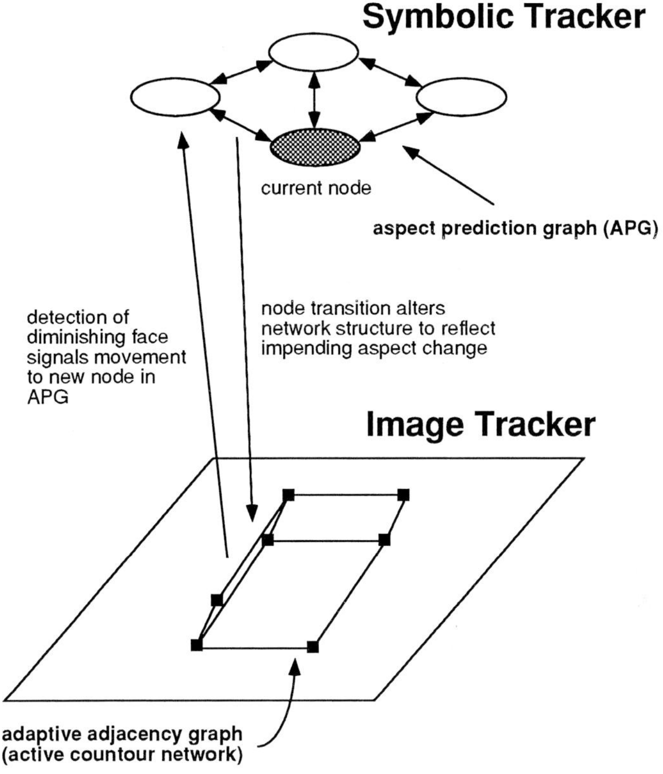


Fig. 13. Qualitative object tracking.

size of the zone of influence (potential well) around each image feature. Selection of $s$ depends on the expected density of features in the image and the disparity between successive images.

The AAG encodes the topology of the network's regions, as defined by minimal cycles of contours. Contours in the AAG can deform subject to both internal and external (image) forces while retaining their connectivity at nodes. Connectivity of contours is achieved by imposing constraints (springs) between the contour endpoints. If an AAG detected in one image is placed on another image that is slightly out of registration, the AAG will be "pulled" into alignment using local image gradient forces.

The basic behavior of the AAG is to track image features while maintaining connectivity of the contours and preserving the topology of the graph. This behavior is maintained as long as the positions of active contours in consecutive images do not fall outside the zones of influence of tracked image features. This, in turn, depends on the number of active contours, the density of features in the image, and the disparity between successive images. If either the tracked object or the camera moves between successive frames, the observed scene may change due to disappearance of one of the object faces. The shape of the region corresponding to the disappearing face will change and eventually the size of the region will be reduced to zero. The image tracker monitors the sizes and shapes of all regions in the AAG and detects such events. When such an event is detected, a signal describing the event is sent to the symbolic tracker.

### 5.2. Symbolic Tracker

The symbolic tracker tracks movement from one node to another in a representation called the aspect prediction graph.[10] Each of the nodes in this representation, derived from an aspect graph[19] and the aspect hierarchy, represents a topologically different viewpoint of the object, while arcs between nodes specify the visual events or changes in image topology between nodes. The role of the symbolic tracker is to:

1. Determine which view or aspect of the object is currently visible (current node).
2. Respond to visual events detected by the image tracker by predicting which node (aspect) will appear next (target node).
3. From the visual event specification defined by the current and target nodes, add or delete structure from the active contour network (predictions).
4. If aspect predictions cannot be verified by the image tracker, or visual event predictions cannot be recognized by the symbolic tracker, the symbolic tracker must be able to bootstrap the system to relocate itself in the aspect prediction graph.

### 5.3. Visual Event Recognition

The symbolic tracker specifies the criteria for which a visual event will be detected by the image tracker. Currently, we use the region area as the single event criteria. If at any time during the image tracking of an aspect, one or more of its faces' areas falls below some threshold, we interpret that to mean that the face is undergoing heavy foreshortening and will soon disappear. When a region's area drops below the threshold, the image tracker sends a signal to the symbolic tracker. Given its current position (node) in the aspect prediction graph, the symbolic tracker compares the outgoing arcs, or visual events, with the events detected by the image tracker. The arc in the aspect prediction graph matching the observed visual event defines a transition to a new aspect.

The transition between the current aspect and the predicted aspect defines a set of visual events in terms of the faces in the aspect defined by the current APG node. If one or more faces disappear from the current aspect to the predicted aspect, the symbolic tracker directs the image tracker to delete those contours from the adaptive adjacency graph which both belong to the disappearing faces and are not shared by any remaining faces. Alternatively, if one or more new faces are expected to appear, the symbolic tracker directs the image tracker to add structure to the adaptive adjacency graph. Since the symbolic tracker knows along which existing contours new faces should appear, it can specify between which nodes in the adaptive adjacency graph new contours should be added.

### 5.4. Example

In Fig. 14, we demonstrate our tracking technique on a sequence of images taken of a rotating block. Note that for the first frame, the AAG was created from the recovered aspect. For subsequent frames, a blurred, thresholded, gradient image is used to exert external forces on the AAG. Moving left to right, top to bottom, we can follow the AAG as it tracks the image faces. When the foreshortened face's area falls below a threshold, the visual event is signaled to the symbolic tracker. Consequently, the nodes and contours belonging to the disappearing faces are removed while nodes and contours belonging to the face predicted to appear are added. Note that in order to ensure that new contours and old contours do not "lock on" to the same image gradient ridge, the contours are automatically "pulled apart", so that they will converge to the correct edges in the image. We are currently investigating the use of repulsion forces that would more effectively prevent network contours from converging.

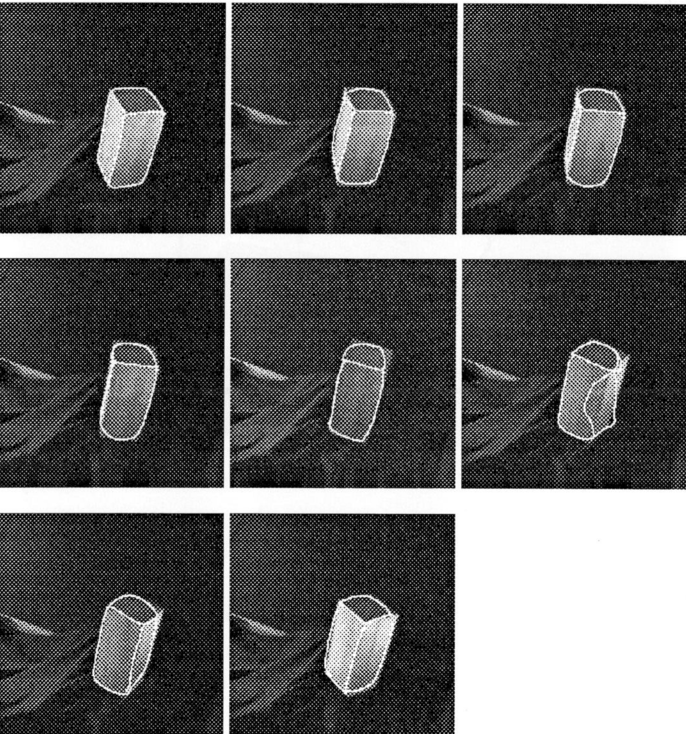

Fig. 14. Tracking a rotating block. There were 11 images in the sequence with 10 iterations of the AAG per image, for a total of 110 snapshots of the AAG. Working left to right and top to bottom, we show snapshots 1, 23, 32, 41, 70, 82, 90, and 110. Note that when the disappearing face is detected (70), the new face is predicted and contours are added (82). The added contours are automatically "pulled apart" to ensure that they do not converge to the same image edge; final position of the new edge is shown in frame 90.

## 6. QUANTITATIVE SHAPE TRACKING

Our approach to quantitative tracking[3,4] makes use of our frameworks for qualitative and quantitative shape recovery described in previous sections, as well as a physics-based framework for quantitative motion estimation.[22] To be able to track multiple objects, initialization of the models is performed in the first frame of the sequence based on our quantitative shape recovery process. For successive frames, the qualitative shape recovery process can be avoided in favor of a physics-based model updating process requiring only a gradient computation in each frame, as shown in Fig. 15. Assuming small deformations between frames, local forces derived from stereo images are sufficient to update the positions, orientations, and shapes of the models in 3D; no costly feature extraction or correspondence is necessary.

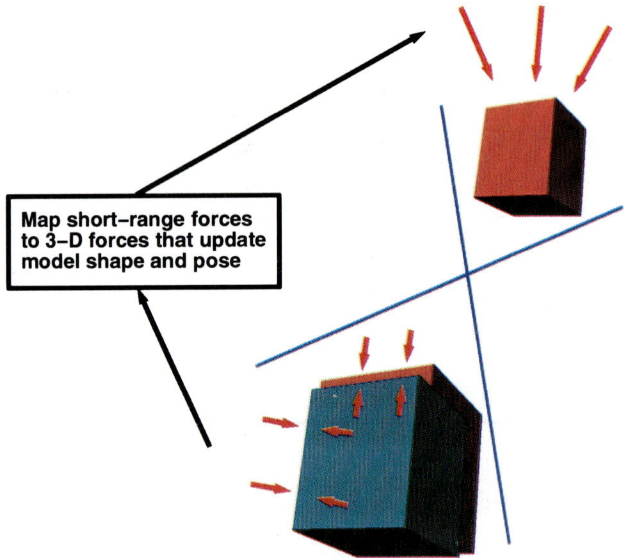


Fig. 15. Quantitative object tracking.

### 6.1. Tracking and Prediction

Kalman filtering techniques have been applied in the vision literature for the estimation of dynamic features[7] and rigid motion parameters[17,2] of objects from image sequences. We use a Kalman filter to estimate the object's shape and motion in a sequence of images. This allows us to predict where the object will appear in the image at some future time, thereby increasing the likelihood of the projected model falling within the local gradient field.

We incorporate a Kalman filter into our dynamic deformable model formulation by treating the model's Lagrangian equations of motion (10) as system models. Based on the use of the corresponding extended Kalman filter, we perform tracking by updating the model's generalized coordinates $\mathbf{q}$ according to the following equation:

$$\dot{\hat{\mathbf{u}}} = \mathbf{F}\hat{\mathbf{u}} + \mathbf{g} + \mathbf{P}\mathbf{H}^\top \mathbf{V}^{-1}(\mathbf{z} - \mathbf{h}(\hat{\mathbf{u}})), \tag{12}$$

where $\mathbf{u} = (\dot{\mathbf{q}}^\top, \mathbf{q}^\top)^\top$ and matrices $\mathbf{F}, \mathbf{H}, \mathbf{g}, \mathbf{P}, \mathbf{V}$ are associated with the model dynamics, the error in the given data, and the measurement noise statistics.[22] Since we are measuring local short range forces directly from the image potential, the term $\mathbf{z} - \mathbf{h}(\hat{\mathbf{u}})$ represents the 2D image forces. Using the above Kalman filter, we can predict at every step the expected location of the data in the next image frame, based on the magnitude of the estimated parameter derivatives $\dot{\mathbf{q}}$.

### 6.2. Computing Forces on the Model

Only those nodes on the model surface that are visible should respond to image forces. A modal node is made active if: (1) it lies on the occluding contour of the model from that viewpoint,[27] or (2) the local surface curvature at the node is sufficiently large and the node is visible. Visibility of the nodes can be determined in two ways. Since we have a 3D model, we can easily test the visibility of each node on the model, turning off those nodes that are self-occluded. A more elegant approach involves the symbolic tracker used in the qualitative tracker. By maintaining which aspect prediction graph node is visible, the symbolic tracker can activate only those nodes corresponding to visible faces. Determining which aspect is visible can be computed directly from knowledge of the model's exact pose. Alternatively, we can also pursue a data-driven approach to determining which aspect is visible. Analogous to our qualitative tracker, local image events can be used to detect a change in aspect with the aspect governing which nodes on the model are active (visible). In this case, a sudden vanishing of forces along a contiguous set of projected model nodes belonging to a face would signify an aspect change.

We must also deal with occlusion due to both known and unknown objects passing in front of the object being tracked. If the occluding object geometry and pose is known, then node visibility of the tracked object can be easily computed. Forces at occluded nodes can be simply turned off until they become visible again. For occlusion by an unknown (untracked) object, we can monitor changes in the image forces exerted on the tracked model's nodes. If the local forces at a particular node suddenly vanish or greatly increase, this erratic behavior can be used to suggest local occlusion, resulting in deactivation of those nodes. The Kalman filter can still maintain the track based on prior motion as well as other active nodes until the object becomes disoccluded.

### 6.3. Examples

We demonstrate our approach in a series of tracking experiments involving real stereo image sequences. Figure 16(a) shows the first pair of stereo images. The initial pose and shape of both objects are recovered using a stereo extension of our quantitative shape recovery algorithm. The objects are subsequently tracked using only image gradient forces, shown as a set of blurred edges in the image. Figures 16(b)–(f) show snapshots of the two objects being tracked with the

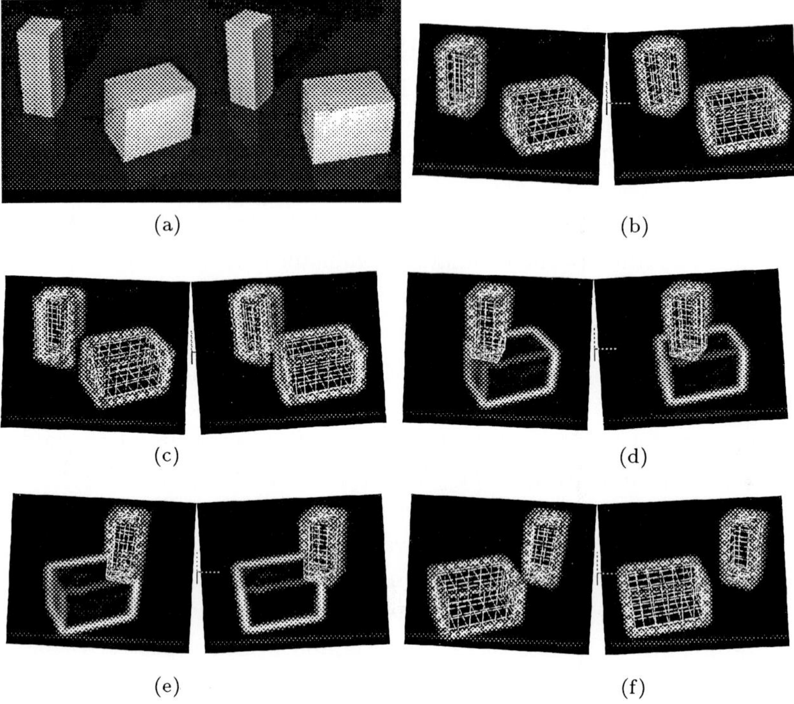


Fig. 16. Tracking two independently moving blocks in a sequence of stereo images: (a) stereo pair, (b) initialized models, (c) start of occlusion, (d) taller block partially occluded (occluding model not shown), (e) taller block becoming disoccluded (occluding model not shown), (f) end of occlusion. Note that only the active model nodes are marked, with occluded nodes at the bottom of the taller block unmarked.

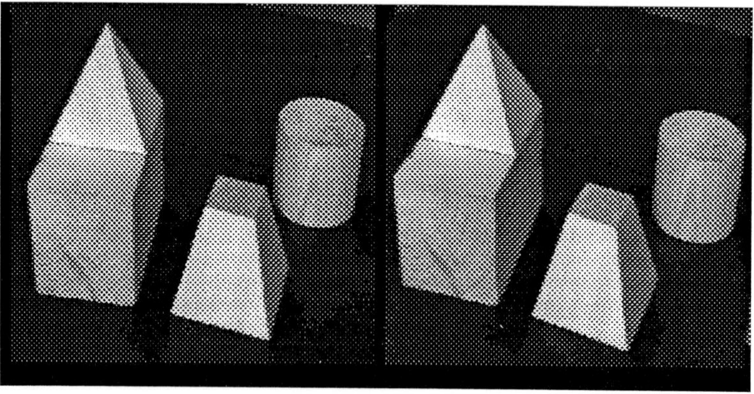

Fig. 17. Initial stereo images of the multi-object scene.

wire-frame models overlaid on the image potential. This example illustrates our ability to track an object when a known object partially occludes it. The nodes on either model which are determined to be occluded (through either self-occlusion or occlusion by another known model) are deactivated until they become visible.

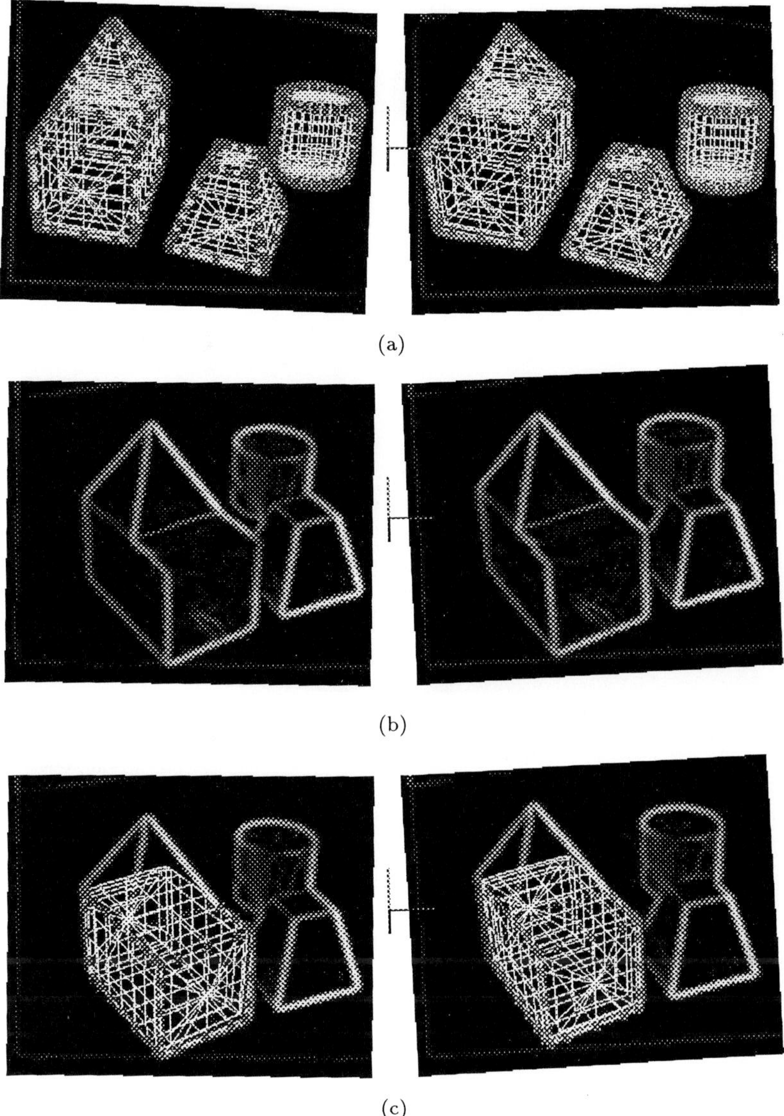

(a)

(b)

(c)

Fig. 18. Tracking multiple objects in a sequence of stereo images: (a) initialized models, (b) image potentials of an intermediate frame (both occlusions and visual events have occurred), (c) each object part correctly tracked with part model overlaid on the image potentials. Note that only the active model nodes are marked.

In the second experiment, we consider a sequence of stereo images (24 frames) of a scene containing multiple objects, including a two-part object. Figure 17 shows the initial stereo images of the multi-object scene. Figure 18(a) shows the initialized models using the same technique as before. Figure 18(b) shows the image potentials at an intermediate time frame where the aspects of some parts have changed and some parts have become partially occluded. Figures 18(c)–(f) show that each

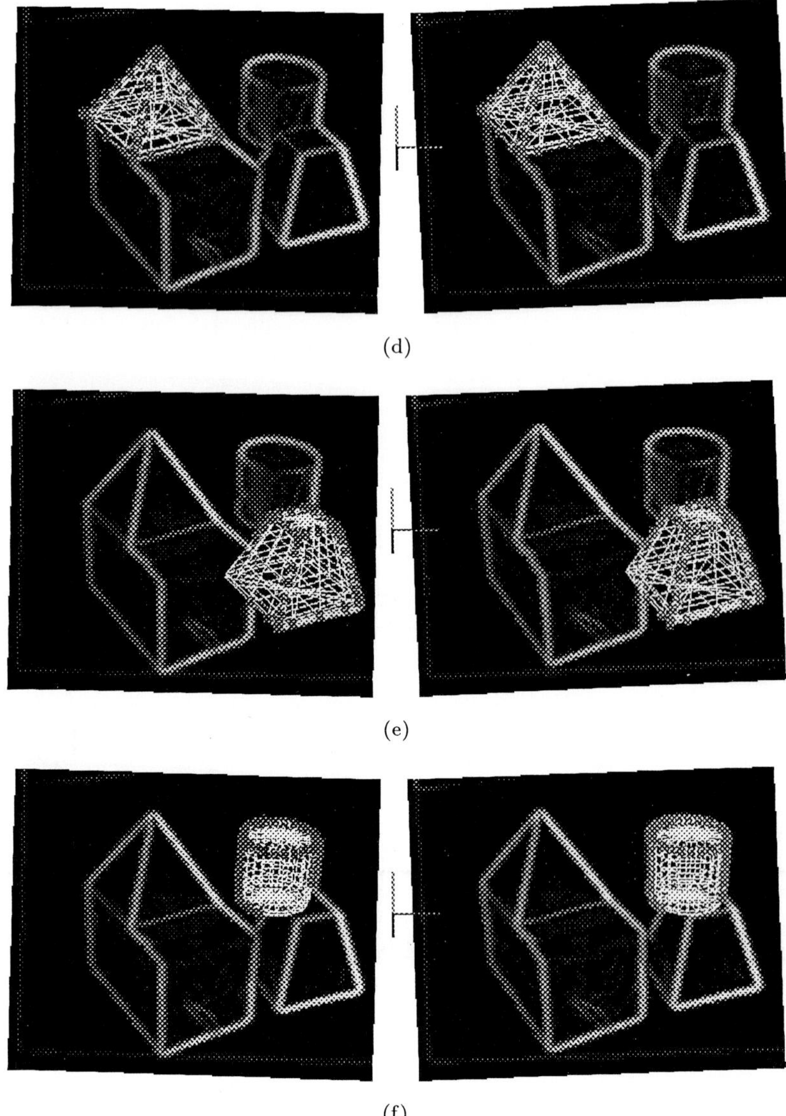

(d)

(e)

(f)

Fig. 18. (*Cont'd*). (d)–(f) each object part correctly tracked with part models overlaid on the image potentials. Note that only the active model nodes are marked.

object is still successfully tracked under these circumstances with the individual part models overlaid on the image potentials.

## 7. CONCLUSIONS

Data-driven, deformable models allow models to adapt their shapes according to the image data. This is in stark contrast to typical CAD-based vision systems which attempt to model the exact geometry of an object. However, by effectively weakening the models to such an extent, they are not left with enough constraints to support segmentation, recognition, or tracking beyond simple translation. In this paper, we have shown how a qualitative object representation, integrating both object-centered and viewer-centered models, provides the missing constraints necessary to overcome these problems. Specifically, our probabilistic part-based aspect hierarchy:

(1) provides the missing constraints on physics-based deformable model recovery, allowing more accurate shape recovery from both 2D and 3D data,
(2) provides a control mechanism for an active contour network that can qualitatively track an object's translation *and* rotation in depth, and
(3) provides a control mechanism that can control node activation when quantitatively tracking an object's motion and shape.

The results reported here are still preliminary, with much work remaining. The techniques are still sensitive to region segmentation performance, and the objects used in the experiments are simplified. Our goal has been to explore a number of closely-related object recognition behaviors that must be addressed by an active agent in a dynamic environment. Our object representation has so far provided a common framework for novel algorithms for these and other behaviors (e.g., active object recognition.[10]) We continue to refine these algorithms while at the same time attempting to work with more complex scenes containing more realistic objects.

## REFERENCES


1. A. Barr, "Superquadrics and angle-preserving transformations", *IEEE Computer Graphics and Applications* **1** (1981) 11–23.
2. T. J. Broida, S. Chandrashekhar, and R. Chellappa, "Recursive 3D motion estimation from a monocular image sequence", *IEEE Trans. Aerospace and Electronic Systems* **26**, 4 (1990) 639–656.
3. M. Chan, D. Metaxas, and S. Dickinson, "A new approach to tracking 3D objects in 2D image sequences", in *Proc. AAAI '94*, Seattle, WA, Aug. 1994.
4. M. Chan, D. Metaxas, and S. Dickinson, "Physics-based tracking of 3D objects in 2D image sequences", in *Proc. 12th Int. Conf. on Pattern Recognition*, Jerusalem, Israel, Oct. 1994, pp. 326–330.
5. R. Cipolla and A. Blake, "Motion planning using image divergence and deformation", in *Active Vision*, eds. A. Blake and A. Yuille, MIT Press, 1992, pp. 189–201.
6. R. Curven, A. Blake, and R. Cipolla, "Parallel implementation of Lagrangian dynamics for real-time snakes", in *Proc. British Machine Vision Conf. (BMVC '91)*, Sept. 1991, pp. 27–35.
7. R. Deriche and O. Faugeras, "Tracking line segments", *Image and Vision Computing* **8**, 4 (1990) 261–270.
8. S. Dickinson, "The recovery and recognition of three-dimensional objects using part-based aspect matching", Technical Report CAR-TR-572, Center for Automation Research, University of Maryland, 1991.
9. S. Dickinson, "Part-based modeling and qualitative recognition", in *Three-Dimensional Object Recognition Systems*, eds. A. Jain and P. Flynn, Advances in Image Communication and Machine Vision Series, Elsevier, Amsterdam, 1993.

10. S. Dickinson, H. Christensen, J. Tsotsos, and G. Olofsson, "Active object recognition integrating attention and viewpoint control", in *Proc. ECCV '94*, Stockholm, Sweden, May 1994.
11. S. Dickinson, P. Jasiobedzki, H. Christensen, and G. Olofsson, "Qualitative tracking of 3D objects using active contour networks", in *Proc. IEEE Conf. on Computer Vision and Pattern Recognition*, Seattle, June 1994.
12. S. Dickinson and D. Metaxas, "Integrating qualitative and quantitative shape recovery", *Int. J. of Computer Vision* **13**, 3 (1994) 1–20.
13. S. Dickinson, D. Metaxas, and A. Pentland, "Constrained recovery of deformable models from range data", in *Proc. 2nd Int. Workshop on Visual Form*, Capri, Italy, May 1994.
14. S. Dickinson, A. Pentland, and A. Rosenfeld, "A representation for qualitative 3D object recognition integrating object-centered and viewer-centered models", in *Vision: A Convergence of Disciplines*, ed. K. Leibovic, Springer Verlag, New York, 1990.
15. S. Dickinson, A. Pentland, and A. Rosenfeld, "From volumes to views: An approach to 3D object recognition", *CVGIP: Image Understanding* **55**, 2 (1992) 130–154.
16. S. Dickinson, A. Pentland, and A. Rosenfeld, "3D shape recovery using distributed aspect matching", *IEEE Trans. on Pattern Analysis and Machine Intelligence* **14**, 2 (1992) 174–198.
17. E. D. Dickmanns and V. Graefe, "Applications of dynamic monocular machine vision", *Machine Vision and Applications* **1** (1988) 241–261.
18. M. Kass, A. Witkin, and D. Terzopolous, "Snakes: Active contour models", *Int. J. of Computer Vision* **1**, 4 (1988) 321–331.
19. J. Koenderink and A. van Doorn, "The internal representation of solid shape with respect to vision", *Biological Cybernetics* **32** (1979) 211–216.
20. D. Metaxas, "Physics-based modeling of nonrigid objects for vision and graphics", Ph.D. thesis, Dept. of Computer Science, Univ. of Toronto, 1992.
21. D. Metaxas and S. Dickinson, "Integration of quantitative and qualitative techniques for deformable model fitting from orthographic, perspective, and stereo projections", in *Proc. Fourth Int. Conf. on Computer Vision*, Berlin, Germany, May 1993.
22. D. Metaxas and D. Terzopoulos, "Shape and nonrigid motion estimation through physics-based synthesis", *IEEE Trans. on Pattern Analysis and Machine Intelligence* **15**, 6 (1993) 580–591.
23. A. Pentland and S. Sclaroff, "Closed-form solutions for physically based shape modeling and recognition", *IEEE Trans. on Pattern Analysis and Machine Intelligence* **13**, 7 (1991) 715–729.
24. D. Terzopolous and R. Szeliski, "Tracking with Kalman snakes", in *Active Vision*, eds. A. Blake and A. Yuille, MIT Press, 1992, pp. 3–21.
25. D. Terzopoulos and D. Metaxas, "Dynamic 3D models with local and global deformations: Deformable superquadrics", *IEEE Trans. on Pattern Analysis and Machine Intelligence* **13**, 7 (1991) 703–714.
26. D. Terzopoulos, A. Witkin, and M. Kass, "Symmetry-seeking models and 3D object recovery", *Int. J. of Computer Vision* **1** (1987) 211–221.
27. D. Terzopoulos, A. Witkin, and M. Kass, "Constraints on deformable models: Recovering 3D shape and nonrigid motion", *Artificial Intelligence* **36** (1988) 91–123.

**Sven Dickinson** received the B.A.Sc. degree in systems design engineering from the University of Waterloo, Canada, in 1983, and the M.S. and Ph.D. degrees in computer science from the University of Maryland, in 1988 and 1991, respectively. He is currently Assistant Professor of Computer Science at Rutgers University, where he also holds a joint appointment in the Rutgers Center for Cognitive Science (RuCCS). He also currently holds or has held affiliations with the MIT Media Laboratory (Visiting Scientist, 1991–1994), the University of Toronto (Visiting Assistant Professor, 1994 to present), and the Center for Automation Research at the University of Maryland (Visiting Assistant Professor, 1992 to present). From 1991 to 1994, he was a Research Associate at the Artificial Intelligence Laboratory, University of Toronto. From 1985 to 1991, he was a Graduate Research Assistant in the Computer Vision Laboratory, Center for Automation Research, University of Maryland. Prior to this he worked in the computer vision industry, designing image processing systems for Grinnell Systems Inc., San Jose, CA, and optical character recognition systems for DEST, Inc., Milpitas, CA.

His major field of interest is computer vision with an emphasis on object recognition and mobile robot navigation. Dr. Dickinson is Co-Chair of the *1997 IEEE Workshop on Generic Object Recognition*, and in 1996 received the NSF CAREER award for his work in generic object recognition.

*Biography and photograph of Dr. D. Metaxas are not available.*

# THE ROLE OF MACHINE LEARNING IN BUILDING IMAGE INTERPRETATION SYSTEMS

TERRY CAELLI*

*Department of Computer Science, Curtin University of Technology*
*Perth, WA 6001, Australia*

WALTER F. BISCHOF†

*Department of Psychology, University of Alberta*
*Edmonton, Alberta T6G 2E9, Canada*

Machine learning has been applied to many problems related to scene interpretation. It has become clear from these studies that it is important to develop or choose learning procedures appropriate for the types of data models involved in a given problem formulation. In this paper, we focus on this issue of learning with respect to different data structures and consider, in particular, problems related to the learning of relational structures in visual data. Finally, we discuss problems related to rule evaluation in multi-object complex scenes and introduce some new techniques to solve them.

*Keywords*: Object recognition, machine learning, scene understanding, image labelling.

## 1. INTRODUCTION

In this paper, we discuss applications of machine learning (ML) techniques to the development and optimization of image interpretation systems. Image interpretation refers to the process of labeling image data with respect to a set of criteria that can either be known *explicitly* to the observer or system or may be encoded *implicitly* in the specific algorithms and constraints used by the system. In both cases, machine learning techniques are useful for making generalizations from training data, such as predicting labels for newly observed image data, for estimating parameters of sub-processes, such as parameters controling image segmentation, or for optimizing the procedures for searching and labeling images.

In the following, we discuss some general issues regarding the application of machine learning to image interpretation. We introduce different approaches to unsupervised and supervised learning and consider several fundamental issues regarding the representation of (a) image data, (b) knowledge required to interpret image data, and (c) rules used for interpreting image data. Next, we study the application of machine learning in low-level and high-level vision and discuss evaluation criteria and design issues that arise at both levels. Finally, we present several systems that were designed to learn image interpretation rules, both in low-level and high-level vision applications.

*Supported by a grant from the Australian Research Committee.
†Supported by Grant OGP38521 from the Natural Sciences and Engineering Research Council of Canada.



Spatial Computing: Issues in Vision, Multimedia and Visualization Technologies (1997) 143–168

### 1.1. Learning Paradigms

A representative sample of general ML techniques already in use for image interpretation is shown in Table 1. The techniques can be grouped into "supervised" and "unsupervised" learning. In the case of supervised learning, the output states of the image interpretation system (for example, the labels to be assigned to different image parts) are known explicitly and the system is aimed at predicting these states. In the case of unsupervised learning, the output states are defined only implicitly in the specific algorithms and constraints that are used.

Table 1. Representative machine learning techniques for computer vision.

| | Unsupervised learning<br>Model | Major application |
|---|---|---|
| Parametric | Bayesian classifiers | Segmentation |
| | Radial basis functions | Image synthesis |
| Non-parametric | K-means | Feature grouping |
| | Kohonen maps | Segmentation |
| | Vector quantization | Image compression |
| | COBWEB | Visual taxonomies |

| | Supervised learning<br>Model | Major application |
|---|---|---|
| Attribute-indexed | Discriminant functions | Classification |
| | Decision trees | Recognition |
| | Neural networks | Feature extraction |
| | Evidence-based systems | Recognition |
| Part-indexed | Rulegraphs | Recognition by parts |
| | Conditional rule generation | Recognition by parts |
| | FOIL | Symbolic descriptions |

*Unsupervised Learning.* Classic examples of unsupervised learning models include clustering techniques where input data is grouped into sets of similar examples using proximity analysis of example attributes. The result of the grouping process depends on the particular characteristics of the proximity models. Both parametric and non-parametric techniques have been used extensively. Parametric techniques include parametric Bayesian clustering where (probabilistic) cluster membership is modeled using, for example, multivariate Gaussian functions.[1] Alternatively, the functions can be used to synthesize observed data (images), as is the case with the radial basis function formulation.[2] In both cases, clustering involves determining position and shape parameters of the best fitting functions for modeling the clusters, and the algorithms for finding them typically use gradient descent with respect to the function parameters.

Parametric clustering techniques have several drawbacks, including the complexity of the search procedure required, the lack of unique solutions and, most importantly, the assumption that such functions actually do represent the data. For these reasons, non-parametric clustering techniques have been more popular. Clustering is aimed at partitioning data such that within-cluster distances are minimized and between-cluster distances are maximized. The well-known methods shown in Table 1 share common features to achieve this goal. For the K-means method, the formulation is direct in that the search for clusters is guided by the minimax constraint (i.e. minimizing within-cluster distances and maximizing between-cluster distances). Kohonen maps enact a similar process[3] through the formation of attractors in the data-attribute space. In vector quantization[4] clustering is achieved through binning techniques[5] while conceptual clustering systems like COBWEB[6] create partitions in attribute space by maximizing category utility measures.

*Supervised Learning.* Supervised learning differs from unsupervised in so far as criteria for labeling data (e.g. classification labels) are known explicitly. Given some training data described in terms of a set of features (attributes) and their class labels, the goal of supervised learning is to find a (simple) partitioning of the feature (attribute) space that allows correct classification of all training data, as well as generalization from training data to unseen, similar data. Supervised learning methods differ with respect to the feature space partitioning they produce, as illustrated in Fig. 1. Given that each region in the partition defines an area of generalization, the methods therefore differ with respect to the produced generalizations.

One class of procedures partition the attribute space using perceptron-like linear decision functions. These include classical discriminant function methods,[7] linear decision trees and decision trees based on neural networks.[8] Elaborations of these methods involve neural network-based approaches such as cascade-correlation,[9] radial basis functions,[2] or vector quantization.[4]

A second class of methods, rule-based methods, also partition attribute spaces with respect to class labels but the partition boundaries are constrained to orientations parallel to the axes. This is done to allow extraction of simple rules of the form

```
if <conditions on feature states>
then <evidence weights for each class>
```

where the rule condition is defined by a conjunction of attribute bounds (and associated labels) and the rule actions are defined in terms of fuzzy class memberships, Bayesian posterior probabilities, or weights in a neural network.[10] The more popular rule-based methods include decision trees[11] and evidence-based systems.[12,10]

### 1.2. Representation

Image information can be represented in at least two different schemes. In one scheme, patterns are encoded as images, per se, in an image coordinate system (Cartesian, log-polar, or coordinates of transforms such as Fourier or Hough) with

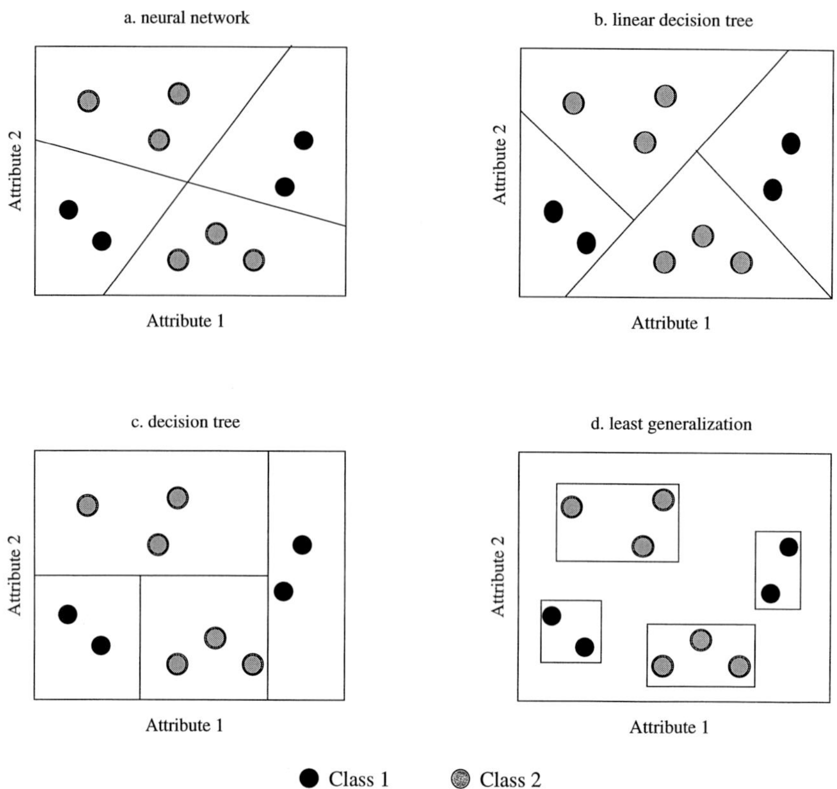


Fig. 1. Feature space partitioning produced by four different methods. (Top left) Neural network: Lines correspond to zeros of perceptron-type (hidden) units. (Top right) Linear decision tree: For each polygonal region splits are introduced recursively to maximize class evidence. (Bottom left) Decision tree: Splits are made at orientations orthogonal to feature axes. They maximize class evidence in each region and introduce an ordering of attributes. (Bottom right) Least generalization: Bounding boxes determine limits for class evidence.

attribute values (e.g. intensity, color, amplitude, phase, or frequency) defined at each coordinate. In the other system, patterns are defined in terms of coordinate values in an abstract attribute (sometimes called 'feature') space. The feature space is not necessarily related directly to the initial encoding of the image data and may include attributes of pixels, of pattern parts, or of complete patterns.

In this latter representation an image composed of multiple parts can be described in terms of (unary) features of single parts, as well as (binary) features of relations between different parts. For example, the parts of an image may correspond to segmented image regions, unary features may include area or average brightness of each region, and binary features may include center–center distance or length of shared boundaries between different regions. In some of the representations, it is made explicit that a given unary or binary relation holds for specific parts (e.g. "Image part 12 and image part 15 have a center–center distance of 300 pixels"), i.e. the connection between unary and binary attributes and labels of pattern parts is made explicit. In other representations, this information is not represented (e.g. "Two of the image parts have a center–center distance of 300 pixels"). The former representation is referred to as a *part-indexed* or label-compatible representation, whereas the latter is referred to as an *attribute-indexed* representation. In general, part-indexed representations have a greater representational power but are inferior to attribute-indexed representations with respect to the efficiency of the associated matching procedures.[13]

Attribute-indexed systems rely on a single representational domain, the attribute domain. Part-indexed systems can rely also on information about image coordinates due to the fact that part label information is preserved. This allows part-indexed systems to operate in a joint image-attribute domain. In a sense, this is similar to classical Gabor-representations of spatial information[14] in that they generate representations based on minimal descriptions in terms of image parts while, at the same time, minimizing joint occurrences of different classes in attribute space (corresponding to Gabor representations minimizing joint uncertainty in the image and attribute domains).

## 2. MACHINE LEARNING IN LOW-LEVEL VISION

In discussing applications of ML to low-level vision, we restrict our attention to edge extraction and region segmentation, even though ML has also been used in other areas, such as image restoration or image enhancement.[15] Approaches to low-level vision involve the development of operators for the detection of features such as edges, corners or lines using filter-based, statistical or geometric techniques. Most *classical approaches* have been essentially "open-loop" in the sense that the output of an operator is not used to estimate or adjust operator parameters, or, in general, that image-dependent statistics are used to optimize these parameters. For example, although edge operators at multiple scales produce evidence for different types of image gradients or edges the resultant edge maps are typically not used to adjust the range of scales used.[16] In other words, such an approach does not "solve" a clear problem such as determining edges that are acceptable to a human observer or edges that satisfy particular physical constraints.

In *adaptive signal analysis*, on the other hand, operator parameters are estimated and adjusted to optimize image-dependent constraints. For example, parameters of edge detectors can be adjusted so as to maximize, in a statistical sense, the explained image variance in local image regions.[17] However, the design characteristics of the operators remain fixed and specific to given images. It is desirable that image operators can be trained to produce outputs that correspond to known features as close as possible and that the resultant operators can be applied to new data, i.e. that they can generalize from the training examples. This is precisely what can be achieved using ML approaches.

In recent years there has been considerable interest in using *connectionist learning procedures* for low-level vision. Specifically, feed-forward neural networks have been used to learn edge extraction, image enhancement and texture segmentation.[15,18] They can be used in both supervised and unsupervised modes to determine the types of pixel window values which evidence different feature types. Indeed, it can be shown that hidden layers of a neural network can compute both stationary or non-stationary adaptive filters depending on how the weight matrices are formulated in the formation of the filter point-spread functions.[19] The development of non-stationary adaptive operators, i.e. of operators whose parameters can vary for different image regions, constitutes a major development over past models which were based on classical stationary signal processing even though they may have been adaptive.

Recently, we have extended this type of machine learning approach to low-level vision using a *"model-based" neural network* (MBNN) approach.[20] MBNNs differ from usual neural networks in that connection weights as well as the (non-linear) transducer functions are parameterized and modeled in such a way to guarantee an output which satisfies given constraints. For example, we have developed modules of MBNNs which can compute eigenvectors or quantize histogram data. This type of network is illustrated in Fig. 2 which has been developed for encoding the degrees to which patterns are invariant to rotations, shift and scale, i.e. for encoding the invariance signature of a shape. Such signatures have recently been used successfully in invariant optical character recognition.[20]

We argue that machine learning techniques have significant uses in the development of robust low-level segmentation and feature extraction processes. However, they must take into account the following constraints. First, input to the ML models must reflect desired output properties, such as, for example, rotation invariance of operators. Second, the ML models must be capable of operating directly on image pixels and regions, preferably in a parallel fashion and at multiple scales. Third, cost functions and model parameters should be chosen to reflect domain knowledge. Finally, we believe that model-based and modular ML systems are particularly promising given that their behavior can be analyzed more clearly and learned rules can be more easily described than is the case with standard neural nets.

## 3. MACHINE LEARNING IN HIGH-LEVEL VISION

High-level vision is concerned with the interpretation of patterns and images, in the sense of determining classifications and other labels for image and pattern parts, and possibly determining mappings between given patterns and stored models to determine the pose of objects or to predict position and existence of occluded pattern parts. Machine learning has received most attention in this area, given that — *ab initio* — classical pattern recognition problems have been posed in terms of supervised learning and classification. More recently, analytic parametric classifiers, such as linear discriminant functions, have been replaced by methods based on multiple evidential systems and search techniques such as neural networks, least squares and nearest neighbor algorithms. The problem remains, however, the same.

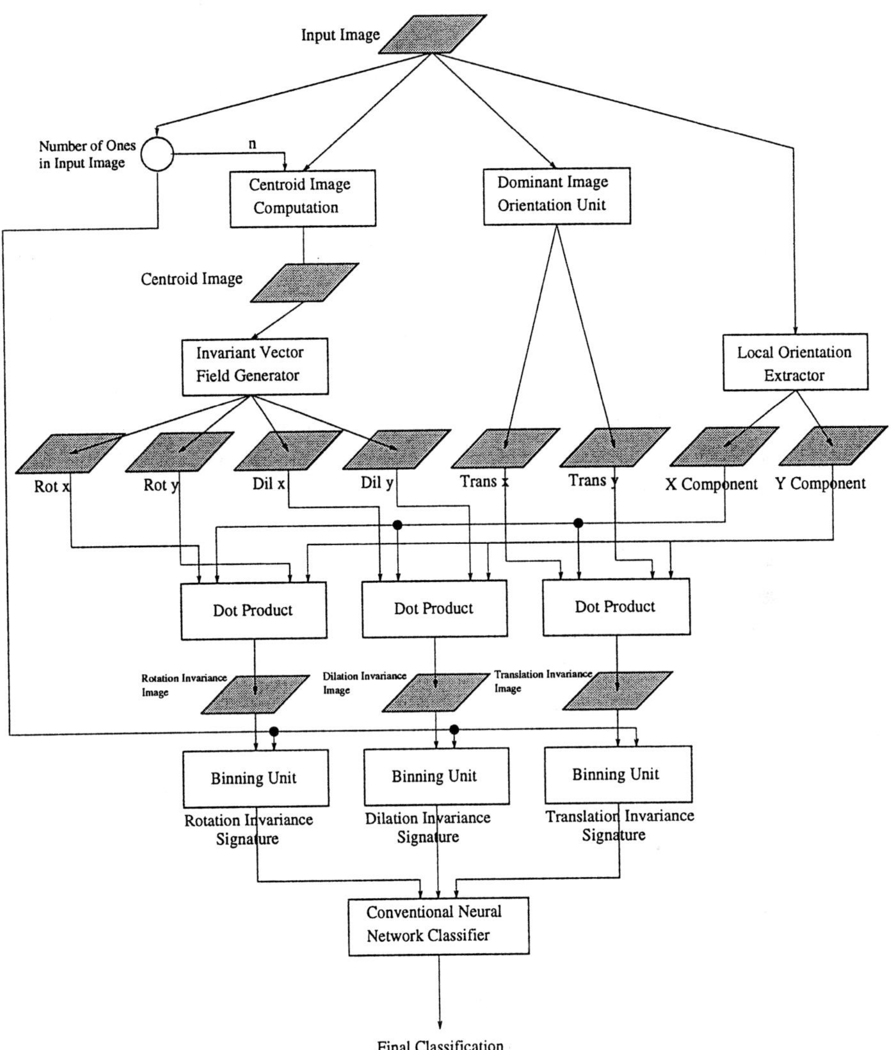


Fig. 2. The idea of model-based neural networks is to constrain or model the weights in such a way that, at particular levels of processing, different operations are guaranteed to occur. In this example, the extraction of directional derivatives of curves, their invariance signatures are used to recognize patterns invariant to rotations, translations and scale. Here, the network computes the products of local curve orientations $(X, Y components)$ with the vectors corresponding to invariant vector fields for rotations (Rot $x, y$), dilations (Dil $x, y$) and translations (Trans $x, y$). The histograms of such scalar products are computed, quantized and then used as input to a classifier — all within a standard feed-forward neural network architecture (see Ref. 20).

That is, we are concerned with the problem of identifying known and novel patterns or structures in simple or complex ("scene") image data and the power of such systems lies in their ability to generalize from training data while still retaining classification accuracy.

## 3.1. Design Issues

The design and application of ML techniques in high-level vision revolves around the four major issues, pattern decomposition, feature selection, rule generation and rule application.

*Pattern Decomposition.* Patterns have been typically represented by one of three methods. The first, *template representation* encodes the pattern by an image, per se, albeit normalized, pre-processed for edges and related features and at multiple scales. The major problems with such representations are that they are not rotation and scale invariant nor lack the ability to readily encode the required variability in structure. The second, *global feature representation* uses features of image transforms to encode shape.These include Fourier, Hough and moment generating function-based transformations. Typical problems with these methods include their lack of invariance, uniqueness with limited numbers of components and their derivation from the complete image: they do not apply to complex multiple-object scenes. The third, *encoding-by-parts* represents patterns by their labeled parts, relations and their associated unary and binary attributes. Though dependent on segmentation/feature extraction processes, we argue that this method proves to be the most useful for invariant pattern recognition, the generation of structural descriptions of shape and the recognition of patterns in complex scenes.

*Rule Generation and Application.* Whether the decomposition is defined by templates, global image transforms or part-decompositions, the issues related to feature/attribute selection and generalization have common characteristics and involve some type of learning strategy. As discussed in Sec. 1, supervised learning methods differ with respect to the features space partitioning model employed (Fig. 1). Linear discriminant functions, linear decision trees, Voronoi tesselations produce different types of partitions which, in turn, determine different types of pattern "rules" or "generalizations" from training data. On the other hand, techniques which generate rules with Horn clause conditions (conjunctions of attribute bounds), so-called "rule-based methods", impose constraints on the partition boundaries. This is done to enable rapid rule evaluation and to allow the derivation of symbolic descriptions, even if it is achieved at the cost of obtaining less efficient feature space partitions.

Application of classification rules that are acquired in a supervised learning paradigm is complicated by several factors. In typical applications, the number of rules and/or classes is large and exhaustive search through all classification rules may not be feasible. Schemes for *efficient rule evaluation* have to be devised that may include pre-compiling of search strategies or the use parallel search methods.

*Recognition from partial data*: Many real recognition problems involve the recognition of patterns from partial data. We claim that in order to optimize this process, rule generation and recognition methods are required that are based on a "recognition-by-parts" approach. In this approach, pattern fragments or individual pattern parts (and their associated attributes) are learned to provide sufficient evidence for the classification of patterns.

*Recognition from distorted data*: Most realistic recognition problems involve identification of known classes or patterns in data which is not identical to any of the training data. Solutions involve the ability of learning systems to generalize from training data. The problem is to optimize generalization while retaining recognition accuracy.

*Finding patterns in complex data*: Perhaps one of the more difficult problems in recognition is that of finding patterns (or objects) in complex multiple object scenes. Solutions must involve evidencing distinct pattern regions in an efficient way. One may find efficient solutions in specific applications but, in general, the problem is ill-posed.

*Correspondence between data parts and model parts*: Beyond a mere classification of patterns or objects, it may be required to determine the correspondence between the parts of a pattern and those of stored model patterns. This may be required to determine the pose of objects or in order to predict the existence of (hidden) pattern parts. Solutions to this problem depend on whether learning or encoding training data also includes pattern or object part labels. Part-indexed data structures implicitly solve the pose problem while simple attribute-indexed systems, such as evidence-based systems[12] do not. These methods may have to be supplemented by methods for additional hypothesis testing or model projection to solve the pose problem. This will be explored further in the following sections.

### 3.2. Non-Inductive Recognition Systems

Most recent recognition systems are based on the recognition-by-parts approach. This allows the (range- or intensity-based) encoding of objects by parts over different views. Further, global features are rarely appropriate for highly variable or for fragmented 2D patterns: Fourier or Karhunen–Loéve transforms of complete patterns cannot easily be used to identify fragments nor find patterns embedded in complex scenes. For these reasons, most recent recognition systems assume the recognition-by-parts representation where pattern and data are in the form of labeled graphs or labeled and attributed graphs. Consequently, methods are required for efficient instantiation of known model graphs in observed data.

One group of methods, including those developed by Grimson[21] and Bunke,[22,23] use, essentially, traditional graph matching methods for solving correspondences between model and data graphs, and rely on constraint propagation to improve the efficiency of the matching procedure. An alternative approach is geometric hashing: unary and binary features of model parts and their relations are stored in a hash table where each entry consists of an $n$-tuple of feature states and a list of training patterns that satisfy these feature states.[24]

From a machine learning perspective, there are several problems with these non-inductive approaches. They do not explicitly deal with generalization (induction) in the sense that they do not determine parts, relations and their associated attribute bounds that are necessary and sufficient for recognizing training patterns and similar, unseen patterns. They do not typically use part indexing as a constraint in compiling the hash functions. However, they "pre-compile" the ways in which parts or attributes need to be checked for efficient evaluation of different models.

### 3.3. Inductive Recognition Systems

Induction or generalization is concerned with summarizing data in such a way that the resultant indexing system can efficiently evidence different classes or patterns. ML is involved in generalization, in the selection of parts and attributes, and the optimization of the resulting rules.

Many methods reduce encoding and recognition processes to creating rules or tables where specific feature values are used to index classes of patterns that were present in training data. Machine learning is concerned with issues related to the form of such rules, their automatic generation, and their optimization. There are many different systems to attain these goals, and one of the aims of this paper is to point out domains where these systems work and where they fail.

An important issue is the amount of relational information that is needed to encode patterns. This is important for the development of robust and efficient recognition systems in both 2- and 3-dimensional domains. As discussed before, representational schemes can be classified as either attribute-indexed or as part-indexed. In part-indexed representations, connections between unary and binary features or predicates are made explicit, and structural pattern information is thus completely preserved. In attribute-indexed representations this connection is lost and, consequently, structural pattern information can be represented only to a limited extent. In the following sections, we present first an example of an attribute-indexed inductive system, followed by two different types of part-indexed inductive systems.

### 3.4. Attribute-Indexed Inductive Systems: EBS

In many applications, data is essentially non-relational and attribute-indexed systems are perfectly adequate. This is the case with many of the datasets used in the machine-learning literature. It is also true in spatial computing, remote sensing, or in image classification problems, where classifications are often based on simple feature vectors, such as intensity, color or spectral values. It also applies to pattern and object recognition models where morphological or global attributes are used to define shapes. Furthermore, attribute-indexed systems are capable of encoding a limited amount of structural information, as discussed below.

Evidence-based systems ("EBS") are an example of attribute-indexed systems that have been used for 3D object recognition. We have developed an EBS for range-based object recognition[10] as an extension of earlier work by Jain and Hoffman.[12] In this approach, learning of a set of training images or patterns is achieved in three steps: feature extraction, rule generation, and evidence combination.

*Feature Extraction.* In a first step, each image or pattern of a training set is segmented into parts. Pattern features are extracted that include global features of the whole pattern, unary features of pattern parts, and binary features of relations between pattern parts. The features are collected into three separate feature spaces. A point in the unary feature space, for example, represents a feature vector of a single pattern part, and is labeled with the class of the corresponding pattern.

*Rule Generation.* Given that all training patterns are encoded in multiple feature spaces, an attempt is made to capture the predominant characteristics of the training samples by grouping them into spatially-delimited regions or clusters in feature space. The bounds on such regions can be used as conditions for the activation of rules, and they define the degree of generalization from samples. Each rule has associated evidence-weights that correspond to the likelihood that activation of the rule contributes evidence for the existence of an object or class of objects.

Generation of rules and evidence weights involves the use of clustering algorithms. For reasons discussed above, such clusters are defined by hyper-rectangles and oriented along the feature space axes to allow for rules of the conjunctive form. Since clusters need not be disjoint, more complex definitions of rule conditions can be constructed. For example, non-convex regions can be defined logically by rules which include some regions of feature space but explicitly exclude others.

In the EBS system developed by Jain and Hoffman,[12] rules were generated by clustering the samples in feature space using a minimum spanning tree technique. In our work,[25] we have used minimum entropy clustering which adjusts the position and size of a fixed number of rectangles (clusters) to maximally separate the occurrences of class samples per cluster. In other words, we relabel the cluster membership of each sample to minimize the entropy function:

$$H_{min} = \min_{i \in j} \left\{ - \sum_{j} \sum_{k} p_{jk} \ln p_{jk} \right\} \tag{1}$$

where $p_{ij}$ is the probability of class $i$ occurring in cluster $j$ and the probability is determined from the relative frequency of class samples within a given cluster solution.

*Evidence Combination.* All the evidence provided by the global, the unary, and the binary features must be combined into a composite evidence value. Rather than use a predetermined scheme for evidence combination, we use supervised learning to estimate optimal weights of features, and, at the same time, to learn the relationships between unary and binary features. To achieve this, we have used a neural network with input nodes corresponding to activated rules (defined by the presence of given part and part relational attributes) which are combined during training via connection weights to maximize known classifications of objects (see Fig. 3). Generalization comes from two sources, first, the cluster bounds in attribute spaces determined by the clustering procedure, and, second, the degrees to which different observed attributes of parts and their relations can activate network weights

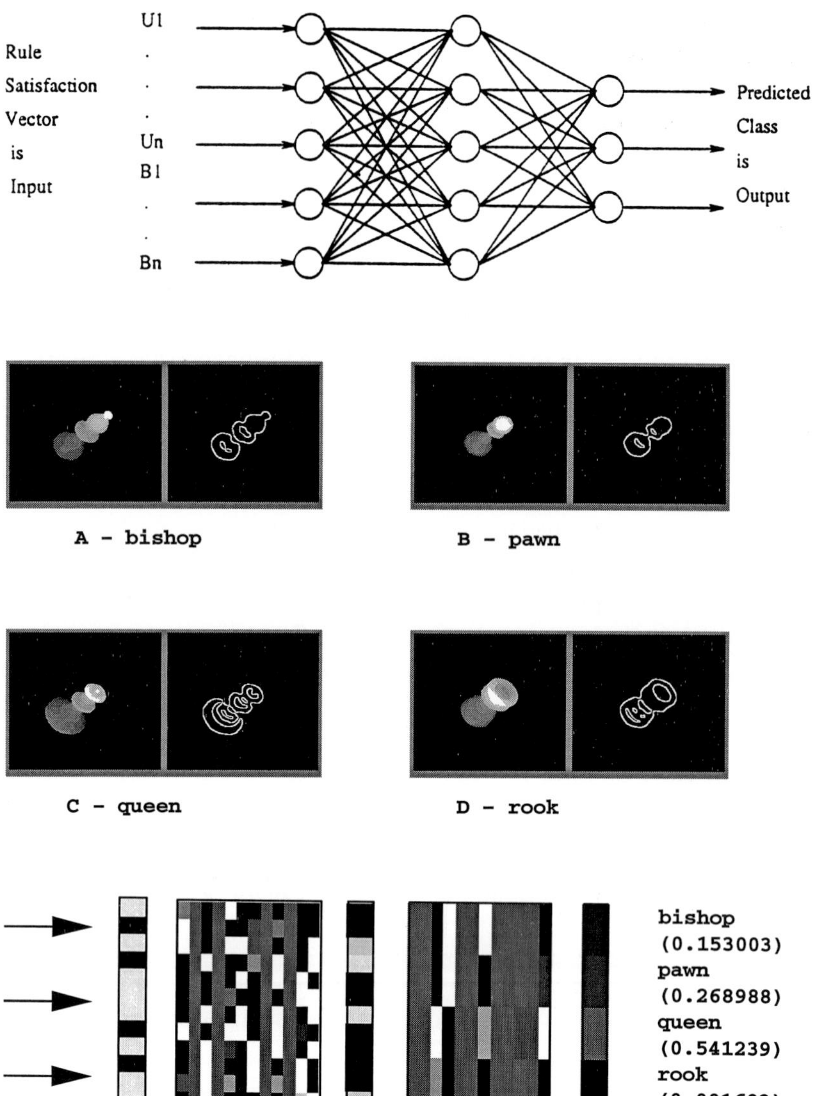


Fig. 3. Object recognition using an evidence-based neural network system. (Top) Rules are generated for objects involving the presence of part (unary feature bounds) and relational attributes (binary feature bounds) whose evidence weights are determined via a neural network. (Bottom) New views are classified according to the rules activated by the presence of parts and relations and evidence weights propagated via the network hidden units (from Ref. 10).

to result in the same class evidence vector. Figure 3 shows the case for classifying different chess pieces using this method. For both training and testing, input range data was initially partitioned in terms of convexity, concavity and planarity. For these parts, attributes were computed that included unary attributes such as curvature or area and binary attributes such as angle between surface normals or distance. These attributes were clustered using a minimum entropy method and formed the (0,1) input to a simple feed-forward neural network to estimate the weights of such evidence in recognizing objects. The actual weights and states of the hidden units during the recognition phase are shown at the bottom of Fig. 3.

The evidence weights are determined by the connections between input, hidden, and output layer nodes. Each hidden layer node is connected to every unary and binary cluster. This allows for the reinforcement of co-occurrences between unary and binary feature states and thus allows implicit learning of relational structures. It does, however, not guarantee unique representation of structural relations.

EBS is an efficient and powerful method for learning classifications of complex patterns. Its main limitation is the fact that structural representation is not unique, i.e. rules are generated without *explicitly* considering the relationships between specific unary and binary feature values that define specific objects. Limited representation of structural information is attained *implicitly* via the hidden units in the neural network, but it does not *guarantee* a unique representation of structural relations in the data.

There are two principal ways to improve EBS-like systems with respect to the ability to represent structural pattern information. The evidence mechanism can be supplemented by a posterior test of structural pattern identity. Alternatively, evidence rules can be elaborated to contain (*a priori*) structural pattern information. The first path is chosen in the rule graph method,[26] and the second is chosen in the conditional rule generation (CRG) method.[13]

### 3.5. Part-Indexed Inductive Systems: Rulegraphs

The idea behind rulegraphs[26] is to use EBS evidence weights together with *explicit* structural pattern information to prune the search space in matching model graphs to data graphs. The technique relies on two simple principles: First, sets of model graphs and their vertices are reduced by generalization, collecting like features for different classes into clusters in feature space. Second, search for subsets of compatible labels between rules is constrained using evidence weights produced by an EBS. The matching process involves graphs of cardinality no greater than the number of unary rules and thus is more efficient than classical graph matching procedures.

A rulegraph is a graph of rules in which vertices correspond to unary rules and edges correspond to binary rules according to the following connection criterion: two unary rules $U_i$ and $U_j$ are connected by a binary rule $B_k$ if there exist labels $X$, $Y$ such that $X \in U_i$ and $Y \in U_j$ and $XY \in B_k$ (see Fig. 4).

The basic idea of graph matching using rulegraphs is illustrated in Fig. 4. Given a set of training patterns, a set of unary and binary rules are generated (Fig. 4(a)). Unary and binary rules that share common labels are connected by a rulegraph edge, according to the connection criterion (Fig. 4(b)). When a new pattern is presented to the system, several rules are activated (Fig. 4(c)), each evidencing different parts of the training patterns: Sample part $X$ could correspond to parts $A$ or $D$, $Y$ could correspond to $B$, $C$, $E$, or $F$, and the binary relation $B(XY)$ could correspond to $B(AC)$ or $B(EF)$. Among these, only one interpretation is consistent with the

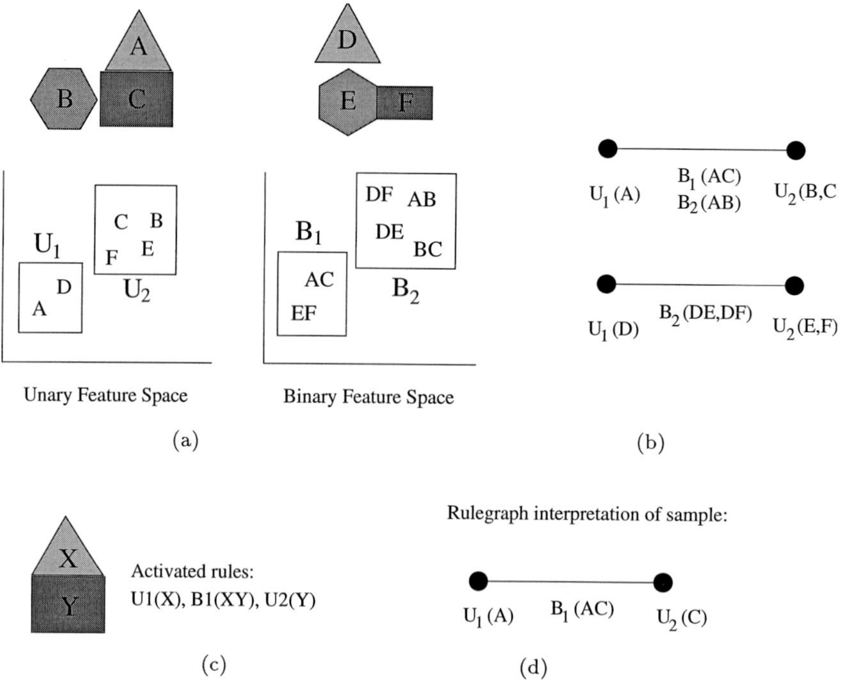


Fig. 4. Training patterns are used in (a) to label the unary and binary rules according to the mapping of the parts and their relationships into each feature spaces. Unary rules are labeled with single labels and binary rules are labeled with label pairs. Rulegraph models may then be formed, according to the connection criterion, and these are shown in (b). At run time, parts in the sample pattern activate unary and binary rules based on their feature states as shown shown in (c). The search for label-compatible rules between the sample and the model results in rulegraph interpretation (best match) as is seen in (d) (from Ref. 26).

rulegraph model, namely the label mapping $X \rightarrow A$ and $Y \rightarrow B$, and this is the interpretation accepted by the rulegraph system.

In rulegraphs, several labels may exist in each rule vertex and this gives rise to multiple mapping states involving the same labels. To determine label-compatibility between *rules* instead of *parts* we use a method which proceeds in five steps. In Step 1, all possible mapping states are created for all the labels in the sample and model rules. In Step 2, all incompatible label mappings between sample rulegraph and model rulegraphs are eliminated. In Step 3, the (multiple) remaining mapping states are updated by instantiation (if the label is *not* yet mapped) or elimination (if the label *is* mapped) using the mappings generated in Step 2 and the old mapping states. In Step 4, the mapping states are updated in order of decreasing evidence of rules into which they map. This ensures that labels which have strongest evidence for a particular class will be mapped first. Finally, in Step 5, we check that at least one binary rule is satisfied.

This method offers a technique for checking compatibility between rules. The problem of finding the *best* match now reduces to that of finding the largest evidenced set of rules which are all pairwise compatible. The cardinality of the search problem has already been reduced to the number of unary rules instead of the number of primitive parts. Furthermore, the evidence weights can be used to direct the search toward rules and models for which strong evidence exists. To achieve this, we use A* search combined with the Bayesian evidence weight metric to allow pruning of the search tree (see Ref. 26).

### 3.6. Part-Indexed Inductive Systems: CRG

The idea of Conditional Rule Generation (CRG) is to generate classification rules that include structural pattern information to the extent that is required for classifying correctly a set of training patterns. CRG searches for the occurrence of unary and binary features states between connected pattern components and creates a tree of hierarchically organized rules for classifying new patterns. Generation of a rule tree proceeds in the following manner.

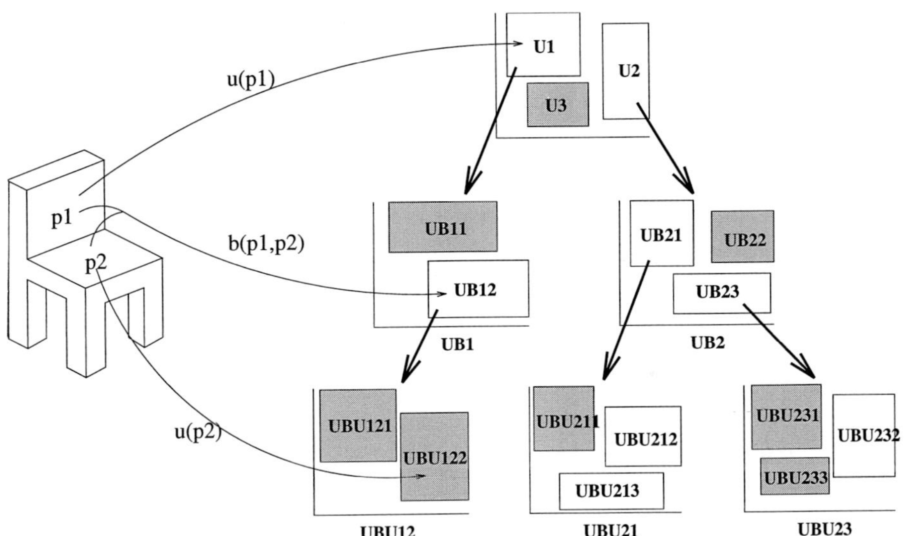


Fig. 5. Cluster Tree generated by the Conditional Rule Generation Procedure (CRG). The unresolved unary clusters ($U1$ and $U2$) — with elements from more than one class — are expanded to the binary feature spaces $UB1$ and $UB2$, from where clustering and expansion continues until either all rules are resolved or the predetermined maximum rule length is reached, in which case rule splitting occurs. Associated graphs are illustrated.

*Cluster Tree Generation.* First, the unary features of all parts of all patterns are collected into a unary feature space $U$ in which each point represents a single part. The feature space $U$ is partitioned into a number of clusters $U_i$. Some of these clusters may be unique with respect to class membership (e.g. $U_3$ in Fig. 5) and provide a classification rule: If a pattern contains a part $p_r$ whose unary features satisfy the bounds of a unique cluster $U_i$ then the pattern can be assigned a unique classification. The non-unique clusters contain parts from multiple pattern classes and have to be analyzed further. For every part of a non-unique cluster (e.g. $U_2$ in

Fig. 5) we collect the binary features of this part with all other parts in the pattern to form a (conditional) binary feature space $UB_i$. The binary feature space is clustered into a number of clusters $UB_{ij}$. Again, some clusters may be unique (e.g. cluster $UB_{11}$ in Fig. 5) and provide a classification rule: If a pattern contains a part $p_r$ whose unary features satisfy the bounds of cluster $U_i$, and there is an other part $p_s$, such that the binary features of the pair $\langle p_r, p_s \rangle$ satisfy the bounds of a unique cluster $UB_{ij}$ then the pattern can be assigned a unique classification. For non-unique clusters, the unary features of the second part $p_s$ are used to construct another unary feature space $UBU_{ij}$ that is again clustered to produce clusters $UBU_{ijk}$. This expansion of the cluster tree continues at additional levels $UBUB$, $UBUBU$, ... involving additional pattern parts until all clusters are completely resolved. Some clusters may, however, never be resolved. In this case, the cluster tree has to be refined by either re-clustering one of the features spaces or by splitting one of the clusters.

Feature space clustering can be obtained using parametric or non-parametric clustering, as discussed in the Introduction, or using fuzzy clustering.[27] Alternatively, one can rely completely on the cluster refinement methods discussed in the next section.

*Cluster Tree Refinement.* Analysis of non-unique clusters can proceed by further expanding the cluster tree, analyzing unary and binary attributes of additional pattern parts. Alternatively, the derived clusters in the tree can be refined or broken into smaller, more discriminating feature bounds or rules as described below. Both approaches have their respective disadvantages. Cluster refinement leads to an increasingly complex feature-space partitioning and thus may reduce the generality of classification rules. Cluster-tree expansion, on the other hand, successively reduces the possibility of classifying patterns from partial data. In the end, a compromise has to be established between both approaches.

One successful approach to cluster tree refinement involves entropy-based splitting procedures. Consider splitting the elements of an unresolved cluster $C$ along a (unary or binary) feature dimension $F$. The elements of $C$ are first sorted by their feature value $f(c)$, and then all possible cut points $T$ midway between successive feature values in the sorted sequence are evaluated. For each cut point $T$, the elements of $C$ are partitioned into two sets, $P_1 = \{c \mid f(c) \leq T\}$ with $n_1$ elements and $P_2 = \{c \mid f(c) > T\}$ with $n_2$ elements. We define the partition entropy $H_P(T)$ as

$$H_P(T) = (n_1 H(P_1) + n_2 H(P_2))/(n_1 + n_2).$$

The cut point $T_F$ that minimizes $H_P(T_F)$ is considered the best point for splitting cluster $C$ along feature dimension $F$. The best split of cluster $C$ is considered the one along the feature dimension $F$ that minimizes $T_F$.[5] For an unresolved leaf cluster $C_L$, one can split $C_L$ or any cluster in the parent chain of $C_L$. Among these clusters, the one that minimizes $T_F$ is considered the optimal point for refining the cluster tree.

A completely resolved cluster tree provides a set of deterministic rules for classification of patterns. In addition, partial rule instantiations (such as, for example, the classification associated with cluster $UB_{23}$ in Fig. 5) can provide partial evidence for class membership of incomplete or distorted patterns.

*Evidence Combination.* Every cluster element in the cluster tree corresponds to a sequence $U_i - B_{ij} - U_j - B_{jk} \ldots$ of unary and binary features associated with a non-cyclic chain of pattern parts. CRG thus produces classification rules for (small) pattern fragments and their associated unary and binary features whereas EBS and rulegraphs producc classification rules for sets of unary and binary features. When CRG rules are applied to some pattern, one obtains one or more (classification) evidence vectors for each pattern fragment. These evidence vectors have to be combined into a single evidence vector for the whole pattern. Difficulties arise when a test scene contains multiple patterns where it is unclear whether a sequence $p_i - p_j - \ldots - p_n$ of pattern parts belongs to the same pattern or whether it is "crossing the boundary" of different patterns. In the former case, CRG rule can be expected to produce correct classifications, whereas in the latter case classification may be arbitrary.

In this section, we present a simple scheme for evidence combination in CRG-type schemes for classification of pattern fragments. In the next section, we will analyze more complex schemes for classifying scenes containing multiple patterns or objects.

Pattern identification and classification begins with the extraction of all non-cyclic paths up to a certain length $l$. These paths, termed *chains*, constitute the basic units for pattern classification. A chain is denoted by $S = \langle p_i, p_j, \ldots, p_n \rangle$ where each $p_i$ denotes a pattern part. For some chains, all parts belong to a single pattern, but other chains cross the boundary between different patterns.

Each chain $S = \langle p_i, p_j, \ldots, p_n \rangle$ is classified using the CRG classification rules. Depending on the unary and binary feature states, a chain may or may not instantiate one (or more) classification rules. In the former case, rule instantiation may be partial (with a non-unique evidence vector $\vec{E}(S)$), or complete. As discussed above, the evidence vector for each rule instantiation is derived from the empirical class frequencies of the training examples.

The evidence vectors of all chains $\langle p_{i_1}, p_{j_1}, \ldots, p_n \rangle$, $\langle p_{i_2}, p_{j_2}, \ldots, p_n \rangle, \ldots$ terminating in $p_n$ must be combined to obtain a classification for part $p_n$. This is a problem related to "stacked generalization",[28] with the added difficulty that some of the evidence vectors may be mutually incompatible.

A simple scheme for evidence combination is the *winner-take-all* solution: the evidence vectors of all chains terminating in $p_n$ are averaged to give $\vec{E}_{av}(p_n)$, and the most likely class label is used to classify part $p_n$. This solution does not take into account that, for a chain $S = \langle p_i, p_j, \ldots, p_n \rangle$, the average evidence vectors $\vec{E}_{av}(p_i)$, $\vec{E}_{av}(p_j), \ldots, \vec{E}_{av}(p_n)$ may be very different and possibly incompatible. If they are very different, it is plausible to assume that the chain $S$ is crossing a boundary. In this case, $S$ and its evidence vectors should be disregarded.

Compatibilities between evidence vectors are taken into account in the *relaxation labeling* solution. Here, the weight of an evidence vector $\vec{E}(p_i)$ of part $p_i$ depends on the similarity (compatibility) of $\vec{E}(p_i)$ to the evidence vectors of neighboring parts. The constraints on evidence vectors are propagated throughout the pattern using a standard relaxation labeling technique.[29] More precisely, the relaxation-labeling solution is given by

$$\vec{E}^{t+1}(p_i) = \Phi\left[\sum_{S=\langle p_i \ldots p_n \rangle} \vec{E}^t(p_i) C(p_i, p_n)\right] \tag{2}$$

where $\vec{E}^t(p_i)$ corresponds to the evidence vector of $p_i$ at iteration $t$, with $\vec{E}^0(p_i) = \vec{E}_{av}(p_i)$. Further, $C(p_i, p_n)$ corresponds to the compatibility between parts $p_i$ and $p_n$, and $\Phi$ is the logistic function

$$\Phi(z) = (1 + \exp[-20(z - 0.5)])^{-1}. \tag{3}$$

The compatibility function is defined in terms of the scalar product between the evidence vectors of parts $p_i$ and $p_n$,

$$C(p_i, p_n) = \vec{E}(p_i) \cdot \vec{E}(p_n). \tag{4}$$

For identical evidence vectors $\vec{E}(p_i)$ and $\vec{E}(p_n)$, $C(p_i, p_n) = 1$, and for incompatible evidence vectors, for example $\vec{E}(p_i) = [1, 0, 0]$ and $\vec{E}(p_n) = [0, 1, 0]$, $C(p_i, p_n) = 0$.

Compatibility of evidence vectors is a weak constraint for updating the evidence vectors of each part. Much stronger constraints can be derived from the comparison of test patterns to model patterns and the establishment of correspondence mappings between the two. This is further considered in the next section in the context of complex scene analysis.

## 4. COMPLEX SCENE ANALYSIS

As discussed before, identifying specific shapes in scenes composed of multiple objects or patterns cannot be directly accomplished using attribute-indexed pattern recognition systems such as neural networks or decision trees. Attempts to solve such problems using windowing or "perceptual grouping" methods are typically heuristic, unreliable and inefficient though, in some limited domains this can be of some use.[21,30] Here, we discuss a solution in the context of a rule-based system that makes only weak and general assumptions about the structure of scenes and objects. Our solution is based on the analysis of the relationships within (intra) and between (inter) instantiated rules generated by the CRG system. CRG has the advantage of actually "pre-compiling" the cliques or groupings of parts which, from the training data, are necessary and sufficient for discriminating between different models. The proposed solution method is based on the *sequential* evaluation of constraints described below.

*Initial Rule Evaluation.* The first stage involves direct activation of the CRG rules in a parallel, iterative deepening method. Starting from each scene part, all possible sequences of parts, termed *chains*, are generated and classified using the CRG rules. Expansion of each chain $S = \langle s_1, s_2, \ldots, s_n \rangle$ terminates if at least one of the following conditions occurs:

(1) the part sequence $s_1, s_2, \ldots, s_n$ cannot be expanded without creating a cycle,
(2) all CRG rules instantiated by $S$ are completely resolved, or
(3) the binary features $\vec{b}(s_n, s_{n+1})$ do not satisfy the features bounds of any CRG rule.

If a chain $S$ cannot be expanded, the evidence vectors of all rules instantiated by $S$ are averaged to obtain the evidence vector $\vec{E}(S)$ of the chain $S$. Further, the initial evidence vector of a part $p$ is obtained by averaging evidence vectors over the set $\mathcal{S}_p$ of all chains that start at $p$,

$$\vec{E}(p) = |\mathcal{S}_p|^{-1} \sum_{S \in \mathcal{S}_p} \vec{E}(S). \tag{5}$$

where $|\mathcal{S}_p|$ denotes the cardinality of the set $\mathcal{S}_p$. This initial estimate is improved in the next few steps by identifying "crossing" snakes and eliminating their contribution to the evidence vector $\vec{E}(p)$.

*Chain Permutation Constraint.* The chain permutation constraint is based on the assumption that rule instantiations are invariant to permutations, i.e. if two chains are permutations of each other, for example $S_1 = \langle A, B, C \rangle$ and $S_2 = \langle B, A, C \rangle$, their parts must index the same set of model parts, independent of chains and independent of instantiated rules.

*Single Classification Constraint.* The single classification constraint is based on the assumption that *at least one* chain among all chains starting at a scene part does not cross an object boundary and that at least one instantiated rule indexes the correct model parts. Given this, if there is any scene part that initiates a single chain $S_i$ and this chain instantiates a single classification rule then the model parts indexed by $S_i$ can be used to constrain all chains that touch $S_i$.

These two deterministic constraints are very powerful in terms of eliminating inconsistent (crossing) chains. Their usefulness breaks down, however, for cases where the assumptions are not met by training and test data sets.

*Inter-chain Compatibility Analysis.* The idea of the inter-chain compatibility analysis is as follows. The less compatible the evidence vector of a chain $S_i$ is with the evidence vectors of all chains that $S_i$ touches, the more likely it is that $S_i$ crosses an object boundary. In this case $\vec{E}(S_i)$ is given a low weight in the computation of (5). Let $S_i$ and $S_j$ be touching chains, and let $T_{ij}$ be the set of parts common to the two chains. A compatibility measure $C(S_i, S_j)$ between $S_i$ and $S_j$ can be defined based on the overlap of model parts instantiated by $T_{ij}$ and the overall compatibility of a chain $S_i$ is then defined as the average compatibility of $S_i$ with all chains that $S_i$ touches:

$$w_{inter}(S_i) = |\mathcal{S}_T|^{-1} \sum_{S \in \mathcal{S}_T} C(S_i, S). \qquad (6)$$

where $\mathcal{S}_T$ denotes the set of chains that touch $S_i$.

*Intra-Chain Compatibility Analysis.* The last rule for detecting boundary-crossing chains is based on the following idea. If a chain $S_i = \langle s_{i1}, s_{i2}, \ldots, s_{in} \rangle$ does not cross boundaries of objects then the evidence vectors $\vec{E}(s_{i1})$, $\vec{E}(s_{i2})$, ..., $\vec{E}(s_{in})$ are likely to be similar, and dissimilarity of the evidence vectors suggests that $S_i$ may be a "crossing" chain. Similarity of any pair of evidence vectors can be measured by their dot product 4 and similarity of all intra-chain evidence vectors $w_{intra}(S)$ is obtained by averaging the evidence vectors of all pairs of parts in the chain $S_i$.

*Evidence Combination.* Combining inter- and intra-snake compatibilities, the evidence vectors of a part $p$ can be computed using the following iterative relaxation scheme:

$$\vec{E}^{(t+1)}(p) = \Phi\left[Z^{-1} \sum_{S \in \mathcal{S}_p} w_{inter}(S) w_{intra}^{(t)}(S) \vec{E}(S)\right] \qquad (7)$$

where $Z$ is a normalizing factor and $\Phi$ the logistic function (3). Iterative computation of (7) is required since recomputation of $\vec{E}(p)$ affects the intra-chain compatibility. As indicated above, the four rules presented in this section are evaluated sequentially, and the final part classification is given by the iterative scheme (7).

For illustration purposes we consider the problem of identifying compound blocks in complex scenes.

### 4.1. Colored Blocks Example

Examples of isolated block configurations were presented during training in a supervised learning procedure (Fig. 6). Each block configuration consisted of three training examples, and the test arrangements of complex block combinations consisted of up to 20 blocks (Fig. 7).

Images of the training and test scenes were captured with a color camera. Preprocessing was fairly simple, consisting of a *segmentation* stage and a *feature extraction* stage. Segmentation was achieved using a form of K-means clustering on position $(x, y)$ and color $(r, g, b)$ attributes.[31] For the resulting clusters, small clusters were merged with larger neighbor clusters in order to eliminate spurious image regions. Given the rich image information, it is not surprising that the resulting image regions correspond fairly well to the individual blocks.

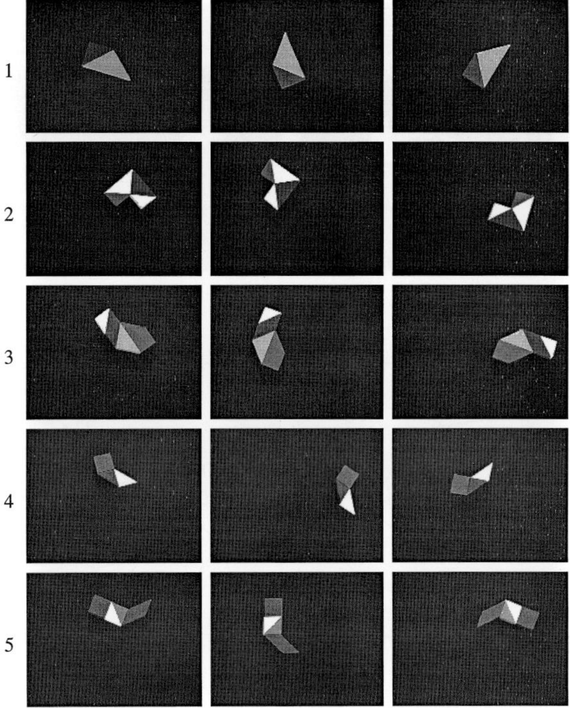


Fig. 6. Images of five classes of toy block configurations with three views each. The image parts are described by the unary features size, eccentricity and the three normalized color coordinates. Pairs of image parts are described by the binary features of midpoint distance, area-normalized midpoint distance, minimum distance and normalized shared boundary length.

In the feature extraction stage the following unary features were extracted for each image region: size (in pixels), compactness ($perimeter^2/area$), and the normalized color signals $R/(R+G+B)$, $G/(R+G+B)$, and $B/(R+G+B)$. For pairs of image regions the following binary features were computed: absolute distance of region centers, minimum distance between the regions, distance of region centers normalized by the sum of the region areas, and length of shared boundaries normalized by total boundary length.

For the training data, CRG analyzed 276 different chains of pattern parts and produced 32 rules: 9 *U*-rules, 4 *UB*-rules, 12 *UBU*-rules, 3 *UBUB*-rules, and 4 *UBUBU*-rules. From the distribution of rule types, it is evident that CRG used predominantly unary features for classification. Classification performance was tested on the complex configurations of block patterns, two of which are shown in Fig. 7 together with the classification results. Classification proceeded as described above, using the chain analysis and relaxation labeling solution. For both scenes, all parts (11 and 17 for the left and right scenes of Fig. 7, respectively) were classified correctly with the exception of a single part from the class-4 configuration.

For comparison purposes, we have analyzed the block example using classical decision trees.[32] In the first analysis, a *UBB*-triple analysis, each image part $P$ of

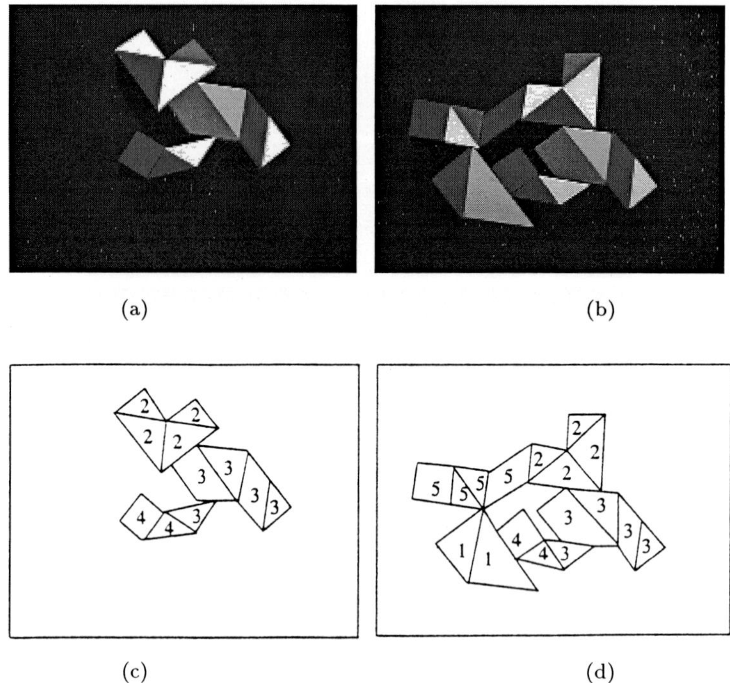


Fig. 7. Two block scenes and their classifications. (a) Block scene consisting of 11 blocks corresponding to examples of classes 2, 3, and 4. (b) Block scene consisting of 17 blocks corresponding to examples of all classes. (c) Classification result for block scene in (a) with region labels corresponding to classes. (d) Classification result for block scene in (b) with region labels corresponding to classes.

the training and test images was described by 13 features. These features consisted of the five unary features of $P$ (see above), the four binary features (see above) of the relation between $P$ and its closest neighbor, and another four binary features of the relation between $P$ and its second-closest neighbor. For the class-1 cases which consisted of two parts only, the feature values for the second binary relation were set to "unknown". A decision tree was generated using C4.5 with default parameters,[32] and the resulting tree was used to classify all parts of the test scenes in Fig. 7. In each of the two scenes, three parts were misclassified. The good performance obtained with C4.5 is consistent with the observation that the use of higher-order relational information does not seem to be crucial for successful classification of this data set.

The first comparison using C4.5 employed features of all *UBB*-triples (unary features and binary features of relations with two other parts) for classification. A second analysis, using *UBU*-triples (with 14 features: the same five unary features of all pairs of parts, as well as the same four binary features of their relation) was performed, but the results cannot be interpreted as easily. For the scene in Fig. 7(a), 33 out of 110 *UBU*-triples or 30% were misclassified, and for the scene in Fig. 7(b), 103 out of 272 *UBU*-triples or 37.8% were misclassified. One reason for the error rate being so high is the fact that no analysis corresponding to the chain analysis described above was performed with the C4.5 results. However, the error rates seem to be too high to be corrected using the relaxation scheme proposed there.

A general point is, however, more important. The CRG method generates rules of (minimal) variable length *optimized for a given training set*, whereas the decision tree (C4.5) *fixes* the dimensionality of the feature space and rule length. Indeed, C4.5 does not use part-indexing and so the relational structure has to be encoded implicitly in the attributes extracted from different parts and part relations. The choice of *UBB*-triples for the block example lead to a C4.5 performance that was essentially the same as that of CRG, but for the *UBU*-triples the C4.5 performance was much worse. This choice has to be done *a priori* whereas it is adjusted dynamically in the CRG method. Further, CRG is designed to exploit structural information of patterns and dependencies between feature states, whereas C4.5 analyzes a fixed set of features that are assumed to be independent. In this sense, the application of C4.5 to the blocks data was somewhat misleading in the sense that the necessary and relevant structural information was generated manually. This example of forcing C4.5 to function with RS and complex scene data emphasizes the very need for systems like CRG.

## 5. CONCLUSIONS

In this paper we have considered issues related to how knowledge can be used to develop strategies for the interpretation of image data. Although the examples have been visual, it is clear that such technologies can also be applied to other domains including the range of data types that exist in GIS, visualization and multi-media. Indeed, we claim that such technologies need to be explored for the development of content-based image queries of current interest in many commercial applications.

The main points of this paper are that ML has to be considered in the context of the data structures required to solve specific problems and the development of efficient and robust search procedures especially at the recognition stage. For example, if the data structure is a labeled and attributed graph then the aim of ML is to generalize on such relational structures and to find optimal subgraphs which are suited for evidencing one structure and not others. Equally, if the data structure is non-relational then standard attribute-indexed systems are sufficient.

Other ways in which knowledge can be introduced into visual learning resides in the notion of "model-based" processes. Even "unsupervised" learning models use this in so far as the spatial contiguity assumption, the cost functions and parameters used to model the clustering processes all assume data models. Equally, in the area of low-level vision, the modeling of windowing functions and the requirements for extraction of specific features are all examples of how specific domain knowledge and constraints are used in the generation of rules for interpreting image data.

This perspective competes with "black-box" learning models where arbitrary attributes, decision functions are used to enable generalization from observed data. Ml offers essentially, a methodology for summarizing and generalizing from observed data and such processes have to be firmly embedded in the data structures or domain knowledge types. Further work must also proceed on the integration of low and high-level learning modules where the performance of recognition or interpretation can be used to update even low-level feature extraction and attribute selection.

## REFERENCES


1. P. Cheeseman, J. Kelly, M. Self, J. Stutz, W. Taylor, and D. Freeman, "AUTOCLASS: A Bayesian classification system", in *Proc. Fifth Int. Conf. on Machine Learning*, San Mateo, CA, 1988, pp. 54–64.
2. T. Poggio, "Networks for approximation and learning", *Proc. IEEE* **78** (1990) 1481–1497.
3. S. Amari and K. Maginu, "Statistical neurodynamics of associative memory", *Neural Networks* **1** (1988) 63–73; also found as a technical report at this site.
4. P. C. Cosman, K. L. Oehler, E. A. Riskin, and R. M. Gray, "Using vector quantization for image processing", *Proc. IEEE* **81** (1993).
5. U. Fayyad and K. Irani, "On the handling of continuous-valued attributes in decision tree generation", *Machine Learning* **8** (1992) 87–102.
6. D. Fisher, "Knowledge acquisition via incremental conceptual clustering", *Machine Learning* **2**, 2 (1987) 139–172.
7. R. O. Duda and P. E. Hart, *Pattern Classification and Scene Analysis*, John Wiley, New York, 1973.
8. Y. Park, "A comparison of neural net classifiers and linear tree classifiers: Their similarities and differences", *Pattern Recognition* **27**, 11 (1994) 1493–1503.
9. S. E. Fahlman and C. Lebiere, "The cascade-correlation learning architecture", in *Advances in Neural Information Processing Systems 2*, ed. D. S. Touretsky, Morgan Kaufmann, San Mateo, CA, 1990, pp. 38–51.
10. T. Caelli and A. Dreier, "Variations on the evidence-based object recognition theme", *Pattern Recognition* **27**, 2 (1994) 185-204.
11. J. Quinlan, "Induction of decision trees", *Machine Learning* **1** (1986) 81–106; reproduced in *Readings in Machine Learning*, Ref. 33, pp. 57–69.
12. A. K. Jain and R. Hoffman, "Evidence-based recognition of 3D objects", *IEEE Trans. on Pattern Analysis and Machine Intelligence* **PAMI-10**, 6 (1988) 783–802.
13. W. F. Bischof and T. Caelli, "Learning structural descriptions of patterns: A new technique for conditional clustering and rule generation", *Pattern Recognition* **27**, 5 (1994) 689–697.
14. D. Gabor, "Theory of communication", *J. of the Institute of Electrical Engineers* **93**, 6 (1946) 429–459.
15. H. Kong and L. Guan, "A neural network adaptive filter for the removal of impulse noise in digital images", *Neutral Networks* **9** (1996) 373–378.
16. W. F. Bischof and T. Caelli, "Parsing scale-space and spatially stability analysis", *Computer Vision, Graphics and Image Processing* **42** (1988) 192–205.
17. B. McCane, T. Caelli, and O. de Vel, "Multi-scale adaptive segmentation using edge and region based attributes", submitted, 1996.
18. A. Jain and K. Karu, "Texture analysis: Representation and matching", in *Image Analysis and Processing, 8th Int. Conf. ICICAP '95*, eds., C. Braccini, L. DeFloriani, and G. Vernazza, San Remo, Italy, 1995, pp. 3–10.
19. T. Caelli, D. Squire, and T. Wild, "Model-based neural networks", *Neural Networks* **6** (1993) 613–625.
20. D. Squire and T. Caelli, "Shift, rotation and scale invariant signatures for two-dimensional contours in a neural network architecture", *Annals of Mathematics and Artificial Intelligence*, 1997 (in press).

21. W. E. L. Grimson, *Object Recognition by Computer*, MIT Press, Cambridge, MA, 1990.
22. H. Bunke and B. Messmer, "Efficient attributed graph matching and its application to image analysis", in *Image Analysis and Processing, 8th Int. Conf. ICICA '95*, eds., L. DeFloriani and G. Vernazza, San Remo, Italy, 1995, pp. 45–55.
23. H. Bunke and B. Messmer, "Recent advances in graph matching", in *Spatial Computing*, eds., T. Caelli, H. Bunke, and P. Lam, World Scientific, Singapore, 1997.
24. P. J. Flynn and A. K. Jain, "BONSAI: 3D object recognition using constrained search", *IEEE Trans. on Pattern Analysis and Machine Intelligence* **13**, 10 (1991) 1066–1075.
25. T. Caelli and A. Pennington, "An improved rule generation method for evidence-based classification systems", *Pattern Recognition* **26**, 5 (1993) 733–740.
26. A. R. Pearce, T. Caelli, and W. F. Bischof, "Rulegraphs for graph matching in pattern recognition", *Pattern Recognition* **27**, 9 (1994) 1231–1247.
27. B. McCane, T. Caelli, and O. de Vel, "A fuzzy machine learning approach to recognizing 3D objects and 2D scenes", in *Proc. 2nd Asian Conf. on Computer Vision: ACCV '95*, vol. 3, 1995, pp. 106–111.
28. D. H. Wolpert, "Stacked generalization", *Neural Networks* **5** (1992) 241–259.
29. A. Rosenfeld and A. C. Kak, *Digital Picture Processing*, Academic Press, Orlando, Florida, 1982.
30. D. G. Lowe, *Perceptual Organization and Visual Recognition*, Kluwer Academic Publishers, Boston, 1995.
31. A. K. Jain and R. C. Dubes, *Algorithms for Clustering Data*, Prentice Hall, Englewood Cliffs, NJ, 1988.
32. J. R. Quinlan, *C4.5 Programs for Machine Learning*, Morgan Kaufmann, San Mateo, California, 1993.
33. J. W. Shavlik and T. G. Dietterich, eds., *Readings in Machine Learning*, Morgan Kaufmann, San Mateo, CA, 1990.

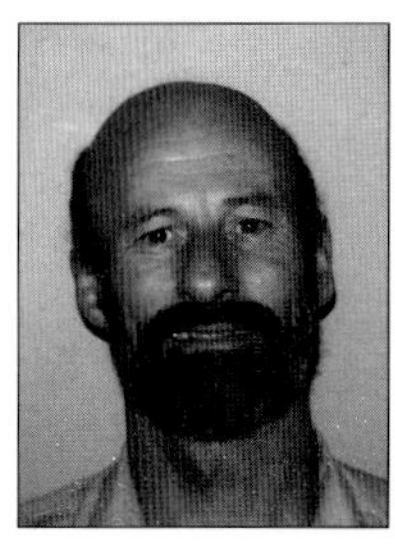

**Terry Caelli** is Professor of computer science and Head of the School of Computing at Curtin University of Technology. Professor Caelli completed his Ph.D. at the University of Newcastle in the area of visual pattern recognition in 1975.

His current interests lie in computer vision, machine learning as they apply to building image interpretation and annotation systems for both static and dynamic spatial data and the inference of actions and function. Professor Caelli is actively involved in the International Association for Pattern Recognition and the IEEE and retains interests in understanding and modeling human vision.

His current application domains include human surveillance, environmental and industrial monitoring, and domain-specific multi-media query and annotation systems. Current research is funded via the Australian Research Council, Defence and local industries.

**Walter F. Bischof** received his Ph.D. degree in psychology in 1982 from the University of Bern, Switzerland. He is currently Associate Professor of psychology and Adjunct Professor of computer science at the University of Alberta and Adjunct Associate Professor of computer science at Curtin University.

His research interests are equally distributed between human and computer vision. In human vision, he works on early spatiotemporal analysis in the visual system with an emphasis on mechanisms of motion detection and motion integration. In computer vision his interests are focussed on object recognition and visual learning.

# RECENT ADVANCES IN GRAPH MATCHING

H. BUNKE and B. T. MESSMER

*Institut für Informatik und Angewandte Mathematik, Universität Bern*
*Neubrückstr. 10, CH-3012 Bern, Switzerland*
*E-mail: bunke@iam.unibe.ch; messmer@vptt.ch or messmer@iam.unibe.ch*

A powerful and universal data structure with applications in various subfields of science and engineering is graphs. In computer vision and image analysis, graphs are often used for the representation of structured objects. For example, if the problem is to recognize instances of known objects in an image, then often models, or prototypes, of the known objects are represented by means of graphs and stored in a database. The unknown objects in the input image are extracted by means of suitable preprocessing and segmentation algorithms, and represented by graphs that are analogous to the model graphs. Thus, the problem of object recognition is transformed into a graph matching problem.

In this paper, it is assumed that there is an input graph that is given on-line, and a number of model, or prototype, graphs that are known *a priori*. We present a new approach to subgraph isomorphism detection which is based on a compact representation of the model graphs that is computed off-line. Subgraphs that appear multiple times within the same or within different model graphs are represented only once, thus reducing the computational effort to detect them in an input graph. In the extreme case where all model graphs are highly similar, the run time of the new algorithm becomes independent of the number of model graphs. We also describe an extension of this method to error-correcting graph matching. Furthermore, an approach to subgraph isomorphism detection based on decision trees is proposed. A decision tree is generated from the models in an off-line phase. This decision tree can be used for subgraph isomorphism detection. The time needed for decision tree traversal is only polynomial in terms of the number of nodes of the input graph. Moreover, the time complexity of the decision tree traversal is completely independent on the number of model graphs, regardless of their similarity. However, the size of the decision tree is exponential in the number of nodes of the models. To cut down the space complexity of the decision tree, some pruning strategies are discussed.

*Keywords*: Graph matching, graph isomorphism, subgraph isomorphism, error tolerant graph matching, decision tree.

## 1. INTRODUCTION

A powerful and universal data structure with applications in various subfields of science and engineering is graphs. In computer vision and image analysis, graphs are often used for the representation of structured objects. For example, if the problem is to recognize instances of known objects in an image, then often models, or prototypes, of the known objects are represented by means of graphs and stored in a database. The unknown objects in the input image are extracted by means of suitable preprocessing and segmentation algorithms, and represented by graphs that are analogous to the model graphs. Thus the problem of object recognition is transformed into a graph matching problem.

Generally, the term *graph matching* refers to the process of comparing two (or more) graphs with each other. There are several classes of graph matching



Spatial Computing: Issues in Vision, Multimedia and Visualization Technologies (1997) 169–203

problems. In the *graph isomorphism* problem, we want to determine if two given graphs are isomorphic to each other. An isomorphism is a bijective mapping between the nodes of the two graphs such that the structure of the edges is preserved. In the *subgraph isomorphism* problem, we are given two graphs $G_1$ and $G_2$, and want to find out if $G_2$ contains a subgraph that is isomorphic to $G_1$. Finally, in *error-tolerant graph matching*, we want to establish a graph or subgraph isomorphism in the presence of some distortions. The admissible distortions are often problem dependent. A general distortion model may include, for example, the deletion, insertion, and substitution of both nodes and edges. These distortions are also called *edit operations*. In order to model the fact that certain distortions are more frequent than others, one can assign a cost to each individual edit operation. Error-tolerant graph matching can be used to calculate a measure of similarity, or dissimilarity, for a given pair of graphs. This measure of similarity is based on the sequence of edit operations that has the minimum cost among all possible sequences that transform one of the given graphs into the other. Thus, approximate graph matching is a generalization of string edit distance computation.[1] For a more comprehensive introduction to graph matching, see Refs. 2 and 3.

It is still an open question whether the graph isomorphism problem is in the complexity class P or NP.[4] In this paper, we will consider only subgraph and error-tolerant graph matching as these problems are more important in computer vision. They are known to be in NP. This means that all available methods have an exponential time complexity. Consequently, graph matching algorithms that are guaranteed to yield the correct solution are applicable only if the underlying graphs are relatively small. Graph matching for large graphs becomes computationally intractable. The only choice to deal with large graphs are approximate algorithms. These have usually a computational complexity that is lower than exponential, but they are no longer guaranteed to find the correct solution for a given problem.

The best known algorithm for subgraph isomorphism detection is that of Ullman.[5] It is based on tree search with backtracking. In order to speed up the search, a particular lookahead technique is used, which allows to detect and prune dead ends in the search tree early. Another well-known method for subgraph isomorphism detection is based on maximal clique detection in a compatibility graph.[6] The algorithms that have been proposed for error-tolerant matching are based on tree search, similar to Ullman's algorithm.[7–10] As the search space in error-tolerant matching is even larger than in regular subgraph isomorphism detection, the use of good heuristics together with $A^*$-like search techniques[11] becomes indispensable.

Ullman's method, the technique based on maximal clique detection, and tree search based error-tolerant graph matching are optimal algorithms in the sense that they are guaranteed to yield the correct solution to a given problem. In the area of approximate algorithms, on the other hand, methods like simulated annealing,[12] neural networks,[13] genetic algorithms,[14] continuous optimization[15] and probabilistic relaxation[16] have been proposed. The idea underlying all these methods is to iteratively minimize an objective function that represents the distance of the current solution to the correct solution. The most serious problem of these approaches is that the minimization procedure may either not converge or get trapped in a local minimum.

In this paper, it is assumed that there is an input graph that is given on-line, and a number of model, or prototype, graphs that are known *a priori*. We present a new approach to subgraph isomorphism detection which is based on a compact representation of the model graphs that is computed off-line. Subgraphs that appear multiple times within the same or within different model graphs are represented only once, thus reducing the computational effort to detect them in an input graph. In the extreme case where all model graphs are highly similar, the run time of the new algorithm becomes independent of the number of model graphs. We also describe an extension of this method to error-tolerant graph matching. Furthermore, an approach to subgraph isomorphism detection based on decision trees is proposed. A decision tree is generated from the models in an off-line phase. This decision tree can be used for subgraph isomorphism detection. The time needed for decision tree traversal is only polynomial in terms of the number of nodes of the input graph. Moreover, the time complexity of the decision tree traversal is completely independent on the number of model graphs, regardless of their similarity. However, the size of the decision tree is exponential in the number of nodes of the models. To cut down the space complexity of the decision tree some pruning strategies are discussed.

Numerous applications of graph matching in image analysis and computer vision have been described in the literature. These include character classification,[17,18] schematic diagram and shape analysis,[7,19,20] 3D object recognition,[21–25] stereo vision,[6] dynamic scene analysis[26] and muscle tissue classification.[27] Other interesting applications of graph matching can be found in the domain of machine learning for computer vision. For example, in Refs. 28 and 29 graph matching is combined with clustering techniques and rule generation in order to learn and classify new shapes and in Ref. 30 substructure discovery is conducted by means of graph matching. Finally, in Ref. 31 the application of the error-tolerant graph matching algorithm introduced in Sec. 4 of this paper to schematic diagram interpretation and automatic learning of symbols is described.

## 2. DEFINITIONS AND NOTATIONS

The algorithms presented in this paper work on labeled graphs. Let $L_V$ and $L_E$ denote the set of vertex and edge labels, respectively.

**Definition 1:** A *graph* $G$ is a 4-tuple $G = (V, E, \mu, \nu)$, where

- $V$ is the set of vertices,
- $E \subseteq V \times V$ is the set of edges,
- $\mu : V \rightarrow L_V$ is a function assigning labels to the vertices,
- $\nu : E \rightarrow L_E$ is a function assigning labels to the edges.

□

In this definition, the edges are directed, i.e. there is an edge from $v_1$ to $v_2$ if $(v_1, v_2) \in E$. For graphs with undirected edges, we require $(v_2, v_1) \in E$ for any edge $(v_1, v_2) \in E$. The empty graph, i.e. the graph with an empty set of vertices, will be denoted by $\emptyset$.

**Definition 2:** Given a graph $G = (V, E, \mu, \nu)$, a *subgraph* of $G$ is a graph $S = (V_s, E_s, \mu_s, \nu_s)$ such that

1. $V_s \subseteq V$
2. $E_s = E \cap (V_s \times V_s)$
3. $\mu_s$ and $\nu_s$ are the restrictions of $\mu$ and $\nu$ to $V_s$ and $E_s$, respectively, i.e.,

$$\mu_s(v) = \begin{cases} \mu(v) & \text{if } v \in V_s \\ \text{undefined} & \text{otherwise} \end{cases}$$

$$\nu_s(e) = \begin{cases} \nu(e) & \text{if } e \in E_s \\ \text{undefined} & \text{otherwise} \end{cases}$$

□

From this definition it is easy to see that, given a graph $G$, any subset of its vertices uniquely defines a subgraph of $G$. We use the notation $S \subseteq G$ to indicate that $S$ is a subgraph of $G$.

**Definition 3:** Given a graph $G = (V, E, \mu, \nu)$ and a subgraph $S = (V_s, E_s, \mu_s, \nu_s)$ of $G$, the *difference* of $G$ and $S$ is the subgraph of $G$ that is defined by the set of vertices $V - V_s$. We denote the difference of $G$ and $S$ by $G - S$.

□

**Definition 4:** Given two graphs $G_1 = (V_1, E_1, \mu_1, \nu_1)$, $G_2 = (V_2, E_2, \mu_2, \nu_2)$, where $V_1 \cap V_2 = \emptyset$, and a set of edges $E' \subseteq (V_1 \times V_2) \cup (V_2 \times V_1)$ with a labeling function $\nu : E' \to L_E$, the *union* of $G_1$ and $G_2$ with respect to $E'$ is the graph $G = (V, E, \mu, \nu)$ such that

1. $V = V_1 \cup V_2$
2. $E = E_1 \cup E_2 \cup E'$
3. $\mu(v) = \begin{cases} \mu_1(v) & \text{if } v \in V_1 \\ \mu_2(v) & \text{if } v \in V_2 \end{cases}$
4. $\nu(e) = \begin{cases} \nu_1(e) & \text{if } e \in E_1 \\ \nu_2(e) & \text{if } e \in E_2 \\ \nu(e) & \text{if } e \in E' \end{cases}$

□

The union of two graphs $G_1$ and $G_2$ with respect to a set of edges $E$ according to Definition 4 will be denoted by $G_1 \cup_E G_2$.

**Definition 5:** A bijective function $f : V \to V'$ is a *graph isomorphism* from a graph $G = (V, E, \mu, \nu)$ to a graph $G' = (V', E', \mu', \nu')$ if:

1. $\mu(v) = \mu'(f(v))$ for all $v \in V$.
2. For any edge $e = (v_1, v_2) \in E$ there exists an edge $e' = (f(v_1), f(v_2)) \in E'$ such that $\nu(e) = \nu(e')$, and for any $e' = (v_1', v_2') \in E'$ there exists an edge $e = (f^{-1}(v_1'), f^{-1}(v_2')) \in E$ such that $\nu(e') = \nu(e)$.

□

**Definition 6:** An injective function $f : V \to V'$ is a *subgraph isomorphism* from $G$ to $G'$ if there exists a subgraph $S \subseteq G'$ such that $f$ is a graph isomorphism from $G$ to $S$.

□

Notice that graph isomorphism is a special case of subgraph isomorphism. For the remainder of this paper, we will assume that there is a number of *a priori* known graphs, the so-called *model* or *prototype graphs*, and an *input graph* that is given on-line. The input and model graphs will be also referred to as input and models, for short.

## 3. SUBGRAPH ISOMORPHISM — A GRAPH DECOMPOSITION APPROACH

### 3.1. Basic Idea

Given a set of model graphs $G_1, \ldots, G_L$ and an input graph $G_I$, we want to find all subgraph isomorphisms from any of the models to the input graph. Under a naive strategy, we would match the input graph sequentially to each model using, for example, Ullman's algorithm. The main disadvantage of this approach is that it is linearly dependent on the number of model graphs. Moreover, it is inefficient if different model graphs have common substructures, because these substructures will be matched with the input graph for each model repeatedly. In order to overcome this inefficiency, we propose a different approach.

Instead of matching each model graph individually onto the input graph, we recursively decompose the model graphs off-line into smaller subgraphs. At run time, these subgraphs are matched onto the input graph, and all detected subgraph isomorphisms are combined into subgraph isomorphisms for complete model graphs. This idea is similar to the RETE matching algorithm for forward chaining production systems.[32,33] The main advantage of this scheme is that subgraphs that appear multiple times in the same or in different model graphs must be matched only once onto the input. Consequently, the corresponding subgraph isomorphism detection process will be more efficient than the sequential matching of the input graph with each of the models.

The new approach consists of two parts. First, there is an off-line process in which the model graphs are recursively decomposed and the resulting subgraphs are represented by a special data structure. The second part is an on-line process, in which an input graph is matched with the model graphs, which are represented by the data structure generated in the first step.

### 3.2. Decomposing the Model Graphs

The main idea of the new approach is to recursively decompose the model graphs into smaller subgraphs in an off-line processing step. At run time, the subgraph isomorphism problem is solved in a divide-and-conquer fashion. That is, we first look for subgraph occurrences of parts of the models in the input graph. All such occurrences are then successively combined into subgraph isomorphisms for the complete models.

**Definition 7:** Let $B = \{G_1, \ldots, G_L\}$ be a set of model graphs. A *decomposition* of $B$, $D(B)$, is a finite set of 4-tuples $(G, G', G'', E)$, where

1. $G, G'$ and $G''$ are graphs with $G' \subset G$ and $G'' \subset G$
2. $E$ is a set of edges such that $G = G' \cup_E G''$
3. For each $G_i$ there exists a 4-tuple $(G, G', G'', E) \in D(B)$ with $G = G_i$; $i = 1, \ldots, L$.
4. For each 4-tuple $(G, G', G'', E) \in D(B)$ there exists no other 4-tuple $(G_1, G_1', G_1'', E_1) \in D(B)$ with $G = G_1$.
5. For each 4-tuple $(G, G', G'', E_1) \in D(B)$
   (a) if $G'$ consists of more than one vertex then there exists a 4-tuple $(G_1, G_1', G_1'', E_1) \in D(B)$ such that $G' = G_1$
   (b) if $G''$ consists of more than one vertex then there exists a 4-tuple $(G_2, G_2', G_2'', E_2) \in D(B)$ such that $G'' = G_2$
   (c) if $G'$ consists of one vertex then there exists no 4-tuple $(G_3, G_3', G_3'', E_3) \in D(B)$ such that $G' = G_3$
   (d) if $G''$ consists of one vertex then there exists no 4-tuple $(G_4, G_4', G_4'', E_4) \in D(B)$ such that $G'' = G_4$.

□

Informally speaking, a decomposition is a recursive partitioning of graphs into smaller subgraphs, starting with complete models and terminating at the level of single vertices. The first component in a 4-tuple $(G, G', G'', E)$ is the graph to be decomposed, $G'$ and $G''$ are its two parts, and $E$ are the edges in $G$ between $G'$ and $G''$ (see Conditions 1 and 2 in Definition 7). Condition 3 in Definition 7 makes sure that every model in $B$ is decomposed, and Condition 4 implies that a decomposition is unique. By means of Condition 5 it is guaranteed that a decomposition is complete, i.e. the process of partitioning a graph into two parts is continued until individual vertices are reached. If several models $G_i, G_j, \ldots$ have a common subgraph $G$, or if $G$ occurs multiple times in one model $G_i$, it is sufficient to represent $G$ just by one 4-tuple $(G, G', G'', E)$ in $D(B)$. This property not only leads to a compact representation of a set of models, $B$, by means of the decomposition $D(B)$, but it also is the key to an efficient matching procedure at run time.

The decomposition of a set of models will be used to guide the search for subgraph isomorphisms from the models to the input. If there is a 4-tuple $(G, G', G'', E)$ in $D(B)$, then subgraph isomorphisms from $G'$ and $G''$ to the input will be searched

DECOMPOSITION($B$)

1. let $B = \{G_1, \ldots, G_L\}$ and $D(B) = \emptyset$
2. for $i = 1$ to $L$
   decompose($G_i$)

Fig. 1. Algorithm *decomposition*.

DECOMPOSITION($G$)

1. let $D$ be a decomposition and $S_{max} = \emptyset$.
2. if $G$ consists of only one vertex then exit.
3. for all $(G_i, G'_i, G''_i, E_i)$
   if $G_i$ is a subgraph of $G$ and $S_{max}$ is smaller than $G_i$ then let $S_{max} = G$.
4. if $S_{max}$ is isomorphic to $G$ then exit.
5. if no subgraph $S_{max}$ was found and $G$ consists of more than one vertex then
   (a) choose randomly a subgraph $S_{max}$ of $G$.
   (b) decompose($S_{max}$)
6. decompose($G - S_{max}$)
7. add $(G, S_{max}, G - S_{max}, E)$ to $D$ where $E$ is the set of edges between $S_{max}$ and $G - S_{max}$ in $G$.

Fig. 2. Procedure *decompose*.

for first. Once such subgraph isomorphisms have been found, they will be combined, whenever possible, into subgraph isomorphisms from $G$ to the input. This procedure is started with subgraphs $G'$ and $G''$ that consist of single vertices only, and is recursively continued until the level is reached where $G$ represents a complete model.

Apparently, there exist many different decompositions for a given set of models. This property holds even in the case where the set of models consists of only a single graph. One could now define an optimal decomposition being, for example, one that contains the minimum number of 4-tuples, or one where the largest subgraph $G$ that occurs in all models is represented by a 4-tuple $(G, G', G'', E)$. However, the computation of such an optimal decomposition is a highly exponential problem[30]. In this paper we propose a decomposition algorithm which usually does not generate an optimal decomposition but is computationally inexpensive.

In Fig. 1 the algorithm *decomposition* is displayed. The input to the algorithm is a set $B$ of models and the output is their decomposition $D(B)$. The procedure *decompose* is given in Fig. 2.

Although the algorithm *decomposition* will usually not generate an optimal decomposition, it was shown in practical experiments that this has no significant influence on the performance of the run time algorithm. Very importantly, however, is the fact that the algorithm *decomposition* is incremental, i.e., given a set $B$ of model graphs that are represented by the decomposition $D(B)$, a new model graph $G_{L+1}$ can be added to the database by simply calling *decompose*($G_{L+1}$). Thus, $D(B)$ can be updated incrementally without the need for a complete recomputation of $D(B)$ from scratch. This is of particular interest in applications where large databases of graphs are involved and new model graphs must be added to the database at run time.

### 3.3. Subgraph Isomorphism Detection

The decomposition of a set of model graphs presented in the previous section is the basis for an efficient algorithm that detects subgraph isomorphisms from a set of model graphs to an input. Instead of matching each model individually onto a given input, the new algorithm first finds all occurrences of the individual vertices of the model in an input graph. These occurrences are then recursively merged into larger structures until the level of complete model graphs is reached. There are two basic problems that must be solved in this scheme. First, as the smallest component of a graph is a single vertex, there must be a procedure for the detection of subgraph isomorphisms from single vertices to an input graph. Secondly, given a decomposition $D(B)$ and a 4-tuple $(G, G', G'', E) \in D(B)$, if all subgraph isomorphisms from $G'$ and $G''$ to the input graph have been found, they must be combined into subgraph isomorphisms from $G$ to the input graph. The solution to the first problem is straightforward. In order to detect subgraph isomorphisms of graphs that consist of single vertices only, we just need a procedure that tests if the labels of the two vertices are identical. Next, if subgraph isomorphisms for two graphs $G'$ and $G''$ to the input graph have been found, and there is a 4-tuple $(G, G', G'', E)$ in the decomposition, two conditions are tested. First, the instances of $G'$ and $G''$ in the input graph must be disjoint. Secondly, for each edge in $E$ there must exist a correct mapping to the input graph and vice versa. If both conditions are satisfied, the subgraph isomorphisms for $G'$ and $G''$ can be combined into a subgraph isomorphism for $G$. Recursive application of this procedure for all quadruples in a decomposition eventually yields all subgraph isomorphisms for a given set $B$ of model graphs.

It is easy to see that any subgraph $S$ that is part of several models or occurs more than once in the same model will be matched only once to the input if it is represented by a 4-tuple $(S, S_1, S_2, E)$.

### 3.4. An Example

In order to illustrate the new algorithm, we give an example. In Fig. 3 two model graphs, $g_1$ and $g_2$, and an input graph, $g_3$, are shown. In Fig. 4 the decomposition of $g_1$ and $g_2$ is graphically represented by a network. The network is displayed with vertices of the model graphs in the top layer. Below are subgraphs of the models that consist of more than one vertex. The complete models are represented

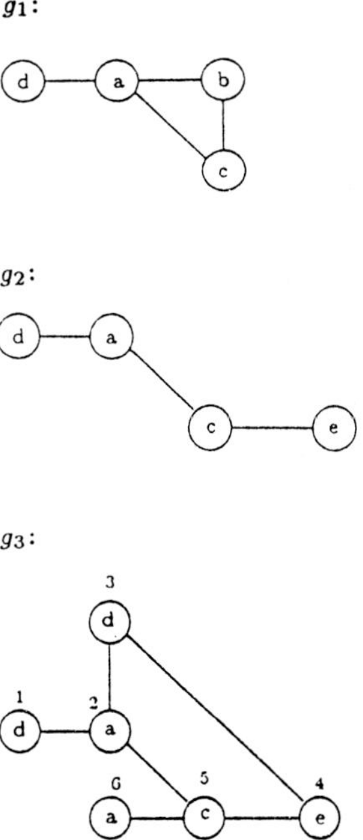


Fig. 3. Two model graphs $g_1$, $g_2$ and an input graph $g_3$.

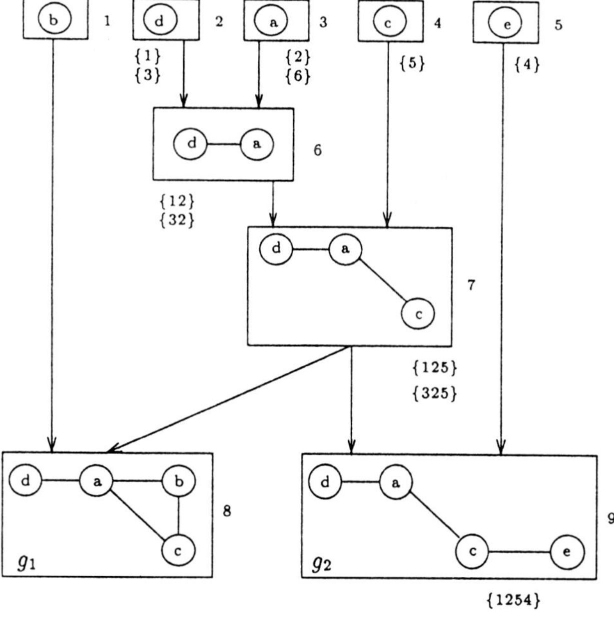


Fig. 4. Decomposition of graphs $g_1, g_2$ from Fig. 3 displayed as a network structure.

at the bottom of the network. The numbers to the right of each network node are identifiers. At the top of the network, the five different vertex labels occurring in $g_1$ and $g_2$ are represented. Notice that, for example, the vertex with label $d$ represented in node 2 appears in both $g_1$ and $g_2$. It appears, however, only once in the decomposition. On the second level in Fig. 4, a subgraph that is decomposed into two vertices with label $d$ and $a$, respectively, and an edge connecting them is represented. This subgraph occurs in both $g_1$ and $g_2$. In network node 7, the largest common subgraph of $g_1$ and $g_2$ is represented. It is decomposed into the subgraph represented in node 6, a vertex represented in node 4, and an edge. Finally, network nodes 8 and 9 represent models $g_1$ and $g_2$, respectively.

At run time, given the input graph $g_3$, the matching algorithm described in the previous section first tries to find all subgraph isomorphisms for the vertices represented in the top nodes of the network. For example, the vertex labeled $d$ can be matched onto the vertices 1 and 3 of $g_3$. Consequently, there are two subgraph isomorphisms associated with node 2 (denoted by $\{1\}$ and $\{3\}$ below the node 2 in Fig. 4). Next, for each subgraph in the decomposition whose components have already been successfully tested, the algorithm tries to combine the subgraph isomorphisms of its components. In node 6, the subgraph isomorphisms $\{1\}$ and $\{3\}$ associated to node 2, and $\{2\}$ and $\{6\}$ associated to node 3 are combined. However, only the combinations $\{12\}$ and $\{32\}$ are valid subgraph isomorphisms from the graph in network node 6 to the input graph $g_3$. Because of the existence of these two subgraph isomorphisms, the subgraph in node 7 will be tested next. This process continues until a single subgraph isomorphism, $\{1254\}$, has been found from the graph $g_2$ to the input graph $g_3$. It can be easily verified that no other subgraph isomorphism from either $g_1$ or $g_2$ to $g_3$ exists.

Table 1. Best and worst case complexities of the new and the traditional algorithm.

| | New algorithm | Ullman's algorithm |
|---|---|---|
| | All models are completely different: $n_1 = 0$, $n_2 = M$ | |
| Best case | $O(Lmn)$ | $O(Lmn)$ |
| Worst case | $O(Lm^n n^2)$ | $O(Lm^n n^2)$ |
| | All models are similar; in the limit: $n_1 = n$, $n_2 = 0$ | |
| Best case | $O(mn)$ | $O(Lmn)$ |
| Worst case | $O(m^n n^2)$ | $O(Lm^n n^2)$ |

### 3.5. Computational Complexity Analysis

In Ref. 34, a detailed complexity analysis of the algorithm described in the previous sections is given. In the present paper, we only give the results of this analysis, see Table 1. The following quantities are used in Table 1:

$L$ = the number of model graphs in the database,
$n_1$ = the number of vertices of a subgraph that is common to all models,
$n_2$ = the number of vertices that are unique to each model,
$n$ = the total number of vertices of a model graph, i.e. $n = n_1 + n_2$,
$m$ = the number of vertices in the input graph.

The complexity of Ullman's algorithm is given for the purpose of comparison. For both algorithms, the best case arises when each of the vertices of the model graphs is uniquely labeled. On the other hand, the worst case occurs when all vertices in the model graphs have the same label and each vertex is connected to each other vertex. In the upper part of Table 1, it was assumed that all models are completely disjoint. In this case, both algorithms have the same complexity. The lower part of Table 1 corresponds to the case where all models have a common subgraph of size $n_1$. In the limit, when all models become identical, i.e. $n_1 = n$ and $n_2 = 0$, the complexity of the decomposition based algorithm is no longer dependent on the number of models, $L$. Notice that in this case, Ullman's algorithm still depends on $L$.

### 3.6. Experimental Results

In order to examine the performance of the new algorithm in practice, we have performed a number of experiments with randomly generated graphs. The new algorithm (NA) and Ullman's refinement procedure (UA) were both implemented in C++ and run on a SUN Sparc10 Workstation. The code of NA consists of roughly 7000 lines compared to 2500 lines of UA.

All model and input graphs were randomly generated. The parameters in the random graph generation process were the number of vertices, the number of edges, the number of different vertex labels (all edges were unlabeled and undirected), the number of graphs in the database and the size of the common subgraph that was contained in all models. In our experiments, we automatically generated model graphs based on these parameters. From each model graph a corresponding isomorphic input graph was derived by copying and permuting its vertices and edges. Both NA and UA were then used to detect all graph isomorphisms from the models to the inputs. In order to account for the random nature of the underlying graphs, each experimental run was repeated ten times and the average computation time was recorded as a result. By varying different parameters in the graph generation process, the behavior of the new algorithm was studied.

In the first experiment, we were interested in measuring the influence of the size of the graphs and the database on the performance of both algorithms. We started with a database consisting of a single graph with 10 vertices and 12 edges. The number of vertex labels was set to 10. We gradually increased the number of graphs in the database to 20 and we also increased the number of vertices from 10 to 50 together with the number of edges from 12 to 60. In Fig. 5 the results for NA (lower plane) and UA (upper plane) are shown; see also Figs. 6 and 7. Apparently, the performance of UA became worse than that of NA with an increasing graph as well

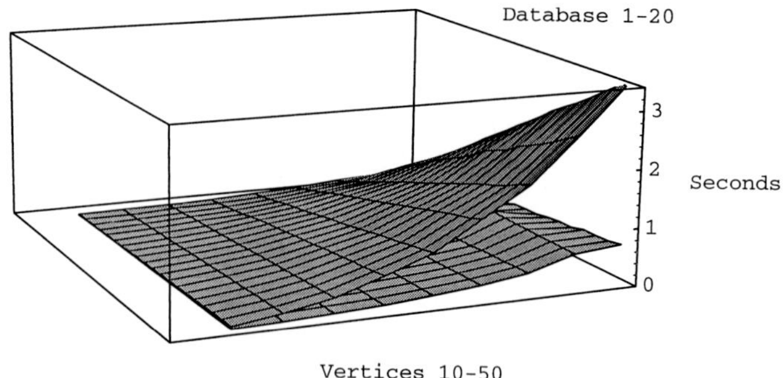


Fig. 5. Time in seconds for increasing the number of vertices and the size of the database. (The lower plane denotes the time of NA, while the upper plane represents the time of UA.)

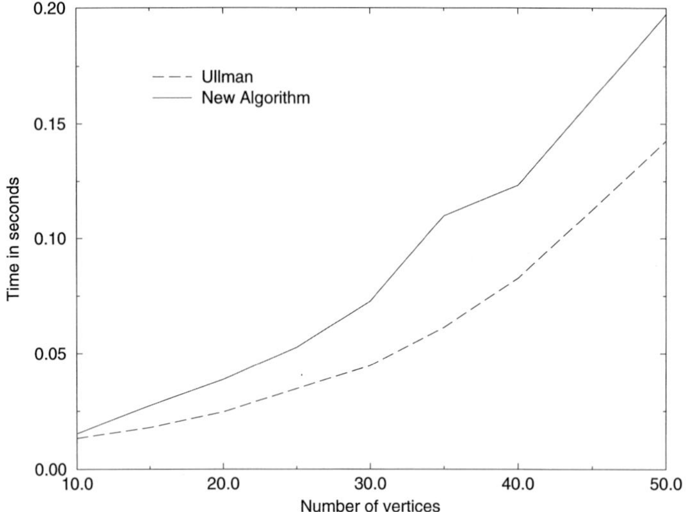


Fig. 6. Cut through Fig. 5 along the vertex axis for one model graph in the database.

as an increasing database size. This behavior can be explained by the fact that by increasing the size of the model graphs while leaving the number of labels constant, there will be a growing number of substructures that occur multiple times within the same or different models. These substructures need to be considered only once by NA. UA, however, must search for these substructures each time they appear in a model graph.

In the first experiment, there were between one and five vertices with identical labels in each graph on the average. Therefore, many of the generated model graphs had some random substructures in common. In the second experiment, the effect of sharing common substructures among models was examined more closely. For this purpose, we generated model graphs consisting of 50 vertices and approximately 60 edges and increased the number of models from 1 to 20 and the size of the common subgraph from 5 to 45 vertices. Except for the common subgraph, all models were

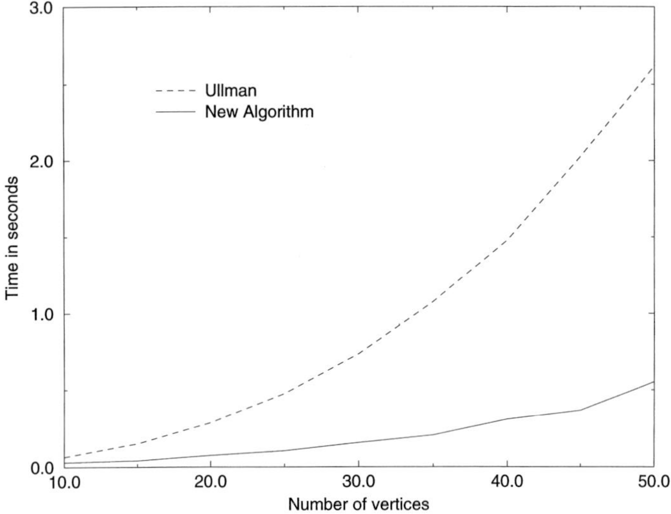


Fig. 7. Cut through Fig. 5 along the vertex axis for 20 model graphs in the database.

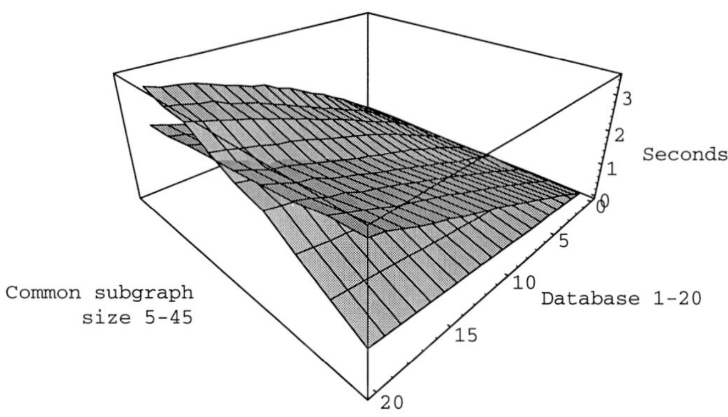


Fig. 8. Time in seconds for an increasing number of vertices in the common subgraph and an increasing size of the database. (The lower plane in the front corner denotes the time of NA, while the upper plane represents the time of UA.)

disjoint, i.e., except for the vertices of the common subgraph for which 15 different labels were allocated, the vertices of the model graphs were all uniquely labeled. The results of the second experiment are given in Fig. 8 where the lower plane at the front corner denotes the times of NA while the upper plane represents UA. Clearly, the intersection of the two planes indicates that for a small or uncommon subgraph in the different models the performance of NA was slightly worse than that of UA. But for an increasing size of the common subgraph, the time needed by NA decreased and became much less than that required by UA.

In Fig. 9, a cut through Fig. 8 along the common subgraph axis is displayed. The size of the database was set to 20. We observe that if the common subgraph

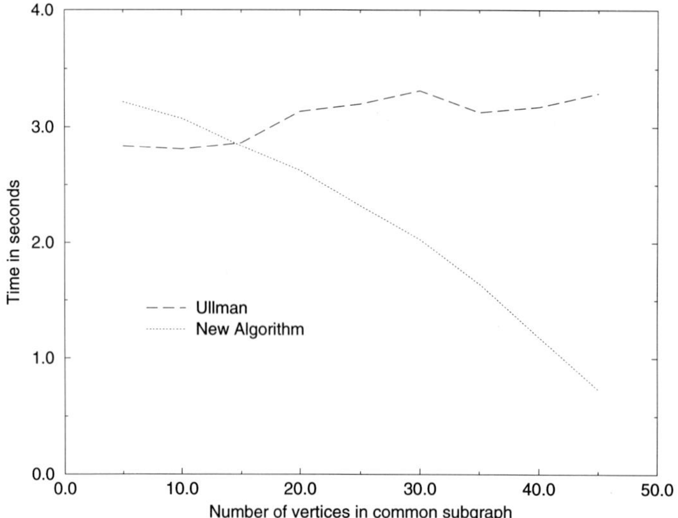


Fig. 9. Cut through Fig. 8 along the common subgraph axis with the size of the database set to 20.

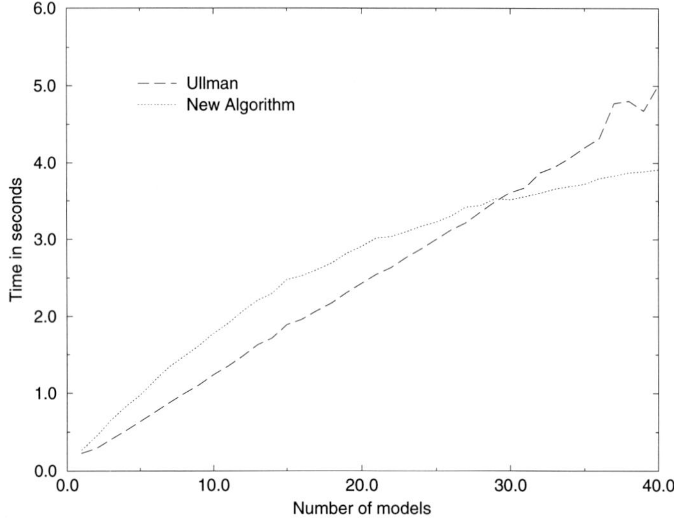


Fig. 10. Cut through Fig. 8 along the database axis with the size of the common subgraph set to 5.

contained less than 15 vertices, NA performed worse than UA. However, for larger common subgraphs the time required by NA decreased rapidly while UA's time requirement increased. Note that in both Figs. 8 and 9 the database contained at most 20 models. It may be expected that even for small subgraphs there is a size of the database for which NA outperforms UA. Figure 10 demonstrates this behavior. It shows a cut through Fig. 8 along the database axis with the common subgraph size set to five vertices. As an extension of the results shown in Fig. 8, the size of the database was varied between 1 and 40. For a database size of 30 models the run time of the two algorithms was identical and for larger databases NA performed better than UA. This indicates that NA is more efficient than UA even for small common subgraphs provided that the number of models in the database is sufficiently large.

In the first and second experiments, the model graphs and databases were of moderate size. The next experiment was devoted to testing the behavior of both algorithms for large graphs on the one hand and large databases on the other hand. In Fig. 11 the size of the model and input graph was increased from 50 to 500 vertices along with the number of edges that was increased from 60 to 600 edges. There were 30 different vertex labels used, i.e., for a graph with 300 vertices there were on average 10 vertices with the same label. The database consisted of a single model graph. We can observe that the performance of UA decreased much faster than NA's performance. While UA matched graphs with 250 vertices within 30 seconds, NA was capable of matching graphs twice as large in the same time. This behavior can again be explained by the fact that with an increasing number of vertices (and a constant number of labels) the number of substructures that appear multiple times inside the same model graph grows.

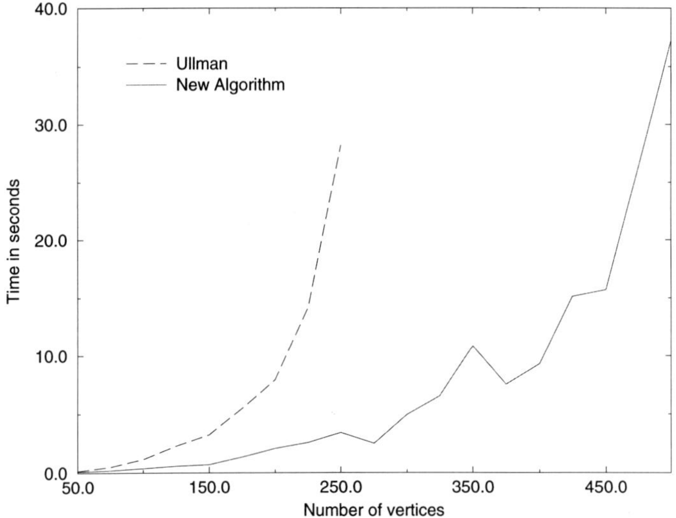


Fig. 11. Computation time for an increasing number of vertices in the model graphs.

Next, in Fig. 12, the number of model graphs in the database was increased from 1 to 100. As in the very first experiment (Fig. 5) the graphs consisted of 50 vertices and 60 edges with 10 vertex labels. Note that with NA even large databases remain tractable (about 1 sec) while UA requires time that is linearly dependent on the database (15 sec for 100 models).

In summary, the experiments reported in this section confirm the results of the theoretical computational complexity analysis. Further experiments are reported in Ref. 34.

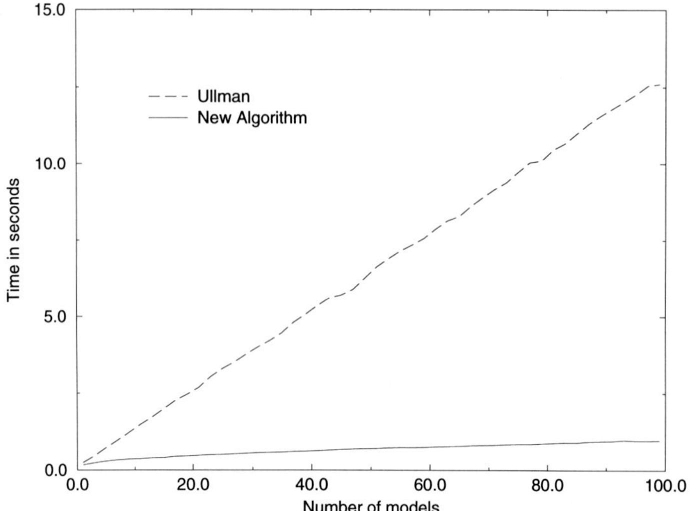


Fig. 12. Computation time for an increasing number of models in the database.

## 4. ERROR-TOLERANT SUBGRAPH ISOMORPHISM

Real world objects which are represented by graphs may be affected by noise and distortions. In order to compare the undistorted model graphs to a distorted input graph and to decide which of the models is most similar to the input, it is necessary to define a distance measure for graphs. Similar to the string matching problem where edit operations are used to define the string edit distance,[1] we define a subgraph edit distance that is based on the idea of compensating the distortions in the input graph by means of edit operations that are applied to the model graphs,[7] i.e., the graph edit operations are used to alter the model graphs until there exist subgraph isomorphisms to the input graph. To each of the graph edit operations, a certain cost is assigned. The subgraph distance from a model to an input graph is then defined to be the minimum cost taken over all sequences of edit operations that are necessary for the compensation of the distortions in the input graph. It can be concluded that the smaller the subgraph distance between a model and an input graph is, the more similar they are. We consider the following distortions in a graph: vertex and edge label distortions, missing vertices, and missing or extraneous edges. Notice that it is not necessary to consider extraneous vertices in the input graph as we are searching for subgraph isomorphisms from the model to the input graph. Thus extraneous vertices in the input graph are automatically ignored. For each type of distortion given above, a corresponding graph edit operation is defined.

**Definition 8:** Given a graph $G = (V, E, \mu, \nu)$, a *graph edit operation* $\delta$ on $G$ is any of the following:

- $\mu(v) \rightarrow l$, $v \in V$, $l \in L_V$: substituting the label $\mu(v)$ of vertex $v$ by $l$ (for the correction of vertex label distortions).

- $\nu(e) \to l'$, $e \in E$, $l' \in L_E$: substituting the label $\nu(e)$ of edge $e$ by $l'$ (for the correction of edge label distortions).
- $v \to \$$, $v \in V$: deleting the vertex $v$ from $G$ (for the correction of missing vertices).[a]
- $e \to \$$, $e \in E$: deleting the edge $e$ from $G$ (for the correction of missing edges).
- $\$ \to e = (v_1, v_2)$, $v_1, v_2 \in V$: inserting an edge between two existing vertices $v_1$, $v_2$ of $G$ (for the correction of extraneous edges).

In order to model the fact that certain distortions are more likely than others, each graph edit operation $\delta$ is assigned a certain cost $C(\delta)$. The costs of the graph edit operations are strongly application dependent and must be defined on the basis of heuristic knowledge.

The five edit operations in Definition 8 are powerful enough to transform any graph $G$ into a subgraph of any other graph $G'$. Therefore, it is always possible to find a sequence of edit operations that transform a model graph $G$ into another graph $G'$ such that a subgraph isomorphism $f$ from $G'$ to a distorted input graph $G_I$ exists.

**Definition 9:** Given a graph $G = (V, E, \mu, \nu)$ and an edit operation $\delta$, the edited graph, $\delta(G)$, is a graph $\delta(G) = (V_\delta, E_\delta, \mu_\delta, \nu_\delta)$ with

1. $V_\delta = \begin{cases} V - \{v\} & \text{if } \delta = (v \to \$) \\ V & \text{otherwise} \end{cases}$

2. $E_\delta = \begin{cases} E \cup \{e\} & \text{if } \delta = (\$ \to e) \\ E - \{e\} & \text{if } \delta = (e \to \$) \\ E \cap (V_\delta \times V_\delta) & \text{otherwise} \end{cases}$

3. $\mu_\delta(v) = \begin{cases} l & \text{if } \delta = (\mu(v) \to l) \\ \mu(v) & \text{otherwise} \end{cases}$

4. $\nu_\delta(e) = \begin{cases} l & \text{if } \delta = (\nu(e) \to l) \\ \nu(e) & \text{otherwise} \end{cases}$

□

**Definition 10:** Given a graph $G = (V, E, \mu, \nu)$ and a sequence of edit operations $\Delta = (\delta_1, \delta_2, \ldots, \delta_k)$, the edited graph, $\Delta(G)$, is a graph

$$\Delta(G) = \delta_k(\ldots \delta_2(\delta_1(G))) \ldots)$$

□

The total cost of the transformation of $G$ into $\Delta(G)$ is given by $C(\Delta) = \sum_{i=1}^{k} C(\delta_i)$. We can now combine the concepts of edited graph and subgraph isomorphism into the concept of error-correcting subgraph isomorphism.

**Definition 11:** Given two graphs $G$ and $G'$, an *error-correcting* (ec) *subgraph isomorphism* $f$ from $G$ to $G'$ is a 2-tuple $f = (\Delta, f_\Delta)$ where

[a]Note that all edges in $G$ that are incident with the vertex $v$ are deleted, too.

1. $\Delta$ is a sequence of edit operations such that there exists a subgraph isomorphism from $\Delta(G)$ to $G'$,
2. $f_\Delta$ is a subgraph isomorphism from $\Delta(G)$ to $G'$.

□

The cost of an *ec* subgraph isomorphism $f = (\Delta, f_\Delta)$ is the cost of the edit operations $\Delta$, i.e. $C(f) = C(\Delta)$. It is easy to see that there is usually more than one sequence of edit operations $\Delta$ such that a subgraph isomorphism from $\Delta(G)$ to $G'$ exists and, consequently, there is usually more than one error-correcting subgraph isomorphism from $G$ to $G'$. For our distance measure, we are particularly interested in the error-correcting subgraph isomorphism with minimum cost. The subgraph distance is thus defined as follows.

**Definition 12:** Let $G$ and $G'$ be two graphs. The *subgraph distance* from $G$ to $G'$, $d(G,G')$, is given by the minimum cost taken over all error-correcting subgraph isomorphisms $f$ from $G$ to $G'$:

$$d(G,G') = MIN_\Delta\{C(\Delta) \mid \text{there is an } ec \text{ subgraph isomorphism } f = (\Delta, f_\Delta) \text{ from } G \text{ to } G'\}$$

□

It is possible to generalize the method introduced in Sec. 3 to error-tolerant subgraph isomorphism detection. The decomposition algorithm that compiles a network from a set of model graphs remains the same. But the dynamic procedure that finds instances of network units in the input graph has to be extended. In the error-tolerant version, each network unit also accepts distorted subgraphs of the input graph $g$. Together with each distorted instance of a network unit, the corresponding edit costs are stored. The network nodes are no longer activated strictly from top to bottom, i.e. from smaller to larger units, but in a best-first manner where the subgraph with the smallest edit cost is considered first. It is possible to integrate a lookahead procedure that takes into regard a lower bound estimate of the future cost when selecting the unit with the smallest edit cost. This lookahead procedure can be implemented such that almost no additional computational overheads arise. Thus, we get a very efficient error-tolerant graph matching procedure. For more details of this method including an analysis of its computational complexity and experimental results see Ref. 34.

## 5. A POLYNOMIAL MATCHER FOR PREPROCESSED MODEL GRAPHS

In this section we describe another new method for subgraph isomorphism detection. Contrary to Secs. 3 and 4, however, we consider the problem to find a subgraph isomorphism from an input graph to any of the models. The proposed method is based on an intensive preprocessing step in which the model graphs are used to create a *decision tree.* At run time, the input graph is then classified by the decision tree and all model graphs for which there exists a subgraph isomorphism from the input are detected. If we neglect the time needed for preprocessing, the computational complexity of the new subgraph isomorphism algorithm is only polynomial in the number of input graph vertices. Furthermore, it is independent of the number of model graphs and the number of edges in any of the graphs. However, the decision tree that is constructed in the preprocessing step is of exponential size in terms of the number of vertices of the model graphs. Therefore, we also present several pruning techniques which aim at reducing the size of the decision tree. A brief description of the method described in this chapter has also been given in Ref. 35.

### 5.1. Problem Formulation

Let $L_V$ and $L_E$ denote the sets of vertex and edge labels, respectively (see Sec. 2). Furthermore, let $G = (V, E, \mu, \nu)$ be a graph with $V = \{v_1, v_2, \ldots, v_n\}$. Then $G$ can also be represented by its adjacency matrix $M = (m_{ij})$, $i, j = 1, \ldots, n$, where $m_{ii} = \mu(v_i)$ and $m_{ij} = \nu((v_i, v_j))$ for $i \neq j$. Apparently, the adjacency matrix representation of a graph does not take into account loops at a vertex. However, this isn't a real restriction as loops can be represented by means of an extended set of vertex labels.

Clearly, the matrix $M$ is not unique for a graph $G$. If $M$ represents $G$, then any permutation of $M$ is also a valid representation of $G$.

**Definition 13:** A $n \times n$-matrix $P = (p_{ij})$ is called a *permutation matrix* if

1. $p_{ij} \in \{0, 1\}$ for $i, j = 1, \ldots, n$
2. $\sum_{i=1}^{n} p_{ij} = 1$ for $j = 1, \ldots, n$
3. $\sum_{j=1}^{n} p_{ij} = 1$ for $i = 1, \ldots, n$

□

If graph $G$ is represented by an $n \times n$ adjacency matrix $M$ and $P$ is an $n \times n$ permutation matrix, then the $n \times n$ matrix

$$M' = PMP^T \tag{1}$$

where $P^T$ denotes the transpose of $P$, is also an adjacency matrix of $G$. If $p_{ij} = 1$ then the $j$th vertex in $M$ becomes the $i$th vertex in $M'$. Let $G_1$ and $G_2$ be two graphs and $M_1$ and $M_2$ their corresponding adjacency matrices. Apparently, $G_1$ and $G_2$ are *isomorphic* if there exists a permutation matrix $P$ such that

$$M_2 = PM_1P^T \tag{2}$$

Notice that the matrix $P$ can be understood as a bijective function $f$ that maps the vertices of $G_1$ to $G_2$, and vice versa. That is, $f(v_j) = v_i$ iff $m_{ij} = 1$. We will call both $P$ and $f$ a *graph isomorphism* between $G_1$ and $G_2$. Thus, the problem of finding a graph isomorphism between two graphs $G_1$ and $G_2$ is equivalent to finding a permutation matrix $P$ for which (2) holds true.

**Definition 14:** Let $M = (m_{ij})$ be an $n \times n$ matrix. Then $S_{k,m}(M)$ denotes the $k \times m$ matrix that is obtained from $M$ by deleting rows $k+1, \ldots, n$ and columns

$m+1,\ldots,n$, where $k,m \leq n$. That is, $S_{k,m}(M) = (m_{ij})$; $i = 1,\ldots,k$ and $j = 1,\ldots,m$.

□

Using the notation introduced in the last definition, not only the concept of graph isomorphism but also subgraph isomorphism can be described in terms of adjacency matrices. Let $G_1$ and $G_2$ be graphs with adjacency matrices $M_1$ and $M_2$ of dimension $m \times m$ and $n \times n$, respectively, where $m \leq n$. There is a subgraph isomorphism from $G_1$ to $G_2$ if there is an $n \times n$ permutation matrix $P$ such that

$$M_1 = S_{m,m}(PM_2P^T). \tag{3}$$

Thus, the problem of finding a subgraph isomorphism from $G_1$ to $G_2$ is equivalent to finding a permutation matrix $P$ for which (3) holds. Notice that

$$S_{m,m}(PM_2P^T) = S_{m,n}(P)M_2(S_{m,n}(P))^T.$$

### 5.2. Subgraph Isomorphism by Means of Decision Trees

We assume again that there is a set of model graphs that are known *a priori* and an input graph that becomes accessible at run time only. For each model graph we compute all possible permutations of its adjacency matrix and transform these adjacency matrices into a decision tree. At run time, the matrix of the input graph is then used to find those adjacency matrices in the decision tree that are identical to it. The permutation matrices that correspond to these adjacency matrices represent the graph or subgraph isomorphisms that we are looking for.

Let $G = (V, E, \mu, \nu)$ be a model graph and $M$ its corresponding $n \times n$-adjacency matrix. Furthermore, let $A(G)$ denote the set of all permuted adjacency matrices of $G$,

$$A(G) = \{M_P | M_P = PMP^T \text{ where } P \text{ is an } n \times n \text{ permutation matrix}\} \tag{4}$$

Now the subgraph isomorphism problem can be restated in terms of $A(G)$. For a model graph $G$ with corresponding $n \times n$-adjacency matrix $M$ and an input graph $G_I$ with an $m \times m$-adjacency matrix $M_I$ and $m \leq n$, we want to determine whether there exists a matrix $M_P \in A(G)$ such that $M_I = S_{m,m}(M_P)$. If such a matrix $M_P$ exists, the permutation matrix $P$ corresponding to $M_P$ describes a subgraph isomorphism from $G_I$ to $G$, i.e. $M_I = S_{m,m}(M_P) = S_{m,m}(PMP^T)$. If $G$ and $G_I$ are of equal size, the permutation matrix $P$ represents a graph isomorphism between $G_I$ and $G$, i.e. $M_I = PMP^T$.

Apparently, the set $A(G)$ can be organized in a decision tree. The features that will be used for the classification process are the individual elements in the adjacency matrices, arranged in a particular way. We say that matrix $M$ consists of an array of so-called *row–column* elements $a_i$, where each $a_i$ is a vector of the form

$$a_i = (m_{1i}, m_{2i}, \ldots, m_{ii}, m_{i(i-1)}, \ldots, m_{i1})$$

The matrix can then be written as

$$M = (a_1, a_2, \ldots, a_n); \quad i = 1, \ldots, n.$$

Figure 13 illustrates the representation of an adjacency matrix $M$ by its row–column elements. Notice that the $a_i$'s are of different dimension, depending on $i$.

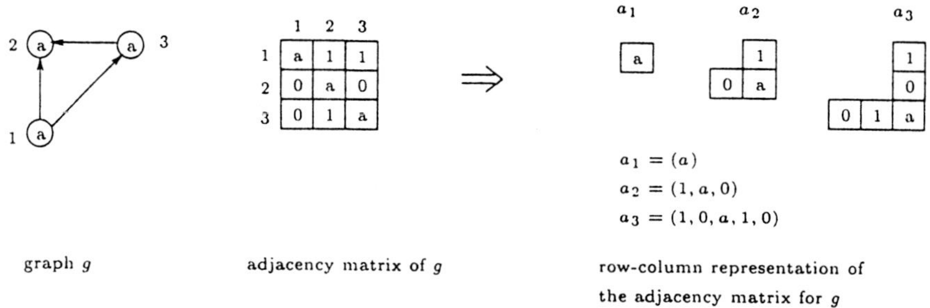


Fig. 13. The row–column representation of an adjacency matrix.

The decision tree for a model graph with adjacency matrix $M$ is now built according to the row–column elements of each adjacency matrix $M_P \in A(G)$. At the top of the decision tree there is a (dummy) root node. Its direct successors constitute the first level of the decision tree. On the first level, the classification is done by comparing the first row–column element of the input graph to the first row–column element $a_1$ of each matrix $M_P \in A(G)$. The element $a_1 = (m_{11})$ represents the label of the first vertex in each matrix in $A(G)$, with $m_{11} \in L_V$ (see Sec. 5.1). Thus, on the first level of the decision tree we simply check if the label of the first vertex of the input graph matches any of the vertex labels of the model graph. Next, on the second level of the decision tree, the second row–column element $a_2$ of each matrix is used for the classification. This means that we check if the label of the second vertex of the input graph and the edges between the second and the first vertex have identical occurrences in any of the model graphs. This process is continued on the subsequent levels in the decision tree. With each matrix $M_P$ that is represented by some node $N$ on level $k$, the corresponding permutation matrix $P$ is also stored. Finally, each leaf node at the bottom of the decision tree represents a set of identical matrices $M_P \in A(G)$. The number of these matrices is equal to the number of automorphisms of $G$.[b] For each matrix, the corresponding permutation matrix is stored.

In Fig. 14, a graph, $g_4$, and its corresponding decision tree is shown. The nodes of the decision tree are represented by shaded circles. Each directed branch from one node to another has a row–column element associated with it. At the top of Fig. 14 the set $A(g_4)$ of permuted adjacency matrices of $g_4$ is listed. It is easy to see that the number of automorphisms of $g_4$ is one. Therefore, each leaf node in the decision tree represents exactly one adjacency matrix.

[b] An automorphism is an isomorphism of a graph to itself.

$$A\ \begin{array}{ccc} 1 & 2 & 3 \\ \hline b & 1 & 1 \\ 0 & a & 1 \\ 0 & 0 & a \end{array} \quad B\ \begin{array}{ccc} 1 & 3 & 2 \\ \hline b & 1 & 1 \\ 0 & a & 0 \\ 0 & 1 & a \end{array} \quad C\ \begin{array}{ccc} 2 & 1 & 3 \\ \hline a & 0 & 1 \\ 1 & b & 1 \\ 0 & 0 & a \end{array} \quad D\ \begin{array}{ccc} 2 & 3 & 1 \\ \hline a & 1 & 0 \\ 0 & a & 0 \\ 1 & 1 & b \end{array} \quad E\ \begin{array}{ccc} 3 & 1 & 2 \\ \hline a & 0 & 0 \\ 1 & b & 1 \\ 1 & 0 & a \end{array} \quad F\ \begin{array}{ccc} 3 & 2 & 1 \\ \hline a & 0 & 0 \\ 1 & a & 0 \\ 1 & 1 & b \end{array}$$

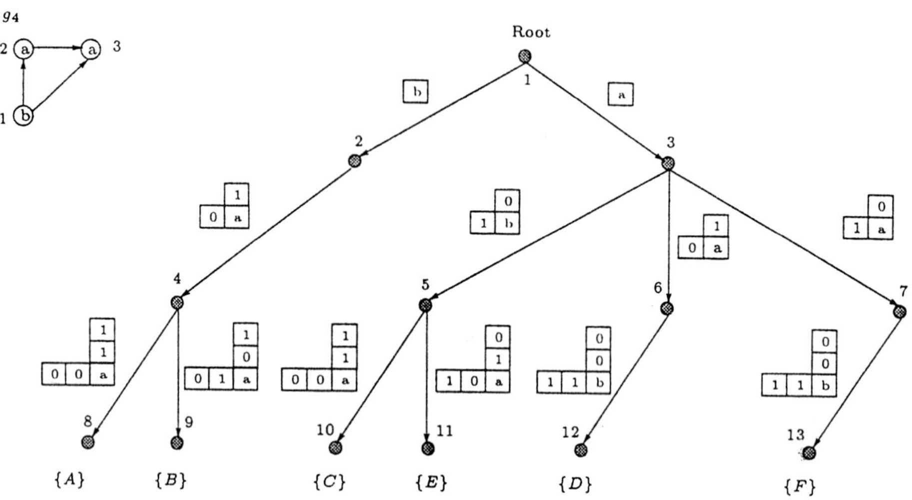


Fig. 14. Decision tree for the classification of the adjacency matrices $A, \ldots, F$ of the graph $g_4$.

An important requirement for a decision tree is that the classification on each level must be easily computable. Therefore, the successor which is reached via an element $a_k$ in the decision tree must be easily decidable. For this purpose, all row–column elements that are associated with the branches pointing from a node on level $k$ to a node on level $k+1$ are collected in a dictionary of strings. This dictionary is organized as an index structure with $2k+1$ indices. There are exactly $2k+1$ elements $m_{ij}$ in a row–column element $a_{k+1}$ and each of these elements is used as an index. Looking up an element in this dictionary can be done in $2k+1$ steps. Thus finding the successor node in the decision tree at level $k$ can be done in $O(2k+1) = O(k)$ steps. As an example, consider node 3 on level 1 of the decision tree in Fig. 14. There are three branches leading from node 3 to nodes 5, 6, and 7, respectively. The row–column elements associated with these branches are organized in a dictionary that is given in Fig. 15. In this example, a three-level index structure is required.

So far we have only discussed the structure of the decision tree with regard to a single model graph. If there are several model graphs in a database then the most trivial solution would be to build a decision tree individually for each of them. However, it is possible to represent several model graphs by the same decision tree. Given model graphs $G_1, G_2, \ldots G_L$, the corresponding sets $A(G_1), A(G_2), \ldots, A(G_L)$ can be treated as if they belonged to the same graph and integrated into the same decision tree. In Fig. 16 the decision tree for the graph $g_4$ of Fig. 14 and another graph, $g_5$, is displayed. The adjacency matrices in $A(g_5)$ are given at the top of

Fig. 16. Only two nodes have to be added to the decision tree that corresponds to the graph $g_4$. As there are three automorphisms of $g_5$, nodes 13 and 15 in Fig. 16 each represents exactly three adjacency matrices.

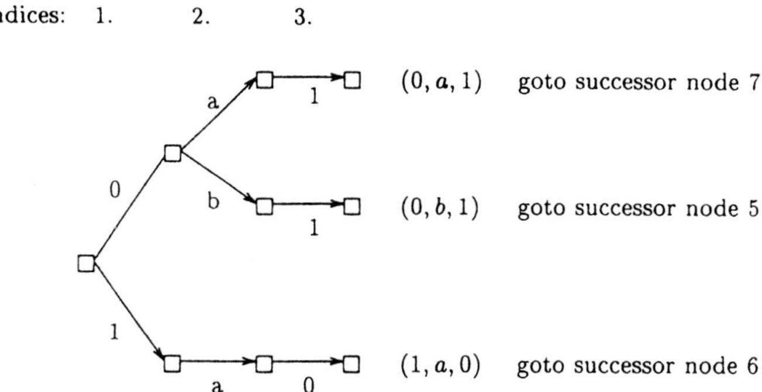


Fig. 15. Dictionary and index for the decision tree node 3 in Fig. 14.

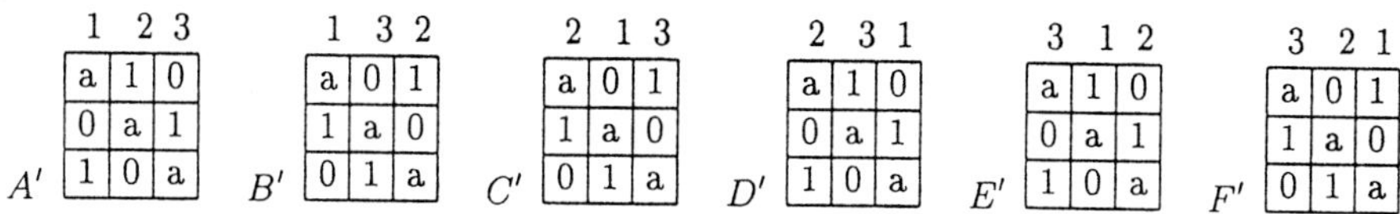


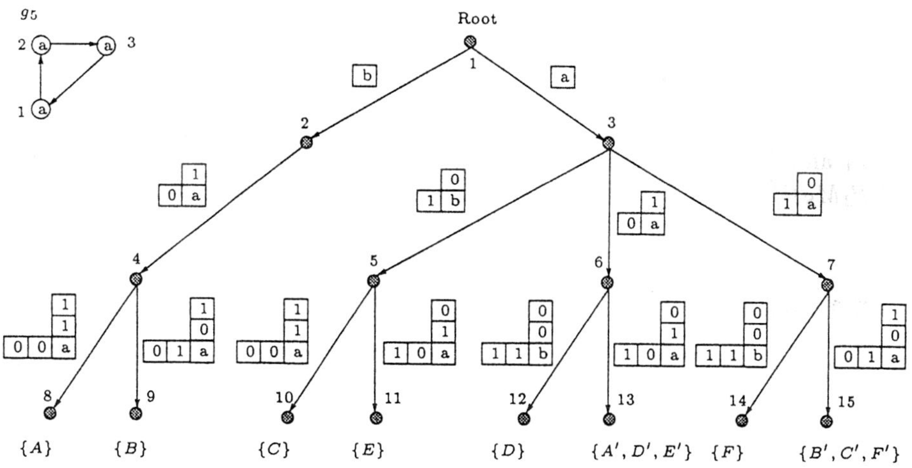


Fig. 16. Decision tree for the graph $g_4$ in Fig. 14 and another graph $g_5$.

At run time, a decision tree is used in order to classify the $m \times m$ adjacency matrix $M_I$ of an input graph $G_I$. The matrix $M_I$ is classified on the first level according to its row–column element $a_{1_I}$. If there is some branch $i$ from the root node to a successor node whose associated element $a_{1_i}$ matches $a_{1_I}$, the algorithm continues with the successor node on the second level, and so on. If at some point no classification is possible, then the input graph $G_I$ is not isomorphic to any subgraph of the model graphs. If each row–column element of $G_I$ has been used in the classification process and some node $N$ in the decision tree has been reached, then each permutation matrix that is associated with $N$ represents a subgraph isomorphism from the input graph to one of the model graphs. If node $N$ is a leaf node, i.e., the input graph and the model graph are of the same size, then each permutation matrix associated with $N$ describes a graph isomorphism between the input graph and one of the models.

In Ref. 34 the computational complexity of the decision tree method is analyzed. In this analysis, it was shown that the size of the decision tree that represents $L$ graphs with $n$ vertices each is $O(Ln^n)$. On the other hand, given an input graph with $m$ vertices, the time required for the tree traversal is only $O(m^2)$.

### 5.3. A More Efficient Representation of Decision Trees

The decision trees described in the last section are unnecessarily large. In this section, we introduce a more compact representation. It is based on the observation that at level $k$ in the decision tree, not only all subgraphs consisting of $k$ vertices are present, but also each of these subgraphs $S$ is represented $k!/\alpha$ times, where $\alpha$ denotes the number of different automorphisms of $S$. For example, in Fig. 14, the subgraph of $g_4$ consisting of the vertices 1 and 2 has two adjacency matrices and is therefore represented twice in the decision tree, namely, by the matrix $\binom{b\ 1}{0\ a} = S_{2,2}(A)$ in node 4 and by the matrix $\binom{a\ 0}{1\ b} = S_{2,2}(C)$ in node 5. Clearly, these representations are equivalent and this kind of redundancy can be avoided. As a result, a more compact representation of the decision trees is obtained.

Let $N_1$ and $N_2$ be nodes of the decision tree that both represent the same subgraph $S$ of a model graph $G$ and let $S$ be given by its adjacency matrix $M_S$. Furthermore, let $M_1$ and $M_2$ be the adjacency matrices belonging to $N_1$ and $N_2$, and $P_1$ and $P_2$ the corresponding permutation matrices such that $P_1 M_S P_1^T = M_1$ and $P_2 M_S P_2^T = M_2$. Then, there exists a permutation matrix $R$ such that

$$M_1 = R M_2 R^T \tag{5}$$

$R$ can be simply obtained as

$$R = P_1 P_2^T \tag{6}$$

because substituting $R$ in Eq. (5) by $P_1 P_2^T$ and also substituting $M_2$ by $P_2 M_S P_2^T$ yields $P_1 P_2^T (P_2 M_S P_2^T)(P_1 P_2^T)^T = P_1 M_S P_1^T = M_1$. Therefore, the adjacency matrix represented in node $N_2$ can be transformed, by means of the matrix $R$, into a matrix that is represented in $N_1$. The most important conclusion from this observation is that it is not necessary to create successor nodes of node $N_2$ in the decision tree. Instead, it is sufficient to introduce a pointer from $N_2$ to $N_1$ that indicates that, whenever decision tree node $N_2$ is reached, the search is to be continued with the successors of $N_1$. Such a pointer will be called a *redirecting branch.* Associated with a redirecting branch is the permutation matrix $R$. In general, for a subgraph $S \subset G$, we choose from the set of decision tree nodes that represent $S$, an arbitrary node $T$ and insert redirecting branches from all the other nodes to $T$. Consequently, only one of the decision tree nodes representing $S$ will be used for the further decision tree traversal. A procedure for compiling a decision tree, including redirecting branches, is described in Ref. 34.

In Fig. 17, the decision tree for the graphs $g_4$ and $g_5$ is displayed. There are two redirecting branches in this decision tree (denoted by dotted lines). Associated with both branches is the permutation matrix $\begin{pmatrix} 0 & 1 \\ 1 & 0 \end{pmatrix}$. When this permutation matrix is applied to the $2 \times 2$ submatrices $S_{2,2}(A)$, $S_{2,2}(B)$ and $S_{2,2}(D)$ of $g_4$, the matrices $S_{2,2}(C)$, $S_{2,2}(E)$ and $S_{2,2}(F)$ result. For the graph $g_5$, the redirecting branch transforms the matrices $S_{2,2}(A')$, $S_{2,2}(D')$ and $S_{2,2}(E')$ into the matrices $S_{2,2}(C')$, $S_{2,2}(F')$ and $S_{2,2}(B')$. Notice that by means of the redirecting branches it is possible to save three decision tree nodes.

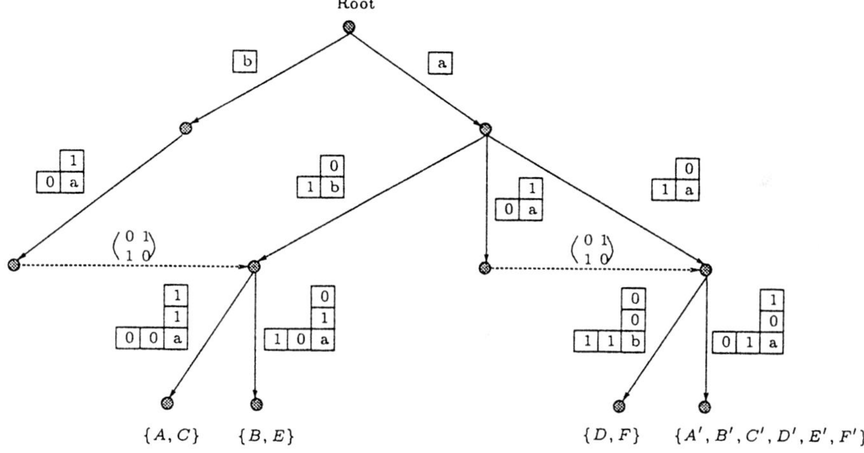


Fig. 17. Compact decision tree for the classification of the adjacency matrices $\{A, \ldots, F\}$ and $\{A', \ldots, F'\}$ of the graphs $g_4$ and $g_5$, respectively (see also Figs. 14 and 16).

So far, we have only discussed the compilation of decision trees for single model graphs. However, the general structure of a decision tree is independent of the number of model graphs that are classified by the tree. Therefore, a decision tree can be extended and used for any number of model graphs in the database. The technique for decision tree construction introduced in this section reduces the space complexity of a decision tree from $O(Ln^n)$ (see Sec. 5.2) to $O(L3^n)$.[34]

### 5.4. Further Pruning Strategies

Without loss of generality, we can require that the vertices of the input graph are ordered such that each vertex is connected to at least one other vertex that appears earlier in the ordering. For the adjacency matrix of the input graph, given as a vector of row column elements $(a_1, \ldots, a_m)$, this means that each row–column element $a_i$ contains at least two non-zero entries. It is straightforward to show that the adjacency matrix of any connected graph can be transformed such that the above condition holds. This problem is equivalent to finding a spanning tree of a graph and can be solved in quadratic time.[36] We can then reduce the number of permutated adjacency matrices $A(G)$ that must be classified by the decision tree. Namely, all permutations of the model matrix for which the above condition does not hold, may be discarded at compilation time. For graphs with a low degree of connectivity, the number of decision tree nodes that are pruned by this technique can be very high. As the transformation of the input graph has only quadratic time complexity, the graph isomorphism algorithm based on the pruned decision tree has the same computational complexity as before. Also, both graph and subgraph isomorphism detection are still supported by a decision tree that was subject to this type of breadth-pruning.

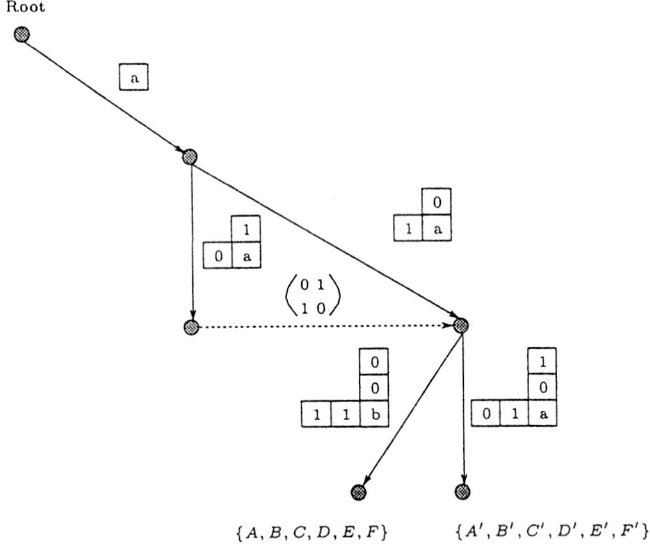


Fig. 18. The decision tree of Fig. 17 (for the graph $g_4$ and $g_5$) after breadth-pruning was performed.

Another technique for pruning a decision tree is based on the following observation. Let $M_I = (a_1, \ldots, a_m)$ be the adjacency matrix of an input graph $G_I$. Assume that $M_I$ is to be classified by a decision tree that was built for a model graph $G$. Furthermore, assume that $M_I$ has been classified up to the level $k$ and node $N$ is the current node in the decision tree. In the next step, the algorithm will try to find a successor node of $N$ according to the $k+1$th element of $M_I$, $a_{k+1}$. Note that there are exactly $(m-k)!$ different permutation matrices of $G_I$ for which the first $k$ row–column elements $(a_1, \ldots, a_k)$ are identical. Consequently, when $M_I$ has been classified up to the element $a_k$, there are in fact $m-k$ different successor nodes, each representing a permutation of $M_I$ for which the element $a_{k+1}$ is different but the elements $a_1, \ldots, a_k$ are identical. Therefore, a modified version of the graph isomorphism algorithm may rotate the $m-k$ last columns and rows of the input matrix $M_I$ and try each of the $m-k$ row–column elements $a_{k+1}$ in order to classify the matrix. Naturally, in a complete decision tree, each of the row–column elements will allow a successful classification. However, with the modified version of the graph isomorphism algorithm it is no longer necessary to incorporate all $m-k$ successors, but it is sufficient to build a single successor node. The modified algorithm will still be able to classify the input matrix by trying all $m-k$ possible rotations of the last rows and columns of the input matrix.

If this pruning scheme is applied on each level of the decision tree, then the number of nodes in the tree will be reduced by a factor of $n$, where $n$ indicates the total number of vertices in the model graph. Hence, in the case of $L$ unlabeled, undirected graphs, the size of the decision tree will be bounded by $O(L3^n/n)$. The computational complexity of the graph isomorphism algorithm, on the other hand, is increased by a factor of $I$ due to the permutations of the input matrix which must be performed on each level of the decision tree. Thus, the run time complexity of the new algorithm for undirected, unlabeled graphs on the basis of a pruned decision tree is bounded by $O(m^3)$. The main drawback of this type of breadth-pruning technique, however, is that the resulting decision tree can only be used for graph isomorphism and no longer for subgraph isomorphism detection.

In Fig. 18, the decision tree for the graphs $g_4$ and $g_5$ of Fig. 17 is displayed after pruning has been applied. Pruning reduces the size of the decision tree remarkably. Note that the left branch departing from the root node is no longer necessary since all adjacency matrices can be classified by the right branch at the expense of reordering the vertices. Consequently, the decision tree now contains only 6 nodes instead of 11. Additional pruning techniques are discussed in Ref. 34.

### 5.5. Experimental Results

In order to examine the efficiency of the new algorithm in practice, we performed a number of experiments with randomly generated graphs. All the experiments documented in this section are concerned with graph isomorphism detection and the underlying decision trees were subject to pruning as described in Sec. 5.4. For each experiment, we generated one or more model graphs and used these model graphs to create isomorphic input graphs. All of the graphs generated for the experiments were undirected and unlabeled. The decision tree algorithm was implemented in C++ and run on a SUN Sparc10 workstation. In order to assess its performance, we defined a basic computation step to be the comparison of one model graph vertex and its incident edges to one input graph vertex and its incident edges. The performance was then measured by counting the number of basic computation steps that were executed while searching for all graph isomorphisms. Additionally, we measured the absolute computation times of both algorithms. Each experiment was repeated ten times for different permutations of the vertices of the model and the input graphs and the average number of computation steps and times were taken. The size of the decision tree in terms of the number of nodes was also recorded for each experiment. For the purpose of comparison, we ran the same experiments with Ullman's algorithm.

In the first experiment, we wanted to investigate the run time efficiency of the decision tree algorithm, but also its limits with regard to the size of the graphs

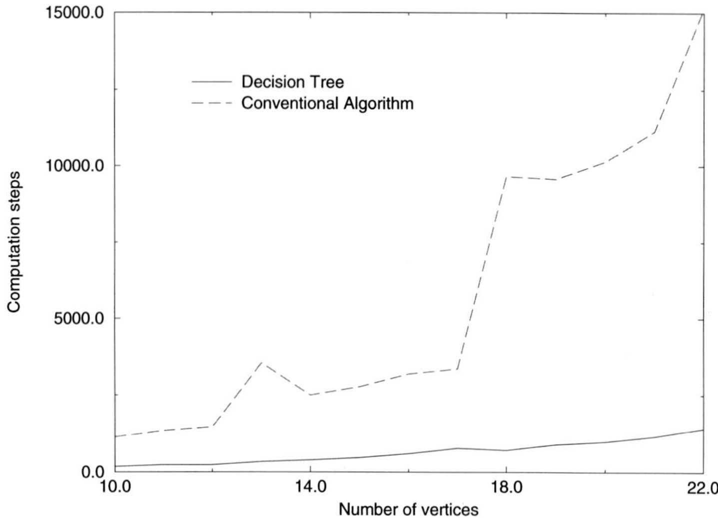


Fig. 19. Computation steps for a growing number of vertices (first experiment).

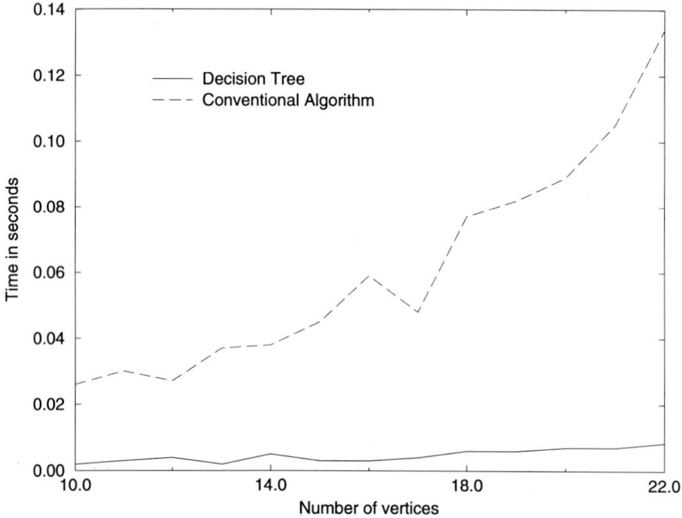


Fig. 20. Computation time in seconds for a growing number of vertices (first experiment).

that can be handled. For this purpose, we randomly generated a sequence of model graphs with a growing number of vertices. A copy of each model graph with randomly permuted vertices was used as an input graph. We started with a graph consisting of 10 vertices and 15 edges and ended up with a graph consisting of 22 vertices and 33 edges. The number of computational steps that were needed by the new and the conventional algorithm in order to find all graph isomorphisms between the model and input graph are plotted in Fig. 19. The corresponding computation times are displayed in Fig. 20. Clearly, the new algorithm is much more efficient

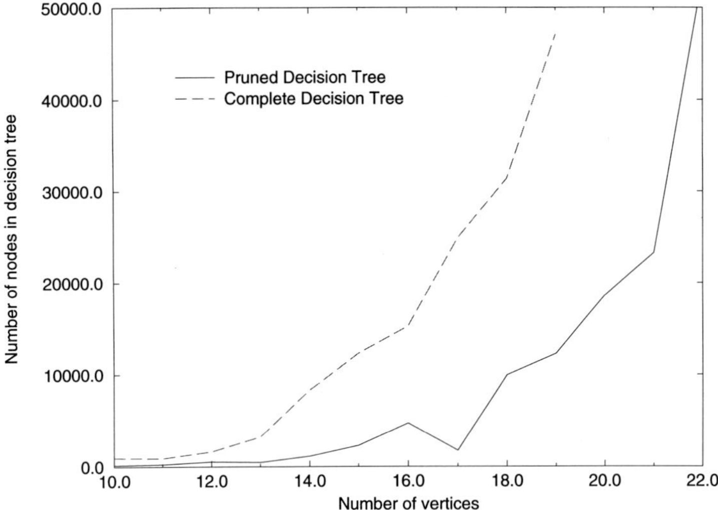


Fig. 21. Number of nodes in the decision tree for a growing number of vertices (first experiment).

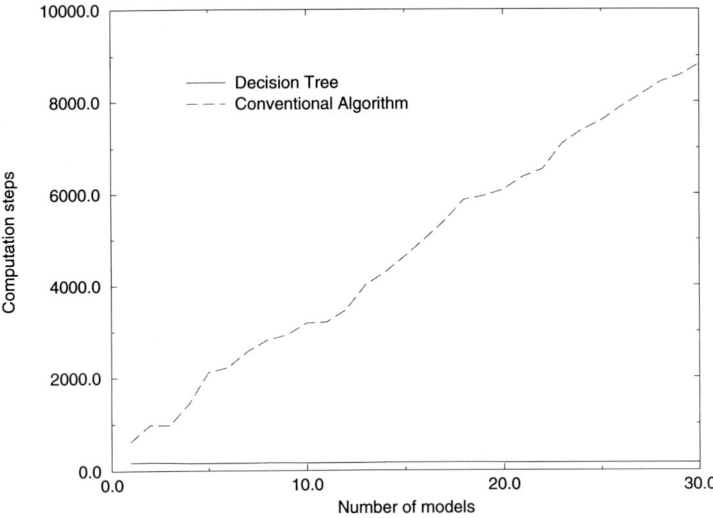


Fig. 22. Computation steps for a growing number of model graphs (second experiment).

than the backtracking algorithm, as predicted. Notice that the computation time for a graph with 22 vertices and 33 edges was ten times longer with the conventional algorithm than with the new algorithm.

The cost of the run time efficiency of the new algorithm is, however, the size of the decision tree. In Fig. 21, the number of nodes in the breadth-pruned and the complete decision tree for a growing number of vertices in the model graphs are displayed. The largest model graphs our implementation can deal with consist of 19 vertices when the underlying decision tree is complete and 22 vertices when the decision tree is pruned. The growth of the complete decision tree is clearly exponential. While there were only 174 nodes in a complete decision tree for a graph with 10 vertices, there were already 47,050 nodes in a tree for a graph with 19 vertices. The pruned decision tree, on the other hand, is much smaller, i.e., for a graph consisting of 19 vertices, there were only 12,207 nodes in the decision tree. A breadth-pruned decision tree consisting of 50,000 nodes can represent model graphs with up to 22 vertices, compared to only 19 vertices in the case of the complete decision tree. The compilation of a pruned decision tree for a model graph with 10 vertices took only two seconds, while for a model graph with 22 vertices roughly 30 minutes were needed.

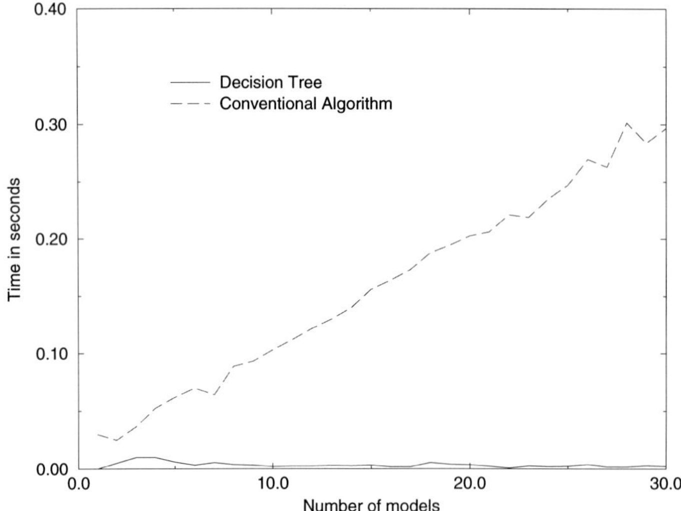


Fig. 23. Computation time in seconds for a growing number of model graphs (second experiment).

In the second experiment, we were interested in the influence of the database size on the performance of the new algorithm. We first generated a single model graph consisting of 11 vertices and 33 edges and then gradually added new model graphs of the same size until there were 30 graphs in the database. With every new model that was added to the existing database, a corresponding input graph was generated and the computational effort for finding all graph isomorphisms from the input graph to the model graphs in the database was measured. The results of the second experiment are documented in Figs. 22 and 23. As expected, the decision tree algorithm's performance was completely independent of the number of models in the database. The conventional algorithm, on the other hand, had to perform a graph isomorphism search for each model in the database individually and was, therefore, linearly dependent on the size of the database. While the computation time of the decision tree algorithm varied between 0.005 and 0.01 seconds, the conventional algorithm needed approximately 0.3 seconds for 30 model graphs.

From the computational complexity analysis, we expect that the size of the decision tree is linearly dependent on the number of model graphs. In practice,

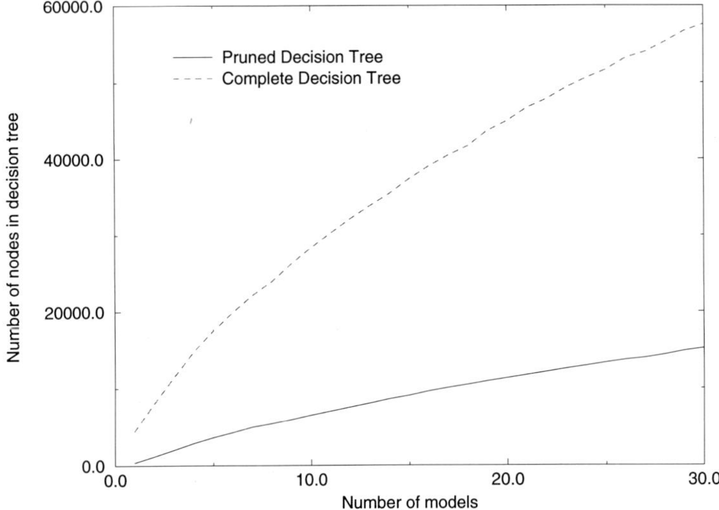


Fig. 24. Number of nodes in the decision tree for a growing number of model graphs (second experiment).

however, due to the fact that common subgraphs of different model graphs are represented by the same part of the decision tree, the size is usually only sublinearly dependent on the number of model graphs. In Fig. 24, this effect can be clearly observed. Consequently, with the run time being independent of the number of model graphs, the new algorithm is an interesting option for applications where graphs are restricted in size but the number of models is large. Further experiments are reported in Ref. 34.

## 6. CONCLUSIONS

In this paper we first briefly reviewed the existing literature on graph matching. Then, a new method for exact and error-tolerant subgraph isomorphism detection was introduced. This method is based on a compact network representation of model graphs. With several models in the database, the network represents identical subgraphs of the different model graphs only once, thus reducing the number of computational steps necessary in order to detect exact and error-tolerant subgraph isomorphisms from a model graph to an input graph. The efficiency of the new algorithm was analytically shown and practically demonstrated in experiments.

Furthermore, a new approach to subgraph isomorphism detection based on decision trees was proposed. Given a set of model graphs, a decision tree is generated that represents, for each model graph, all possible permutations of the vertices. At run time, the isomorphisms or subgraph isomorphisms from an input graph to all models can be found by a simple decision tree traversal. This approach has a time complexity that is only quadratic in the number of vertices of the input graph. Moreover, it is completely independent of the number of model graphs, and of the connectivity, i.e. the number of edges of the input graph and the models. However, the size of the decision tree grows exponentially with the size of the model graphs. In order to cut down the space complexity of a decision tree, different pruning techniques were discussed.

From the experiments reported in this paper, the following conclusions can be drawn. The decision which graph matching algorithm is best suited for a particular application depends on the size of the underlying graphs, the kind of labels that occur in the graphs, and the type of matching that is required. If the graphs (labeled or unlabeled) are small (up to 20 vertices) and exact graph or subgraph isomorphisms from the input to the models must be found then the decision tree method will perform best in terms of execution time. Otherwise, if the direction of matching is reversed, i.e. exact subgraph isomorphisms must be detected from the models to the input, then Ullman's algorithm or, in case of errors, an $A^*$ based algorithm must be used. If the model graphs and the input graph are of medium size (up to 500 vertices) and labeled (at least more than five different vertex or edge labels) then the decomposition based algorithm is expected to perform better than any conventional algorithm for both exact and error-tolerant graph and subgraph isomorphism detection from the models to the input. However, in case of unlabeled graphs and if subgraph isomorphisms must be found from the input to the models then it is again advisable to apply either Ullman's algorithm or an $A^*$ based method. Finally, in the case of very large graphs (more than 500 vertices) only approximate algorithms such as simulated annealing,[12] neural networks,[13,37] genetic algorithms[14] or probabilistic relaxation[16] will be able to solve the exact or error-tolerant graph matching problem in reasonable time, albeit at the cost of occasionally missing the optimal solution.

The graph matching algorithms described in this paper are very general and powerful. As a matter of fact, there are no problem dependent assumptions included. The nodes and edges of the underlying graph may represent anything, and there are no restrictions on the node and edge labels. Our distortion model consists of the deletion, insertion and substitution of both nodes and edges, which is powerful enough to model any type of error that may be introduced into an input graph. Adapting the error-tolerant matching algorithm to a particular application requires the solution of two concrete tasks. First, a suitable graph representation of the objects in the problem domain has to be developed. Secondly, appropriate costs of the graph-edit operations have to be found. It is anticipated that there are many applications where both tasks are not really difficult if a set of sample pattern is given.

There are a number of open problems in graph matching that deserve further research. Examples include the extension of the decision tree approach to error-tolerant matching, the parallelization of the algorithms presented in this paper, the learning of edit cost from a set of sample graphs, and the combination of optimal and approximate algorithms.

## ACKNOWLEDGEMENT

This work is part of a project of the Priority Program SPP IF, No: 5003-34285, funded by the Swiss National Science Foundation.

## REFERENCES

1. R. A. Wagner and M. J. Fischer, "The string-to-string correction problem", *J. of the Association for Computing Machinery* **21**, 1 (1974) 168–173.
2. H. Bunke, "Structural and syntactic pattern recognition", in *Handbook of Pattern Recognition and Computer Vision*, eds., C. H. Chen, L. F. Pau, and P. Wang, World Scientific Publ. Co. Singapore, 1993, pp. 163–209.
3. L. Shapiro, "Relational matching", in *Handbook of Pattern Recognition and Image Processing: Computer Vision*, ed. T. Y. Young, Academic Press, 1993, pp. 475–496.
4. M. R. Garey and D. S. Johnson, *Computers and Intractability: A Guide to the Theory of NP-Completeness*, Freeman and Company, 1979.
5. J. R. Ullman, "An algorithm for subgraph isomorphism", *J. of the Association for Computing Machinery* **23**, 1 (1976) 31–42.
6. R. Horaud and T. Skordas, "Stereo correspondence through feature grouping and maximal cliques", *IEEE Trans. on Pattern Analysis and Machine Intelligence* **PAMI11**, 11 (1989) 1168–1180.
7. H. Bunke and G. Allerman, "Inexact graph matching for structural pattern recognition", *Pattern Recognition Lett.* **1**, 4 (1983) 245–253.
8. M. A. Eshera and K. S. Fu, "A graph distance measure for image analysis", *IEEE Trans. on Systems, Man, and Cybernetics* **14**, 3 (1984) 398–408.
9. A. Sanfeliu and K. S. Fu, "A distance measure between attributed relational graphs for pattern recognition", *IEEE Trans. on Systems, Man, and Cybernetics* **13** (1983) 353–363.
10. W. H. Tsai and K. S Fu, "Error-correcting isomorphisms of attributed relational graphs for pattern recognition", *IEEE Trans. on Systems, Man, and Cybernetics* **9** (1979) 757–768.
11. N. J. Nilsson, *Principles of Artificial Intelligence*, Tioga, Palo Alto, 1980.
12. L. Herault, R. Horaud, F. Veillon, and J. J. Niez, "Symbolic image matching by simulated annealing", in *Proc. British Machine Vision Conf.*, Oxford, 1990, pp. 319–324.
13. J. Feng, M. Laumy, and M. Dhome, "Inexact matching using neural networks", in *Pattern Recognition in Practice IV: Multiple Paradigms, Comparative Studies and Hybrid Systems*, eds., E. S. Gelsema and L. N. Kanal, North-Holland, 1994, pp. 177–184.
14. K. A. De Jong and W. M. Spears, "Using genetic algorithms to solve NP-complete problems", in *Genetic Algorithms*, ed. J.D. Schaffer, Morgan Kaufmann, 1989, pp. 124–132.
15. P. Kuner and B. Ueberreiter, "Pattern recognition by graph matching — combinatorial versus continuous optimization", *Int. J. of Pattern Recognition and Artificial Intelligence* **2**, 3 (1988) 527–542.
16. W. J. Christmas, J. Kittler, and M. Petrou, "Structural matching in computer vision using probabilistic relaxation", *IEEE Trans. on Pattern Analysis and Machine Intelligence* **PAMI17**, 8 (1995) 749–764.
17. S. W. Lu, Y. Ren, and C. Y. Suen, "Hierarchical attributed graph representation and recognition of handwritten Chinese characters", *Pattern Recognition* **24** (1991) 617–632.

18. J. Rocha and T. Pavlidis, "A shape analysis model with applications to a character recognition system", *IEEE Trans. on Pattern Analysis and Machine Intelligence* **16**, 4 (1994) 393–404.
19. S. W. Lee, J. H. Kim, and F. C. A. Groen, "Translation- rotation- and scale invariant recognition of hand-drawn symbols in schematic diagrams", *Int. J. of Pattern Recognition and Artificial Intelligence* **4**, 1 (1990) 1–15.
20. A. Pearce, T. Caelli, and W. F. Bischof, "Rulegraphs for graph matching in pattern recognition", *Pattern Recognition* **27**, 9 (1994) 1231–1246.
21. E. Gmuer and H. Bunke, "3D object recognition based on subgraph matching in polynomial time", in *Structural Pattern Analysis*, eds., R. Mohr, T. Pavlidis, and A. Sanfeliu, World Scientific, 1990, pp. 131–147.
22. E. K. Wong, "Three-dimensional object recognition by attributed graphs", in *Syntactic and Structural Pattern Recognition — Theory and Applications*, eds., H. Bunke and A. Sanfeliu, World Scientific, 1990, pp. 381–414.
23. J. K. Cheng and T. S. Huang, "Image recognition by matching relational structures", in *IEEE PRIP*, 1981, pp. 542–547.
24. A. W. Wong, S. W. Lu, and M. Rioux, "Recognition and shape synthesis of 3D objects based on attributed graphs", *IEEE Trans. on Pattern Analysis and Machine Intelligence* **PAMI11**, 3 (1989) 279–290.
25. M. S. Costa and L. G. Shapiro, "Analysis of scenes containing multiple non-polyhedral 3D objects", in *Lectures Notes in Computer Science 974: Image Analysis and Processing*, eds., C. Braccini, L. DeFloriani, and G. Vernazza, Springer Verlag, 1995.
26. H. Bunke, T. Glauser, and T.-H. Tran, "Efficient matching of dynamically changing graphs", in *Theory and Applications of Image Analysis*, eds., P. Johansen and O. Olsen, World Scientific Publ., 1992, pp. 110–124.
27. A. Sanfeliu, K. S. Fu, and J. M. S. Prewitt, "An application of a graph distance measure to the classification of muscle tissue patterns", *Int. J. of Pattern Recognition and Artificial Intelligence* **1**, 1 (1987) 17–42.
28. W. F. Bischof and T. Caelli, "Learning structural descriptions of patterns: A new technique for conditional clustering and rule generation", *Pattern Recognition* **27**, 5 (1994) 689–699.
29. T. Caelli and W. Bischof, "The role of machine learning in building image interpretation systems", published in this volume.
30. D. J. Cook and L. B. Holder, "Substructure discovery using minimum description length and background knowledge", *J. of Artificial Intelligence Research*, 1994, pp. 231–255.
31. B. T. Messmer and H. Bunke, "Automatic learning and recognition of graphical symbols in engineering drawings", in *Proc. Int. Workshop on Graphics Recognition*, University Park, Pennsylvania, 1995, pp. 33–43.
32. C. L. Forgy, "Rete, a fast algorithm for the many pattern/many object pattern match problem", in *Artificial Intelligence* **19** (1982) 17–37.
33. H. S. Lee and M. I. Schor, "Match algorithms for generalized Rete networks", *Artificial Intelligence*, 1992, pp. 255–270.
34. B. T. Messmer, "Efficient graph matching algorithms for preprocessed model graphs", Ph.D. thesis, Institut für Informatik und angewandte Mathematik, Universität Bern, Switzerland, 1995.
35. B. T. Messmer and H. Bunke, "Subgraph isomorphism detection in polynomial time on preprocessed model graphs", in *Proc. of the Asian Conf. on Computer Vision ACCV*, 1995, pp. 151–155.
36. S. Even, *Graph Algorithms*, Pitman Publ., 1979.

37. L. Xu and E. Oja, "Improved simulated annealing, Boltzmann machine, and attributed graph matching", in *Lecture Notes in Computer Science 412*, ed., L. Almeida, Springer Verlag, 1990, pp. 151–161.

---

**Horst Bunke** received his M.S. and Ph.D. degrees in computer science from the University of Erlangen, Germany in 1974 and 1979, respectively. He was a member of the scientific staff at the University of Erlangen from 1974 to 1984. From 1980 to 1981 he was on a postdoctoral leave visiting Purdue University, West Lafayette, Indiana, and in 1983 he held a temporary appointment at the University of Hamburg, Germany. In 1984, he joined the University of Bern, Switzerland, where he is a full professor in the computer science department. He was department chairman from 1992–1996. In 1997 he became dean of the Faculty of Science at the University of Bern. Professor Bunke held visiting positions at the IBM Los Angeles Scientific Center (1989), the University of Szeged, Hungary (1991), the University of South Florida at Tampa (1991 and 1996), the University of Nevada at Las Vegas (1994), and the Kagawa University, Takamatsu, Japan (1995).

Professor Bunke is a Fellow of the International Association for Pattern Recognition (IAPR), editor-in-charge of the *International Journal of Pattern Recognition and Artificial Intelligence*, and editor-in-chief of the book series on *Machine Perception and Artificial Intelligence*. From 1982 to 1986 he was the chairman of the technical committee on Structural and Syntactic Pattern Recognition of the IAPR. He was on the program and organization committee of many conferences and served as a referee for numerous journals and scientific organizations.

He has about 300 publications, including 16 books. He is a member of the AAAI, the IEEE Computer Society, the Pattern Recognition Society, the European Association for Signal Processing, and other scientific organizations. His current interests include pattern recognition, machine vision, and artificial intelligence.

**Bruno Messmer** is an artificial intelligence expert currently working for Swiss Telecom in the domain of network planning, design and optimization.

His main interests include graph matching, pattern recognition, case-based reasoning and search algorithms. In 1992, he received his masters in computer science from the University of Bern for his work on applying the RETE algorithm to graph matching. For this work, he won the 1992 IBM Switzerland artificial intelligence prize. After having worked for one year in a software company designing financial real-time applications, he continued his work on graph matching at the University of Bern. In 1995, he received a Ph.D. in computer science for developing new algorithms for efficient graph matching.

Dr. Messmer has published over 15 articles. He has also implemented a general graph matching toolkit in C++ that has been integrated in a number of different applications.

# COOPERATIVE SPATIAL REASONING FOR IMAGE UNDERSTANDING

TAKASHI MATSUYAMA
*Department of Electronics and Communication*
*Kyoto University, Sakyo, Kyoto 606-01, Japan*

TOSHIKAZU WADA
*Department of Information Technology, Okayama University*
*Tsushima Naka, Okayama 700, Japan*

*Spatial Reasoning*, reasoning about spatial information (i.e. shape and spatial relations), is a crucial function of image understanding and computer vision systems. This paper proposes a novel spatial reasoning scheme for image understanding and demonstrates its utility and effectiveness in two different systems: region segmentation and aerial image understanding systems. The scheme is designed based on a so-called *Multi-Agent/Cooperative Distributed Problem Solving Paradigm*, where a group of intelligent *agents* cooperate with each other to fulfill a complicated task. The first part of the paper describes a cooperative distributed region segmentation system, where each region in an image is regarded as an agent. Starting from seed regions given at the initial stage, region agents deform their shapes dynamically so that the image is partitioned into mutually disjoint regions. The deformation of each individual region agent is realized by the snake algorithm[14] and neighboring region agents cooperate with each other to find common region boundaries between them. In the latter part of the paper, we first give a brief description of the cooperative spatial reasoning method used in our aerial image understanding system SIGMA. In SIGMA, each recognized object such as a house and a road is regarded as an agent. Each agent generates hypotheses about its neighboring objects to establish spatial relations and to detect missing objects. Then, we compare its reasoning method with that used in the region segmentation system. We conclude the paper by showing further utilities of the Multi-Agent/Cooperative Distributed Problem Solving Paradigm for image understanding.

*Keywords*: Spatial reasoning, cooperative distributed problem solving, multi agent system, image understanding, region segmentation, hypothesis and test analysis.

## 1. INTRODUCTION

A primary objective of *image understanding* is to construct a symbolic description of the scene depicted in an image(s), while image processing transforms an image into another and pattern recognition classifies and labels objects represented by feature vectors. An image understanding system (IUS in short) analyzes an image(s) to *interpret* the scene in terms of the object models given to IUS as the knowledge about the world. Here the *interpretation* refers to the correspondence (i.e. mapping) between the description of the scene and the structure of the image. It associates objects in the scene (e.g. houses, roads) with *image features* segmented from the image (e.g. points, lines, regions). Once the description of the scene is constructed, computer systems can answer various queries about the scene (e.g. how many houses exist in the scene?), perform physical operations by controling robot manipulators



Spatial Computing: Issues in Vision, Multimedia and Visualization Technologies (1997) 205–227

(e.g. pick up and move physical objects), and if needed, generate explanations of the scene in natural languages. It is in this sense that we can say IUS *understands* the scene.

Generally speaking, the information used by IUSs can be classified into the following two types:

1. *Attributes*: intrinsic properties of objects such as color, texture, size, and shape.
2. *Relations*: relational constraints between objects such as spatial relations, *part-of* relations, and generalization/specialization relations.

Note that the shape information can be represented by either attributes or relations depending on applications; while moment features[1] and Fourier descriptors[2] characterize shape attributes of a region, the shape of a complex (e.g. articulated) object is represented structurally by using *part-of* relations.[3]

The success of our former aerial image understanding system[4] can be attributed to versatile image analysis modules which analyze various spectral and spatial attributes of segmented regions. This system, however, makes little use of relational information between objects, and hence its capability of *spatial reasoning*, reasoning based on spatial relations, is very limited. Most (statistical) pattern/image recognition systems share this limitation.

In the late 1970s, many IUSs with various spatial reasoning capabilities were developed.[5] They used spatial relations mainly in the *bottom-up* way. That is, consider a binary spatial relation $REL(O_1, O_2)$ between two object classes, $O_1$ and $O_2$: e.g. $FACING(HOUSE, ROAD)$. In the bottom-up analysis, this relation is used as a *constraint* to recognize object instances of these two classes:

1. First extract image features which satisfy intrinsic properties of $O_1$ and $O_2$, respectively. Suppose we have two sets of such image features: $\{a_1, a_2, ..., a_m\}$ for $O_1$ and $\{b_1, b_2, ..., b_n\}$ for $O_2$. They are considered as candidate object instances of $O_1$ and $O_2$, respectively.
2. Next select a pair of image features $(a_i, b_j)$ which satisfy the spatial relation $REL$. Recognize such pair(s) of image features as object instances of $O_1$ and $O_2$ and reject the others as errors.

In this bottom-up recognition scheme, relations are considered as constraints to *filter out* erroneous image features. This is the reasoning performed by relaxation labeling[6] and constraint filtering/satisfaction procedures.[7] Practical utilities of this scheme were shown by several modern IUSs,[8,9] where the probabilistic relaxation[6] was incorporated to determine the most plausible global interpretation: i.e. minimize a cost function associated with a network of constraints.

As the complexity of scenes increases, however, the purely bottom-up spatial reasoning scheme finds its limitation. That is, the scheme assumes that all meaningful image features are extracted by the initial segmentation; while erroneous image features can be filtered out, no mechanism is supported to detect new correct ones when they are missed by the initial segmentation. As is well known, however, this assumption is not valid in practical image understanding; missing image features as well as erroneous ones are inevitable because the image quality and complexity vary dynamically over an image and the information about local image quality and complexity is not available at the initial segmentation.

To overcome the limitation of the bottom-up spatial reasoning, modern IUSs[10-13] incorporated so-called *top-down hypothesis-and-test* analysis. It uses spatial relations to generate hypotheses about missing objects (i.e. predict their locations and (appearance) models) and activates the top-down image analysis (i.e. re-segmentation) to find image features corresponding to the missing objects.

The use of relations is very different in the two analysis processes: consistency examination in the bottom-up analysis and hypothesis generation in the top-down analysis. Although several IUSs[10-12] incorporated both these analysis processes, they had no unified reasoning scheme for integrating the bottom-up and top-down analyses. They used *ad hoc* rules to control the analysis processes.

In this paper, we propose a novel spatial reasoning scheme for image understanding and demonstrate its utility and effectiveness in two different systems: region segmentation and aerial image understanding systems. The scheme is designed based on a so-called *Multi-Agent/Cooperative Distributed Problem Solving Paradigm*, where a group of intelligent *agents* cooperate with each other to fulfill a complicated task. We will show that the agent cooperation realizes the flexible integration of bottom-up and top-down spatial reasoning processes.

The first part of the paper describes a cooperative distributed region segmentation system, where each region in an image is regarded as an agent. Starting from seed regions given at the initial stage, region agents generate hypotheses about their own goal states (i.e. expected region shapes) in parallel. Then neighboring region agents cooperate with each other to find common region boundaries between them. Following such cooperation, each region agent deforms its shape so that the image is partitioned into mutually disjoint regions. The region deformation is realized by the snake[14] algorithm.

In the latter part of the paper, we first give a brief description of the cooperative spatial reasoning method used in our aerial image understanding system SIGMA.[13] In SIGMA, each recognized object such as a house and a road is regarded as an agent which generates hypotheses about neighboring objects to establish spatial relations and to detect missing objects. Then we compare its reasoning method with that used in the region segmentation system.

We conclude the paper by showing further utilities of Multi-Agent/Cooperative Distributed Problem Solving Paradigm for image understanding.

## 2. COOPERATIVE DISTRIBUTED REGION SEGMENTATION SYSTEM

The goal of region segmentation is to partition an image into a group of mutually disjoint homogeneous regions. Many different algorithms for region segmentation have been proposed: Region merging(growing),[15-19] region splitting,[20] split and merge method,[21,22] and feature clustering.[23]

From a viewpoint of the information type discussed before, all these algorithms mainly use attributes of regions: examination of color and texture homogeneity, and evaluation of shape compactness and boundary smoothness. The relational constraint such as "a group of regions to be detected must form a disjoint union of the image space" is used only indirectly.

Here we propose a cooperative distributed region segmentation system which partitions an image by taking account of both attributes of, and spatial relations between, regions.

### 2.1. Agent Behavior

In our system, each region in an image is considered as an *agent*. It has a *temporary region* as its internal state and changes the state (i.e. deforms the shape) dynamically. A temporary region represents a singly connected component in an image (Fig. 1).

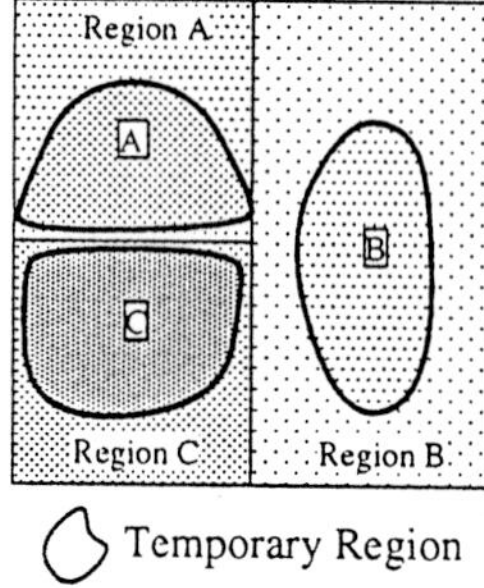


Fig. 1. Temporary regions.

We assume that at the initial stage a seed temporary region is placed well inside each target region to be detected. Such seed regions may be given by hand or extracted by an ordinary region segmentation method.

Each agent iterates the following processes to realize its dynamic shape deformation.

1. Region Boundary Estimation: Probe its surrounding environments and estimate the goal state (expected region boundary[a]). The environments include image data around its current temporary region and states (temporary regions) of neighboring agents. This process corresponds to the top-down hypothesis generation discussed before.
2. Generation of Intention and Cooperation with Other Agents: The estimated region boundary is considered as representing the intention of an agent; the agent is going to change its shape toward the estimated boundary. Disclose the intention to the other agents and examine the consistency between its intention and those generated by the others. Then, if needed, modify the intention to resolve the inconsistency. It is through this process that multiple agents cooperate with each other.

[a]Here we use 'boundary' to denote a dividing line between adjacent regions and 'contour' to denote an enclosing line of an isolated (temporary) region.

3. Shape Deformation: Change the state (i.e. deform the temporary region) based on the modified intention as well as the attributes of the current temporary region.

Note that since all information available at early stages (i.e. the shape and location of a temporary region, and the estimated region boundary) is not reliable, an agent should not deform its shape rapidly. Instead, it should iterate the above processes to realize the gradual shape evolution.

The following sections describe technical details of these processes.

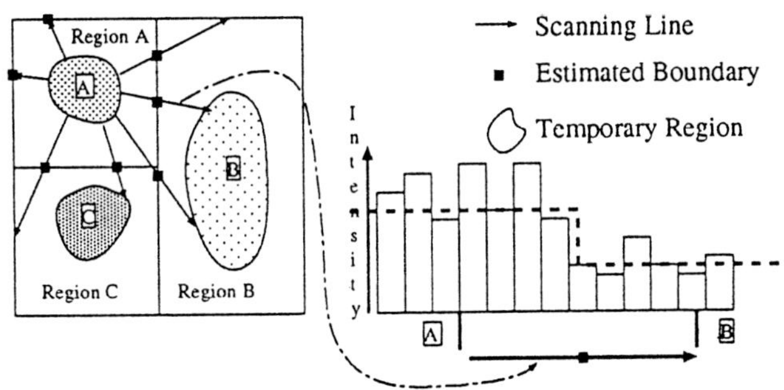


Fig. 2. Boundary estimation.

## 2.2. Boundary Estimation

Since each agent can assume that its temporary region is located well inside a target region, it first extends a group of *scanning lines* emanating right outward from its current temporary region contour[b] (Fig. 2). Then it locates a boundary point on each scanning line. Such a boundary point is the embodiment of a hypothesis generated based on the spatial relation between target regions: "there exists a common region boundary between two adjacent target regions".

Note that since this spatial relation holds only for target regions to be detected, hypotheses generated from a temporary region may not be correct. That is, a scanning line, first of all, may not reach at the correct neighboring temporary region. At the early stage of the shape deformation, especially, most of the hypotheses may be incorrect because temporary regions do not evolve close enough to their corresponding target regions.

Taking such possible incorrectness into account, scanning lines can be classified into the following three types, and different boundary point estimation methods are employed depending on their type:

- Type 1: A scanning line reaches at another temporary region. In this case, the agent assumes that the correct neighboring region is detected and locates the boundary point by fitting a step edge model to the intensity profile along the scanning line (Fig. 2).

[b]Where to locate starting points of the scanning lines will be described later.

- Type 2: A scanning line ends at the image frame. In this case, the agent also applies the same boundary point estimation method as above, assuming that the image frame is surrounded by a background region with zero intensity.
- Type 3: A scanning line crosses its own temporary region. This means that its starting point is located on a deep concave region contour. In this case, the agent regards the starting point of the scanning line as the boundary point.

### 2.3. Intention Line Generation

By connecting a set of detected boundary points, an estimated region boundary is formed, toward which a temporary region is going to deform. However, since each agent estimates the region boundary independently of the others, conflicts, i.e. gaps and overlaps, may be introduced among a group of estimated region boundaries (Fig. 3). In what follows, we describe how such conflicts are detected and resolved through the cooperation among agents.

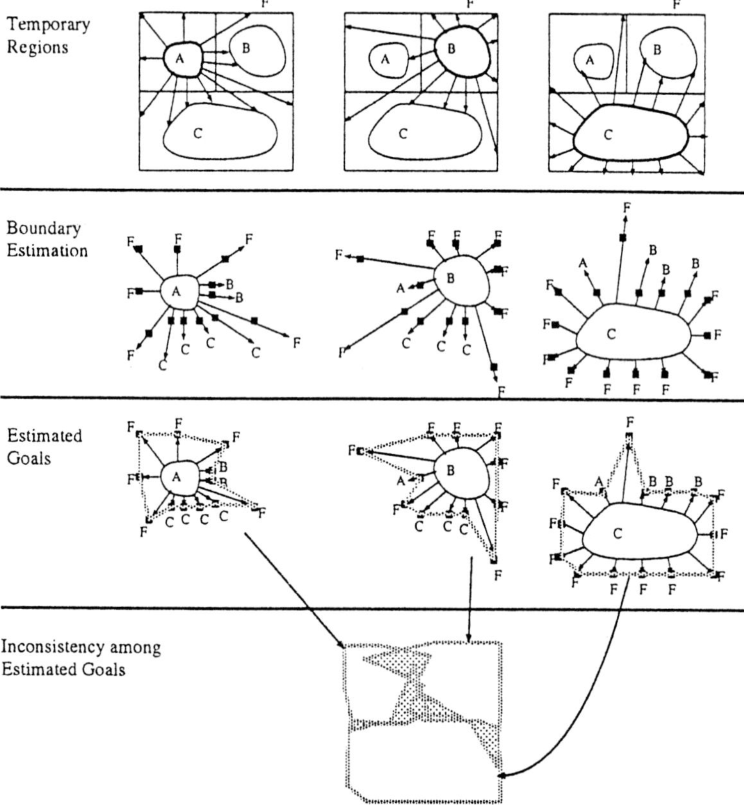


Fig. 3. Inconsistency among estimated region boundaries.

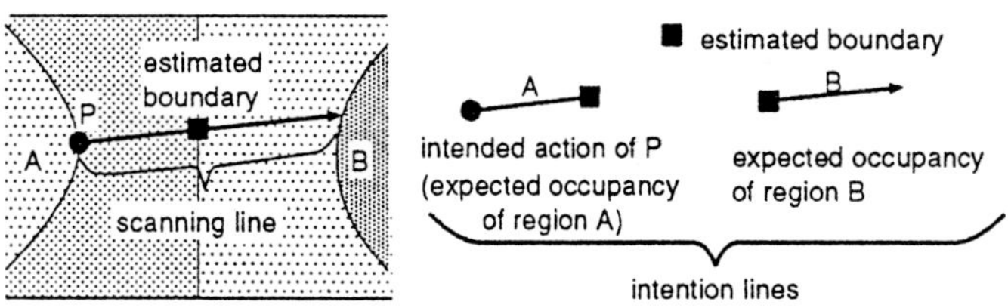


Fig. 4. Intention lines of an agent.

First, a scanning line is divided into a pair of segments at the estimated boundary point (Fig. 4): one from the source temporary region contour (A in Fig. 4) to the boundary point and the other from the boundary point to the neighboring temporary region contour (B in Fig. 4). We associate the former with the source agent label and call it the *intended action* of the source agent. Similarly, the latter associated with the neighboring agent label is called the *expected occupancy* of the neighboring agent:

Intended Action: The source agent intends to deform its temporary region contour toward the boundary point.

Expected Occupancy: The neighboring agent is expected to include this segment into its temporary region after deformation.

We call these two labeled segments *intention lines.* Note that if the source agent reaches the boundary point, the intended action segment will be included into its temporary region. Thus, the segment also represents the expected occupancy of the source agent.

## 2.4. Resolution of Conflicting Intention Lines

After computing intention lines, each agent discloses them to the others and examines the consistency between its own intention lines and those generated by the others. The following two types of inconsistency are detected:

Inconsistency between expected occupancies: This type of inconsistency is detected when intention lines with different agent labels intersect with each other. It means that the intersecting point is expected to be occupied by different agents simultaneously (Fig. 5).

Inconsistency between intended actions: This type of inconsistency is detected when multiple intended actions with the same agent label intersect. It means that the temporary region is expected to be twisted at the intersecting point (Fig. 6).

The inconsistency between expected occupancies is detected and resolved by the following process:

1. An agent traces each scanning line from its starting point to check if another intention line with a different agent label intersects.

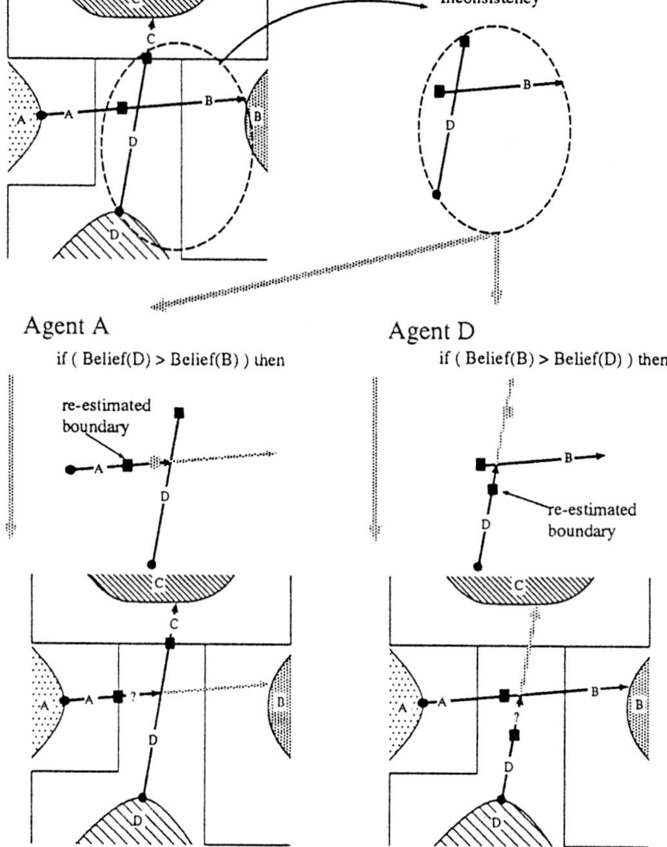


Fig. 5. Inconsistency resolution between intention lines.

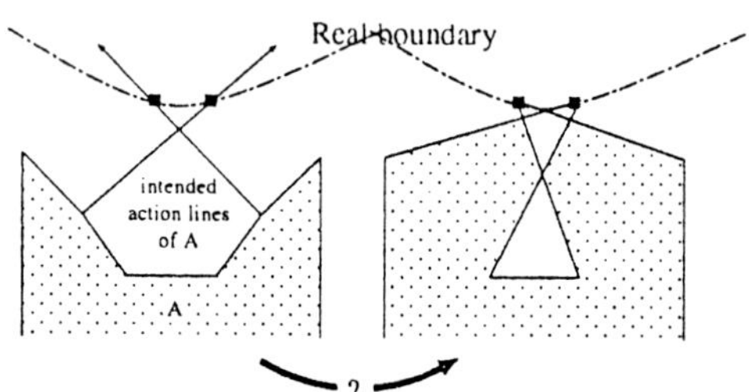


Fig. 6. Twisted region contour.

2. If such an intersection is detected, the agent compares reliability values of the pair of intersecting intention lines. Consider the situation illustrated in Fig. 5, where the expected occupancy labeled with B, which was generated by agent A, intersects with the intended action labeled with D. The reliability of the former $Belief(B)$ is defined by

$$\text{Belief(B)} = 1/\{\sum_i (I_i - < \textit{average intensity of temporary region } B >)^2\}$$

and that of the latter $Belief(D)$ by

$$\text{Belief(D)} = 1/\{\sum_j (I_j - < average\ intensity\ of\ temporary\ region\ D >)^2\},$$

where $I_i$ and $I_j$ denote intensity values along the expected occupancy segment labeled with B and those along the intended action segment labeled with D, respectively. Note that the inconsistency detection, the reliability computation, and the following inconsistency resolution are conducted by both agents A and D in parallel.

3. If $Belief(B)$ is less than $Belief(D)$, agent A, which generated the less reliable intention line, cuts off the scanning line at the intersecting point and locates a new boundary point on the shortened scanning line (The left column in Fig. 5). Then the agent takes this new boundary point as fixed and finishes the consistency examination of that scanning line. The rationale behind this processing is as follows. Since an intention line may intersect with other intention lines with different labels, an agent checks their intersection points sequentially along the scanning line, starting from the temporary region contour of the agent (Fig. 7). Such sequential processing guarantees that the newly detected boundary point by the above conflict resolution process can be considered as consistent with the other intention lines.

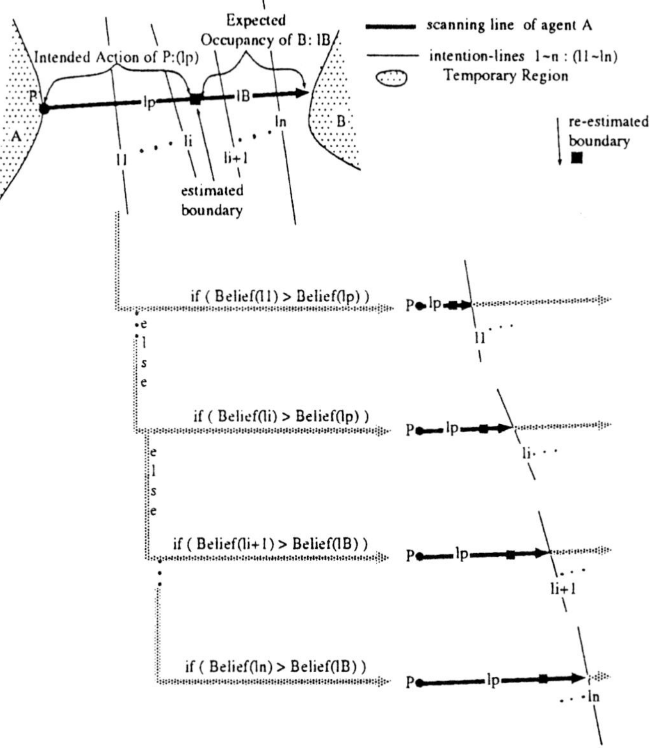


Fig. 7. Inconsistency resolution between multiple intention lines.

Inconsistency between intended actions, on the other hand, is resolved by the following process (Fig. 8). When an agent finds a pair of intersecting intended action segments with the same label, it cuts off the segments at the intersection point. This means that the agent considers the intersection point as the new boundary points on the two scanning lines, respectively. By this conflict resolution, the temporary region of the agent cannot be twisted even if its contour reaches the newly determined boundary point.

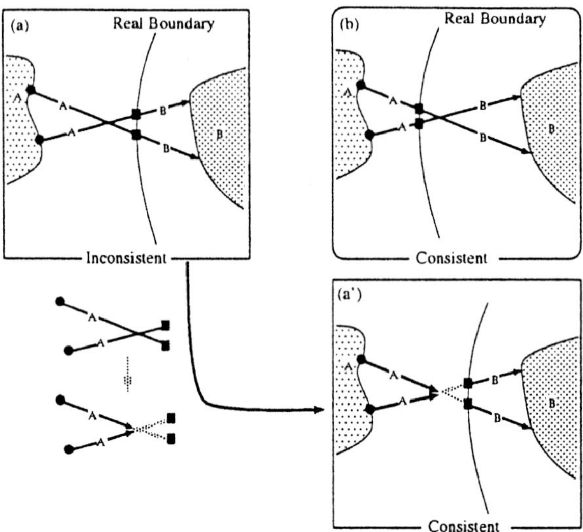


Fig. 8. Inconsistency resolution between intended actions.

## 2.5. Shape Deformation

When an agent finishes the consistency examination of all its intention lines, a set of consistent boundary points are obtained. Then, the agent deforms its temporary region based on its estimated boundary points as well as attributes of the current temporary region.

The temporary region deformation is realized by an algorithm based on the snake.[14] The snake is a deformable contour model to detect a region contour by minimizing an energy function $E_{snake}$ defined on the contour $\vec{v}(s) = (x(s),\ y(s))$ $(0 \leq s < 1)$. $E_{snake}$ is usually defined by the following equation:

$$E_{snake} = \int_0^1 E_{int}(\vec{v}(s)) + E_{image}(\vec{v}(s))\, ds, \tag{1}$$

where

$$E_{int} = (\alpha|\vec{v}_s(s)|^2 + \beta|\vec{v}_{ss}(s)|^2)/2, \tag{2}$$

$$E_{image} = (-|\nabla I(\vec{v}(s))|^2), \tag{3}$$

$$\vec{v}_s = d\vec{v}/ds,\ \vec{v}_{ss} = d^2\vec{v}/ds^2,$$
$\nabla I(\vec{v}(s))$ denotes the intensity gradient at $\vec{v}(s)$,
and $\alpha$, $\beta$ are weighting coefficients.

$E_{int}$ and $E_{image}$ are called *internal energy* and *image energy*, respectively. Minimization of the former makes the contour smooth and that of the latter forces the contour to move toward intensity edges in an image. Note that both of them are computed based on attributes of a temporary region.

In addition to these attribute-based energy functions, we introduce a new energy term $E_{grav}$ into $E_{snake}$, which is defined based on spatial relations to the other regions. That is, it is computed from the estimated region boundary. $E_{grav}$ is defined by the squared distance between a region contour point $\vec{v}(s)$ and the estimated boundary point $\vec{e}(s)$ on the scanning line emanating from $\vec{v}(s)$:

$$E_{grav}(\vec{v}(s)) = |\vec{e}(s) - \vec{v}(s)|^2 \ . \qquad (4)$$

We call this energy *intention energy*. By minimizing this energy function, the region contour is attracted toward the estimated region boundary.

In general, when an objective function to be minimized includes multiple component functions with different physical meanings, weighting coefficients such as $\alpha$ and $\beta$ in Eq. (2) are introduced to balance the component functions. In our case, for example, since $E_{int}$ and $E_{grav}$ compete with each other, some balancing weight should be introduced; the minimization of the former forces the contour to shrink[24] while that of the latter makes the contour expand. As is well known, however, it is hard to determine adequate values of weighting coefficients and the final result is often sensitive to the coefficient values.

In a complex problem, moreover, different weighting coefficients should be used adaptively depending on situations. In our case, when a region contour is wiggled due to noise, a large weight should be given to $E_{int}$ to prevent the contour from being twisted. On the other hand, a small weight should be given to $E_{int}$ for the contour to converge to a sharp corner. Similar arguments hold also for $E_{image}$: that is, while it should be ignored when a temporary region contour is far from the target region boundary, a large weight should be given to place the contour accurately when the contour is close to the boundary.

Ordinary snake-based algorithms[25] use *ad hoc* rules to adjust the coefficients, because they have no concrete basis to discriminate situations. In our system, on the other hand, we can use the estimated region boundary to characterize situations. First we define the *evolution level* $R(s)$ $(0 \leq R(s) \leq 1)$ for each contour point:

$$R(s) = |\vec{v}(s) - \vec{g}|/(|\vec{v}(s) - \vec{g}| + |\vec{e}(s) - \vec{v}(s)|) \ , \qquad (5)$$

where $\vec{g}$ denotes the location of the centroid of the initial temporary region. Note that at the initial stage $0 < R(s) << 1$ and at the final stage $R(s) \approx 1$ .

Then, using $R(s)$, we define $E_{snake}$ as follows:

$$E_{snake} = \int_0^1 (1 - R(s))E_{int}(\vec{v}(s)) + R(s)E_{image}(\vec{v}(s)) + E_{grav}(\vec{v}(s))\, ds. \qquad (6)$$

While at the initial stage, the internal and intention energies are dominant, the weight of the image energy is gradually increased as the shape evolution proceeds.

In addition to the dynamic balancing among the three component objective functions, we employ the following dynamic calibration of the coefficients $\alpha$ and $\beta$ used in $E_{image}$:

- First, make $\alpha$ and $\beta$ vary depending on locations on a region contour: i.e. represent them by $\alpha(s)$ and $\beta(s)$.
- Then, for such contour points where the internal product of a pair of force vectors generated by $E_{grav}$ and $E_{snake}$ becomes negative, decrease $\alpha(s)$ and $\beta(s)$ to weaken the shrinking force produced by $E_{int}$.
- For such contour points where the emanating scanning line reaches its own temporary region or the inconsistency between intended actions is detected, increase $\alpha(s)$ and $\beta(s)$ to remove the excessive concavity from the contour.

With these two coefficient adjustment mechanisms, we can solve the above mentioned problems.

In short, an estimated region boundary, which represents a hypothesis generated based on spatial relations to the other regions, plays two important roles in the shape deformation: one to introduce a relation-based component energy function $E_{grav}$ into $E_{snake}$ and the other to dynamically adjust weights of different component functions. This shows versatile utilities of the top-down hypothesis generation.

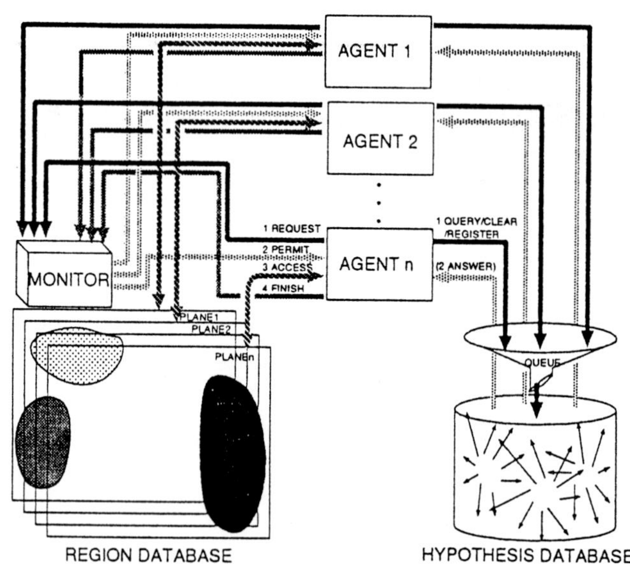


Fig. 9. System organization.

### 2.6. Experimental Results

We developed an experimental system on a UNIX work station, where each agent was implemented as a concurrent UNIX process and two shared databases were prepared to realize interactions among agents (Fig. 9):

Temporary region database: This database stores a group of bit planes. Each plane corresponds to an agent and records its temporary region. The monitor controls concurrent read/write requests from agents.

Intention line database: This database stores all intention lines generated by agents: their geometric attributes, IDs, agent labels, and reliability values. All read/write requests from agents are serialized by a queue.

Note that as is shown in Fig. 9, no direct communication between agents is required; agents cooperate with each other indirectly via their environments. That is, an agent observes its surrounding environments (i.e. the temporary region and intention line databases) and makes a coordinated action with the environments. Such action, in turn, changes environments of the other agents and leads them to cooperative actions.

Thus we can call our cooperation scheme *cooperation without direct communication.* It can be realized when agents (and hypotheses generated by them) have physical bodies (representations); agents can observe behaviors of other agents and understand their intentions without communications. This is in great contrast to ordinary communication-based cooperation mechanisms such as in Ref. 26.

Several artificial images such as shown in Fig. 10(a) and the real image in Fig. 10(c) were analyzed by the system.

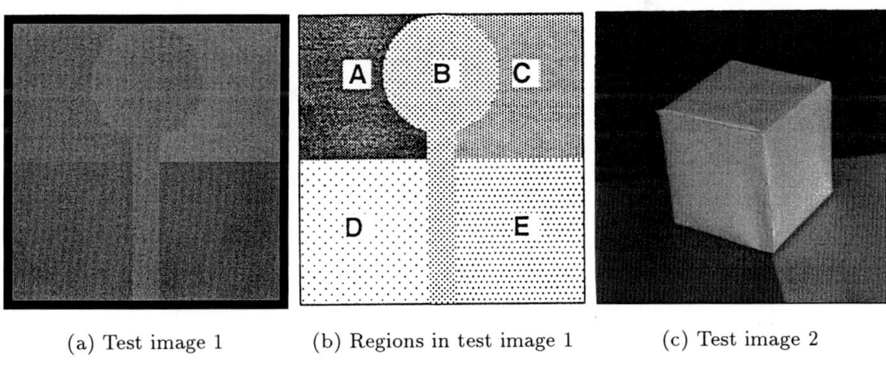


(a) Test image 1 (b) Regions in test image 1 (c) Test image 2

Fig. 10. Test images.

Figure 10(a) consists of five (target) regions as shown in Fig. 10(b). Intensities in the regions are randomly distributed over the following ranges, respectively:

Region A $110 \leq Intensity \leq 149$,
Region B $125 \leq Intensity \leq 164$,
Region C $140 \leq Intensity \leq 179$,
Region D,E $90 \leq Intensity \leq 139$.

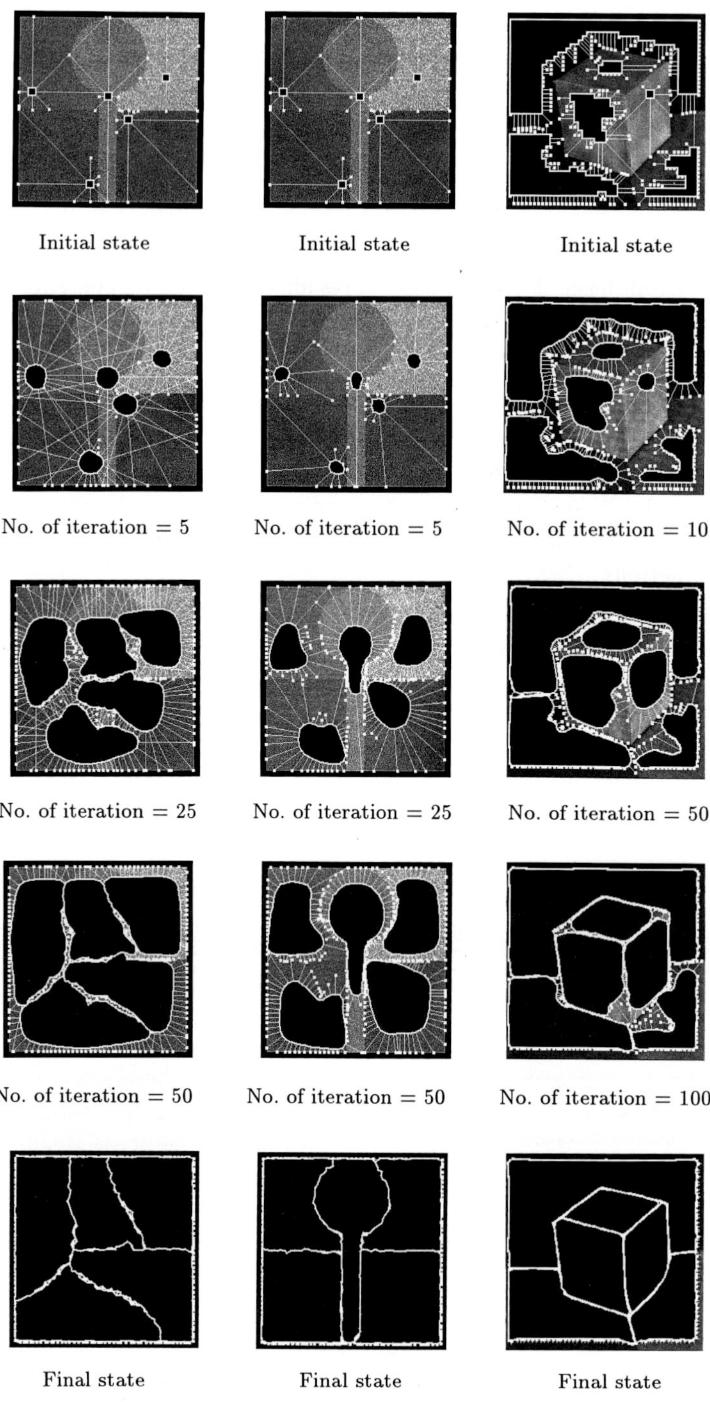


Fig. 11. Segmentation process for test image 1 (without agent cooperation).

Fig. 12. Segmentation process for test image 1 (with agent cooperation).

Fig. 13. Segmentation process for test image 2.

Note that since the intensity ranges overlap with each other, it is hard to segment this image into correct regions by ordinary region segmentation methods. On the other hand, Fig. 10(c) includes six regions with uneven shadings and low contrast boundaries, which also make its segmentation hard.

Figures 11, 12 and 13 illustrate the region deformation processes, where temporary regions are depicted by black regions and intended action segments by white lines. Seed temporary regions were given by hand in Figs. 11 and 12 while those in Fig. 13 were detected automatically.

Figure 11 shows the result when no cooperation between agents is involved. That is, each agent deforms its temporary region independently of the others without checking the consistency of intention lines. As shown in this figure, therefore, intended action segments intersect with each other and rapidly expanding temporary regions invade into others.

Figure 12 shows the result with agent cooperation, where no intended action segments intersect and the invasion is avoided. This result demonstrates the effectiveness of the cooperation between agents.

We also conducted some experiments where different values were assigned to coefficients $\alpha$ and $\beta$. Their results showed that our system is very stable against the change of weighting coefficients. The reason for this can be considered as follows. As defined in Eq. (6), while the internal energy $E_{int}$, which includes $\alpha$ and $\beta$, plays a large role at the early stage of the shape evolution, its weight is gradually decreased and at the final stage, it becomes ineffective. Thus, although $\alpha$ and $\beta$ affect the shape deformation at early and intermediate stages, final region shapes are determined mainly by $E_{image}$ and $E_{grav}$ and hence are insensitive to $\alpha$ and $\beta$.

Figure 13 shows the result for the real image in Fig. 10(c). In this experiment, initial temporary regions were computed by merging $5 \times 5$ rectangular blocks with similar average intensities. While some temporary regions are deeply caved at the initial stage, the dynamic calibration of the coefficients $\alpha$ and $\beta$ gradually removes the excessive concavities. This result demonstrates that the system can work correctly without being affected by uneven shadings or low contrast region boundaries.

In summary, we have shown that the cooperative distributed problem solving paradigm enables us to realize a robust and flexible region segmentation system, where attributes of and spatial relations between regions are integrated to determine region shapes.

However, this system relies heavily on the assumption that an initial temporary region is placed well inside in each target region, respectively. To remove this assumption, we have to augment the system by introducing dynamic agent merging and generation capabilities. Such augmentation requires the incorporation of new knowledge sources to design decision criteria for the agent merging and generation. In fact, Zhu *et al.*[27] used an intensity distribution model in a region to control the dynamic region merging. In the next section, on the other hand, we will show that with rich semantic knowledge, the dynamic agent generation can be realized based on the same spatial reasoning scheme as described in this section. That is, the essential factor that limits the current system capability rests not in its spatial reasoning scheme but in the incorporated knowledge; the relational constraint "the group of regions to be detected must form a disjoint union of the image space" is too weak to determine the number of regions included in an image.

## 3. COOPERATIVE SPATIAL REASONING FOR AERIAL IMAGE UNDERSTANDING

SIGMA is a knowledge-based aerial image understanding system. It analyzes black and white aerial images of suburban areas to construct a structural description of the scene. Its major characteristics are

- Cooperative spatial reasoning by active reasoning agents and
- Knowledge-based top-down image segmentation.

Here, we give a brief overview of its spatial reasoning scheme, where missing object instances (i.e. agents in SIGMA) are dynamically recognized by the top-down hypothesis-and-test analysis. See Ref. 13 for detailed descriptions of SIGMA and experimental results.

### 3.1. Hypothesis Generation by a Reasoning Agent

In SIGMA we used an object-oriented paradigm for representing the world model. The knowledge about a class of objects in the world is represented by an *object class*, where attributes and relational information about that class of objects are stored. A recognized object is represented by an *object instance*: when an object in the scene is recognized, the object class is instantiated to produce an object instance representing the recognized object (Fig. 14).

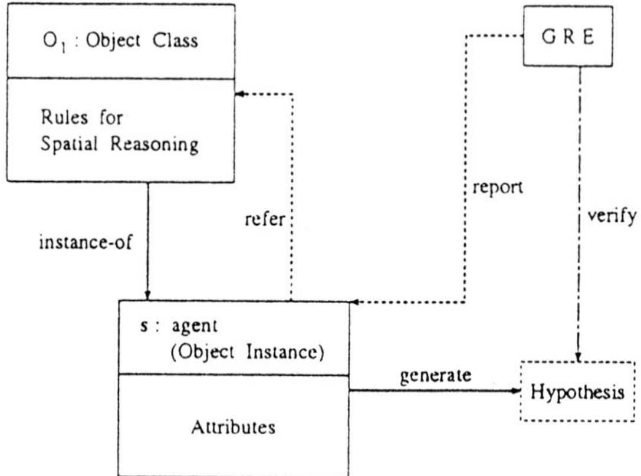


Fig. 14. Mechanism of spatial reasoning in SIGMA.

Once an object instance is generated, it starts spatial reasoning as an active reasoning agent. The knowledge used by the agent is described by a set of rules, which are stored in its corresponding object class (Fig. 14). By applying the rules, the agent first generates hypotheses for its related objects (Fig. 14). For example, a house agent generates hypotheses for its neighboring houses and facing road. Such hypothesis generation is performed concurrently by multiple agents.

A hypothesis is described by

- iconic description (i.e. region) representing the locational constraint on the target object,
- symbolic description (i.e. inequalities) representing constraints on attributes of the target object.

A rule for spatial reasoning is described in the following form:
<*control-condition*>: conditions to activate the rule
<*hypothesis*>: procedure to generate a hypothesis
<*action*>: procedure to be activated when the generated hypothesis is verified or refuted.

A rule is activated by an agent when its attributes satisfy the predicates specified in the <control-condition> part. Then the <hypothesis> part is executed to generate a hypothesis. The activation of the rule, however, is suspended at this stage. That is, the <action> part is not executed until the hypothesis is verified or refuted. Note that since an agent usually generates multiple hypotheses at the same time, the suspension of a rule does not mean the deactivation of the agent; it can conduct reasoning based on non-suspended rules.

GRE in Fig. 14 stands for Geometric Reasoning Expert. It coordinates local spatial reasoning by agents to construct a globally consistent description of the scene. More specifically, it examines the consistency between object instances and hypotheses and reports that result to those agents which generated the hypotheses (Fig. 14).

When an answer to the generated hypothesis is returned from GRE, the agent executes the <action> part of the suspended rule using the returned answer. Note that the <action> part is executed irrespectively of the type of answer: whether or not the hypothesis is verified.

### 3.2. Cooperative Spatial Reasoning by Active Agents

We call object instances (agents) and hypotheses generated by them *evidence*. All partial evidence obtained during the interpretation process is stored in a common database. Each piece of evidence is described in two different forms: the iconic description (region) for representing its location (i.e. occupying space) and the symbolic description for representing attributes and relations to others. GRE examines the consistency among all pieces of evidence in the database and integrates consistent pieces of evidence. Suppose agent $\mathbf{s}$ of class $O_2$ generates a hypothesis $f(\mathbf{s})$ for class $O_1$ using rule $R_1$ about spatial relation REL between $O_1$ and $O_2$. Suppose also the region associated with $f(\mathbf{s})$ overlaps with an instance of $O_1$, $\mathbf{t}$ (Fig. 15(a)). This means that the locational constraint specified by $f(\mathbf{s})$ is satisfied by $\mathbf{t}$. Then, if all attribute constraints associated with $f(\mathbf{s})$ are satisfied by $\mathbf{t}$, these two pieces of evidence are integrated to form what we call a *situation*.

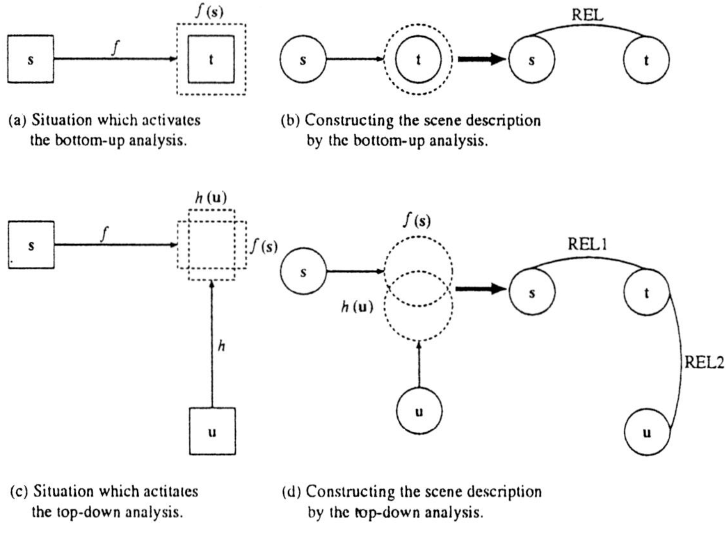


Fig. 15. Cooperative spatial reasoning in SIGMA.

In this case, GRE *unifies* $f(\mathbf{s})$ and $\mathbf{t}$, and returns $\mathbf{t}$ to agent $\mathbf{s}$ as the answer to the hypothesis $f(\mathbf{s})$. Then agent $\mathbf{s}$ executes the <action> part of rule $R_1$, by which a symbolic link representing relation REL is established between $\mathbf{s}$ and $\mathbf{t}$ (Fig. 15(b)). This process of constructing a global scene description (i.e. network) from independent object instances (i.e. nodes) is the bottom-up analysis of SIGMA.

On the other hand, a situation may consist of consistent hypotheses alone: e.g. hypotheses $f(\mathbf{s})$ and $h(\mathbf{u})$ in Fig. 15(c). In this case, their unification makes GRE search for an instance of the hypothesized (missing) object in the image. First GRE unifies all hypotheses included in the situation into a composite hypothesis. In this unification, the sets of constraints (i.e. inequalities) associated with the hypotheses are integrated by computing their intersection: all constraints are ANDed. Then GRE activates a top-down image analysis module to detect the image feature corresponding to the object instance specified by the composite hypothesis.

If the target instance ($\mathbf{t}$ in Fig. 15(d)) is successfully detected from the image, it is inserted into the database. Then, GRE broadcasts the new instance to all source agents which generated the hypotheses ($\mathbf{s}$ and $\mathbf{u}$ in Figs. 15(c), (d)). Agents $\mathbf{s}$ and $\mathbf{u}$, in turn, establish symbolic links to the new instance $\mathbf{t}$ by executing the <action> parts of the suspended rules which were used to generate $f(\mathbf{s})$ and $h(\mathbf{u})$, respectively. This is the top-down analysis to find a missing object instance. Note that the rule executions by independent agents $\mathbf{s}$ and $\mathbf{u}$ are synchronized by GRE. That is, GRE can also be regarded as the synchronization mechanism between multiple independent reasoning agents.

Similar spatial reasoning can be done using *part-of* relations, which enables the system to recognize objects with complex internal structures. For example, SIGMA can recognize a group of regularly arranged houses as a *house group* and a group of smoothly aligned road-pieces as a road.

### 3.3. Elimination of Erroneous Object Instances

As noted early, some recognized object instances may be erroneous. The detection and elimination of such errors is done by GRE in the following way.

Interpretations constructed by GRE are described by *interpretation networks*, where nodes represent recognized object instances and arcs relations among them (i.e. spatial relations and part-of relations, Fig. 16). All object instances in the same network are considered as mutually consistent, because spatial and part-of relations are established only between mutually consistent object instances.

Since the recognition of individual object instances is performed concurrently, multiple different instances may be located at the same place. GRE regards such overlapping instances as conflicting interpretations and establishes an *in-conflict-with* link between those nodes representing the overlapping instances (Fig. 16). Then, reasoning based on conflicting interpretations is performed separately and as a result multiple mutually conflicting interpretation networks are constructed in the database.

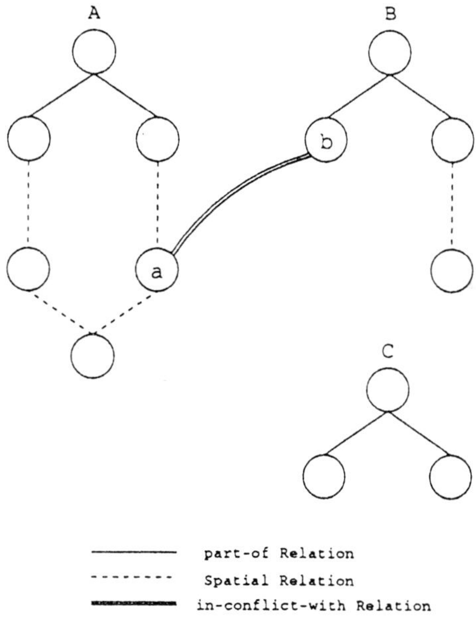


Fig. 16. Interpretation networks.

At the final stage of the analysis, GRE selects the most *plausible* interpretation. By the *interpretation* here, we mean a set of non-conflicting interpretation networks. Note that some interpretation networks may be isolated from the others. For example, Fig. 16 contains three interpretation networks, A, B, and C, and network C is isolated. Since GRE constructs all possible interpretation networks during reasoning, we need to select the most plausible one(s) as the final result. This selection is done as follows:

1. Let FINAL-INTERPRETATION be {} (i.e. empty set) and NETWORKS $\{N_1, ..., N_n\}$ (i.e. set of all constructed interpretation networks).
2. Iterate the following steps until NETWORKS becomes empty.
   (a) Let $N$ be the largest interpretation network among NETWORKS. Remove $N$ from NETWORKS and append it to FINAL-INTERPRETATION. The size of a network is measured by the number of constituent nodes.
   (b) Eliminate all networks in-conflict-with $N$ from NETWORKS.

In Fig. 16, for example, the interpretation networks A and C are selected as the final interpretation and all object instances included in network B are rejected as errors.

In summary, the scheme of cooperative spatial reasoning in SIGMA is almost the same as that used in the region segmentation system described before. The difference is in the meanings of hypotheses; while a hypothesis in the latter only specifies the goal state (expected shape) of a region agent itself, that in the former denotes the *existence* of another agent. Rich semantic knowledge employed in SIGMA allows the generation of such existential hypothesis. For example, knowledge "A spatial relation (e.g., FACING) holds between HOUSE and ROAD" can be represented by

$$\forall x[HOUSE(x) \rightarrow \exists y[ROAD(y) \wedge REL(x,y) \wedge \forall z[ROAD(z) \wedge REL(x,z) \rightarrow z = y]]]. \quad (7)$$

By eliminating the existential quantifier, we have
$\forall x\ [HOUSE(x)\ \rightarrow$

$$[ROAD(f(x)) \wedge REL(x, f(x)) \wedge \forall z\ [ROAD(z) \wedge REL(x,z) \rightarrow z = f(x)]]]. \quad (8)$$

Intuitively speaking, when a house instance **a** is recognized, $HOUSE(\mathbf{a})$ becomes true and the following formula is derived from formula (8).

$$[ROAD(f(\mathbf{a})) \wedge REL(\mathbf{a}, f(\mathbf{a})) \wedge \forall z\ [ROAD(z) \wedge REL(\mathbf{a}, z) \rightarrow z = f(\mathbf{a})]]]. \quad (9)$$

Here $f(\mathbf{a})$ denotes a certain unknown object instance, and its properties are specified by the above formula: $f(\mathbf{a})$ must be an instance of $ROAD$ and must satisfy relation $REL$ to **a**, and such $f(\mathbf{a})$ is unique. Thus, we can say that $f(\mathbf{a})$ stands for a hypothesis generated by agent **a** and that the above reasoning process describes the logical foundation of the hypothesis generation in SIGMA.

In short, with rich knowledge, our cooperative spatial reasoning scheme can realize the dynamic agent generation.

## 4. CONCLUDING REMARKS

This paper proposes a cooperative spatial reasoning scheme for image understanding and demonstrates its utilities and effectiveness in two different systems: region segmentation and aerial image understanding systems. Its major characteristic is the active hypothesis generation based on the knowledge about spatial relations between objects. Although such hypothesis generation requires a lot of computation time and storage space, a robust and flexible spatial reasoning which integrates both bottom-up and top-down analyses can be realized. Our spatial reasoning can be initiated any time based on incomplete information so far obtained, and the integration of hypotheses from different sources increases the reliability of the analysis. That is, we can deform incomplete shaped regions correctly and construct a description of the scene even if some object instances are missing at the initial stage.

In the paper, we also showed that the richer knowledge sources are employed, the more capable spatial reasoning can be realized: the dynamic agent generation capability cannot be realized without rich spatial knowledge that specifies the existence of a related object.

While this paper focuses on spatial reasoning for image understanding, the multi-agent/cooperative distributed problem solving paradigm can also be used in the following applications:

Cooperative Distributed Sensing[28]: Since an area covered by a single sensor is limited, we have to employ a group of locationally distributed sensors to monitor a wide area. In a cooperative distributed sensing system, each sensing station (sensor + signal analysis module) is considered as an agent, which cooperates with each other via a communication network to understand situations and events in a widely spread area. Applications of such a system include security monitoring and traffic flow analysis.

Cooperative Analysis by Heterogeneous Function Modules[4,29]: A complex system like IUS includes a group of analysis modules with different functions: e.g., segmentation, grouping and matching modules. Considering such functional module as an agent, flexible control structures can be realized by the cooperation among agents.

Cooperative Analysis by Multiple Algorithms[30]: To realize a certain analysis function (e.g., stereo matching), a variety of different algorithms have been developed (e.g., template matching, dynamic programming, and edge segment matching). Since each algorithm is designed based on its own specific model and assumption, its performance varies depending on local properties of an image(s) to be analyzed. Thus, considering as an agent a parallel analysis process designed based on a specific algorithm, multiple analysis results by different algorithms can be flexibly integrated through the agent cooperation to increase the reliability and adaptability of the analysis.

In conclusion, we believe that multi-agent/cooperative distributed problem solving paradigm offers a very useful computation scheme to realize flexible and robust IUSs practically usable in real world applications. Toward that goal, we should conduct intensive studies to develop versatile interaction and cooperation mechanisms among agents. Especially, besides designing communication protocols for cooperation, we will investigate further utilities of the cooperation without direct communication proposed in this paper.

## REFERENCES


1. A. Rosenfeld and A. C. Kak, *Digital Picture Processing*, Second Edition, Academic Press, New York, 1982.
2. E. Persoon and K. S. Fu, "Shape discrimination using Fourier descriptors", *IEEE Trans.* **SMC-7**, 3 (1977) 170–179.
3. R. Brooks, "Symbolic reasoning about 3-D models and 2-D images", *Artificial Intelligence* **17** (1981) 285–348.
4. M. Nagao and T. Matsuyama, *A Structural Analysis of Complex Aerial Photographs*, Plenum Publishing Corp., New York, 1980.
5. T. O. Binford, "Survey of model-based image analysis systems", *Int. J. Robotic Res.* **1**, 1 (1982) 18–64.
6. A. Rosenfeld and R. A. Hummel, "Scene labeling by relaxation operations", *IEEE Trans.* **SMC-6**, 6 (1976) 420–433.
7. D. Waltz, "Understanding line drawings of scenes with shadows", in *The Psychology of Computer Vision*, ed., P. Winston, McGraw-Hill, New York, 1975, pp. 19–92.
8. K. E. Price, "Relaxation matching techniques — A comparison", *IEEE Trans.* **PAMI-7**, 5 (1985) 617–623.
9. R. Mohan and R. Nevatia, "Using perceptual organization to extract 3-D structures", *IEEE Trans.* **PAMI-11**, 11 (1989) 1121–1139.
10. D. M. McKeown and W. A. Harvey, "Rule-based interpretation of aerial images", *IEEE Trans.* **PAMI-7**, 5 (1985) 570–585.
11. R. C. Bolles and P. Horaud, "3DPO: a three-dimensional part orientation system", *Int. J. Robotics Res.* **5**, 3 (1986) 3–26.
12. C. H. Wang and S. N. Srihari, "A framework for object recognition in a visually complex environment and its application to locating address blocks on mail pieces", *Int. J. Computer Vision* **2** (1988) 125–151.
13. T. Matsuyama and V. Hwang, *SIGMA: A Knowledge-Based Aerial Image Understanding System*, Plenum Publishing Corp., New York, 1990.
14. M. Kass, A. Witkin, and D. Terzopoulos, "Snakes: Active contour models", *Int. J. Computer Vision* **1**, 4 (1988) 321–331.
15. N. Yokoya *et al.*, "Image segmentation scheme based on a concept of relative similarity", *Proc. of 4th IJCPR*, 1978, pp. 645–647.
16. T. Asano and N. Yokoya, "Image segmentation schema for low-level computer vision", *Pattern Recognition* **14**, 1–6 (1981) 267–273.
17. P. M. Narendra and M. Goldberg, "Image segmentation with directed trees", *IEEE Trans.* **PAMI-2**, 2 (1980) 185–191.
18. T. C. Pong, L. G. Shapiro and R. M. Haralick, "A facet model region growing algorithm", *Proc. of PRIP*, 1981, pp. 279–284.
19. T. C. Pong, L. G. Shapiro, L. T. Watson and R. M. Haralick, "Experiments in segmentation using facet model region grower", *CVGIP* **25**, 1 (1984) 1–23.
20. T. V. Robertson *et al.*, "Multispectral Image Partitioning", LARS Inf., Note 071373, Purdue Univ., 1973.
21. S. L. Horowitz and T. Pavlidis, "Picture segmentation by a directed split-and-merge procedure", *Proc. of 2nd IJCPR*, 1974, pp. 424–433.
22. S. L. Horowitz and T. Pavlidis, "Picture segmentation by a tree traversal algorithm", *JACM* **23**, 2 (1976) 368–388.
23. G. B. Coleman and H. C. Andrews, "Image segmentation by clustering", *Proc. of IEEE* **67**, 5 (1979) 773–785.
24. L. D. Cohen, "On active contour models and balloons", *CVGIP: Image Understanding* **53**, 2 (1991) 218–221.

25. E. Segawa, G. Xu, and S. Tsuji, "Minimal region extraction using expanding active contours", *Proc. of 11th ICPR*, 1992, pp. C688–C691.
26. R. G. Smith, "The contract net protocol: High-level communication and control in a distributed problem solver", *IEEE Trans.* **C-29**, 12 (1980) 1104–1113.
27. S. C. Zhu, T. S. Lee and A. L. Yuille, "Region competition: Unifying snakes, region growing, Energy/Bayes/MDL for multi-band image segmentation", *Proc. of 5th ICCV*, 1995, pp. 416–423.
28. E. H. Durfee, V. R. Lesser, and D. D. Corkill, "Coherent cooperation among communicating problem solvers", *IEEE Trans.* **C-36** (1987) 1275–1291.
29. L. D. Erman, F. Hayes-Roth, V. R. Lesser, and D. R. Reddy, "The Hearsay II speech-understanding system: Integrated knowledge to resolve uncertainty", *ACM Comput. Surveys* **12** (1980) 213–253.
30. M. Watanabe and Y. Ohta, "Cooperative integration of multiple stereo algorithms", *Proc. of 3rd Int. Conf. on Computer Vision*, 1990, pp. 476–480.

**Takashi Matsuyama** received B. Eng., M. Eng., and D. Eng. degrees in electrical engineering from Kyoto University, Japan, in 1974, 1976, and 1980, respectively. He is currently a professor in the Department of Electronics and Communication, Graduate School of Engineering, Kyoto University.

His research interests include knowledge-based image understanding, computer vision, image media processing, and artificial intelligence. He wrote about 100 papers and books including two research monographs, *A Structural Analysis of Complex Aerial Photographs*, 1980 and *SIGMA: A Knowledge-Based Aerial Image Understanding System*, 1990. He won five best paper awards including the Marr Prize at ICCV'95. He is on the editorial board of *Computer Vision and Image Understanding*.

**Toshikazu Wada** received the D. Eng. from Tokyo Institute of Technology in 1990 and became a research associate in the Department of Information Technology, Okayama University. He is currently a Lecturer.

His research interests include pattern recognition, computer vision, and distributed image understanding. In 1995, he won the Marr Prize at ICCV'95.

# HUMAN UNDERSTANDING LIMITS IN VISUALIZATION

ANTHONY J. MAEDER
*School of Engineering, University of Ballarat*
*P.O. Box 663, Ballarat 3353, Victoria, Australia*

Many different techniques for visualizing data exist, and often users must experiment with several before selecting the most effective one for their problem. Knowledge of the characteristics of the human visual system can assist in our choice of visualization techniques. Limits imposed by our visual "cognitive bandwidth" mean that only detail up to these limits needs to be generated in a visualization scene. Some aspects of our visual process will be discussed and an approach will be described for modeling scene detail, which takes visual limits of such aspects into account.

*Keywords*: Human visual system, visualization, visual importance, image display.

## 1. INTRODUCTION

When generating computer graphics or digital image scenes for display, there is often an implicit expectation that providing a greater amount of visual realism will permit better human understanding of the scene. Consequently, visualization becomes a doubly expensive computational task: not only must large volumes of numerical data be processed, but the visual presentation of the data must be undertaken with a high degree of graphical refinement. For example, the presentation may involve fine spatial interpolation and surface smoothing, complex rendering operations for lighting and color, real-time transformation of co-ordinates for motion and interaction. All of these operations require many calculations to be performed in the visualization software, or sometimes in special purpose hardware which may be supplied as an enhancement to the visualization platform. The consequence of this computational load is that visualization is usually regarded as a demanding, expensive application that necessitates the use of complex, high-powered computing resources.

This preoccupation with visual quality and computational expense may be unnecessary for two distinct reasons: the power of *abstraction*, and the limits of human *perception*. Abstraction can be employed in the presentation of data in many circumstances, without severely inhibiting human understanding. Indeed, it may enhance understanding by assisting the viewer to concentrate on the essential information and to suppress less relevant information. The abstraction process seeks to present the data in a form which allows the viewer to make visual assessments of size, position, aggregation, motion etc., without the need to assimilate every fine detail of a "real world" scene. Thus iconic or graphical visualization entities are widely used: scaled symbols for sizes of towns in a map, solid colored regions in chloropleths, streamers for motion properties in fluid flow experiments. Sometimes



Spatial Computing: Issues in Vision, Multimedia and Visualization Technologies (1997) 229–237

these entities are presented with visual cues that make them seem more realistic (e.g. perspective, illumination), but this approach is more directed at visual enjoyment than at deeper understanding. Indeed, these cues may even confuse or bias the understanding obtained, if not properly applied. The usefulness of abstraction in visualization has been widely discussed in the visualization literature (e.g. Tufte,[1] Tufte,[2] and Keller and Keller[3]) and will not be considered further here.

Just as our ability to interpret abstraction determines a minimum amount of information that should be presented for effective visualization, so too does our perception determine a maximum amount of information that can be assimilated by the viewer. Providing excess information to give the impression of realism when generating visualization scenes can be both wasteful and misleading if this amount is exceeded. This point is seldom considered during visualization generation, partly because no accepted general model exists for how the elements of human visual perception interact to provide overall visual understanding of a scene. However, characteristics of individual elements have been studied, and using these it should be possible to set some bounds on the amount of information to be displayed. First we shall review some of the more important physical and mental elements which characterize perception in the human visual system. We shall then proceed to discuss how these elements might be modeled and combined in a straightforward way, to allow a reduction in the amount of information generated for visualization scenes.

## 2. PHYSICAL ELEMENTS

The workings of the human visual system (HVS) have been the subject of considerable investigation by psychologists and cognitive scientists (e.g. Cornsweet,[4] Marr,[5] Spoehr and Lehmkuhle,[6] Sekuler and Blake,[7] DeValois and DeValois[8]), yet in many instances opinions differ on the exact nature of HVS processes. However, a broadly accepted overall model exists, that the eye provides raw data to the brain which combines, analyzes and interprets this data via several different interconnected regions of specialized processing. It is presumed that both the eye and the brain are highly specialized in their respective data handling tasks, and so contribute distinctive *physical* and *mental* elements respectively to our visual perception.

The eye is the source of our entire visual input data stream, providing all physical elements of vision. Light is focused by the cornea and lens onto the retina, where small, densely packed receptors sample its intensity (rods) and color (cones) and feed the data to ganglion cells to be concentrated. In the center of the retina lies the fovea, a small region of about 2 degrees of visual angle where only cones occur and the spatial density of these receptors is highest, so the most detailed data from the scene is acquired. The eye is repeatedly repositioned by small saccadic movements every 200–500 ms and then remains still or "fixated". In this way, detail may be assimilated over time for the whole visual scene. The eye contains well over 100 million receptors, yet the optic nerve which conveys the data from the retina to the brain has only around a million fibers, so considerable data reduction takes place prior to receipt by the brain. We now consider several physical elements of visual perception arising from the above structure, which determine some limitations of HVS performance. These are considered to take place in or near the eye, prior to the brain producing more complex information about the scene (although in fact the brain may be partially involved). They are thus often termed "low level" or "early vision" processes.

### 2.1. Adaptivity, Contrast, Masking

The eye is able to sense a very wide range of intensities covering over $10^8$ units of luminance, from a dark moonless night to bright sun on clouds or snow. However, in any one scene the range is limited to about $10^3$ units, beyond which the receptors saturate on or off. The cones in the eye *adapt* to allow the average intensity in the field of view to be clearly visible, and this average can be positioned anywhere over the full range. At low intensity levels, the cones remain off and only luminance levels are seen (scotopic), but for higher intensities the cones provide most of the information in color (photopic). At any given average intensity level, the eye has varying ability to detect spatial detail based on intensity variation or *contrast*, according to the size of the detail. This relationship is often described by a contrast sensitivity function (CSF), based on a fixed pattern of monotonically varying size (e.g. alternating bars of light and dark). The higher the contrast sensitivity value, the more easily we can detect the presence of the pattern when the contrast is low (i.e. the light and dark intensities are close in value). Typically, maximum contrast sensitivity occurs at between 1 and 5 cycles per degree of visual angle (Fig. 1).

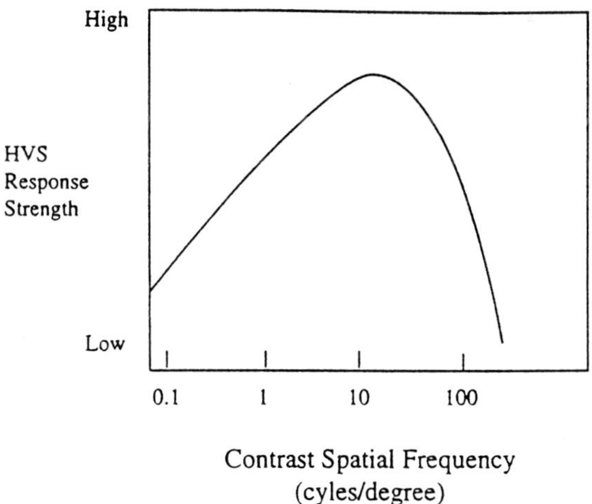


Fig. 1. Human sensitivity to contrast.

A third factor affecting data collection at the eye is the detection or inhibition of parts of the scene by *masking*. The presence of particular patterns of values at neighboring receptors provides a context which invokes a corresponding visual sensation. The detection of orientation of edges is an example of detection masking, and the well-known Mach band effect is an example of inhibition masking.

## 2.2. Distance and Motion

Our binocular vision system provides our primary means of determining the distance to objects in a scene. Of our approximately 200 degrees field of view horizontally, the overlap region covered by both eyes is about 70 percent, so we are able to estimate distances for all objects we can see in any significant detail. When data from the two eyes is brought together, the lateral disparities of parts of the scene as projected on the left and right retinas are calculated, and the distances from the eyes are obtained by simple triangulation. The disparities are found by a combination of feature detection and feature matching activities and are surprisingly accurate: typically 1 part in $10^3$.

In addition to our stereopsis mechanism, our visual system responds to a number of different cues by inferring distance from them. Obscuration of objects, relative sizes, perspective convergence, textural gradients and clarity reduction are all familiar effects and indeed are used frequently in visualization systems where stereo viewing is not available. For a moving viewer and for moving objects, a further cue is provided by the apparent movement of far objects being opposite in direction and slower than that of near objects. Motion also leads to some disadvantageous effects, such as reduced CSF values during motion, so that fine detail becomes lost to view. Due to the fixation process described earlier, we cannot accurately track several objects having different motion, although we can follow a single object moving fairly rapidly, up to about 10 degrees of visual angle per second. Consequently, we tend to neglect assimilation of visual detail over a much higher fraction of the scene once our fixation becomes strongly associated with tracking motion. We are also sensitive to the rate at which we acquire changing scene data, and a flicker sensitivity function may be considered analogously to the CSF. This function peaks at about 10 Hz, and falls to undetectable levels by about 60 Hz, although it is not really objectionable above about 25 Hz.

## 2.3. Color

Color vision occurs because the cone receptors have different ranges and peak sensitivities to the wavelengths of visible light. There are three distinct cone types, providing three "channels" which coincide approximately with red, green and blue sensations. The value for each of the three channels is obtained by averaging the values of intensities detected by all receptors of the same sensation type locally. Of these, red and green are considerably more sensitive. Internally, these channels are recoded by transforming them to a luminance channel and two chrominance channels, the latter being afforded less information capacity. Thus brightness is an inherently stronger scene property than color. Consequently, we are more easily able to distinguish colors being very different hues and very saturated, than subtle shades or mixtures.

Color perception is also subject to certain adaptation processes, such as the surrounding field of colors affecting the value of the color being viewed, or the color of the illuminant being factored out from the color being viewed. There is considerable non-uniformity in the perceived difference between colors which are sampled uniformly in the visible color space, and so standard transformations have been defined by CIE to provide a perceptually uniform space in which all colors are equidistant. The variability between observers, and the wide range of viewing conditions and display device characteristics, make it difficult to achieve a color presentation that will be predictably interpreted by any viewer, so color accuracy is often not a reliable aspect of visualization.

## 3. MENTAL ELEMENTS

Within the brain cortex, more sophisticated understanding of the scene is obtained by more complex processing of the visual data. Objects in the scene are not explicitly identified by the physical elements of the HVS, but by interpretation in the mental elements. The mental elements proceed both bottom up, by amalgamating information from the physical elements (e.g. extracting object boundaries) and top down, by recognition of common or previously seen patterns and forms (e.g. finding features of objects). Certain features are considered important in the amalgamation process: continuous lines, sharp corners, closed regions, homogeneous textures, smooth shading transitions. Such features are often considered to be modeled by "Gestalt" organization of the information into categories which determine the most probable groupings of the features into objects:

- proximity – closer belongs together
- similarity – alike belongs together
- continuation – smooth belongs together
- closure – complete belongs together
- symmetry – balance belongs together

These principles can lead to misinterpretations of reality, so-called "optical illusions", reinforcing the usefulness of this model for explaining the mental visual process. Recognition processes make use of such features as are identified, as indices to narrow the range of choice in identifying the object. A library of "templates" stored in memory is conjectured, with the fundamental features retrieved most readily. All told, we know far less about mental elements of HVS response than the physical elements, and so decisions made on the basis of these are far less reliable.

## 4. VISUAL IMPORTANCE

Considering all of the above HVS elements, we next consider how an estimate could be made of what information in a scene is most significant to enable the viewer to understand the scene. Previous work attempting to define significant scene details has often taken the approach of concentrating on one or two HVS elements only. For example, the spatial frequency distribution can be considered,[9] or selected edge and motion measures can be used.[10] In certain computational situations, such as image coding relative to human observer quality assessment, approaches for combining these factors to construct an overall modified version of the basic technique have been successful.[11] However, these approaches are very specific to the situation and are derived by *ad hoc* means. Another avenue of approach has been to make use of knowledge concerning saccadic eye movements and shifts of visual attention, building on the pioneering work of Yarbus.[12] Some hypotheses have been advanced on the nature of attentional attractors in scene contents[13] and have been used to produce variable spatial quality in image sequences,[14] but only low accuracy has been achieved for attentional shift predictions by this means.

We seek a systematic, general process for obtaining a description for each visible part of the scene, as to the contribution it makes to overall scene understanding. That is, we wish to have a weighting function defined over the scene which provides a quantitative ranking of importance, so that parts of the scene can be selectively degraded or ignored. While all elements are interrelated to some extent, the simplest approach we can adopt is to ignore this interrelationship and assume they are relatively independent. This simplification allows us to combine any estimates of their significance linearly and avoids the combinatorial explosion that would result from trying to establish interrelationships between potentially many elements. In addition, we need to determine the relative significance of each element in the overall visual understanding. In the absence of any other evidence for ranking these elements, we consider each element of equal significance at its average value, and normalize the range of values it takes over the whole scene to the interval [0,1]. At the same time, we must ensure that all elements are mutually combinable without allowing any to dominate others, so they must be linearized through redistribution of values in a process akin to the well-known histogram equalization algorithm.

Our model is based loosely on a *saliency*-based scheme described by Koch and Ullman[15] and others, which produces maps for the prediction and control of viewer attention by combining a fairly large number of low level stimuli into a single map of attention "potential", which in turn provides weights for a simulated neural process. In our model, termed "importance maps", we avoid the use of neural circuits and adopt a simple arithmetic combination of individual "importance factors" which have been linearized and normalized as described below (Fig. 2). These factors may be derived from local properties of the data (e.g. texture, contrast) or global properties (e.g. colorfulness, region size). Generally, local properties correspond to physical elements and global properties to mental elements.

We have applied the above scheme successfully to modifying conventional image analysis operations for application to color images, where visual aspects of the color information were used to provide importance factors.[16] We have also applied it to construct varying quality lossy compressed versions of images,[17] where viewer satisfaction was not affected as strongly at lower bitrates than was the case for uniform image quality schemes, such as standard JPEG. We are currently extending the scheme to cater for motion in image sequences, by adding factors based on motion field characteristics,[18] with an expectation that this will produce acceptable

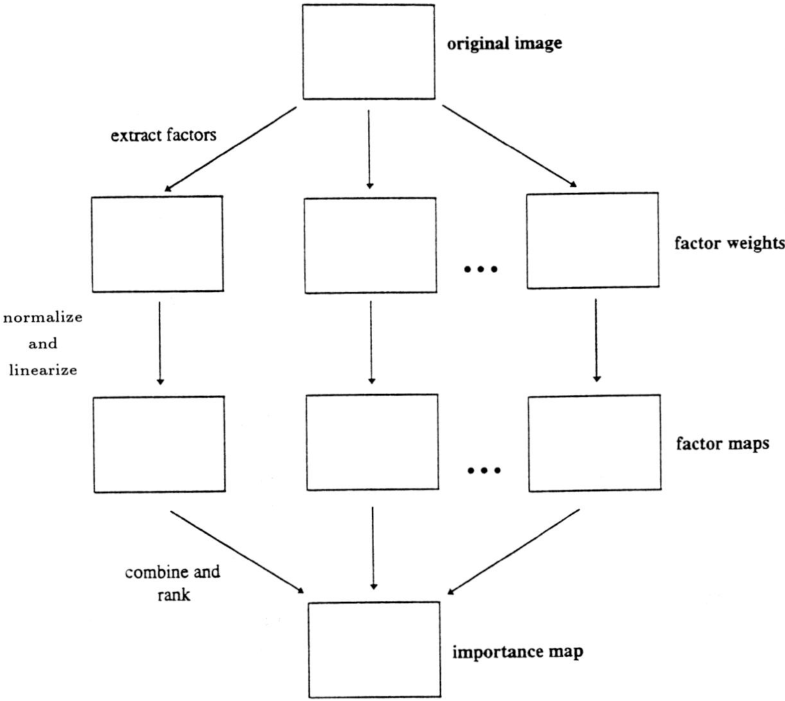


Fig. 2. Constructing an importance map.

quality at reduced delivery bandwidth in various video and multimedia applications. This will be applicable also to moving visualization scenes, as encountered during real-time interaction in simulations and virtual environments.

## 5. CONCLUSION

Some important limitations of the HVS affecting the ability of viewers to comprehend the contents of visualization scenes have been described. An approach which is under development for estimating the importance of all parts of the scene to viewers has been outlined. This approach could be used for both assessment of visualizations for redundancy, and for generating visualizations which minimize redundancy. The approach has the advantage that it is general but can be specialized to suit the circumstances of particular situations. For example, catering for rapid interactive motion or for stereo viewing is no different from catering for static scenes, apart from the actual choice of parameters. Current experiments using our approach suggest that it may be possible to make reductions of the order of 10 (for static scenes) and 100 (for moving scenes) in the amount of information generated for visualization, without suffering unacceptable loss in understanding by the viewer. This would allow many current complex visualization tasks to be performed using PCs, laptops or even TV set-top boxes, rather than on more exclusive workstation platforms.

## ACKNOWLEDGMENTS

This work was supported in part by the Australian Research Council large grant scheme.

## REFERENCES

1. E. R. Tufte, *The Visual Display of Quantitative Information*, Graphics Press, Cheshire CT, 1988.
2. E. R. Tufte, *Envisioning Information*, Graphics Press, Cheshire CT, 1990.
3. P. R. Keller and M. M. Keller, *Visual Cues: Practical Data Visualization*, IEEE Press, Los Alamitos CA, 1993.
4. T. N. Cornsweet, *Visual Perception*, Academic Press, New York, 1970.
5. D. Marr, *Vision*, W. H. Freeman & Co., San Francisco CA, 1982.
6. K. T. Spoehr and S. W. Lehmkuhle, *Visual Information Processing*, W. H. Freeman & Co., San Francisco CA, 1982.
7. R. Sekuler and R. Blake, *Perception*, Alfred A. Knopf, New York, 1985.
8. R. L. DeValois and K. K. DeValois, *Spatial Vision*, Oxford University Press, New York, 1988.
9. A. B. Watson, "Efficiency of an image code based on human vision", *J. Optical Soc. Amer.*, Part A **4**, 10 (1987) 2401–2417.
10. A. A. Webster, C. T. Jones, M. H. Pinson, S. D. Voran and S. Wolf, "An objective video quality assessment system based on human perception", *Procs. SPIE* **1913** (1993).
11. S. A. Klein and D. A. Silverstein, "Image compression, fidelity metrics and models of human observer", *1994 Picture Coding Symp.*, Sacramento CA, Sept. 1994, pp. 96–99.
12. A. L. Yarbus, *Eye Movements and Vision*, Plenum Press, New York, 1967.
13. J. M. Findlay, "The visual stimulus for saccadic eye movements in human observers", *Perception* **9** (1980) 7–21.
14. L. B. Stelmach, W. J. Tam and P. J. Hearty, "Static and dynamic spatial resolution in image coding: An investigation of eye movements", *Procs. SPIE* **1453** (1991) 147–152.
15. C. Koch and S. Ullman, "Shifts in selective visual attention: Towards the underlying visual circuitry", *Human Neurobiology* **4** (1985) 219–227.
16. A. Maeder and B. Pham, "A color importance measure for color image analysis", *IS & T & SID 1st Color Imaging Conf.*, Scottsdale AZ, Nov. 1993, pp. 232–237.
17. A. J. Maeder, "Importance maps for adaptive information reduction in visual scenes", *ANZIIS-95 3rd Australian and New Zealand Conf. on Intelligent Information Systems*, Perth, Nov. 1995, pp. 24–29.
18. A. Maeder, J. Diederich and E. Niebur, "Limiting human perception for image sequences", *Procs. SPIE* **2657** (1996) 330–337.

**Anthony Maeder** is Head of the School of Engineering at University of Ballarat. He holds a Ph.D. in software engineering from Monash University and a MSc. in parallel computation from Natal University in South Africa. He is currently the representative for Australia in the International Association for Pattern Recognition.

His research interests cover a range of topics in computer graphics, digital image processing and data compression.

# A STRATEGY AND ARCHITECTURE FOR THE VISUALIZATION OF COMPLEX GEOGRAPHICAL DATASETS

MARK GAHEGAN and DAVID O'BRIEN

*Department of GIS, Curtin University*
*P.O. BOX U 1987, Perth 6001, Australia*
*E-mail: mark@cs.curtin.edu.au*

The use of computer visualization as a means to analyze complex geographic datasets is discussed. Visualization is a valuable tool for conducting exploratory data analysis on geographical data; making good use of the human eye's unparalleled ability to recognize structure and relationships that may be inherent within the data. Traditional GIS are extremely poor at visualization, being limited to a very restricted set of visual attributes with which to convey information (position, size, color). The use of a more sophisticated approach is discussed in detail. Specifically, a system to visualise complex environmental datasets is described, which makes use of knowledge concerning the problem domain as well as knowledge concerning human cognition.

In the realizations produced, the most salient attributes in the data, for a particular task, are assigned to the most striking visual attributes. Assignments are controlled by heuristics that may be changed to alter system behavior. Results are presented showing the application of this approach on datasets involving several multi-dimensional thematic layers of environmental data, used in mineral exploration.

*Keywords*: Visualization, exploratory analysis, geographical data, knowledge-based.

## 1. INTRODUCTION

The aims of this paper are:

1. To substantiate the need for visualization as a tool with which to conduct exploratory spatial analysis within the geosciences.
2. To provide an approach to visualization, specifically targeted at large and complex geographic datasets, with the aim of increasing the number of data channels that may be viewed simultaneously.
3. To describe a basis by which the behavior of the system can be understood and changed.

The remainder of the paper is organized as follows. The rest of Sec. 1 introduces the datasets used and their characteristics, then describes some alternative strategies for finding or recognizing inherent structure. Section 2 presents the architecture of the approach taken, with particular attention given to the constraints and knowledge that must be brought to bear on the solutions. Section 3 defines the space over which visualizations may be constructed and examines their complexity; this provides the motivation for a more structured approach. Section 4 supplies this structure via constraints and heuristics, and describes their interaction. Some example results are presented in Sec. 5, and the effect of using the various knowledge bases is discussed. Finally, conclusions are given in Sec. 6.



Spatial Computing: Issues in Vision, Multimedia and Visualization Technologies (1997) 239–261

### 1.1. The Nature of the Data

Geographic datasets are traditionally characterized by both their inherent complexity and their sheer volume. The desire to understand the nature of a geographical (or geological) region has led to the development of many different data acquisition techniques that produce a variety of different types of data in several different formats. Imaging sensors are common, such as thematic mapping satellites (SPOT and Landsat TM), as are geo-physically oriented sensors such as those providing gravitational and electro-magnetic anomaly readings. Many other types of data are common, such as seismic line data, transepts, borehole profiles, stream networks, soil samples and 3D forward models of geology. The data differs in format, dimensionality (zero, one, two or three dimensions) and type (quantitative, ordinal, nominal, etc.).

For many classes of problems tackled within the geosciences, it is necessary to use a combination of the data described above in an integrated manner. A single dataset treated in isolation may not contain enough information to provide an insight into the structure of the domain. So, the emphasis of analysis has shifted towards experiments to combine data somehow, with the aim of uncovering structure. This structure may then be used to form more accurate interpretations of the data, perhaps to aid land use classification or to detect candidate regions for mineral exploration. The old approach within the geosciences involved the use of a light table and shaded transparencies, now the use of sophisticated computational tools and visualization environments can be investigated.

### 1.2. Discovering Structure in the Data

Since a good deal of data is now available in digital form, it becomes possible to move from a deductive approach to one that is data driven.[1] So, instead of hypothesizing a model that seems to fit the available (sparse) data, the emphasis has now turned to the data, and the discovery of inherent relationships within it. The spatial variation within the data at fine scales can make the formulation of deductive models extremely difficult, since they must describe a good deal of heterogeneity. Inductive approaches face a similar problem, that of *discovering* relationships that may be partial, variant over space and extremely sensitive to the effects of confounding.

The discovery or uncovering of potentially useful or interesting relationships within complex data sets is a difficult problem for which several approaches are possible. Three examples are:

1. Statistical Approach: Within the spatial sciences, traditional statistics have often proved inadequate[2,3] and a whole series of revised measures of correlation and interpolation are now available.[4] Tools for the analysis of correlation are now available, as are automated techniques to aid in data classification.
2. Evidence Combination Approach: Many evidential approaches exist, and a good review is presented by Bonham-Carter.[5] Since the inherent structures within

the data are not usually known or are not easily describable, techniques can be difficult to select or test without good ground truth data for evaluation. Nonetheless, some sophisticated pattern matching and reasoning tools are available which have shown promising results.[6,7]

3. Visualization Approach: Visualization does not in itself attempt to impose high level structure on the data. Rather it provides an environment where several layers of data may be examined simultaneously. With careful configuration, the realizations produced may enhance the structure that is inherent in the data, but which may be difficult to discover analytically. The actual analysis is then left up to the visual system of the human operator.

Visualization is being used here as a technique for Exploratory Data Analysis; indeed, the term Visual Data Analysis has been coined to describe the use of visual techniques for this purpose.[8] Exploratory Data Analysis is largely hypothesis free.

For many tasks involving the recognition of structure, the human visual system has unparalleled performance. A large portion of the human brain is devoted to vision, and has been shown to possess a bandwidth of about 2 Gbits per second[9]; it is therefore capable of swift and comprehensive analysis of visual imagery.

To exploit our natural ability, the data must be presented in such a way as to maximize the cognitive impact of the phenomenon under investigation. Ideally, the presentation will induce the colloquially termed "pop-out" of the required phenomena; but this requires that the target is characterized in a visual *stimulus space* by unique properties that may be easily distinguished from other distracting properties. Research in psychophysics has demonstrated that human subjects can divide their attention between several different visual stimuli, and furthermore that visual attributes such as position, shape, color, lightness and size can be viewed as orthogonal in stimulus space. A good review of this area is given by Csinger.[10]

Visualization systems offer a means of displaying data in a manner that allows fine control over many different visual parameters, but this in itself is not necessarily sufficient to induce pop-out. With careful selection and configuration however, these parameters can be used to explore the relationships in the data in a variety of novel ways. For all but the psycho-physical expert, the configuration is a far from simple task, requiring considerable skill. Hence the motivation to encapsulate the expertise so that it may be used more widely, and applied by the non-expert in an automated manner.

One might assume that a Geographic Information System (GIS), specifically designed for the manipulation and display of geographic data, might provide a useful environment within which to explore the data visually. But unfortunately, in current GIS, the number of graphical primitives under the direct control of the user is small. On most systems, only 2D or 2.5D is supported, along with a choice of color. Given the best case of position ($x, y$, and $z$) and *color*, we have at most four visual attributes that can be used to display the data. In contrast, the number of attributes within the data may be very large. The use of over twenty channels of data is commonplace for many activities in mineral exploration.

This state of affairs has caused some researchers to define the necessary extensions required to GIS.[11] Others have developed packages external to the GIS, specifically for the visualization of geographic data. Haslett *et al.*[12] address this issue with a series of dynamic graphics tools. An external approach is used here, since this is the only way in which the required visual control can be provided.

In the quest for a more formal approach to the visualization problem, Senay and Ignatius,[13,14] analyze existing approaches and define a solution that categorizes the types of knowledge used into three distinct classes:

(i) knowledge of the data,
(ii) knowledge of computer graphics and visualization tools and
(iii) knowledge of visual perception.

This provides a much needed structure to the problem. Duclos and Grave[15] describe a formal language for visualization, consisting of operators, relationships and variables. Whilst useful as a syntactic basis, it does not address the major problem of *how* data channels should be assigned to visual attributes.

Rogowitz and Treinish[16] propose an approach based on generic tasks, but using rules regarding data definition (meta-data). Specifically, they define two types of rules to control the construction of the visualization; the first set ensures faithful representation of the data, whilst the second provides transforms to enhance or promote various aspects within the data.

Beshers and Feiner,[17] also define a task structure which introduces general operators into the visualization language for tasks such as comparison, directed search and exploration. Again, use is made of meta-data to help select useful techniques. Robertson[18] proposes an orthogonal categorization based on locality; by which visual representations may be selected according to point, local, and global generic tasks. Both of these categorizations are useful and have been included into the approach presented here.

In this paper, the notion of orientation to a user supplied task is taken further. The data to be visualized may be useful for a number of specific purposes; that which may be regarded as a good visualization for one task may at the same time be unsuitable for another. Thus, there is a need for additional knowledge from the domain expert, to allow visualizations to be constructed to suit the requirements of a specialized (as opposed to generic) task. Tasks are described in terms of the required outcome as a triple:

$$< task >< property >< domain > .$$

(a) *Tasks* are of the form described by Beshers and Feiner,[17] and include correlation, exploration and search (identification).
(b) Properties are used to define specific *goals* for which the task is to be constructed. These represent a conceptual *target* to which the visualization is directed. In the field of minerals exploration candidate properties might be

chemistry, electrical potential and geological structure. The selection of data to be used, and its relative importance varies widely with these properties.

(c) *Domains* offer a method of loosely grouping data, so that the task is directed at a particular region in the total data space. Domains are similar to the concept of *views* in relational databases, providing a means of focussing on data that is suitable for some tasks. Again, for minerals exploration, the domains might be chosen to represent the depth from surface: shallow, mid and deep.

The user can issue specific, highly focussed requests, such as:

*explore structure deep*

which presents the data in a way that emphasises geological structure at depth. (Figs. 3–5 give some examples of results from this task and are discussed later.)

Notice that the properties and domains are expressed in the language of the field of application, and are familiar terms to the geoscientist. Applications in other fields of interest require that the properties and domains be restated. Section 3.3 outlines the construction of the task knowledge base.

For a small number of tasks, a fixed set of data and a fixed target environment, the difficulty of producing useful visualizations is not great. Indeed, it may be feasible to hard-code a small number of schemas to provide for the needs of the user. The approach taken here is an attempt to generalize across changing tasks, changing data and changing environments.

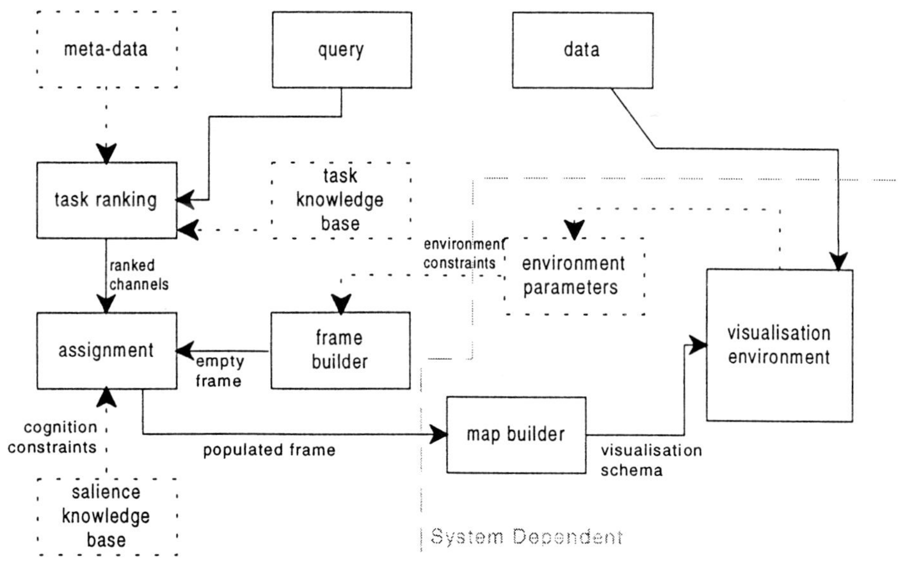


Fig. 1. System architecture.

## 2. SYSTEM ARCHITECTURE

The architecture of the visualization system described in this paper is shown schematically in Fig. 1. The visualization environment is the software that provides the graphical facilities required. Example environments are *IRIS Explorer*, *ArcView* and *Adobe Postscript*. Each supported environment requires its own map builder, to generate valid visualization schemes in the language or script of the environment (for example an *Explorer* Map). Additionally, each environment imposes its own restrictions on the ways in which data may be visually combined. The environment is described in a common format that is used to ensure the production of valid visualization schemas; that is, schemas use only the facilities provided by the environment. Similar to a data definition or meta-data description, the environment parameters represent an operational definition of the package, used as an external-level view onto the functionality. Some example definitions are given in Sec. 4.2.

The components of the visualization system that are dependent upon a particular environment are isolated by a grey dashed line. This represents the extent to which the environment constraints influence the system as a whole. By encapsulating the environmental constraints in this way, the task of changing to another environment is simplified. To illustrate the point, it is often desirable to take the same datasets into the field on a notebook computer, running *ArcView* as opposed to *Iris Explorer*. Only the system dependent modules need to be re-written. Obviously, the resulting visualizations will be more restricted, due to the reduction in dimensionality of the stimulus space. However, the same rules and knowledge still hold.

The key element in the schema is the assignment module. This takes in channels of data and assigns them to the various visual attributes supported by the environment. Assignment is controlled by two knowledge bases. Firstly, knowledge concerning the importance of particular data channels for specific tasks is used to rank the data. Secondly, knowledge concerning human perception is used in the assignment of data properties to visual attributes. The result is an environment capable of adapting its behavior in a task-oriented manner.

Whereas traditional display packages can make use only of position and color, the use of a more advanced environment provides other more subtle attributes such as texture and opacity and a wider range of graphical objects (marks) such as spheres and arrows. This results in an increase in the number of data channels that may be assigned to a single layer in the visualization, but in turn introduces a new and unfamiliar mode of data presentation. Existing conventions for data presentation are ignored in favor of methods allowing the inclusion of more information. It is hypothesized that by careful application of relevant knowledge, the user may perceive structure, even if the visualization looks unfamiliar, i.e. the data is presented in a new and unfamiliar way.

The implementation of the knowledge bases, the rules and the assignment module uses the *CLIPS* expert system package.

### 2.1. The Visualization Problem

The architectures described above show that the problem of visualization can be broken down into two independent issues. The first issue concerns the overall complexity and volume of the data; specifically, that there are often more data available than can be simultaneously visualized by even the most advanced environments.[a] The second issue concerns the assignment of data to the parameters that control the visualization. Of course, the number and type of these parameters is fully determined by the environment chosen.

The automation (or semi-automation) of these two processes requires the application of knowledge concerning data reduction and the assignment of data to visual parameters. Additionally, a number of different types of constraints must be applied concerning the structure of the data and the facilities provided by the visualization environment. The following sections address each of these issues in detail as they relate to the visualization architecture described above.

## 3. THE VISUALIZATION SEARCH SPACE

As the number of data channels and visual parameters increases, the search space of potential visualizations rapidly becomes prohibitively large. This section describes the extents of the resulting search space, under various conditions, in order to make a case for a more 'intelligent' approach.

### 3.1. Data Reduction

The rapid advancement in the development of computer hardware over the last few years has led to a dramatic decrease in price and increase in processing speed of specialized graphics platforms. However, this same technology is also being applied to capture devices, which are producing ever greater volumes of data. It therefore becomes necessary to address the problem of data reduction, since it is unrealistic to hope that the problem will be solved by bigger and better machines. The task of data reduction is governed by two factors: the capabilities of the visualization platform and the capabilities of the human visual system. By carefully engineering the manner in which data is displayed, it is hypothesized that greater amounts of data can be communicated to the user effectively. However, this must be bounded by some theoretical cognitive limit beyond which the human visual system cannot function effectively.

### 3.2. Types of Data Reduction

Data reduction operates in two distinct ways. Firstly, the complexity of datasets may be reduced prior to their use in a number of well-documented ways, including band ratio techniques, principle components analysis (PCA) and sampling strategies, (e.g. Ref. 19). These techniques are designed to minimize information loss whilst maximizing data loss. The resulting dataset is treated as a new and independent source of data, for reasons of simplicity. Secondly, if there remains an excess

[a] It may also be the case that the data volume often exceeds our human capacity for assimilation, and so it becomes necessary to select some channels whilst rejecting others.

of data channels, above that which can be visualized effectively, then some channels must be omitted.

Given that there are a finite number ($r$) of different visual attributes ($v_i$) that may be used, an $r$-dimensional stimulus space is defined $\langle v_1, v_2, \ldots, v_r\rangle$. An assignment of $m$ data channels ($c_i$) to this space produces a visual stimulus ($S$), given by a function mapping as:

$$S = f(\langle c_1, c_2, \ldots, c_m\rangle)\,.$$

An insight into the complexity of the assignment task is provided by examination of the number of permutations and combinations that the above function allows for a database containing $n$ distinct data channels (for example see Ref. 20). If the stimulus space is unordered; that is, all visual attributes have equal importance, then the maximum number of combinations is given by:

$$_cC_r = \frac{n!}{r!(n-r)!}, \qquad r \leq n\,.$$

Databases used in the geosciences for minerals exploration and other forms of spatial analysis are often highly multivariate. As an example, for a database of $n = 20$ channels, but using only $r = 15$ visual parameters, there are 15,504 possible assignments.

In order to reflect the fact that some visual attributes are more immediately understood by the user, the stimulus space may be ordered such that the impact ($\iota$) of one visual parameter is assumed to be greater than another. In this way, visual attributes of higher impact can be assigned to the more important data channels:

$$\langle v_1, v_2, \ldots, v_r\rangle \Rightarrow \iota(v_i) > \iota(v_{i+1})\,.$$

The maximum number of permutations now increases to:

$$_nP_r = r!\,{}_nC_r = \frac{n!}{(n-r)!}, \qquad r \leq n\,.$$

For the same example values of $r = 15$ and $n = 20$, there are now $\cong 2e^{+16}$ possible assignments. If the number of visual parameters is increased to encompass all channels, the number of permutations becomes $n!$. For $r = n = 20$, the number of possible solutions rises to $2.43e^{+18}$. Worse still, if redundant combination[b] is allowed, the maximum number of permutations with repetition becomes $n^r = 20^{15} \cong 3.2e^{+19}$.

The above analysis illustrates two very important points. Firstly, if the number of visual attributes is increased, then for realistically sized data sets the number of potential visualizations grows rapidly. So, any increase in $r$ must be carefully

[b] A redundant combination is where the same data channel may be assigned to more than one visual attribute; the effect is to heighten emphasis on that variable. A common example is where a value may be used to give both the $z$-displacement and the color to a lattice. A colored surface is thus constructed from a 2D planar image.

managed. Secondly, the search space increases rapidly as $n$ increases. A method of reducing $n$ would be highly beneficial.

### 3.3. The Task Knowledge Base

Recall from the introduction that the visualization task is stated as a triple:

$$\langle task \rangle \, \langle property \rangle \, \langle domain \rangle \, .$$

The tasks supported are:

(i) *exploration*, which displays multiple channels of data;
(ii) directed *search*, which displays only a single layer; and
(iii) *comparison*, which combines two or more layers (after Beshers and Feiner[17]).

For the latter two tasks, the visualization requires no knowledge of channels, properties or domains because the operation relates to named channels. Task (i) is less well-defined in terms of the channels required and their relative importance; these will vary with the user's objectives. It is towards the task of (visual) exploration that the remainder of the paper is orientated.

By decomposing the goal of the visualization into two parts (property and domain), considerations of specific task goals are divorced from considerations of the data. The visualization is produced by the interaction of the task knowledge base with other relevant knowledge as described in Sec. 4. Within the task knowledge base, facts are recorded to describe the relevance of a specific data channel to various properties and domains as:

**importance:** ⟨data channel⟩⟨property⟩⟨domain⟩⟨utility⟩ .

Data channels are individually rated for tasks as opposed to the sensors from which they originate; channels from the same sensor often differ in their applicability to various data domains. For example, the facts:

**importance:** airborneEM1, electrical, shallow, 1.0
**importance:** airborneEM1, electrical, mid, 0.4
**importance:** airborneEM1, electrical, deep, 0.1
**importance:** airborneEM1, chemistry, shallow, 0.0 .

state that the utility of channel 1 of airborne electro-magnetics to a task involving investigation of the electrical properties of a region, decreases with depth. Furthermore, the same channel provides no utility for investigation of shallow chemistry, and is therefore redundant. Its inclusion in such a task can only act as a distraction.

Facts are supplied by an expert from the problem domain. Knowledge relating to the task is handled separately from knowledge relating to the construction of the visualization. As a result, the expert supplying the task ranking need understand nothing about visualization.

The utility of a channel ($c$) is dependent on both the property ($p$) and the domain ($d$), and can be described by a function $\mu$:

$$\mu(c, p, d), \qquad 0 \leq \mu \leq 1 .$$

The utility value is then used to order the assignment of data channels to the available visual attributes in a "best first" manner. Channels with little utility will be left until last, and only included if there is spare capacity within the scheme.

The ranking of channels effectively partitions the data into two; those channels which are useful for a particular task, and those which are not. Channels in the latter partition are ignored; they will not be presented to the user even if spare capacity exists in the visualization schema, since they are deemed to add visual clutter. The cutoff point for $\mu$ may be zero or some defined threshold, $\mu_{\text{min}}$. Channels regarded as useful are assigned to available slots in the visualization scheme as described later.

Ideally, all relevant channels are assigned. In the event that some relevant channels are not assigned then a cost penalty is incurred. This can be used as one method of evaluating the usefulness of schemes, and is discussed in Sec. 4.5.

The proposed approach does not necessarily place an upper bound on $r$, since there is no limit on the number of layers that may be added into the visualization. Rather, a (high) cost is associated with the introduction of each layer, since it increases the cognitive effort involved in comprehending the data. More importantly, the ranking of data by task reduces $n$, with minimum loss of information. By making use of the full range of visual parameters available (as detailed in Sec. 4.2), $r$ is increased for each layer. In a visualization environment, just four layers of marks may be sufficient to describe the variance in twenty channels of data.

In summary, for realistically sized datasets, the application of constraints and expertise is necessary to avoid the user being faced with too many initial choices and too many visualizations to evaluate for their usefulness. Further constraints and heuristics are introduced in the following section.

## 4. ASSIGNMENT OF DATA CHANNELS TO VISUAL PARAMETERS

Having shown how the task can be used to impose an order on the channels of data, the next step is to assign these channels to the parameters that define the stimulus space. Three areas of investigation remain (i) the nature of the data, (ii) the nature of the visualization environment and (iii) knowledge of visual perception; these together determine how the assignment should be performed and are discussed in turn below. Section 4.4 shows how the knowledge and constraints within these three areas are used to control the assignment process.

### 4.1. Data Management

Before data can be visualized effectively, various meta-data concerning its structure and type must be known. Data is organized into datasets, where each dataset relates to a particular capturing or acquisition process. For example, the Landsat

TM satellite produces a dataset containing seven bands or channels of data, each one relating to a different range in the electro-magnetic spectrum. The density of data, (coverage) may influence the type of visualization strategies chosen (discussed later in Sec. 4.2). In addition, the dynamic range of the data may also impose limitations.

Beshers and Feiner[17] use meta-data effectively to impose structure on the assignment problem. A similar approach is taken here, with the following information being gathered as a description of each data channel:

- data space: {*spectral, spatial, ...*} — *domain addressed by data*
- coordinates: $\{2D|3D\}$ — *planar or volumetric reference*
- dimensionality: $\{0D|1D|2D|3D\}$ — *points, lines, regions, volumes*
- coverage: {point | local | global} — *locality of the data*
- scale: {nominal | ordinal | quantitative} — *statistical scale*
- dynamic range: $\{x_{\text{min}}, x_{\text{max}}\}$ — *max and min data values*
- precision: $P$ — *precision of data recording*

The dynamic range and precision of the data may influence the mapping from the data values to the visual attribute used for display. However, this issue is not addressed here.

### 4.2. Knowledge Concerning Computer Graphics and the Visualization Environment

Recall that the construction of a visual representation may be regarded as a process of binding channels of data to parameters controlling the visual attributes of the graphical objects, available as part of the visualization library. Examples of graphical objects, referred to as *marks*, are: arrows, spheres, and surfaces (meshes). The visual attributes available are defined by the environment and provide various degrees of control that may be used for display. Examples of visual attributes are: position, shape, size, orientation, value, texture and color[24] and these taken together define the stimulus space. Clearly, from the above description, this component is highly dependent on the visualization environment.

The facilities offered by visualization environments are described by the environment parameters module, shown in Fig. 1. This specification provides the following constraints:

1. The maximum number of layers that can be displayed in the environment.
2. The maximum number of coordinate dimensions supported by the environment.
3. A description of each type of mark, including its shape dimensionality and all visual attributes that may be controlled.

Each layer of marks contains as free variables a set of $r$ visual properties that may be used to control the appearance of (up to) $r$ channels of data. Additionally, it contains as bound variables a set of properties used to control position. The positional information is given such a high degree of importance that it is treated separately.[c] Typically, a GIS provides only one layer of 2D marks containing only one free visual property (color). Some example mark descriptions from the *Explorer* environment are given below:

| | | |
|---|---|---|
| 2D Mesh: | bound variables: | $(x, y)$ |
| | free variables: | $(z, red, green, blue, alpha)$ |
| | dimensionality: | (2D) |
| | coverage: | (local, global) |
| 3D Mesh: | bound variables: | $(x, y, z)$ |
| | free variables: | (red, green, blue, alpha) |
| | dimensionality: | (3D) |
| | coverage: | (local, global) |
| 2D Sphere: | bound variables: | $(x, y)$ |
| | free variables: | $(z,$ *size*, *color*) |
| | dimensionality: | (2D) |
| | coverage: | (point) |
| 3D Arrows: | bound variables: | $(x, y, z)$ |
| | free variables: | $(x', y', z',$ *color*) |
| | dimensionality: | (3D) |
| | coverage: | (point, local) |

The variables listed describe the control that the developer has over the appearance of a mark set in a specified environment. They may not necessarily represent the most desirable parameters from a cognitive perspective, as can be seen by comparing them with Table 1, which shows a ranking of elementary perceptual tasks.[21,d] For example, color appears as a single property in the table, but is controlled by three variables in the meshes described above. These may not be independently discernible by the user (although they may become so with experience).

Notice that the free variables change depending on the mark set used. For example *size*, *shape* and *orientation* are not explicit attributes in meshes, but *size* is defined for 2D spheres, and *orientation* is defined for 3D arrows. Where these attributes are not explicitly defined they may still be used in the following circumstance. If $c$ has a shape dimensionality of zero then the visual attributes of *size*, *shape*, and *orientation* remain free. If $c$ has dimensionality of one, two or three, then these attributes must also be bound to $c$ and cannot be used further. This is because they will be implied by the geometry of the data.

The *Coverage* variable describes the coverage of the data within space. *Point* refers to point measurements, *local* refers to localized features and *global* refers to

[c]Obviously, other assignments are possible and could well be useful. The position of data in space has over-riding importance for the task of mineral exploration, so for the present no alternatives are allowed. Using scattergrams, for example, position may be used instead to display frequencies or intensities.

[d]More suitable variables can only be added by creating new mark sets. We have chosen here to work with those mark sets that are supplied as part of a visualization environment, rather than to implement new sets that might meet our needs more precisely.

coverage-type data, such as images and surfaces (after Robertson,[18]). Knowing the spatial extents of a channel is important in determining candidate marks. It is not appropriate to display *image* data using a set of arrows, since the resulting visualization will be too densely filled and most likely cause visual interference, where marks are superimposed.[e]

### 4.3. Knowledge Concerning Human Cognition

Perceptual knowledge is used to impose an order on the available visual attributes, so that the most visually striking attributes are assigned to the most important data. The knowledge is derived from psycho-physical studies which suggest that for classes of perceptual tasks, there is an order in which visual quantities are perceived.[10] The key factor in ranking visual attributes relates to the statistical scale of the data. Data on a nominal scale must be treated differently from data on an interval or ordinal scale. Where there is an ordering or ranking within the data, then the visualization should reflect this. Where it is not present, the visualization should not give the impression that it is.

Table 1 shows the orderings presented by Mackinlay[21] for quantitative, ordinal and nominal data.

Table 1. Ranking of elementary perceptual tasks according to statistical scale (greyed items are not applicable).

| Quantitative | Ordinal | Nominal |
|---|---|---|
| Position | Position | Position |
| Length | Grey Saturation | Colour Hue |
| Angle | Colour Saturation | Texture |
| Slope | Colour Hue | Connection |
| Area | Texture | Containment |
| Volume | Connection | Grey Saturation |
| Grey Saturation | Containment | Colour Saturation |
| Colour Saturation | Length | Shape |
| Colour Hue | Angle | Length |
| Texture | Slope | Angle |
| Connection | Area | Slope |
| Containment | Volume | Area |
| Shape | Shape | Volume |

It is interesting to note that position is rated as the most important visual attribute for all types of data.

By examining the statistical scale used within a channel ($c$), the relevant column in Table 1 can be used to rank a visual attribute ($v$) according to its impact ($\iota$)

[e]A better solution would use some form of density measure, calculated from the number of individual marks to be rendered on the viewing area.

when used to describe the channel. A simple rule is defined:

$$\iota(v, \text{cscale}) \qquad 0 \le \iota \le 1\,.$$

In practice, the rules need only impose a ranking on those perceptual tasks that appear in a mark description as a variable. Since the table only defines a ranking, it is necessary to choose actual values for $\iota$ in keeping with the ranking. This is an ongoing task involving the evaluation of results.

Note that the ranking of visual attributes cannot occur until the statistical scale of data in the channel ($c$.scale) is known. It cannot therefore be computed until a channel is presented for assignment.

At present, further knowledge concerning human perception is not used. However, there is a need to apply some heuristics that govern the *interaction* of visual attributes in order to increase the impact of important channels, particularly with regard to redundant assignment. Some candidates are provided by Rheingans and Landreth.[22]

### 4.4. Controlling the Assignment Process

Data channels are assigned to the visual parameters of marks according to knowledge and constraints described later. If an assignment of a data channel to a set of marks results in some mark attributes not being used, then other channels of data may be assigned to these attributes. This is known as *mark composition.*[13] In the system described here, one of the goals is to utilize all of the available bandwidth within sets of marks. When a set of marks is exhausted, other layers may be used that share the same (geographical) axis. This is known as *axis composition.*

The assignment of channels to marks is treated as a state-space search in which transitions between states (moves) are performed by axis and mark composition. Assignment continues until one of the following conditions is true

(i) all relevant channels are assigned;
(ii) all available layers and visual attributes are exhausted;
(iii) the total cost associated with the visualization exceeds a specified limit $C_{\max}$.

Axis Composition Rule. A new layer is added to the schema, vertically aligned with any existing layers. The positional parameters of the layer $(x, y)$, being the most important, become bound to the coordinates of the channel $c$. Since all layers share the same positional parameters, they are always co-registered in $x$ and $y$. If channels contain 3D data then the $z$ variable also becomes bound to position and so cannot be used further.

For axis composition to be possible, the following conditions must be met:

1. The maximum number of layers (if specified) must not be exceeded. Some environments may support only one layer. For environments where multiple layers are supported, the number of layers may be artificially limited to reduce the visual complexity.

2. The data axes must be compatible, so that composition is possible. The layers must therefore share the same coordinate reference frame (spatial in this case), as given by the *dataspace* attribute in the channel description. They should also be co-incident in space.
3. The dimensionality of the data must be supported by the available layers. A 2D environment cannot support 3D data without projection down to 2D first.

Assuming that the above tests prove positive, the next step is to select appropriate mark sets for the new layer, based on the following conditions:

1. The dimensionality required by the positional data in a channel must be supported by the mark set it is assigned to. This ensures that 3D data is not assigned to 2D marks for example.
2. Marks must be compatible with the *coverage* within the data channel. This ensures that a localized mark such as arrows is not used to display global data such as an image, for example.

Mark Composition Rule. Mark composition soaks up the spare capacity within a layer. Assuming that a layer has already been assigned channel(s), then for mark composition with a further channel to be possible, the following three conditions must be met:

1. There is spare capacity within the layer; that is, some visual attributes remain free.
2. The channel has a coordinate dimensionality which is compatible with the coordinate dimensionality of the layer.
3. The two channels can share the same positional coordinates; either they are co-registered (e.g. two images quantized to the same grid), or may be interpolated onto the same coordinates. The positional attributes in each channel must be assigned to (or interpolated onto) the positional variables of the marks.

Mark composition is generally favored over axis composition, since the introduction of extra layers is hypothesized to increase the cognitive effort required by the user. One goal of the search is therefore to minimize the number of layers.

Figure 2 shows a possible assignment of channels from three datasets to two layers of marks. In this example, datasets 1 and 2 both provide channels to layer 1, by mark composition. Dataset 3 requires a new layer. Not all channels are assigned, indicating that they may not be considered useful for the particular task portrayed.

A valid schema is the result of a series of valid assignments such that either all relevant data is assigned or the capacity of the schema is full (no more channels may be added). The relative merits of one valid schema over another may be determined by the costing functions described below.

### 4.5. Heuristics for Assignment

The assignment of channels to marks as specified above is an under-constrained problem. However, the introduction of further constraints is problematic since it

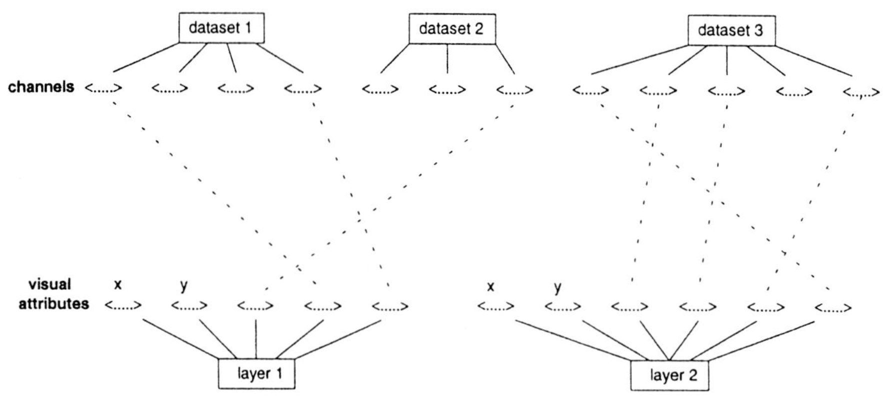


Fig. 2. Assignment of channel properties to layer visual attributes.

will lead ultimately to conflict. Rogowitz and Treinish[16] point out, but do not address, the difficulty caused by unwanted rule interaction, and thus the need for conflict resolution. The approach taken here is to avoid conflict by controling the final part of the assignment problem with heuristics. So, instead of hard-fast rules, the nature of the resulting visualization is controlled by weights that are freely combinable to produce a total score, used to rank possible solutions. Behavior (that is, the types of visualizations that are favored) is changed by altering these weights.

The costs described are cumulative. At any given stage in the construction of a solution (i.e. for any partial solution) a total cost so far is calculated as the sum of the following:

(a) *Unassigned Data.* After each assignment, the sum of all unassigned utility is given, calculated across all $m$ unassigned channels. The purpose of $W_{\text{unassigned}}$ is to encourage the assignment of channels in order of their utility to the given task $t$.

$$C_{\text{unassigned}} = \sum_{j=1}^{m} \mu(c_j, p, d) * W_{\text{unassigned}} .$$

(b) *Additional Layers.* Each layer added (not including the first layer) incurs a penalty. The number of layers used is $p$.

$$C_{\text{layer}} = (p-1) * W_{\text{layer}} .$$

An alternative to provide a sharper increase in cost with the addition of each layer is:

$$C_{\text{layer}} = {W_{\text{layer}}}^{(p-1)} .$$

(c) *Dataset Distribution.* The cognitive cost involved in breaking up the channels from a single dataset and distributing them over a number of layers. A count is made of the number of times that channels from the same dataset are assigned to different layers.

$$C_{\text{distribution}} = \sum_{i=1}^{p}\sum_{j=1}^{p} \text{count}\begin{pmatrix} c_i\cdot\text{ dataset} = c_j\cdot\text{ dataset} \wedge \\ c_i\cdot\text{ layer} \neq c_j\cdot\text{ layer} \end{pmatrix} * W_{\text{distribution}} \quad i < j\,.$$

(d) *Assignment to Visual Attributes.* The importance of the channel should be reflected by the ranking of the visual attribute to which it is assigned. Properties with high utility (as rated by the domain expert for a given task) should be assigned to the most visually striking attributes, shown in Table 1. Properties with low utility should be assigned to less striking visual attributes, or they may dominate the realization. An absolute difference measure is used between the channel utility ($\mu$) and the visual impact ($\iota$). The sum is calculated across all $n$ assigned channels — the goal of the search engine is to find plausible low cost solutions.

$$C_{\text{assignment}} = \sum_{i=1}^{n} (|\mu(c_i, t)| - |\iota(v_i, c_i\cdot\text{ scale})| * W_{\text{assignment}})\,.$$

The total cost of an assignment is given by:

$$C_{\text{total}} = C_{\text{unassigned}} + C_{\text{layer}} + C_{\text{distribution}} + C_{\text{assignment}}\,.$$

The initial values for the weights were selected by experimentation and are in a state of continual refinement as further results are evaluated.

### 4.6. The Search Procedure

To move through the search space, a cost minimization approach is taken. At a given state, the total cost of each move to a new state ($C_{\text{total}}$) is evaluated for all possible moves. The move(s) with the lowest cost is chosen, and the search continues until all channels or assigned, or $p$ or $C_{\max}$ is exceeded. Broadening of the search is achieved by evaluating all partial solutions that are within a certain value of the lowest cost solution so far.

The actual cost of a particular realization is determined by the values of the weights ($W$) used above. To alter the nature of the realizations, these weights may be changed as follows:

To increase the degree of mark composition, $W_{\text{layer}}$ is increased. Increasing $W_{\text{layer}}$ will cause realizations to be preferred where mark capacity is used up, but which may appear visually cluttered. Decreasing $W_{\text{layer}}$ will cause realizations with less information in layers, with the consequence that more layers will be required to convey the same information.

The emphasis on channels with higher utility may be changed by adjusting $W_{\text{assignment}}$. This may allow the role of less important channels to be studied more easily.

The distribution of channels over layers is governed by $W_{\text{distribution}}$. For some tasks, distribution may be desirable, in which case the cost is reduced. For others, it may be important to keep datasets together where possible.

The use of redundant assignments is handled differently. Generally, a channel that has already been assigned to a visual attribute is taken out of the search space. However, for some comparative tasks it may be important to duplicate some channels. Redundant assignment can be controled by the task knowledge base, by supplying more than one channel description for the same channel, with the possibility of each description being assigned a different utility.

## 5. RESULTS

The first issue to address is whether a user can make sense of the visualizations produced, given their quite radical differences from traditional display methods. The first reaction of new users when presented with a realization seems to be one of confusion, but once they have oriented themselves within the visual spaces, and then interacted with them, they rapidly become familiar. The visual correlation of data across several datasets is often of great interest; so much so that the use of animated techniques to promote the impact of correlation are now being investigated. On occasion, the visualizations have uncovered unanticipated structure in the data, which is of great interest to the users.

Experiments conducted so far have been evaluated by a geo-physicist for their usefulness to the task posed. Generally speaking, there is a good correlation between solutions ranked as 'useful' by the expert, and their calculated cost. Further refinement of the heuristics and a richer set of perceptual guidelines are still required however, to improve the success rate.

In some instances, further control over the mapping of data values to visual parameters is required, so that specific ranges or trends within the data are enhanced. In reality, there is a highly complex interplay between the different visual attributes even though they are treated as orthogonal concepts for the purposes of mark composition. Whilst some renderings offer good insight into their designated task, others produce results which are confusing, at least initially. Two areas that still require significant attention are the provision of a legend and the inclusion of further rules and heuristics describing the human cognition process as it relates to mark composition.

### 5.1. Sample Results of Rendered Scenes

Results are shown for four rendered scenes in Figs. 3–6. Details concerning the assignment of channels to visual parameters are given in Appendix 1. Figure 3 shows the result of visualizing the data using no limit on the number of layers and without a defined task. The scene contains four layers, making it difficult for the user to view it as a single entity. Without a task specified, too many channels of data are displayed, requiring extra layers.

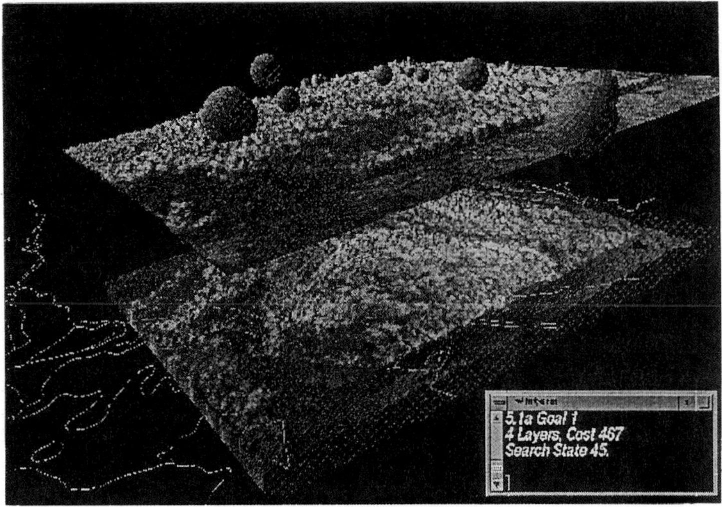


Fig. 3. A visualization with no goal defined.

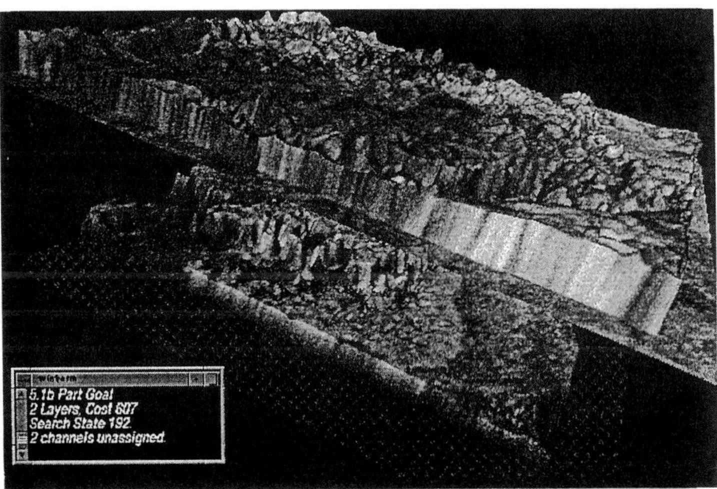


Fig. 4. A visualization restricted to two layers, but with no goal.

Figure 4 again has no task, but a limit of two layers is imposed. The assignment is more dense, with less redundant visual attributes, but the resulting visualization does not provide much insight into the nature of the data.

Figure 5 is given the task of: *explore* (*geological*) *structure deep.* The resulting scene shows good structural correlation in an immediately apparent way. All of the useful data has been assigned using just two layers. The scene is useful for minerals exploration.

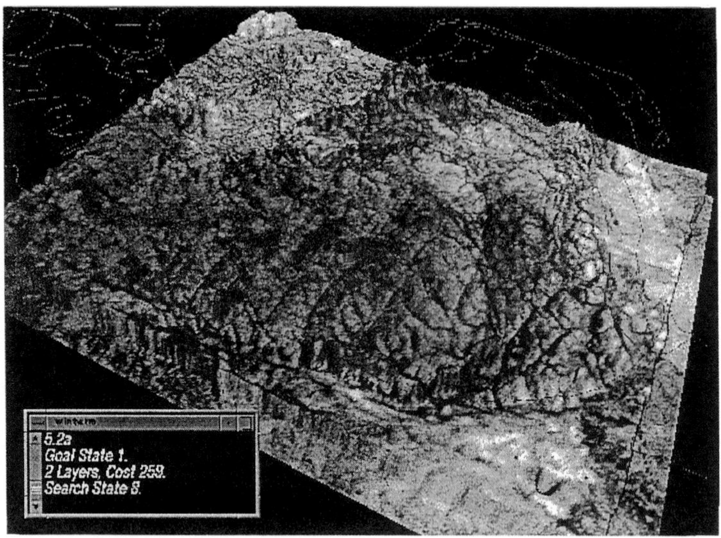


Fig. 5. A visualization using perceptual knowledge and the task: *explore (geological) structure deep*.

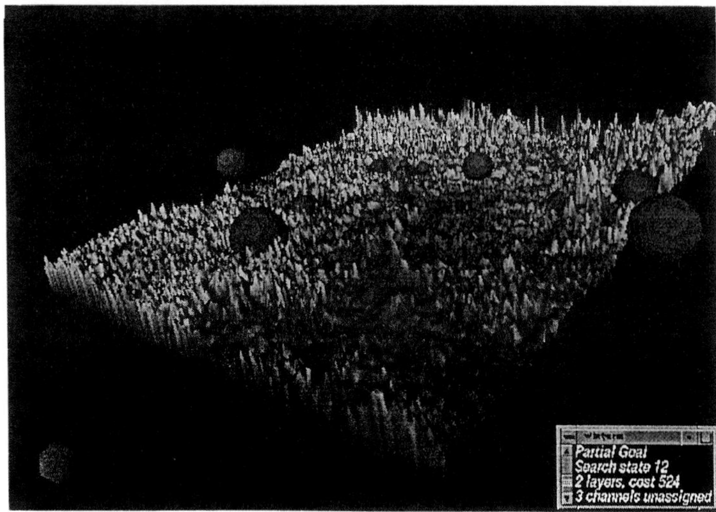


Fig. 6. An alternative task to study surface chemical properties.

For contrast, Fig. 6 shows an entirely different task, that of: *explore chemistry surface*. Appendix A shows that priority has been given to different channels. Note that the assignment of Landsat TM band seven to height ($z$) was probably not a good choice because of its erratic fluctuation coupled with its global coverage in gridded form. Avoiding this type of assignment would involve analyzing the rate of change of data values over space. Extra domain knowledge might also help here, so that the expert could specify the types of visual attributes that they would prefer to see used for a particular data channel (e.g. Ref. 16).

Further results of the application of this architecture to minerals exploration and floristic classification tasks are available over the world-wide-web from "http://www.cs.curtin.edu.au/~gisweb/visualization/".

## 6. CONCLUSIONS AND FUTURE WORK

The requirement for better visualization strategies for the geosciences is clear. One method of achieving an improvement is to closely orient the behavior of a visualization system towards a user-supplied task. This places a reliance on a domain expert for configuration, but in return gives a focussed theme to the realizations produced. The divorcing of knowledge and expertise into discrete units reduces the complexity of system configuration.

The use of the more subtle visual attributes (by broadening the stimulus space) can provide a means of compressing the data into a more coherent realization, but is by no means a trivial task. The search space of potential solutions enlarges rapidly as the number of data channels and visual attributes increases. In order to manage the problem effectively, constraints and heuristics must be carefully chosen.

There is a need for further study of the effects of combining visual attributes in terms of the perceived quality of the renderings produced. This will involve refinement of existing knowledge bases and also the introduction of further domain rules as described in Sec. 5. To this end, the next stage to be developed is a feedback loop, where the ranking of solutions by a user will be applied to modify system behavior, by changing the weights associated with rules and the utility and visual impact values. A learning strategy will be employed to analyze results and modify the knowledge bases and heuristic weights accordingly.[23]

## APPENDIX 1: LEGEND DESCRIBING THE RESULTS

For Fig. 3, the layers are (from the top):

1. Spheres: borehole.sample → *size.*
2. Surface: landsat.7 → *height*, radiometrics.classified → *alpha*, landsat.5 → *red*, radiometrics.potassium → *green*, landsat.7 → *blue.*
3. Vectors: geology → *red.*
4. Surface: landsat.4 → *height*, magnetics → *alpha*, radiometrics.uranium → *red*, landsat.2 → *blue.*

For Fig. 4, the layers are (from the top):

1. Surface: radiometrics.thorium → *height*, radiometrics.classified → *alpha*, radiometrics.Potassium → *green*, landsat.7 → *blue.*
2. Surface: magnetics → *height*, landsat.4 → *alpha*, landsat.2 → *red*, landsat.5 → *green;*

For Fig. 5, the layers are (from the top):

1. Vectors: geology → *red*
2. Surface: magnetics → *height*, landsat.7 → *alpha*, landsat.2 → *red*, landsat.4 → *green*, landsat.5 → *blue*;

For Fig. 6, the layers are (from the top):

1. Spheres: borehole.sample → *size*
2. Surface: landsat.7 → *height*, landsat.5 → *alpha*, radiometrics.uranium → *red*, landsat.2 → *green*, landsat.4 → *blue*.

## REFERENCES

1. Q. Tang, "A personal visualization system for visual analysis of area-based spatial data", in *Proc. GIS/LIS '92*, vol. 2, American Society for Photogrammetry and Remote Sensing, Bethesda, Maryland, USA, 1992, pp. 767–776.
2. L. Anselin, "Discrete space autoregressive models", in *Environmental Modelling with GIS*, ch. 46, eds., M. F. Goodchild, B. O. Parks, and L. T. Steyart, Oxford University Press, New York, 1993, pp. 454–469.
3. N. A. C. Cressie, *Geostatistics, The American Statistician* **43**, 4 (1989) 197–202.
4. N. A. C. Cressie, *Statistics for Spatial Data*, John Wiley and Sons, USA, 1993.
5. G. F. Bonham-Carter, *Geographic Information Systems for Geoscientists*, Pergammon Press, UK, 1994.
6. T. Lee, J. A. Richards and P. H. Swain, "Probabilistic and evidential approaches for multisource data analysis", *IEEE Trans. on Geoscience and Remote Sensing* **25**, 3 (1987) 283–293.
7. S. A. C. Openshaw and M. Charlton, "Building a prototype geographical correlates machine", *Int. J. of Geographical Information Systems* **4**, 3 (1990) 297–311.
8. J. Warner, "Visual data analysis into the 90s", *Pixel* **1**, 1 (1990) 40–44.
9. J. McAlbee, "Spatial modelling and visualization: Methodologies for an integration — Pathways to understanding", *EGIS '91*, vol. 2, EGIS Foundation, Utrecht, Netherlands, 1991, pp. 707–716.
10. A. Csinger, *The Psychology of Visualization*, Technical Report Series, Department of Computer Science, University of British Columbia, 1992.
11. J. L. Hartmann, "Visualization techniques in GIS", *Proc. EGIS '92*, vol. 1, EGIS Foundation, Utrecht, Netherlands, 1992, pp. 406–412.
12. J. Haslett, R. Bradley, P. Craig, A. Unwin, and G. Wills, "Dynamic graphics for exploring spatial data with application to locating global and local anomalies", *The American Statistician* **45**, 3 (1991) 234–242.
13. H. Senay and E. Ignatius, "Compositional analysis and synthesis of scientific data visualization techniques", in *Scientific Visualization of Physical Phenomena*, ed., Patrikalakis, Springer-Verlag, Hong Kong, 1991, pp. 269–281.
14. H. Senay and E. Ignatius, "A knowledge-based system for visualization design", *IEEE Computer Graphics and Applications* **14** (1994) 36–47.
15. A. M. Duclos and M. Grave, "Reference models and formal specification for scientific visualization", in *Scientific Visualization: Advanced Software Techniques*, ed., P. Palamidese, 1993, pp. 3–14.
16. B. E. Rogowitz and L. A. Treinish, "An architecture for rule-based visualization", in *Proc. IEEE Visualization '93*, 1993, pp. 236–243.
17. C. Beshers and S. Feiner, "Autovisual: Rule-based design of interactive multivariate visualizations", *IEEE Computer Graphics and Applications* **13** (1993) 41–49.

18. P. K. Robertson, "A methodology for scientific data visualization: Choosing representations based on a natural scene paradigm", in *Proc. IEEE Visualization '90*, 1990, pp. 114–123.
19. T. M. Lillisand and R. W. Kiefer, *Remote Sensing and Image Interpretation*, John Wiley and Sons, 1979.
20. S. K. Kachigan, *Statistical Analysis*, Radius Press, New York, USA, 1986.
21. J. D. Mackinlay, "Automating the design of graphical presentations of relational information", *ACM Trans. Graphics* **5**, 2 (1986) 110–141.
22. P. Rheingans and C. Landreth, "Perceptual principles for effective visualizations", in *Perceptual Issues in Visualization*, eds., G. Grinstein and H. Levkowitz, Springer-Verlag, Berlin, 1995, pp. 59–69.
23. J. P. Lee and G. G. Grinstein, "An architecture for retaining and analyzing visual exploration of databases", in *Proc. IEEE Visualization*, 1995, pp. 101–108.
24. J. Bertin, *Graphics and Graphic Information Processing*, de Gruyter, Berlin, 1981.

---

**Mark Gahegan** is a lecturer in the Department of Geographic Information Systems (GIS) at Curtin University of Technology in Perth, Western Australia, where he teaches in the graduate and post-graduate degree programmes in GIS. Previously, he was a lecturer in the School of Computing at Leeds University, England. Research interests centre around geographical data and include: spatial data structures, remote sensing, data visualization, data modeling and contextual reasoning.

**David O'Brien** received the B.Sc.(Hons) degree in Cognitive Science from the University of Sussex, England in 1991. After commencing a Ph.D. course at Leeds he transferred to Curtin University of Technology in Western Australia in order to join the recently established Department of Geographic Information Systems. His thesis topic concerns the development and comparison of different visualization strategies applied in the area of minerals exploration.

# VISUALIZING SPATIAL DATA: THE PROBLEM OF PARADIGMS

PHILIP K. ROBERTSON

*Canon Information Systems Research Australia*
*1 Thomas Holt Drive, N. Ryde, NSW 2113, Australia*

This paper describes the problem of developing working paradigms for advanced spatial data applications. The key role of interactive visualization in enabling the expertise of specialists, if effectively integrated into their working environments, is described. The scope for applying intelligence in designing visualizations to support, rather than to supplant, the expert is explored. A systematic framework describing the visualization design process, and an approach to applying intelligence around metavisualizations of the visualization design process, are summarized.

*Keywords*: Visualization, interaction, spatial data, intelligent systems.

## 1. INTRODUCTION

Advanced applications, such as geological modeling and geophysical exploration, push computational and display technologies to their limits. This applies not only to hardware performance but also to the software and system support. Significantly, available display and computational capabilities are often not utilized effectively because of poor linking to the working environment of application specialists. Specialists thus currently spend much effort struggling with computational tools and associated displays of data, side issues such as data format interchange, explicit functionality descriptions, and other tasks that distract from the main task of high value work in the application domain. New technologies and functionalities exacerbate the problem: "working paradigms", such as the cartographic paradigm in spatial data handling, are generally based on established work practices and associated specifications of tasks the user performs in an application domain. These work practices and associated tasks, however, may constrain or preclude taking effective advantage of emerging technologies.

Graphical interfaces can provide easier access to these computational functionalities but seldom map the functionalities effectively into the working paradigm of an application specialist. Interactive visualization has the potential to make a strategic impact by enabling the expertise of specialists but needs sufficient integration with the working paradigm of an application domain to be usable and adopted by existing specialists. Thus the design of visualizations, and more generally of interaction, is critical to whether integration with an application working paradigm is achieved. Effective design requires knowledge of an application domain and associated tasks. Capturing and applying such knowledge for a broad range of tasks, and for a set of possible interactions, is a major exercise.

*This work was performed while the author was with CSIRO Division of Information Technology, Canberra, Australia.



Spatial Computing: Issues in Vision, Multimedia and Visualization Technologies (1997) 263–273

This paper looks at the underlying needs in advanced applications for environments supporting a specialist's working paradigm. The evolution of paradigms of using technology in spatial data applications is summarized. The importance of interactive visualization, the need to integrate its design into an application environment, the evolution of visualization systems, and systematic design approaches, are described. The scope for introducing artificial intelligence to help guide the design of visualizations, and an incremental approach to drawing on artificial intelligence, are proposed as a practical step towards intelligent support to help enable, rather than supplant, the expertise of application specialists.

## 2. THE PROBLEM OF PARADIGMS

Computing systems should support the normal working environment of application specialists, allow specialists to work on problems in a manner consistent with this environment, and make the underlying tools or technologies transparent to their use. For example, an ideal working environment for a geoscientist would allow interaction with the data on a large format, scale-accurate 3D display or its virtual equivalent, with appropriate support for visualization, for accessing networked data sets and for querying or formulating hypotheses in domain-specific terms.

### Integrating new technologies

The integration of new technologies into an application environment is rarely a one-step process. This is partly because new technologies seldom cover all components of existing practices, and so require integration with possibly incompatible processes, but also because practices evolve under the impact of new technologies. The start point is usually close to the working practices that already exist but, because the technologies often have a capacity to streamline or replace existing practices, changes are often rapid. This poses a problem: leading users adapt practices quickly to best utilize emerging capabilities but other users not participating in this rapid evolution still expect tools to support traditional practices. The traditions of cartography still underpin current map-making processes, whereas in mineral exploration, pen and paper techniques have been largely supplanted by workstations using remotely-sensed data.

The path to changing or evolving work practices is not straightforward. Revising old practices to incorporate new capabilities does not necessarily lead to increased efficiencies. The standard way of developing new practices, by developing a task and usage model, does not necessarily capture key elements of an often complex process, many components of which are implicit to working patterns rather than easily articulated.

Unfortunately effective evaluation of revised practices, or of new practices, is seldom performed. In some cases where it is performed earlier low-technology practices are reinstated. This indicates the magnitude of the problem of how to integrate new technology capabilities into complex working environments that have often evolved over many years and have strongly entrenched practices and training approaches.

This prompts a look at the evolution of integrating new computing technologies in applications associated with spatial data.

### Evolving working paradigms associated with spatial data

Current computing environments for the most part promote a paradigm of use that is many steps away from the natural or preferred paradigm of use. Most specialists work in an environment that can best be described as a "computational systems and tools" paradigm. That is, they struggle with tools, systems, networks, incompatibilities, different data formats, primitive data-flow representations of their processes, minimal automatic documenting and logging of operations they perform on their data, minimal backtrack or "undo" capability, minimal capture of the algorithm just applied to the data, and often even minimal support for preserving data integrity. Hand-recorded log books are still crucial.

Even if data integrity is better preserved, under a "database update" paradigm, database languages are not sufficient for describing often complex modeling or comparison operations. And this is still not the working context that is easy or natural for an application specialist. A "visualization-centred" paradigm, based on the recognition that pictures often provide the most effective and influential form of communication, both in static and dynamic form or even in "hot-spot" enquiry mode can be an improvement.

Even this is several steps away from a "working-application environment" paradigm. One step closer might be a "task-driven" paradigm such as a document or report for policy advice or positional analysis. An interface that supports such a document as a working component, and where visualizations and other information provide linked access to data and models transparently, can get close to an "working-application environment" paradigm. But the actual working environment of application specialists really needs to reflect not just one end result or task associated with producing the result, but the full expected range of end results and associated sets of tasks.

### Multiple paradigms

Advances in networking have introduced the additional problem that many data sets are now being accessed by specialists from different disciplines. Data structuring and derived data or metadata, must increasingly be accessible to a range of fields with different expectations and practices. There may also be requirements for different views of the data for different tasks within a discipline. This increasingly calls for intelligent conversion layers for any given field with specific requirements.

## 3. THE EVOLUTION OF INTERACTIVE VISUALIZATION SYSTEMS

Interactive visualization is central to enabling the expertise of application practitioners. Why visualization? Because visualization is the process of using a picture of data to help build a better understanding — to mentally "visualize" the data. It helps give insights into data, problems and processes by exploiting the eye's direct access to the brain. It takes advantage of the brain's powerful capacity to see patterns and trends, and to detect anomalies, in large amounts of complex data. And why interactive? Because interaction allows a user to reach in and adjust the picture. Interaction exploits hand-eye coordination and short-term memory capabilities by drawing a user into exploring the data and problems. Parameters of models and views of the data can be adjusted with immediate feedback on the result. This is how we explore real-world objects: we pick them up, turn them around, take them apart, and put them back together.

Visualization is thus more than a display; it implies the building of a mental model linking the display with its context. This causes consideration not just of the perceived display, but also of its interpretation, which depends on the mental model or internal representation that the user has built, which in turn depends on the context and environment of use. Considering the needs for interactive visualization thus helps to focus on the broader needs for developing application-sensitive working environments.

Visualization systems are gradually evolving to come closer to meeting the needs of advanced applications.[1] This prompts a closer look at the evolution of visualization systems and the types of capability that have emerged or might be expected to emerge. Three major advances in capabilities stand out:

- Geometric transformations: the capability to perform spatial transformations on screen sized data sets, ideally at interactive rates. This provides users with a capability to manipulate their data for ease of viewing and, when modeling techniques are suitable, manipulating model parameters directly.
- Perceptual addressing: the capability to specify and control display parameters such as color in perceptual terms with associated modeling of display devices to ensure accurate realization. This provides users with the capability to specify enhancements in meaningful terms, and achieve increasingly device independent display and interpretation of colors.
- Guidance for design of visualizations: the capability to incorporate intelligence in helping a user decide what visualization technique and tools to use for a specified task, and to apply domain specific constraints. More generally, it can help the user work in terms relevant to an application environment.

Of these three needs, only the first has been effectively integrated with application software and even then often only in specialized systems. Early systems provided geometrical transformation capabilities increasingly embedded as part of display functionality. Examples include polygon transformation pipelines with associated scan-conversion support, and image transformation for geometrical warping in specialized image processing systems used for remote sensing applications. Even still, performance is not sufficient for practical modeling or simulation tasks.

Perceptual color addressing has been accessible in a small number of application systems for some years but has not been supported as a display functionality. As a result it is not performed at interactive rates for screen sized images. Systems have provided hardware support for simplified perceptual addressing in device dependent terms but perceptual addressing in device-independent terms has not been supported even though the requirements for perceptual color control are now fairly well understood.

The requirements for increased intelligence in visualization systems, however, are far from being well understood at present; they are really only just being considered at a generic level. Thus whilst the future path for visualization systems clearly hinges around exploiting intelligent support, possible architectures and implications for display designs are still being worked out. How then do we move towards such a target capability, elicit the system requirements to make it possible, and map these requirements to the underlying display and computational architectures and technologies?

## 4. A SYSTEMATIC FRAMEWORK FOR DESIGNING VISUALIZATIONS

Expertise will only be enabled if the data or processes are presented in appropriate ways that avoid or resolve ambiguity, are sufficiently consistent for reproducible results, but are sufficiently flexible to allow exploratory work. This suggests developing systematic approaches to determining first, the visualizations and interactions that are necessary or desirable, and second, what visualizations and interactions may be undesirable or introduce ambiguity. Often such approaches are based on a clear understanding, or reference model, of the underlying processes of visualization and interaction, and the resulting assumptions about the user.[2,3]

### Choosing visual representations

There are many different alternative visualizations for data, or combinations of data variables, ranging from various ways of using color to structural representations. Similarly interaction can be applied in a range of different ways. The problem is one of choosing the best for a given set of data, interpretation task, and domain of application. The process of choosing corresponds to traversing a decision tree of possible representations, or at a lower level determining meaningful parameters for each representation.

What is needed first is an understanding, in generic perceptual terms, of what characteristics of a data variable are portrayed by any particular representation that is used to convey the information to an observer. This means determining the information conveying capabilities of the various representations used. Possible ways of describing these capabilities have emerged from graphics; there is not necessarily any unique or best way, but rather a sufficient set of descriptors can allow a basis for systematically determining the capabilities of any particular representation. One such set of descriptors can be stated in terms of the degree of locality of the information[4]:

- values at a point (elementary);
- local neighborhoods of values (intermediate);
- global distribution of values (advanced).

To illustrate the use of such attributes, we can look at visualizations that are depictions of plausible real-world objects or scenes, the so-called natural scene paradigm for visualization.[5] This paradigm is based on recognizing that we are experienced at abstracting, and thus understanding intuitively, the properties of real scenes. This is the same requirement which we have for individual data variables represented within a visualization: the ability to abstract variables while also looking at their correlation. So, for example, an overhead relief-shaded surface representation of data makes evident the local attributes of a particular value (such as gradients), and the global structure (such as undulations), but not necessarily values at a point because there is no absolute reference for surface height. On the other hand, we can introduce an interactive dipstick to give a reading of surface height at any point, or interactively rotate the surface for a perspective view and improve the ability to estimate the height and thus data value at any point.

These generic point, local and global attributes can be applied more broadly to, for example, vector and tensor field representations with consistent interpretation.[6] They provide a basis for systematically describing attributes of a data variable that can be made evident in any given representation. And in each case, if the data type represented by the scene property is known (for example ordinal scalar field represented by surface height), a formalized description of the representation can be made.

### Understanding the interpretation task

Interpretation tasks are generally couched in domain-specific terms that often have a particular contextual meaning. But that does not preclude the specialist from making the bridge to generic terms, such as the above described point, local and global attributes of a data variable, to describe the attributes that a representation can convey. So for example a specialist could indicate interest in the absolute values of one variable at any point in a field, perhaps in relation to the gradient (or local distribution of values) of another variable. Although not all interpretation tasks are necessarily so easy to specify, usually a specialist has a sufficient idea of what is being sought to describe it in generic terms. If the data type is also known this then provides a formalized description of the data and interpretation task.

### Matching the representation to the interpretation

If the representation capability and the interpretation task are both described in generic terms, designing the visualization and interaction is reduced to a process of matching the representation capabilities to the task requirements, and thus steering the choice of representation. For a given set of available representations in a software visualization package these representation capabilities can be predetermined. A best match approach, taking into account any specified priorities, can be used.

It is unlikely that such a choice would be a one-pass process. Rather a specialist might choose one of a number of recommended representations, look at some tabular depiction of the degree to which the task and representation capabilities are matched, and then perhaps refine the priority or focus of the interpretation aims. The important point is that this type of systematic approach to design need not be complex to generate consistency and better user feedback than is achieved without it. Neither does it have to be formalized and implemented in software — it can be a set of guiding steps for realizing such representations with the information about representation capability built up through experience.

The need to develop such systematic approaches to design is being increasingly realized in the area of intelligent information presentation systems: unless there is some systematic base rationale for how intelligence or guidance is applied, it is very difficult to apply it usefully. Top-down approaches, such as the one outlined above, and bottom-up (compositional) approaches have been developed, as have rule-based, or case-based matching approaches.[5,7–12] What is increasingly clear is that with improvements in functionality and performance of visualization systems the need for designing visualizations is becoming more evident. The emphasis is very much on moving from pretty pictures to informative pictures, where informative implies that the information can be unambiguously decoded, which in turn implies that the encoding approach must be based on systematic design methodologies.

Underpinning all these approaches are several key components:

- characterizing the data properties;
- characterizing the presentation capabilities;
- identifying user-defined and contextual interpretation tasks;
- supporting user-defined interpretation tasks as some kind of relationship between data and presentation spaces.

The last step relies on finding a relatively robust approach to providing intelligent support.

## 5. AN INCREMENTAL APPROACH TO INTELLIGENT SUPPORT

An approach, and associated architecture, for incorporating intelligence into the visualization design process can be based on using autonomous agents to perform well-defined tasks associated with metavisualizations — graphical representations of operations associated with constructing a visualization.[13,14] This allows an incremental approach to incorporating intelligence, and to acquiring and representing knowledge.

The approach relies on first, a mechanism for traversing levels of the decision tree or trees that cover all possible choices of visual representation and associated parameters, and second, a method of making decisions in the absence of sufficient direct information. Underpinning the framework are models that allow knowledge representation in a sufficiently formalized manner that intelligence can be introduced to guide the required decisions by drawing on that knowledge.

### The role of metavisualizations

The metavisualizations provide a complete and encapsulated description of methods of mapping data into a visual representation. Associated with each metavisualization is a set of parameters that must be set (by default or interactively) for the operation to be completed. These methods are designed along perceptual lines and therefore offer constrained interaction. The constraints ensure that arbitrary mappings do not result. Thus if appropriate metavisualizations are designed to represent schematically any required visualization technique, a set of encapsulated mechanisms for performing mappings results. The encapsulation is important — it means that there is a limited set of requirements for invoking a metavisualization.

Metavisualizations may hierarchically invoke lower level metavisualizations which correspond to decisions about the mapping at a lower level in the overall decision tree. All the information necessary to complete the task for a metavisualization can be obtained from one or more of the *device, data, user*, or *project* models defined in the framework. This includes, for example, the definition of the range of producible colors for a color display device, the information carrying capability of specific data mappings, or suitable default points for data mapping definitions such as five-percentile points on a data histogram.

### Exercising intelligence through autonomous agents

A metavisualization has associated with it a set of autonomous agents whose task it is to find, or deduce, the required information to complete the task for a metavisualization. This may include for example, information about the level of interaction to offer, whether specific metavisualizations are even displayed, or whether encapsulated icons are provided to show the resulting mappings for inclusion in a final product. This information is gathered from the system models or deduced in a localized manner. Thus intelligence can be added incrementally around the operation of any particular metavisualization.

### Binding framework — reference models

Underpinning the approach must be a formalized reference model for the visualization process, including models for critical components. The reference model need not include all possible operations initially; rather it must have sufficient flexibility to allow extensions as required. But the core tenet — that knowledge about devices, data, interpretation and tasks can be sufficiently described by the models — requires a degree of formalization beyond that of current systems.

## 6. SUMMARY AND DISCUSSION

This paper has offered an overview of the problem of developing improved application software systems, and more specifically interactive visualization capabilities, for advanced applications involving spatial data. It recognizes that technological advances are increasing the computational resources available to application specialists, but often at the expense of increased complexity of use. An approach to drawing intelligence into the design of visualizations is proposed as a viable and robust step in improving application environments.

The basic premise behind this approach is that offering incremental intelligent support is the best way to help enable the expertise of specialists. This is because the context and direct tasks involved in advanced spatial applications are too complex and variable for traditional rule-based expert systems to assist effectively. Thus the approach is to help the expert in the process of interacting rather than to do the task for the expert. Introducing intelligence requires a systematic and formalized framework for the processes involved in applying techniques. The approach suggested in this paper comprises applying intelligence incrementally around well-defined schematic graphical encapsulations, or metavisualizations, that represent mappings of data into visual representations. This has the advantage that a user can "undo" or adjust decisions or parameters associated with any mapping simply by invoking the relevant metavisualization.

The approach relies on a knowledge base that reflects not the end result the user would want, and therefore what the system should produce, but rather the processes a user would perform on identified generic steps in the data visualization process. This is an important distinction. Existing knowledge engineering focusses on identifying what knowledge the system needs to reason successfully, whereas this approach focusses on identifying what knowledge the user needs to interact effectively. Interaction design is thus based on a model of the application of expertise, rather than on a model of the end purpose behind applying the expertise. This approach can therefore be treated as developing an interaction paradigm, rather than a full working environment paradigm. It is consistent with taking the interim step of enabling a user's expertise, rather than attempting to supplant the user's expertise.

This work is not complete; in this paper key ideas are drawn together to present an overview of the problem and to focus on interactive visualization as part of the process of applying expertise. It also emphasizes the importance of defining the process of interactive visualization in a systematic and thus formalizable manner to allow a systematic approach to incorporating intelligent support towards effective application "working paradigms".

## 7. ACKNOWLEDGMENTS

This paper draws on, integrates, and presents an overview of material from several earlier papers which elucidate aspects of this work independently (see References). It also draws on suggestions from the Ph.D. research of Matthew Hutchins, of the CSIRO Division of Information Technology and the Australian National University. The influence of discussions with David Abel of the CSIRO Division of Information Technology, and David Peters of the Tasmanian Parks and Wildlife Organisation, are acknowledged, as are the contributions of co-authors of earlier papers cited.

## REFERENCES

1. P. K. Robertson, "Applications requirements and the evoluton of displays", in *Display Systems: Design and Applications*, eds., L. MacDonald and T. Lowe, John Wiley & Sons, 1996.
2. R. B. Haber and D. McNabb, "Visualization idioms: A conceptual model for scientific visualization systems", in *Visualization in Scientific Computing*, eds., G. Neilson and B. Shriver, IEEE Computer Society Press, 1990, pp. 74–92.
3. P. K. Robertson and L. De Ferrari, "Systematic approaches to visualization: Is a reference model needed?", *Proc. ONR Workshop on Data Visualization*, Darmstadt, 1993, in *Scientific Visualization: Advances and Challenges*, Academic Press, 1994, pp. 287–305.
4. J. Bertin, *Graphics and Graphic Information Processing*, translated by W. J. Berg and P. Scott, Walter de Gruyter, Berlin, New York, 1981.
5. P. Robertson, "A methodology for choosing data representations", *IEEE Computer Graphics and Applications* **11**, 3 (1991) 56–67.
6. L. Hesselink and T. Delmarcelle, "Visualization of vector and tensor data sets", *Proc. ONR Workshop on Data Visualization*, Darmstadt, 1993, in *Scientific Visualization: Advances and Challenges*, Academic Press, 1993.
7. J. Mackinlay, "Automating the design of graphical presentations of relational information", *ACM Trans. on Graphics* **5**, 2 (1986) 110–141.
8. S. Roth and J. Mattis, "Data characterization for intelligent graphics presentation", *Proc. ACM-CHI '90.*
9. H. Senay and E. Ignatius, "Compositional analysis and synthesis of scientific data visualization techniques", in *Scientific Visualization of Physical Phenomena*, ed., N. M. Patrikalakis, Springer-Verlag, 1991, pp. 269–281.
10. S. Casner, "A task-analytic approach to the automated design of graphic presentations", *ACM Trans. on Graphics* **10**, 2 (1992) 111–151.
11. C. Beshers, "Automated design of virtual worlds for visualizing multivariate relations", *Proc. IEEE Visualization '92*, Boston, MA, 1992, pp. 283–290.
12. B. E. Rogowitz and L. A. Treinish, "An architecture for rule-based visuaization", in *Proc. IEEE Visualization '93*, San Jose, 1993, pp. 236–244.
13. P. K. Robertson, M. Hutchins, D. R. Stevenson, S. Barrass, C. Gunn, and D. Smith, "Mapping data into color gamuts — using interaction to increase usability and reduce complexity", Special Issue on Advanced Interaction, *Computer and Graphics* **18**, 5 (1994) 653–665.
14. P. K. Robertson and M. Hutchins, "Guided color representation using perceptual color spaces", *SPIE Symp. on Electronic Imaging Science and Technology: Human Vision, Visual Processing and Digital Display VI*, San Jose, Feb. 1995.

**Philip K. Robertson** is General Manager of Research and Development at Canon Information Systems Research Australia (CISRA), a research subsidiary of Canon with 150 staff working in image processing, color graphics and multimedia R&D. He was previously Manager of R&D Strategies, at the CSIRO Division of Information Technology in Australia where he was Leader of the Human-Computer Interaction and Visualization Program.

Dr. Robertson's research covers algorithms, architectures, systems and methodologies for image processing, multimedia, human-computer interaction and visualization, color modeling and displays, and massively parallel computing.

He holds a BE and MSc. in Electrical Engineering, and a Ph.D. in computer science from the Australian National University. He is a member of the editorial boards of *IEEE Computer Graphics & Applications, IEEE Transactions on Visualization and Computer Graphics*, and Pergamon's *Computers and Graphics*, and has been on the Program and Technical committees of international conferences and workshops. He has been an invited speaker and panelist at international conferences, and edited special issues of several journals.

# THE VISITORS GUIDE: A SIMPLE VIDEO REUSE APPLICATION

KIM SHEARER, SVETHA VENKATESH, DOROTA KIERONSKA
*Department of Computer Science*
*Curtin University of Technology, Perth, Western Australia 6001*

One of the results of the surge in interest in the internet is the great increase in availability of pictorial and video data. Web browsers such as Netscape give access to an enormous range of such data. In order to make use of large amounts of pictorial and video data, it is necessary to develop indexing and retrieval methods. Pictorial databases have made great progress recently, to the extent that there are now a number of commercially available products. Video databases are now being researched and developed from a number of different viewpoints. Given a general indexing scheme for video, the next step is to reuse clips in further applications.

In this paper we present an initial application for the reuse of video clips. The aim of the system is to resequence video clips for a particular application. We have chosen a well-constrained application for this purpose, the aim being to produce a video tour of a campus between designated start and destination points from a set of indexed video clips. We use clips of a guide entering and leaving buildings on our campus, and when visitors select a start location and a destination, the system will retrieve clips suitable for guiding the visitor along the correct path. The system uses an index of spatial relationships of key objects for the video clips to decide which clips provide the correct sequence of motion around the campus.

Although the full power of the indexing notation is unnecessary for this simple problem, the results from this initial implementation indicate that the concept could be applicable to more complex problems.

*Keywords*: Video reuse, indexing, video similarity, subsequences.

## 1. INTRODUCTION

Video indexing systems of the future will require a number of components which index sequences from different points of view. Just as journal articles are indexed by author, citation, keyword and title to allow retrieval by people with different starting points and goals, so video must have more than one index. The indices proposed already provide a generous spread of methods and query schemes.

The simplest level is detection of cuts and camera operations, which is amply described in literature.[1,11] This work detects a number of the features of video production in an automated fashion. In particular, cuts may be detected with a high degree of reliability using very simple image processing algorithms. The majority of camera motions can also be detected in a reliable fashion, although there are difficulties yet to be resolved in this area of the work.

Simple visual features are the base of the next level of indexing. A number of systems use easily evaluated image features, such as color histograms or global texture, to produce indices for images. There is also some work being done on extending this to videos. The difficulty with this work is in the query interface.



Spatial Computing: Issues in Vision, Multimedia and Visualization Technologies (1997) 275–301

While image similarity is simple to provide, it is difficult to provide a raw interface to the query mechanism. The current systems require the user to describe their query in rather arbitrary terms, usually represented by numbers and often related to example sets. Even assuming the quantities used as a metric are useful measures, direct user queries are ungainly and difficult, requiring a certain amount of user skill. The final problem is that of applying this form of metric to temporal based data such as video; there is no clear approach to solving this difficulty.

Using more complex visual processing we may produce an index based on spatial relationships between objects. The task of object detection and tracking through a video sequence is not one which can be fully automated in general. However for some applications it is possible to index video sequences in this manner with limited manual supervision. The application we have chosen falls into this category.

We propose a system to guide visitors about the campus of our university. This system works from a map of the campus, and a set of annotated video clips of a guide traversing the campus. Each of the clips contains only one moving object, the guide. It is thus a much simplified problem to mark items of interest in the initial scene, and track them through the video. There will generally be two areas in each frame with a large difference in image motion between frames.

Given a map containing information about paths and exits, and a collection of annotated clips, how does our guide work? The encoding at the heart of our system is based on a 2D string system for representing spatial relationships.

## 2. 2D STRINGS

The early work on 2D strings was presented in 1987 by Chang, Shi and Yan.[6,9,8] This work was part of a project to produce an iconic indexing system for pictorial databases. Pictures are converted to a pair of strings which are stored in the database and queries are expressed in the same string notation, which allows the database to be searched using a simple matching scheme. Matching strings are then decoded into simple iconic representations of the original picture which may be displayed as a response to the queries.

Strings in this work have as their alphabet a set $V$ of object labels and a set $A$ containing the operators $\{=, <, :\}$.

**Definition 1.** A 1D string, defined over a set $S$, is any string $x_1, x_2, \ldots x_n$ where $n \geq 0$ and $\forall j : x_j \in S$.

**Definition 2.** A 2D string over $V$ is defined to be

$$(x_1, y_1, x_2, y_2, \ldots y_{n-1}, x_n, x_{p(1)}, z_1, x_{p(2)}, \ldots z_{n-1}, x_{p(n)})$$

where

| | |
|---|---|
| $x_1 \ldots x_n$ | is a 1D string over $V$ |
| $p : \{1..n\} \rightarrow \{1..n\}$ | is a permutation function over $\{1 \ldots n\}$ |
| $y_1 \cdots y_{n-1}$ | is a 1D string over $A$ |
| $z_1 \ldots z_{n-1}$ | is a 1D string over $A$ |

Here $p$ is a permutation function which maps a symbol in the first string of a 2D string pair to its corresponding symbol in the second string.

The first string in a 2D string pair expresses object relations along the $u$ axis, the second string relations along the $v$ axis. The usual convention is that $u$ is the horizontal axis, with values increasing left to right, and the $v$ axis is vertical with values increasing bottom to top. The operators '=' and '<' have the usual meanings of equality and less than, with less than being to the left of for the $u$ axis, and below for the $v$ axis. The operator ':' is slightly unusual and means that two objects are in the same set.

The matching algorithm for strings defined by Chang *et al.* is based on a simple ranking scheme for the object symbols in strings. The rank of a symbol in a string is defined to be one plus the number of $<$ operators which precede the symbol. The ranks of the symbols in the string $a < b : c < d = e$ are given in Table 1.

Table 1. Ranks for Chang *et al.*

| a | < | b | : | c | < | d | = | e |
|---|---|---|---|---|---|---|---|---|
| 1 | | 2 | | 2 | | 3 | | 3 |

Using this simple ranking Chang *et al.* define three different types of matching, providing three levels of strictness of match, with type-2 being an exact match and type-1 and type-0 being progressively less strict. The three types of matches have the following definition:
A string $S$ is a type-$i$ subsequence of a string $T$ if

1. $S$ is contained in $T$
2. If $a_1 w_1 b_1$ is a substring of $S$, $a_2 w_2 b_2$ is a substring of $T$, where $a_1$ matches $a_2$ and $b_1$ matches $b_2$ then

$$\begin{aligned}
&\text{Type-0 } rank(b_2) - rank(a_2) \geq rank(b_1) - rank(a_1) \\
&\quad \text{or } rank(b_1) - rank(a_1) = 0 \\
&\text{Type-1 } rank(b_2) - rank(a_2) \geq rank(b_1) - rank(a_1) \geq 0 \\
&\quad \text{or } rank(b_2) - rank(a_2) = rank(b_1) - rank(a_1) \\
&\text{Type-2 } rank(b_2) - rank(a_2) = rank(b_1) - rank(a_1)
\end{aligned}$$

This matching scheme is simple to evaluate and is intuitive. The major problem with this work is that the method of encoding the string is point based and discards extent information, object position being determined by the object's centroid. Using this encoding pictures that are very different can generate the same strings. The initial attempts to remedy the shortcomings of the Chang system were 2D E-strings[7] and G-strings.[5]

Jungert's E-strings (for extended strings) extended Chang's work by adding operators derived from work in temporal reasoning by Allen.[2] Unfortunately the new operators can no longer be expressed in a unified structure. G-strings use a cutting mechanism to break objects into smaller pieces, allowing the expression of relationships in a simple string form once again. The cutting produces a greater number of objects, leading to greater complexity in matching. As each object may have more that one piece, objects are no longer directly comparable, but may require comparison of a number of sub-objects. The advantage of Chang's original system over later systems is that, being point based, all symbols are either equal, less than or greater than each other symbol. The cost of this simplicity is the loss of extent information.

A system which provides a compromise between Chang's point based system and the latter interval based systems, is 2D B-strings.[10] In B-strings objects are represented by two symbols, one representing the start point along an axis, and another representing the end point along the axis. The advantage of this representation is that all symbols in the strings are simply comparable, unlike the segmented objects of interval based systems, yet extent information is represented. The cost of this improvement is that each object requires two symbols in each string. This is partially balanced by the reduced number of operators required.

Matching for B-strings uses three types, similar to Chang *et al.* These types are calculated from the ranks of symbols in the string, and are based on relationship categories and orthogonal relationships. Symbols in B-strings are assigned a rank using the following equation

$$\text{rank}(s_i) = \sum_{j=1}^{i} f(s_j)$$

where

$$f(s) = \begin{cases} 1 & \text{if } s \neq \text{`}=\text{'} \\ -1 & \text{if } s = \text{`}=\text{'} \end{cases}$$

Type-0 matching is based on the five relationship categories. Taking each of the 13 spatial relationships along each axis, there are a total of 169 possible 2D spatial relations. These are categorized into five partitions, *disjoint*, *meet*, *contain*, *inside* and *partly overlap*. The partitions are defined by:

**Definition 3.** The relationship category of the spatial relationship between two objects $a$ and $b$ is:

1. *Disjoint*: if $\mathit{end\_rank}(a) < \mathit{begin\_rank}(b) \vee \mathit{end\_rank}(b) < \mathit{begin\_rank}(a)$ along either axis
2. *Meet*: if $\mathit{end\_rank}(a) = \mathit{begin\_rank}(b) \vee \mathit{end\_rank}(b) = \mathit{begin\_rank}(a)$ along one axis and the condition for disjoint is not satisfied on the other axis
3. *Contain*: $\mathit{begin\_rank}(a) \leq \mathit{begin\_rank}(b) \wedge \mathit{end\_rank}(b) \leq \mathit{end\_rank}(a)$ along both axes
4. *Inside*: $\mathit{begin\_rank}(b) \leq \mathit{begin\_rank}(a) \wedge \mathit{end\_rank}(a) \leq \mathit{end\_rank}(b)$ along both axes
5. *Partly overlap*: if no other relationship category holds

Essentially these partitions are:

| | |
|---|---|
| *disjoint* | the two objects do not touch or overlap |
| *meet* | the objects touch but do not overlap |
| *contain* | the first object completely surrounds the second object |
| *inside* | the second object completely contains the first object |
| *partly overlap* | the objects overlap, but neither is completely contained by the other |

Two objects which are a type-0 match between two pictures must have the same overlap properties, but the match is invariant under rotation and reflection. This is the least strict of the three matching types.

Type-1 matching uses orthogonal relationships between objects. The orthogonal relationship between two objects expresses the direction in which one object lies from the viewpoint of the other object. Orthogonal relationships are defined as follows:

**Definition 4.** Object $a$ is said to be to the *east*(*west*) of another object $b$ iff there is some part of $a$ to the *east*(*west*) of the whole of $b$.

**Definition 5.** Object $a$ is said to be to the *north*(*south*) of another object $b$ iff there is some part of $a$ to the *north*(*south*) of the whole of $b$.

The orthogonal relationship between two objects may be derived from symbol ranks using the following rules:

1. $a$ is to the east of $b$ if $u$: $end\_rank(a) > end\_rank(b)$
2. $a$ is to the west of $b$ if $u$: $begin\_rank(a) < begin\_rank(b)$
3. $a$ is to the north of $b$ if $v$: $end\_rank(a) > end\_rank(b)$
4. $a$ is to the south of $b$ if $v$: $begin\_rank(a) < begin\_rank(b)$

We use the notation $aC_{ab}b$ to denote the relationship category for two objects $a$ and $b$, $aO_{ab}b$ to denote orthogonal relationships and $aR_{ab}b$ to denote the exact spatial relationships between the objects. B-string matching may then be defined as follows:

**Definition 6.** Picture $f'$ is a type-$i$ subpicture of $f$ if

1. All objects in $f'$ are also in $f$
2. For any two objects, $a, b \in f'$

   $aC_{ab}b$, $aO_{ab}b$ and $aR_{ab}b$ are in $f$ and $aC_{ab}'b$, $aO_{ab}'b$, and $aR_{ab}'b$ are in $f'$

$$C_{ab}' = C_{ab} \Rightarrow \text{Type-0 match}$$
$$C_{ab}' = C_{ab} \wedge O_{ab}' = O_{ab} \Rightarrow \text{Type-1 match}$$
$$C_{ab}' = C_{ab} \wedge O_{ab}' = O_{ab} \wedge R_{ab}' = R_{ab} \Rightarrow \text{Type-2 match}$$

For type-2 matching, $R_{ab}' = R_{ab}$ clearly subsumes both relation category and orthogonal relation matching.

The matching scheme described provides a flexible, efficient picture matching method, which should prove useful in a number of application areas.

## 3. INDEXING VIDEO

The use of 2D strings to index video was first suggested by Arndt and Chang.[3] They use the original Chang 2D-strings as the base for constructing a compressed notation for encoding video sequences. The notation retains the strings representing the initial frame of the video, then represents the rest of the video as edits to these initial strings.

The edit notation is based on membership of sets of objects of equal rank. For each axis all objects which have the same rank are placed in the same set. If we convert the strings representing each frame of the video to these sets, we can then express the changes caused by object motion as changes to the membership of the sets. Arndt and Chang's operators are therefore based on adding and deleting set members and sets.

The main criticism of this notation is that it is essentially only a method for compressing a sequence of 2D strings. Each time a query is performed for a video, the strings representing the video must be uncompressed, using a two stage process, then ranked fully for each frame and compared to the query. The system we propose does not involve expansion of the compressed encoding, as changes to the ranks of objects may be read directly from the notation.

### 3.1. Notation

Our system is based upon B-strings which, as discussed earlier, incorporates extent information which is not included in the Chang string system. This increases the descriptive power of the representation. The major improvement is that the query process is not based on the expansion to and evaluation of a sequence of 2D strings, rather spatial relationship changes may be read directly from the edit sequence. This allows us to easily discard edits which do not affect the objects in the query, greatly reducing the processing required during querying.

Most queries are subpicture matches, that is, finding a database element, or *reference picture*, which contains a match for the *query picture.* For similarity retrieval we may extract the objects common to the query picture and the reference picture, and form a reduced query picture from these. Generally query pictures will be significantly smaller than reference pictures.

Let $\mathcal{Q} = q_1 \ldots q_m$ denote the query string and $\mathcal{R} = r_1 \ldots r_n$ the reference string. Then let $q_f$ denote the first symbol of $\mathcal{Q}$ to occurring $\mathcal{R}$, and let $q_l$ denote the last symbol of $\mathcal{Q}$ to occurring $\mathcal{R}$. Then $\mathcal{R}$ can be expressed as $[r_1 \ldots r_{f-1}][q_f \ldots q_l][r_{l+1} \ldots r_n]$. The first or last sets may be empty, and $q_f \ldots q_l$ will usually contain elements not in $\mathcal{Q}$. The first and third sets contain no query symbols and therefore changes to these sets have no effect on the spatial relationships of the query objects. In Arndt and Chang notation edits to these portions of the string are evaluated to recreate the string, and then $r_1 \cdots r_{f-1}$ is parsed when obtaining the ranks of query elements. We propose an algorithm which does not require parsing of the 2D string, but reads changes to the spatial relationships of the query objects directly from the edit sequence notation. This allows edits which do not affect the query objects to be discarded.

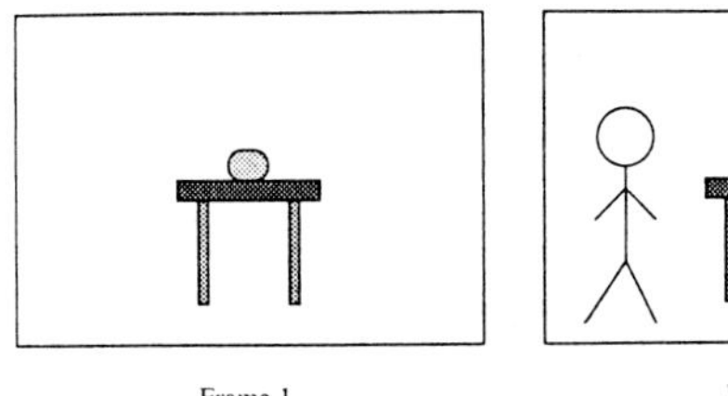
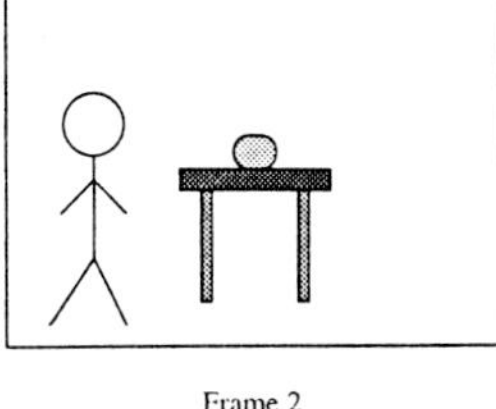

Fig. 1. Three frame video sequence.

The new notation is similar to the Arndt and Chang notation in that there is an initial string representing the first frame in the video, then a sequence of edits to the initial string. The edit operations however differ, and are outlined below:

| | |
|---|---|
| **u** | the next sequence of edits should be performed on the $u$ axis of the string |
| **v** | the next sequence of edits should be performed on the $v$ axis of the string |
| m $i, j$ | move a symbol from position $i$ to position $j$ |
| d $i$ | delete the symbol in position $i$ of the $u$ string, also deletes the corresponding end point in the $u$ string and both symbols in the $v$ string |
| i $ch, i$ | insert the character $ch$ into the string at position $i$ |
| * | the previous edit completed the transformation to the representation of the next frame in the video |

The sequence in Fig. 1 can be expressed as the following sequence of B-strings:

$$\begin{array}{c} table\ \ box\ \ BOX\ \ TABLE\,,\ table\ \ TABLE\ \ box\ \ BOX \\ man\ \ MAN\ \ table\ \ box\ \ BOX\ \ TABLE\,,\ man\ \ table\ \ TABLE\ \ box\ \ BOX\ \ MAN \\ table\ \ TABLE\ \ man\ \ box\ \ MAN\ \ BOX\,,\ man\ \ table\ \ box\ \ BOX\ \ TABLE\ \ MAN \end{array}$$

This sequence is represented in our notation as:

$$\begin{array}{l} table\ \ box\ \ BOX\ \ TABLE, table\ \ TABLE\ \ box\ \ BOX \\ \mathbf{u}\ i\ man, 0\ i\ MAN, 1\ \mathbf{v}\ i\ man, 0\ i\ MAN, 5* \\ \mathbf{u}\ m\ 2,0\ m\ 5,1\ m\ 3,4\ \mathbf{v}\ m\ 2,4* \end{array}$$

## 4. VIDEO RETRIEVAL

In order to optimally use storage space we would prefer to store data in a compressed format. In order to minimize response time we would prefer not to uncompress data as a preprocessing step. Ideally we would like to read the information required directly from its compressed form, and this facility is provided by the notation we propose.

### 4.1. Finding Frames in a Video Sequence

The query resolution algorithm takes as inputs the edit notation for a sequence and a query string. The edit notation for a sequence may be expressed as:

initial $u$ string
initial $v$ string
$e_1e_2 \dots e_n$

where $e_1e_2 \dots e_n$ are the edits to the initial string. The query string is a 2D B-string derived from the users query, usually a pictorial query by example. As the query string does not vary throughout the matching process we can eliminate recalculation of the relationships between query objects by producing *relationship tables.* There are three types of relationship tables, one for each type of match.

For type-0 matching a relationship table is created containing the relationship category for each pair of objects. As there are five distinct relationship categories (see Sec. 2), this table requires three bits for each element of the upper triangular matrix, as shown in Table 2.

Table 2. Relationship table.

| | $o_1$ | $o_2$ | $o_3$ | $\dots$ | $o_n$ |
|---|---|---|---|---|---|
| $o_1$ | | $r_{1,2}$ | $r_{1,3}$ | $\dots$ | $r_{1,n}$ |
| $o_2$ | | | $r_{2,3}$ | $\dots$ | $r_{1,n}$ |
| $\vdots$ | | | | $\ddots$ | $\vdots$ |
| $o_{n-1}$ | | | | | $r_{n-1,n}$ |

Type-1 matching requires orthogonal relationship information as well as relationship categories, so a relationship table containing orthogonal relationships is created in addition to the type-0 table. There are four orthogonal directions used: north, south, east and west, therefore requiring four bits per entry. We must also keep the orthogonal relationships for the reverse order of objects, as both $a$ *orth_rel* $b$ and $b$ *orth_rel* $a$ must be compared. We therefore keep two tables.

When type-2 matching is required a relationship table is created to store the exact relationship, along each axis, between each pair of objects. There are 13 basic relationships, requiring four bits for each axis, therefore requiring one byte for each object pair. For $n$ objects, the space consumed by relationship tables, for each type of matching is:

$$\text{Type-0} \quad 3 \cdot \frac{n^2}{2} \text{ bits} \tag{1}$$

$$\text{Type-1} \quad (3+8) \cdot \frac{n^2}{2} \text{ bits} \tag{2}$$

$$\text{Type-2} \quad (3+8+8) \cdot \frac{n^2}{2} \text{ bits} \tag{3}$$

For 40 objects this represents a space requirement of less than 2 kb.

The initial string from the edit notation of the sequence is used to instantiate the *object rank table* (ORT). This table contains an entry for each object in the query and records, for each object, the position within the reference string of the begin and end symbols along each axis, and the rank of each symbol. Once the object rank table has been instantiated, matching may proceed for the first frame from the reference sequence.

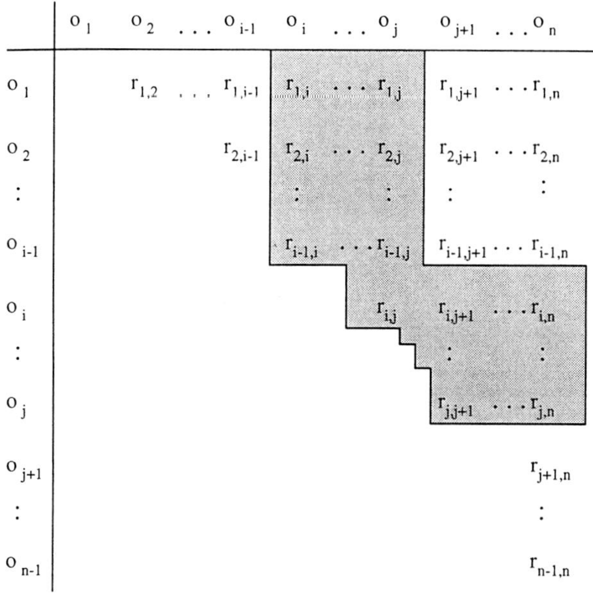

Fig. 2. Match table.

Matching uses another table, called the *match table* (Fig. 2), which has a one bit entry for each object pair in the query. This entry is set if the object pair are a type-$n$ match in the query and reference string. The match is determined by comparing the entry for the object pair in the appropriate relationship table, or tables, with the relationship determined from the object rank table. Thus for type-2 matching for query object $o_i$ and $o_j$, we would compare the type-2 relationship table entry $r_{i,j}$ with the relationship category determined using the ranks from entries $o_i$ and $o_j$ in the object rank table. If $o_i$ and $o_j$ are found to match, entry $r_{i,j}$ in the match table is set, otherwise entry $r_{i,j}$ is cleared. A frame in which all objects match will set all bits in the match table.

Figure 3 shows the tables used in matching and their derivation. In Fig. 3 we can see the relationship tables, which are invariant through the matching process, being compared with the ORT to decide on frame matches. The ORT is updated by the queue of edits. The *compare* process is not performed after every edit, but only after a frame completion marker. There is no way to interpolate between frames without making a number of arbitrary assumptions, which may or may not be valid. We therefore assume that the video has been sampled at a rate consistent with the level of detail required in retrieval.

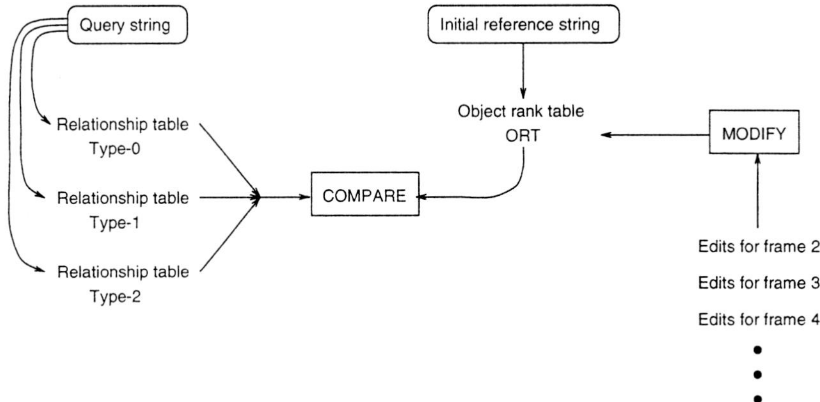


Fig. 3. Derivation of tables used in matching.

If we examine the elements contained in the ORT we see that each may be altered directly from the edits read, without creating and parsing the reference string. Given a symbol having a rank $r$ and position within the string of $p$, if we read an edit: $\text{ic}, p-1$, we can clearly increase both $r$ and $p$ by one to account for the edit. Similar deductions may be made for each of the other edit types. In implementation we must keep the actual reference strings as we process the edits in order to determine whether a symbol being moved or deleted is an object or equality symbol. However the reference strings are at no time parsed once the ORT has been instantiated from the initial string.

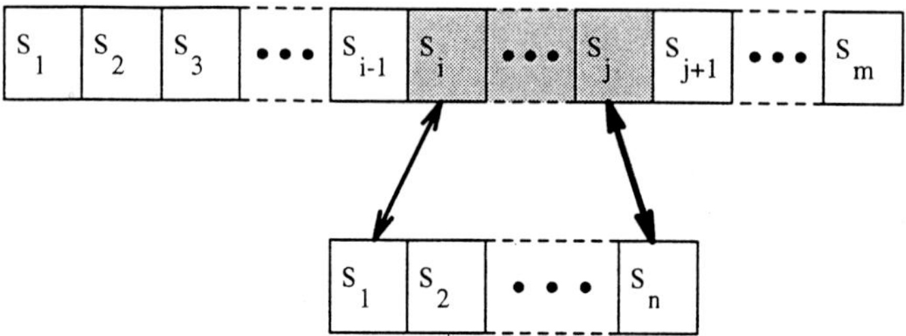

Fig. 4. Segments of the reference string.

Due to the nature of the data kept in the ORT, it is possible to discard a number of edits without applying their effects to object rank. If an edit does not alter the relative positions of objects which have entries in the ORT, then the changes it does produce have no influence on the matching process. Figure 4 depicts a reference string with the region of the string containing objects which match those in the query shaded. Any edits which affect only unshaded parts of the reference string cannot change relationships between objects involved in the query and so may be discarded. Edits which may be discarded for a reference string $S : s_1 \ldots s_n$, with $s_f$

being the first object involved in matching and $s_l$ being the last are:

| | |
|---|---|
| m $i, j$ | if $(i < q_f \vee i > q_l) \wedge (j < q_f \vee j > q_l)$ |
| d $i$ | if $i < q_f \vee i > q_l$ |
| i $ch, i$ | if $i < q_f \vee i > q_l$ |

Given that we wish to apply this work to sequences of images we may look at adapting this algorithm to matching a number of query frames. The simplest method would be to apply the entire matching process for each frame. However, for a sequence of $n$ frames representing a motion query by example, we would construct an ORT $n$ times, each ORT being very similar to the others, and read and process the edits $n$ times. This is repeated work that we wish to avoid.

We may indeed avoid this work by creating the reference tables for all query frames before beginning matching, and using these to create an extended ORT which contains every object from all query frames. Then for each frame of the reference sequence, rather than calculate and compare relations from the ORT for each query frame on the fly, we calculate relationship tables for each frame once, before matching with the first query frame, and store them as we do for query frames. These tables for the current reference string may then be compared against each query frames relationship tables in turn without further calculation. In this way we calculate the relationship between objects in the reference string only once, and parse the edit sequence only once.

It is also useful to create relationship tables for the reference string when the query string contains entries which do not specify an exact object, but indicate attributes the object must have. In this case there may be more than one object in the reference string which could be associated with the entry. This leads to a number of possible query strings which may be treated in the same manner as the multiple frames for a motion query.

## 4.2. Video Subsequence Similarity Matching

The ability to find video frames which contain objects in a given spatial relationship to one another is useful. However the essence of video is that it captures movement of objects, so it makes sense to allow searching for changing object relationships within video sequences. In its simplest form this is not difficult to implement, but there are problems in producing a complete solution.

A video query is a sequence of video frames, each containing a number of objects. We expect the objects contained in separate frames to be reasonably consistent throughout the sequence, if this is not the case we have a collection of unrelated image matches, rather than a sequence. The matching scheme is based on multiple applications of subpicture matching, essentially matching each query frame against each reference frame, optimized for sequences. We can optimize the matching process by using a strategy similar to that used for matching multiple queries generated by attribute matching. For subsequence matching we generate a relationship table for each frame in the query sequence, and each frame in the reference sequence. We can then proceed to test each query frame against each reference frame by a simple table comparison. Frame against frame matches are performed using standard types of subpicture matching for B-strings, either type-0, type-1 or type-2 as the user chooses. The result is a list of frame matches for each query frame, from which we wish to extract a longest sequence of matching frames. This longest sequence is the longest common subsequence of the query sequence and the reference sequence. It is important to note that under this matching scheme, each reference frame may match more than one query frame.

In searching for a query subsequence in a video, we define three forms of matching, which we call type-0, type-1 and type-2 subsequence matching. We therefore have three types of subpicture match, and three types of subsequence match. A type-2 subsequence match is defined as follows: let $\mathcal{Q} = q_1 \ldots q_m$ be a query subsequence, where $q_1 \ldots q_m$ are the frames making up the query. Let $\mathcal{R} = r_1 \ldots r_n$ be the reference video sequence, where $r_1 \ldots r_n$ are the frames of the video. A sequence of frames $r_i r_{i+1} \ldots r_{j-1} r_j$ is a type-2 match for a query if

$$\forall k : i \leq k \leq j \Rightarrow r_k \equiv_t q_k$$

where $a \equiv_t b$ indicates $a$ is a type-$t$ subpicture match for $b$. Thus a type-2 subsequence match displays a frame for frame equivalence between the two sequences compared, as shown in Fig. 5.

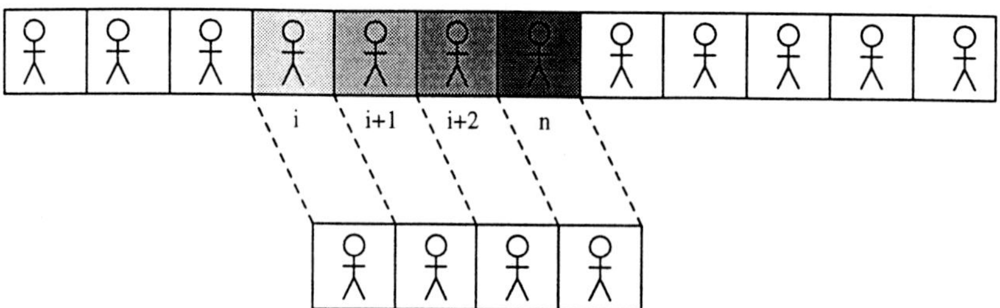


Fig. 5. Type-2 subsequence matching.

We define a type-1 subsequence match as follows: Assuming the earlier definitions for $\mathcal{O}$ and $\mathcal{R}$, the frames $r_{1_1} \ldots r_{1_{max_1}}, r_{2_1} \ldots r_{2_{max_2}}, \ldots, r_{m_1} \ldots r_{m_{max_m}}$ are a type-1 video subsequence match if

$$\forall a : 1 < a < m \Rightarrow \forall b : 1 \leq b \leq max_a : r_{a_b} \equiv_t q_a$$

This relaxes type-2 matching by allowing repetitions of matching frames. We do not expect repeated frames in a query sequence, however in such cases we would allow repetitions in the query to be matched by a single reference frame for type-1 matching, but not for type-2 matching. Figure 6 is a diagram of type-1 matching.

Using the definitions for $\mathcal{Q}$ and $\mathcal{R}$ provided above, a type-0 subsequence match is defined as follows: the frames $r_{match_1}, r_{match_2}, \ldots, r_{match_m}$ are a type-0 subsequence

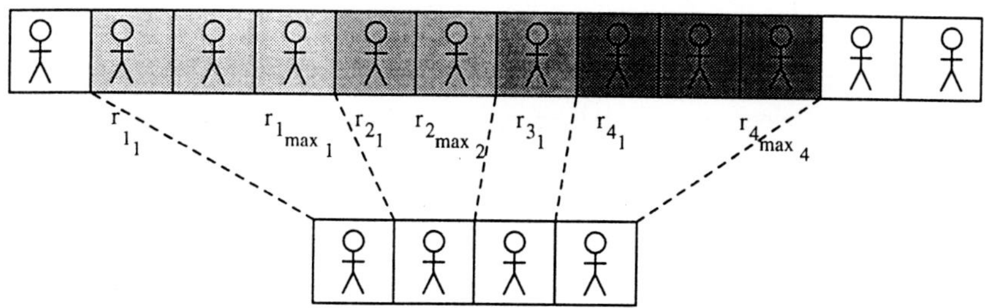


Fig. 6. Type-1 subsequence matching.

match for the query $\mathcal{Q}$ if

$$\forall a : 1 < a < m \Rightarrow r_{match_a} \equiv_t q_a \text{ and } match_1 < match_2 < \ldots < match_m$$

This states that the frames must appear in the correct order, but does not insist on consecutive frames, as shown in Fig. 7.

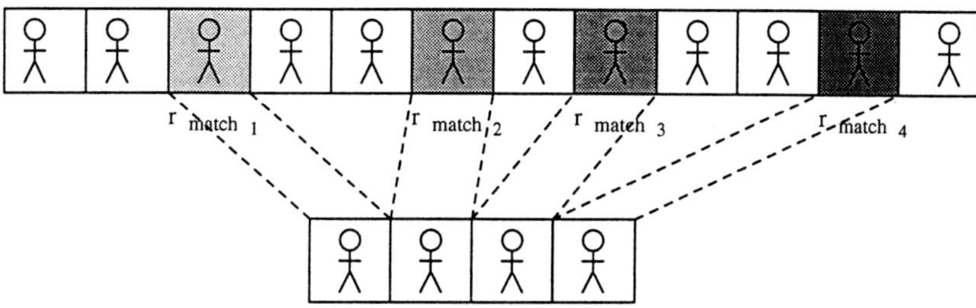


Fig. 7. Type-0 subsequence matching.

If we have a query sequence $q_1, q_2, q_3$ and a reference sequence $r_1, \ldots, r_8$, with subpicture matches

| Query frame | Reference frame matches |
|---|---|
| $q_1$ | $r_2, r_4, r_5, r_8$ |
| $q_2$ | $r_1, r_3, r_6$ |
| $q_3$ | $r_2, r_7$ |

the type-2 subsequence match is $r_5, r_6, r_7$. There are two type-1 matches, these are

$$r_5 r_6 r_7 \qquad r_4 r_5 r_6 r_7 \,.$$

The type-0 matches contained in this subsequence would be

$$\begin{array}{ll} r_2 r_3 r_7 & r_2 r_6 r_7 \\ r_4 r_6 r_7 & r_5 r_6 r_7 \,. \end{array}$$

We now have two forms of matching when applied to a video sequence. There are three types of subsequence matching available, but each of these relies on one of the three string matching types to provide its frame to frame matching. Thus we may have a subsequence match of type-1, which uses type-2 string matching. The notation we shall use for this is to write the string matching type, followed by a slash, then the subsequence matching type. Thus the previous example would be type-2/1 matching.

Given that we use the optimized algorithm, with all relationship tables precalculated the space requirement is: let $\mathcal{Q} = q_1 \dots q_m$, $\mathcal{R} = r_1 \dots r_n$ and let the number of objects in the queries be $O_q$, then referring to Eq. (1), the space requirement is

$$m \cdot \frac{O_q^2}{2} \cdot (3 + 8 + 8) \text{ bits}$$

for query tables and

$$n \cdot \frac{O_q^2}{2} \cdot (3 + 8 + 8) \text{ bits}$$

for the reference strings. Further time optimization can be achieved by maintaining a permanent match table for each frame of the string, at a space cost of

$$m \cdot \frac{O_q^2}{2} \text{ bits}$$

In cases where there are few matches for query frames against reference frames, the cost of producing relationship tables may be greater than the cost of recalculating relationships. This will be the case when most matches fail in the first few relationship comparisons, provided the number of query frames is not large.

Enumeration of subsequence matches is performed by a simple depth first recursive search.

## 5. VIDEO RESEQUENCING

### 5.1. Introduction

Once the difficulties in producing indices for videos are resolved, and segments retrieved, a second problem that confronts us is that of consistency. The movie industry spends considerable time and effort ensuring consistency in productions. We may string together a number of video segments which contain the semantic elements required to tell a story, but inconsistency can obscure or totally derail the story line. Essentially the study of continuity is based around the task of ensuring narrative continuity, that is "*to tell a story* coherently and clearly, to map out the chain of characters' actions in an undistracted way".[4]

Reisz and Millar[12] break the study of continuity into the following sections:

1. Matching consecutive actions
2. Extent of change in image size and angle
3. Preserving a sense of direction
4. Preserving a clear continuity

5. Matching tone
6. Making sound flow over a cut.

We are most directly concerned with *Matching consecutive actions*, a large part of which is ensuring the directions of movement of characters remain consistent with the environment and other clips. Extent of change in image size and angle may influence the choice of camera location for filming, as the rule is to make objects of interest either the same size, or completely different, but not almost the same size. Matching tone could also have an impact on the current system as it discusses the necessity of using similar lighting and coloring conditions for sequences of clips.

Complete automation of consistency checking in a general domain is clearly far from feasible today, however in selected domains we can test techniques which may have more general applications. By solving these smaller domains we can hope to build tools that may be used to decompose the larger problem.

We have chosen a small application, a campus tour guide system, in order to test the use of 2D string methods in video consistency. In this application we are given a map of the campus and a collection of video clips of a guide traversing the campus, the system must select and sequence clips which show the guide traveling along an appropriate route. Here the system is being asked to decide which of the clips form a sequence which is consistent with the task of navigating between points on the campus.

## 5.2. Video Indexing Revisited

The work presented in the previous section shows how we may index and retrieve videos using 2D strings. The notation is compact and matching may be performed in an efficient and flexible manner. Given that we can query the position of key objects over time we seek to apply this to retrieving video segments and arranging them in a consistent order, to tell a simple story. In this case the story narrated is how to get from one place on campus to another. The method chosen is to show the user a sequence of video clips showing a guide person departing from the starting point, passing any appropriate landmarks, and finally arriving at the required destination.

The guide system has a number of video clips in its database, each showing the guide traversing some part of the campus. We want to retrieve the subset of these clips which best illustrates the path between a chosen start point, and destination point on campus. Each clip falls into one of three categories:

1. Clips of the guide exiting and moving away from a building.
2. Clips of the guide approaching and entering a building.
3. Clips of the guide walking past a landmark.

There may be a number of clips for each exit on a building, as there may be paths approaching the building from a number of directions, and the guide may enter and leave each of the exits. There may also be clips showing the guide walking past a building without entering on the way to another destination. We shall call clips that are in category 1 *entry clips*, clips in category 2 *exit clips* and those in category 3 *transit clips*. The point of exit or entry from a building will be termed an *exit*, whether it is used as one, or as an entrance.

There are three main key objects, two of which will appear in every clip: the guide, an exit and a *way point*. A way point is a special landmark used when a clip shows a joining of paths where there is no exit. A crossroad would be a way point, as there are a number of paths approaching a point that is simply a transfer to another path. This aids the system in determining the direction of paths into and out of the way point. Often there are objects other than these three main objects in a video that are prominent. These prominent objects are also annotated as this provides further reference points for motion in the video. These further objects are particularly useful when there are large numbers of paths incident on the same exit or way point.

### 5.3. Data Structures for a Campus Guide

The major problem in the field of reuse for multimedia systems is annotation. In general, producing the index data in an efficient manner is currently impossible. For indexing schemes which are based on object position there is the likelihood that the video surveillance field may soon provide results which allow efficient indexing.

In some environments it is possible, using existing techniques, to largely automate the annotation of a video sequence. In the case of our guide it is relatively simple to distinguish the actual guide. In cases where the camera is fixed on the exit, the guide may be distinguished through simple frame differencing. The other key objects may be annotated in the first frame, and then propagated to further frames as they do not move. If the camera pans to follow the guide through a scene, then there will be two widely variant optic flow fields, a largely stationary and small field for the guide, and a larger more rapidly moving field for the background. The position of the guide is determined by the pixels contributing to the smaller optic flow partition. Key object positions may again be annotated in the initial frame, we then adjust these positions according to the optic flow of the background. These positions provide us with the bounding boxes which enclose objects of interest, which are used to produce the string representation.

Table 3. Record from clips database.

| Location | Exit Id | Number of clips | Camera orientation | String file |
|---|---|---|---|---|
| Library | 0 | 2 | 0 | liblr.mv |
| | | | 0 | librl.mv |

The string representation forms part of the database record stored for each video clip. A record from the database is shown in Table 3. The primary key for the clips database is location. Each location may have multiple exits, each of which may have multiple clips. For each clip, we also record the camera orientation during filming. This orientation is recorded in degrees clockwise from north, and is used in conjunction with exit directions and path directions to determine the desired direction of movement in the video.

In order to use these video clips we must have a method of deciding on the route to use between two locations. This requires a map of the campus. The map data provided consists of a list of locations on the campus. For each of these locations we record the direction each exit faces. Each exit has a record for each path leaving the exit which stores the direction taken from the exit, the other end point of the path, and the direction of arrival at the other end of the path. Again directions are recorded as degrees clockwise from north. The example map in Fig. 8 would be encoded as in Table 4.

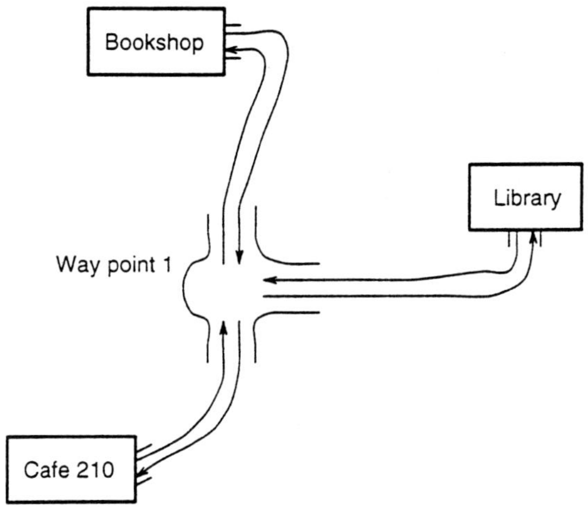


Fig. 8. Campus map.

Table 4. Table representing map.

| Location | Exit face | Destination | Exit direction | Arrive direction |
|---|---|---|---|---|
| Bookshop | East | Way point 1 | South | North |
| Library | South | Way point 1 | West | East |
| Cafe 210 | South east | Way point 1 | North east | South |
| Way point 1 | North | Bookshop | North | South |
| | East | Library | East | West |
| | South | Cafe 210 | South | South west |

This data is sufficient to allow paths to be planned for travel from any one location to another. Currently there has been no weighting placed on the paths, there are properties of paths, such as wheel chair access, which would be appropriate for such an application, and facilities could be added to allow some paths to be declared as under maintenance. Furthermore, the videos used may not be entirely consistent. As new buildings and paths are added to the campus, new videos will be required.

If the original guide is not available, or no longer has the same clothes, or even if the weather is dissimilar, there will be inconsistency in the video clips. These inconsistencies should be minimized, which could again affect path planning, requiring the same guide and similar conditions of brightness be maintained. However path planning is not the main concern of this project and so the path planning algorithm has been kept as simple as possible.

Given the map data it would of course be possible to solve the campus guide problem using a simple look up table. The advantage our implementation has over a look up table approach is that we do not need to indicate clips for paths to new locations. For example assume we take Fig. 8, and add a new location *Administration* so that the map now appears as in Fig. 9. If we were to code this as a look up table we would need to find the entries for the clips for entering and leaving the *Bookshop*, and entering and leaving *Way point 1* on the north, and enter these in the database for the new location. The existing path from the *Bookshop* to *Way point 1* would be deleted and replaced with paths from the *Bookshop* to *Administration*, and from *Administration* to *Way point 1*. This all requires much manipulation of the information on clips.

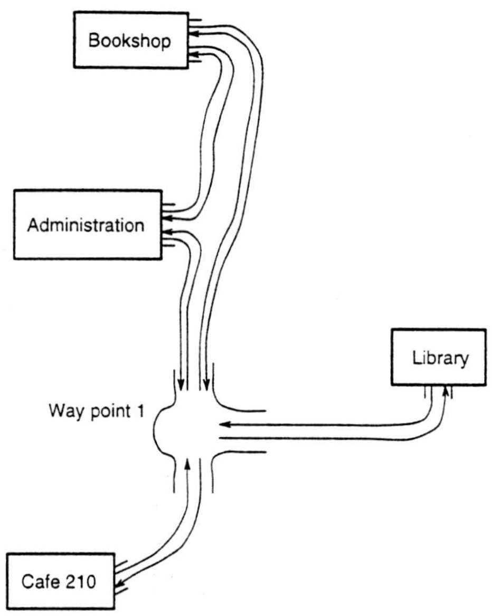


Fig. 9. Altered campus map.

Our approach dissociates the clip information from the map by making the system choose clips at run time. Table 5 representing the new map from Fig. 9 has only two entries altered from the initial table, the locations of the other ends of the

Table 5. Table representing map.

| Location | Exit face | Destination | Exit direction | Arrive direction |
|---|---|---|---|---|
| Bookshop | East | Administration | South | North |
| Library | South | Way point 1 | West | East |
| Cafe 210 | South east | Way point 1 | North east | South |
| Way point 1 | North | Administration | North | South |
| | East | Library | East | West |
| | South | Cafe 210 | South | South west |
| Administration | East | Bookshop | North | South |
| | East | Way point 1 | South | North |

paths from the *Bookshop* and the north path of *Way point 1*. An additional entry is added for the new location.

While this increased data independence may be useful, the main thrust of our approach is more ambitious. The problems we attempt with our solution include some that are less structured than those that can be solved using other methods. For example given an environment with no strictly defined paths we can choose the entrance or exit that demonstrates motion in a direction that best resembles the direction required. There is also application for a more general solution of this work in video resequencing applications which are less restrictive than the guide system, as mentioned above.

## 5.4. Finding the Right Clip

A path retrieved from the map is defined by a sequence of locations on campus, which are landmarks in the order they would be encountered when traveling along the desired route. The task we require of the system is to find and sequence clips of these locations with the guide walking in the correct direction. To do this we use the camera orientation provided with each clip and the directions provided in the map file. Given a direction of motion in the map, and the angle the camera is facing, the corresponding motion in the video image can be deduced. For example an exit direction of 270° and a camera angle of 0°, gives a motion of right to left in the image.

In many of the cases for the guide system, the camera points more or less directly at an exit, and the movement required is either simple left to right, or right to left. This makes the task of deciding upon the correct clip reasonably simple. Decisions in these cases are made using four condition variables: *left before*, *left after*, *right before* and *right after*. These variables are set to represent the position of the guide before and after the guide overlapped with the exit, or way point. Clearly for the guide approaching the *Library* from *Way point 1*, we would be interested in a clip with the four condition variables having values:

| | | |
|---|---|---|
| *left before* | $\leftarrow$ | true |
| *left after* | $\leftarrow$ | false |
| *right before* | $\leftarrow$ | false |
| *right after* | $\leftarrow$ | false |

Given a simple Cartesian environment, with paths at right angles, we can clearly characterize all paths involving exits with the four condition variables above plus a final variable pair, *below before* and *below after.* In fact for our example application all paths involving exits may be decided upon using the variables defined for left and right.

The question is, how do we determine the values of the variables? To answer this we return to the previous section, and similarity matching for video subsequences. For each condition variable we wish to determine if a particular nonoverlapping relationship occurs, either before or after the guide overlaps the exit. Under our assumption of a well-behaved path system, each of these variables may be solved by a simple type-1/0 subsequence query. For example *left before* is true if the query in Fig. 10 returns a non-empty set of matching frames. Similar motion queries may be constructed for each of the variables. If we wish to discover the frames in which the guide overlaps the exit we can use a simple type-0/0 subsequence match.

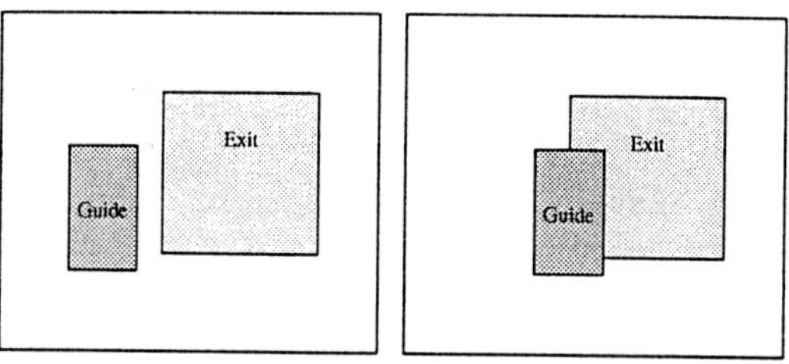


Fig. 10. Motion query for *left before.*

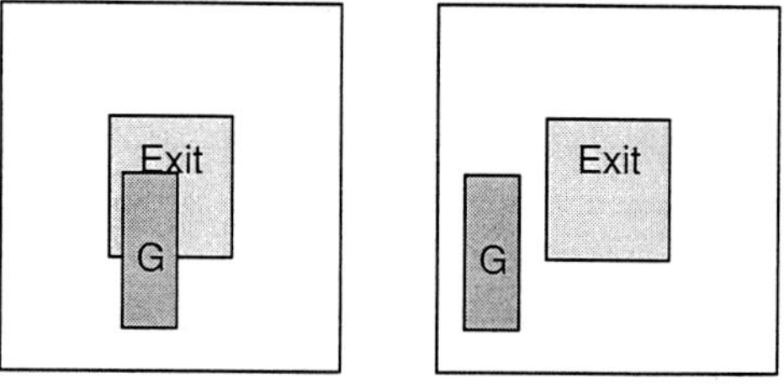


Fig. 11. Query for *exit* then move left.

In fact, in the simplest case where we have a path running across the exit, we can find the correct clip using type-1 subsequence matching. Assume we need an exit clip where the guide departs by moving left. A suitable clip is one which contains a type-1/1 match for the query frames in Fig. 11. A type-1 subsequence match allows repetition of frames, but insists that the final frame that matches the initial query frame, and the first frame that matches the subsequent query frame are contiguous.

Having produced a subsystem to decide on simple exit and entry clips, the majority of the locations on campus are catered for, as most indeed do have paths which run either directly towards, or tangentially across the exit. A more difficult problem however is way points. By definition a way point must have at least three paths leading to it. If we once again assume our Cartesian environment, we can use a similar approach, however the examples of paths we are presented with indicate that not only are way points unlikely to fit our Cartesian model, but also that the paths are less likely to be well-behaved, or even well-tempered, when approaching the way point.

Way points also do not have the built-in restrictions on possible directions found in exits. The guide is constrained to approach, or depart from, and exit from the front, this means that not only can we ignore the possibility of the guide being above the exit in a clip, but also we can rely on the guide being slightly lower than the exit when nearing it. A way point, which we denote as being the central area of an intersection of paths, imposes no such constraints. Way points therefore represent an environment that is considerably more free than that of exits and entries.

Consequently we must gather more information about way point clips in the form of additional condition variables. Apart from the obvious addition of *up before* and *up after*, we also add variables encoding the diagonals. The full list of conditional variables used for way points is:

| Before conditions | After conditions |
|---|---|
| *left before* | *left after* |
| *right before* | *right after* |
| *up before* | *up after* |
| *down before* | *down after* |
| *up left before* | *up left after* |
| *up right before* | *up right after* |
| *down left before* | *down left after* |
| *down right before* | *down right after* |

In this more general environment it is important to note that the *left* and *right* variables may not be determined as they were in the simple case of exits. For exit and entry clips we relied on spatial constraints to guarantee that the guide approached from slightly in front of the exit, however these constraints do not hold for way points. In a general environment there are actually five possible positions of the guide to one side of the way point. The five possibilities for the guide to the right of the way point are shown in Fig. 12. We may use these possible positions to partition the plane into 16 zones, representing likely approach directions of the guide as shown in Fig. 13(a). In this figure each zone represents the approximate area of the plane which the guide must be in to generate a particular spatial relationship with the way point or exit. For example zone 0 corresponds to the relationship in

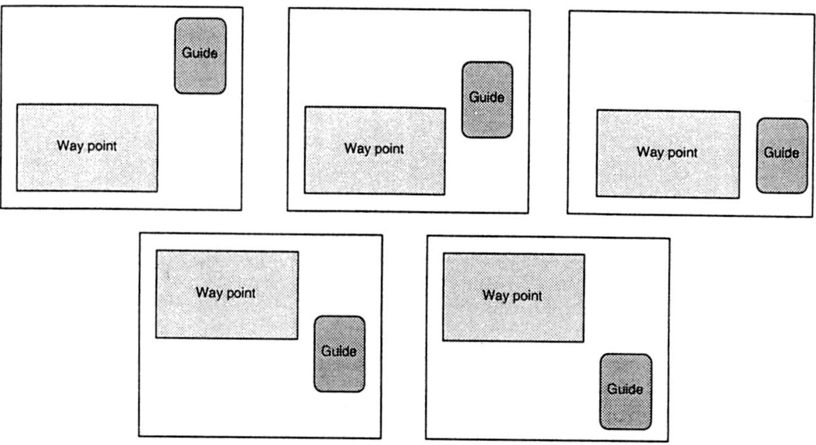


Fig. 12. Five relationships for right.

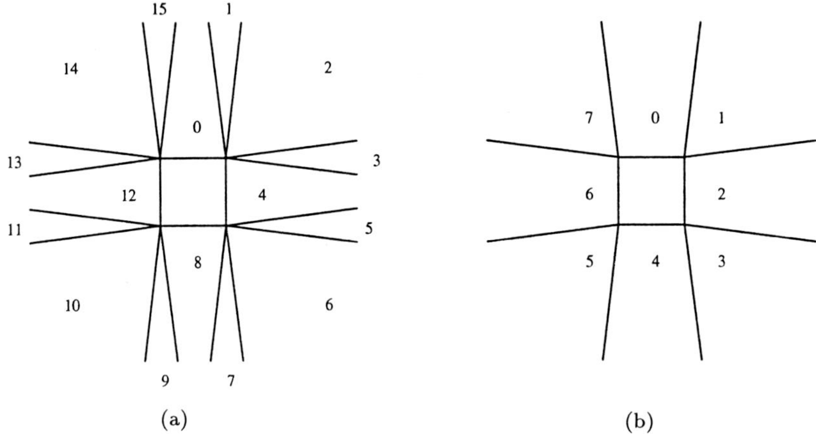


Fig. 13. Partitions of the plane.

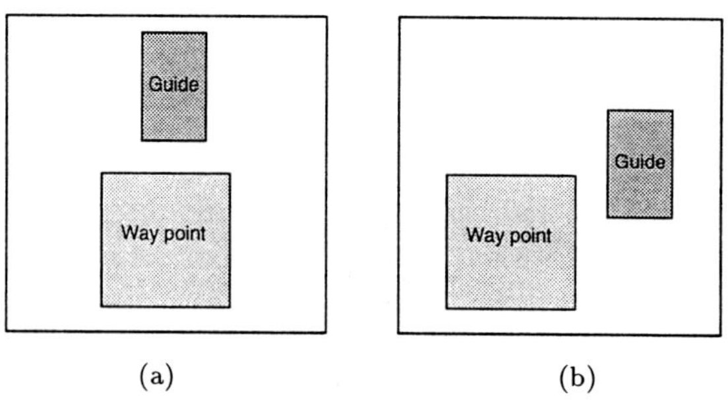


Fig. 14. Relationships corresponding to zones.

Fig. 14(a), while zone 3 corresponds to Fig. 14(b). For the current project the zones to either side of zones 0, 4, 8 and 12 are merged, to produce the eight zones shown in Fig. 13(b), which defines the zones that correspond to the condition variables listed above. To determine these variables we use type-2/1 matching with the appropriate motion queries.

The eight variables give us a high degree of discriminatory power when examining paths. In a case where this is insufficient we could apply the finer grained partition of the plane, however for all the examples in the current study the lesser level of segmentation has been sufficient.

Given the incident direction required of a clip, we may easily deduce which variables are desired, which allowable and which are clearly wrong. For example, given a direction of arrival of 45°, we would desire the condition variable *up right before* to be true, and expect one of *up before* or *right before* to also be true. Any other condition variables would in this case be unacceptable. If we were using the finer grained partitioning, we would desire relationships from partition 2 to be present in the clip, with relationships from partition 1 or 3 highly likely and partitions 0 and 4 possible. Given paths of, perhaps 30° and 60°, we would expect the first to involve partitions 0, 1 and 2, while the second passes through partitions 2, 3 and 4.

An application which could use the finer partitions is to provide a metric for choosing a suitable clip if a precise match does not exist. A cost could be associated with the number of partitions separating the observed partition, and the desired partition. Weighting this by the number of frames spent in the partition, and averaging by the total number of frames, would produce a reasonable metric for choice.

## 6. RESULTS

Figures 15 and 16 show two clips of the same location, *Way point 1*, with the guide approaching along different paths. The camera orientation from the database and condition variables for each clip of *Way point 1* are shown in Tables 6 and 7.

Table 6. Condition variables for video *way1rd.mv*.

| Camera orientation : | 315 |
|---|---|

| | Before | After |
|---|---|---|
| *left* | false | false |
| *right* | false | true |
| *up* | true | false |
| *down* | false | false |
| *up left* | false | false |
| *up right* | true | false |
| *down left* | false | false |
| *down right* | false | false |

Fig. 15. Frames from sequence *way1rd.mv.*

Fig. 16. Frames from sequence *way1dl.mv.*

Table 7. Condition variables for video *way1dl.mv.*

| Camera orientation : | 315 |
|---|---|

| | Before | After |
|---|---|---|
| *left* | false | false |
| *right* | true | false |
| *up* | false | false |
| *down* | false | true |
| *up left* | false | false |
| *up right* | false | false |
| *down left* | false | true |
| *down right* | false | false |

If we examine the map file represented in Table 4, we see that the journey from the *Bookshop* to the *Library* requires a clip passing through *Way point 1*, approaching from the north and departing to the east. Given a camera orientation of 315°, this translates to an approach direction of 45° to the right of the camera line, and a depart direction of 135° to the right of the camera line. We would therefore expect that the guide should approach to the right of and above the way point, and depart to the right and perhaps below the way point. Inspection of the variables in Table 6 reveals that *up* and *up right* are true before the guide reaches the way point, *right* is true after, indicating that this is an appropriate clip. The results in Table 7 provide a possible match for the entry direction, but the lack of *up right before* when compared with the previous clip makes it less acceptable. It is the exit direction however that disqualifies the clip. We desire a clip with the guide departing to the right, but clip *way1dl.mv* depicts the guide departing down toward the left. Clearly the best sequence for this situation is *way1rd.mv.*

## 7. DISCUSSION

The system described in this paper is able to examine video clips, annotated by object relationships, and decide which displays the best match for a desired trip across a campus. The paths in this example are generally well-spaced as they approach an intersection or location, so that we can distinguish between them without testing the limits of the method used.

In future work we plan to apply the system in a less structured environment, in order to determine the full capabilities of our method.

There are two principal reasons for more complex paths occurring. One is that there may be a larger number of paths meeting at an intersection. As the number of paths increases, the separation of course decreases, leading to greater difficulty in deciding exactly which path is best. The other complicating factor is simple geography.

Fig. 17. A difficult path arrangement.

The video frame in Fig. 17 shows a location on campus that has a short path running from the exit to the main path. This path does not run directly away from the exit, but curves away sharply. We would like the exit and entry clips to show the exits clearly, so ideally the camera angle should be orthogonal to the plane of the exit. If we in fact use this camera angle for the exit in Fig. 17, the guide will move to the right of the door before reaching the main path. This will mean that the guide will pass from the exit to the right regardless of the final direction of travel.

Problems such as those posed above could perhaps best be solved with the addition of a reasoning system. Such a system could use not only the relationship of the guide to the exit, or way point over time, but also the relationship of the guide to objects which are common to the clips of the same location. The ability to include deductions about such peripheral objects could greatly increase the applicability of such a system, and represents the next portion of this work.

## REFERENCES

1. A. Akutsu, Y. Tonomura, H. Hashimoto, and Y. Ohba, "Video indexing using motion vectors", in *SPIE Proc. of Visual Communications and Image Processing* **1818** (1992) 1522–1530.
2. J. F. Allen, "Maintaining knowledge about temporal intervals", *Commun. ACM* **26**, 11 (1983) 832–843.
3. T. Arndt and S.-K. Chang, "Image sequence compression by iconic indexing", in *1989 IEEE Workshop on Visual Languages*, 1989, pp. 177–182.
4. D. Bordwell and K. Thompson, *Film Art: An Introduction*, 4th edn., McGraw Hill, Inc., 1993.
5. S. Chang, E. Jungert, and T. Li, "Representation and retrieval of symbolic pictures using generalized 2D strings", in *SPIE Proc. of Visual Communications and Image Processing IV* **1199** (1989) 1360–1372.
6. S. Chang, Q. Shi, and C. Yan, "Iconic indexing by 2D strings", in *Proc. of the IEEE Workshop on Visual Languages*, Dallas, Texas, USA, June 1986; also in *IEEE Trans. on Pattern Analysis and Machine Intelligence* **9**, 3 (1987) 413–428.
7. E. Jungert, "Extended symbolic projections as a knowledge structure for spatial reasoning", in *4th BPRA Conf. on Pattern Recognition*, March 1988, pp. 343–351.
8. S. Lee, M. Shan, and W. Yang, "Similarity retrieval of iconic image database", *Pattern Recognition* **22**, 6 (1989) 675–682.
9. S. Lee and Y. G. Shin, "A cooperative planning system for flexible assembly", in *Proc. of the 2nd Int. Conf. on Computer-Integrated Manufacturing*, Los Alamos, CA, May 1990, pp. 306–313.
10. S. Lee, M. Yang, and J. Chen, "Signature file as a spatial filter for iconic image database", *J. Visual Languages and Computing* **3** (1992) 373–397.
11. K. Otsuji, Y. Tonomura, and Y. Ohba, "Video browsing using brightness data", in *SPIE Proc. of Visual Communications and Image Processing '91: Image Processing* **1606** (1991) 980–989.
12. K. Reisz and G. Millar, *The Technique of Film Editing*, 2nd enlarged edn., The Focal Press, 1968.

**Kim Shearer** holds a Bachelor of Science degree, with honours in computer science, from The University of Western Australia. On completing this degree, he worked for two years in the computing industry, before returning to The University of Western Australia as a tutor. In his time as a tutor Kim undertook research in the distributed systems area. He is now studying for a Ph.D. at the Curtin University of Technology.

His area of study is indexing and retrieval for image and video databases, with associated interests in graph theory and other formal representations.

**Svetha Venkatesh** holds a Bachelor of Engineering from Roorkee University and a Masters of Technology degree from the Indian Institute of Technology in India. She received her Ph.D. from the University of Western Australia in Perth.

She is currently an associate professor at the School of Computing in Curtin University, Perth. She has worked in the areas of active vision, object recognition systems, biological based vision systems, and is currently working on the application of computer vision to image and video database indexing and retrieval.

She is the co-director of the MARVIN group at Curtin University. She is a Senior Member of the IEEE, and was the President of the Australia Pattern Recognition Society in 1991. She is the author of about 80 papers, and is the co-author of the book *From Living Eyes to Seeing Machines* to be published in 1996.

*Photograph of S. Venkatesh is not available.*

**Dorota Kieronska** obtained her B.Sc. and Ph.D. in computer science from University of Western Australia in 1986 and 1990, respectively. She is a senior lecturer in the Department of Computer Science at Curtin University of Technology.

Her research interests include knowledge indexing and representation for multimedia, spatial reasoning and parallel algorithms.

*Photograph of D. Kieronska is not available.*

# CONCEPTUAL REPRESENTATION FOR MULTIMEDIA INFORMATION

ROGER W. SMITH, DOROTA KIERONSKA, SVETHA VENKATESH

*Department of Computer Science, Curtin University Of Technology*
*GPO Box U1987, Perth, Western Australia 6001*
*E-mail: {roger, dorota, svetha}@cs.curtin.edu.au*

Multimedia information is now routinely available in the forms of text, pictures, animation and sound. Although text objects are relatively easy to deal with (in terms of information search and retrieval), other information bearing objects (such as sound, images, animation) are more difficult to index. Our research is aimed at developing better ways of representing multimedia objects by using a conceptual representation based on Schank's conceptual dependencies. Moreover, the representation allows for users' individual interpretations to be embedded in the system. This will alleviate the problems associated with traditional semantic networks by allowing for coexistence of multiple views of the same information. The viability of the approach is tested, and the preliminary results reported.

## 1. INTRODUCTION

The creation, control, and use of information is shifting from organization oriented repositories, to include local collections belonging to individual users. This is due to technological advances in both hardware and communication network services. Furthermore, the information is available in a plethora of formats. Multimedia technologies such as the World Wide Web, allow users to link dissimilar formats in a ubiquitous fashion. However, these links are associative in nature, and do not provide a structure for formal querying or navigation, except via brute force techniques.

This work describes part of the ongoing research on the UMART (Unified, Mental Annotation and Retrieval Tool) project. Multimedia information is now routinely available in the forms of text, pictures, animation and sound. Although text objects are relatively easy to deal with (in terms of information search and retrieval), other information bearing objects (such as sound, images, animation, and data manipulating agents) do not possess the standardized, representational qualities that text objects do.

Our aim is to develop methods for providing users with a means of creating *conceptual maps* of underlying information. Although the conceptual structure of each map is unique to individual users, the underlying structure of the map is a deep, formally defined semantic net. This allows manipulation of the knowledge structure by users as well as automata such as information gathering agents. The main contribution of this work is the development of the underlying framework to allow for the construction of such conceptual maps. None of the existing methods



Spatial Computing: Issues in Vision, Multimedia and Visualization Technologies (1997) 303–327

of knowledge representation, such as found in current hypermedia systems, provide the richness of the structure we propose (refer to Sec. 2.3). Our long term goal is to use the tool not only for knowledge structuring, but also for hypothesis generation.

The outline of this work is as follows: Section 2 surveys the background work. Section 3 introduces the underlying concepts of the UMART, and describes the algorithms for creating and manipulating the representation. Section 4 contains a comparative analysis of the UMART and HTML (Hypertext Markup Language) in creating and utilizing a representation, and an overview of the UMART interface. The conclusions follow in Sec. 5.

## 2. BACKGROUND

### 2.1. Information Retrieval

Information retrieval (IR) systems require the user to enter keywords or phrases in the form of queries, in order to retrieve related information, and IR systems these days must contend with many different media because information is now available in the form of text, pictures, animation and sound. Usually, querying is an interactive process between the user and the system, where the user refines the query for the desired information based on how well a previous query (for the same information) performed.

Although text objects are relatively easy to deal with (in terms of search and retrieval), other information bearing objects (such as sound, images, animation, and data manipulating agents) do not have the canonical representations that text based objects possess.[6] Text is represented in its simplest form by utilizing a set of standard characters (ASCII), and the technology for manipulating, searching and retrieving text is well developed. Unfortunately, still images, audio files, and video sequences have no generalized form, and there are a large number of formats for storing and representing these types of media.

Indexing schemes are therefore used to organize related data objects. To overcome the lack of canonical representation of different knowledge bearing objects, text descriptions can be attached to the objects and these descriptions can then be catalogued for storage and retrieval as desired. However, this leads to a new set of problems in that natural language descriptions are ambiguous.

Providing a human can view the description, the chance of finding the associated information is good, but the number of possible descriptions the user may have to peruse in order to find the information they are looking for does not make this a viable general solution. Instead of free-form descriptions, records that contain a number of enumerated categories can be attached to objects, thereby providing a set of context-free lexical indexes (they are still keywords) to make information retrieval easier. The author selects the category that matches closest the information that the record (frame) is to represent, and the user selects from the category list when searching for information.

In the case of text information objects, the information is returned as the passage or passages of text containing the keywords, and this can be achieved reasonably effectively by searching each information object in a linear fashion. Problems with this method arise however, when the text objects are large, the size of the keyword phrase is large (which can dramatically increase the search time), or there are a large number of text objects to be checked. The large number of objects and their cumulative size make this approach prohibitively expensive in terms of search time, for realistic situations. Also, the keywords that the user chooses for the search might not appear in the text they are looking for, even though the semantic content of the words in the text is equivalent. Synonyms can be substituted for the keywords in an effort to reduce this problem, however this adds additional computational complexity to the search algorithm. For example, assume the user wanted information on "big dogs", but the required article, referred to "big dogs" as "large canines", then the search algorithm would have to search each potential document for both the set of original keywords, and the set of synonyms for each keyword.[7]

Keyword searching alone can be unreliable, even in well defined IR systems such as library databases. Although more advanced systems now utilize semantic categories as well as keyword, author and title searches, depending on the topic, and the degree of user familiarity with the topic, many possible "hits" may be returned by a query, and these must be manually viewed by the user in order to find the information required. IR systems are now coming on-line that also contain "links" to related information. These can be classified as hybrid IR systems because they contain elements of hypertext schemes (refer to Sec. 2.2) that allow the user to search for information in a non-linear fashion. In addition to keyword searches, the objects are linked together in weak, associative, semantic nets.[12,2]

### 2.2. Hypermedia

Hypermedia allows information objects to be represented as nodes in an associative semantic net. The conceptual structure is one of a directed graph.[15] The user is presented with text or other media objects at each node containing markers that lead to other related information objects. Markers are often presented to the user so that they stand out in some way, and the user selects the marker they are interested in to access the node connected to it. Hypermedia documents can exist across networks (the most obvious example of this is the World Wide Web), or in other repositories of information such as CD-ROMs (where once again, both IR and hypermedia technology are utilized to provide the user with many avenues of both reading, and finding information).

Printed text provides a reader with a linear path that must be followed from the first page to the last in order to gain the understanding of the knowledge contained within the text — just as the author intended. Hypermedia however, provides a non-linear path through the knowledge. There may be thousands of possible paths available to the reader of a hypermedia document. Hypermedia documents can be thought of as being partly created by the author (who sets up the information objects and links to other objects), and also the reader, who decides which links to follow when reading the document.[16]

Joyce[4] has identified two types of hypermedia models[a]: exploratory, and constructive. An example of an exploratory hypermedia environment is that of the CD-ROM hypermedia document such as an encyclopaedia. The reader is free to jump into a knowledge representation and move about in that knowledge domain. Eventually, the reader will find themselves on some distantly related topic (after traversing a few links). Assuming that the reader is really interested in the original topic, there is little choice but to go back and try another link. Eventually, the reader will deplete the undiscovered information (although no two readers will probably do this in exactly the same way), which is analogous to reaching the end of a linear document. An example of a constructive hypermedia environment is the WWW. Although readers can still treat web pages in an exploratory manner, they can also create hypermedia documents that transform the original information by providing links to areas of interest in the original representation, by linking other areas in their new document that they feel are associated in some way, and can collaborate with other authors to build larger knowledge domains.

### 2.3. Other Link Systems

*Microcosm*,[3] *Point and Query*,[5] HTML documents, WAIS (an internet service), and *WordNet*,[7] are a cross-section of both exploratory and constructive link systems that are representative of the types of systems available for both constructing knowledge representations, and retrieving information.

Microcosm[3] is a hypermedia system designed by members of the Department of Electronics and Computer Science at Southampton University in the UK. Microcosm allows text, image, video and sound objects to be linked in an associative link structure that can be navigated by users in order to organize and find specific information. One of the most interesting features of this system, is that mark-ups in documents are held externally to the actual document data, meaning that the original information object remains media independent. The user is presented however, with the document contents plus intertextual markers. This in turn means that a number of users can set up their own links (markers) on the same physical document, without altering the contents of the document. The Microcosm model therefore provides both a solution to redundancy of information objects, and to the constraints placed on users when accessing read-only documents that contain internal link markers.

Point and Query[5] is an experimental exploratory system that adds a semantic definition to link markers in the form of questions displayed to the reader in a separate window to the main body of text. It allows a reader a limited form of conversing with the system. Therefore, when a reader is perusing a hypertext document and comes across a link, they can see what questions will be answered by selecting the link and then choose to follow or disregard it. This feature although

[a] Joyce refers to hypertext but the concepts extend to hypermedia.

interesting for manual navigation purposes is not useful for completely automated IR. *Conversational* systems[10] allow users to retrieve information by asking questions about the text as they read it. The hypertext author will have already attempted to foresee all relevant questions the reader may have during the authoring process.

WAIS (Wide Area Information Server) began as a joint project between four information technology oriented companies[b] but has now become a separate company (WAIS Inc.). It is an information retrieval system that has been building its database since the 1980s. WAIS also allows content providers to link remote databases to the system. WAIS Inc. is a company that specializes in electronic publishing services to companies that publish information. The WAIS server allows searching for the documents via web browsers such as Netscape and Mosaic, and also by other client applications such as Gopher. Once information is placed in the WAIS indexes it can be catalogued to provide some semantic depth to queries. WAIS also provides media independence via its indexing system.

HTML is the format used by web navigation software that allows the mark up of links[c] within blocks of text, or on images (e.g., maps, etc.). HTML provides authors of hypermedia documents with a powerful representational syntax that allows a great deal of flexibility in the way that information is displayed. Once a HTML document has been authored it can be linked via a URL (Uniform Resource Locator) to any other HTML document. However, link mark up of a document requires that the information to be marked is captured within the document, and that the link markers are placed in the body of the text around the appropriate words to be marked as links. Therefore, the integrity of the original information object(s) (e.g., a set of related documents) is destroyed, as both the HTML versions and the original objects need to be maintained. It is however, the most widely used hypermedia system in existence at this time, and holds much potential in areas such as education and information retrieval.

WordNet[7] is an example of an online dictionary/thesaurus system where the knowledge representation is organized within the structure of a semantic net. However, WordNet is more than a thesaurus because links between words have semantic relationships such as: synonym (similar meaning), antonym (opposite meaning), hyponym (subsumption), and meronym (which can be described as an ownership type of relation such as *a has-a*). WordNet is an excellent tool in that it can be used to permute queries (refer to Sec. 2.1), providing a range of synonyms for each relevant word in the query. Each of these systems embodies some of the aspects of an ideal hypermedia and information retrieval device. Microcosm's remote link mark-up of text provides users with the ability to set up hypermedia documents on remote knowledge objects, without damaging the integrity of the object. Conversational systems allow readers to ask questions related to objects as they interpret them based on conceptual dependencies that the author sees as important. WAIS allows remote databases of knowledge objects to be indexed categorically and searches for

[b]Thinking Machines Corporation, KPMG Peat Marwick, Apple Computer Inc., and Dow Jones and Company.

[c]Choose or define items within a page that may be marked as links to other items or pages.

information can be carried out on multiple levels. HTML provides authors with powerful representation tools, and is interlinked (via the internet) globally. WordNet utilizes a representation that contains deep semantic relationships (semantic links) between objects (although the objects in this case are only other words or simple combinations of words).

All hypermedia and IR systems rely however, on the syntactic content of the knowledge object in order to find it. As an example, with hypermedia documents (and with respect to knowledge representations), if a contender for a link mark up does not exist in the body of text (or perhaps a feature in an image) then a link cannot be made in that manner. The author must instead create a suitable link contender. In IR systems, if the keywords do not exist (even after query permutation), then the information will not be retrieved. Even by enumerating all possible synonyms within a query (or text) in order to provide keyword search matches, the search, although semantically much deeper, is still extremely limited because it is rigidly tied to the syntax of the query (or text).[10]

### 2.4. Semantic Nets

Semantic nets[11,18] are conceptual data structures that help to model the way knowledge is held in a representation, where objects (the nodes that represent knowledge concepts) are connected with relational links that describe the meaning of the association between them.[17,12] Minsky[8] developed the concept of frames to enhance the representational power of semantic nets. Frames provide defined structures that decrease the complexity of the net.[8,9,1] They allow the objects in the representation to have knowledge of a predefined stereotypical type, and therefore reduce or replace the number of links in the semantic net. This type of information hiding greatly reduces the complexity of the representation, and knowledge about the node is effectively hidden until it is required.

Schank introduced *conceptual dependencies*[13,14] to understand the meaning of natural language text. In these structures, stereotypical situations are represented as a script for a play, where there are slots in the frame for actors, props and scenes. All actions that actors can perform fall in one of 12 predefined categories. Conceptual dependencies define the relationship between entities that can be actors or props, and the primitive actions they perform.

## 3. CONCEPT OF UMART

### 3.1. Description

UMART (Unified Mental Annotation and Retrieval Tool) is a hybrid IR system that allows knowledge objects to be indexed via a semantic category scheme, and utilizes semantic relations to cluster related information together. Further, low level searches can be performed either directly on text media, or on information attached to other media objects (such as category, description, and keyword fields). The ultimate aim of UMART is to provide a system that will allow users to build conceptual maps of chunks of knowledge in such a way that each user is presented with a unique, tailored view of the knowledge, whilst each view maintains a formal internal structure of links between objects that can be manipulated in a computationally tractable way. By utilizing a deep semantic net as the internal skeletal structure of the map, computational reasoning can be achieved together with contextual dependency between objects. The representation allows for combining a domain of shared knowledge objects with personalized structures built by individual users.

UMART does not alter the atomic knowledge objects but is capable of retrieving, displaying, or executing the media types it handles by utilizing both proprietary and third party software. The objectives of UMART are:

1. To provide a canonical representation of knowledge objects. Knowledge objects include:
   (a) Text
   (b) Pictures
   (c) Picture sequences
   (d) Audio
   (e) Other multimedia
   (f) Agents
2. To allow the low-level canonical objects to be represented and linked at a higher level of abstraction in a deep semantic net to achieve useful knowledge representations.
3. To provide methods for building and querying these knowledge representations.
4. To provide agents that can interact between users' representations to perform functions such as information retrieval, removal of redundancy, and knowledge/data gathering.

UMART utilizes three types of frames to represent: low level knowledge objects, links, and high level concepts. Low level common concepts (LLCCs) are frames that are wrapped around atomic knowledge objects such as text, images, videos, etc. LLCCs also are capable of encapsulating URL addresses and executable files (refer to Sec. 3.2). The second type of frame is the high level personal concept (HLPC) that allows user concepts to be represented. They cannot contain atomic knowledge, but can be linked to each other and also to LLCCs (refer to Sec. 3.3). The links between HLPCs and LLCCs have defined semantic meanings, and they represent relationships between objects. The third type of frame is the link frame, that contains the type of link and the address of the nodes being linked (refer to Sec. 3.6).

One of UMART's fundamental aims is to provide tools and mechanisms for the sharing of knowledge between various users, whereby the LLCCs need never be duplicated, and the high level structures can be shared and augmented by other users. The conceptual maps built by individual users is a method of adding value to the information stored in LLCCs.

Due to natural limitations imposed by the fact that each user has the freedom to create arbitrary structures on top of LLCCs, we cannot assume that the structures will bear any similarity or will be able to be merged to create a single global map. Instead, we envisage tools for copying sections of other user's structures that can then be incorporated into one's own conceptual map. Any knowledge can be broadly divided into static concepts and active relations, where static concepts can be thought of as domain knowledge and relations represent properties of concepts that affect or are related to other concepts. What makes knowledge a higher level notion than information is the relationship between information objects — value added information. The user imposed structure is that added value.

In a multi-user scenario, all classical problems of data sharing, such as encountered in distributed databases for example, must be addressed. It must be stressed here that our aim is to share the individualized maps by providing means to access them, and not by merging them into a single structure. An individual user will have the option of maintaining different views, where a view is effectively a separate conceptual map created by a user, or merging them into one view.

### 3.2. Low Level Common Concepts

LLCCs allow information bearing objects to be represented in a generalized form. They are frames that encapsulate information about objects. LLCCs contain five fields: *Concept Name*, *Comment*, and *Time Stamp* fields are of type string; *Data File* must contain a reference to a file that exists, and *Media Type* must contain valid entries selected from an enumerated set. The data type can be one of:

1. Text Documents (e.g., word processor, ASCII format).
2. Images (e.g., GIFs, JPGs, RGBs, etc., formats).
3. Animated Sequences (e.g., MPG format, RGB sequences, etc.).
4. Postscript Formats (e.g., PS format).
5. Sound Files (e.g., WAV, AU, etc., formats).
6. Multimedia Documents (e.g., HTML format).
7. Agents, where an agent in this context can be considered to be a software or hardware device that acts in a deterministic manner to manipulate and/or retrieve data. Agents may interact with users and/or with other agents (e.g., user defined/provided software).

The *Data File* may be one of:

1. The path to the data. This includes paths across local networks, and data may be stored on different hardware platforms and operating systems.
2. URL Addresses. URL addresses can also be set in this field (in which case a web viewer containing the page will be presented to the viewer).
3. Agents. These can be any user defined processes and are executed as independent sibling processes to UMART. Control of any information returned is also user defined (this is easily controlled via scripts etc.).

LLCCs are created, edited and tested, via the UMART interface (refer to Sec. 4.1). Once the user has created an LLCC, it is stored as a node in a graph (refer to Fig. 1).

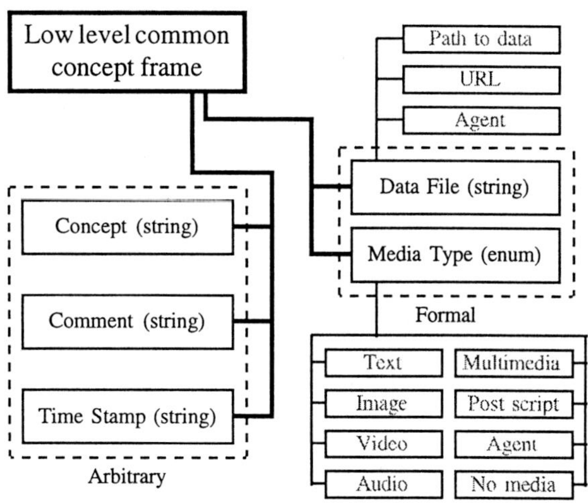


Fig. 1. Schematic of LLCC frame.

### 3.3. High Level Personalized Concepts

Users can define high level concepts at different levels of abstraction, enabling them to structure information object collections. Whilst at the lowest level, atomic information objects are represented as LLCCs (refer to Sec. 3.2), grouping of LLCCs into a higher level of abstraction allows the formation of HLPCs. These high level concepts can be used to link other HLPCs in still higher levels of abstraction. Each HLPC frame is provided with a broad category label, and a more specific sub-category label (relevant to the respective category), so as to enable retrieval of information based on the semantic grouping. The category list is outlined below:

1. Animate – Human, Animal, Plant, Geological, Manufactured.
2. Inanimate – Natural, Manufactured, Fictional.
3. Action.
4. Natural Process – Nuclear, Chemical, Evolutionary, Geological, Living.
5. Location – Global, Continental, Country, State, Locality, Extra terrestrial, Map.
6. Abstract Notion – Thought, Hypothesis, Theory, Concept, Paradigm.

The information about each category is maintained in a category table (Table 1) that contains a list of all nodes belonging to that category. In addition to the category grouping, HLPC frames contain fields that allow the concept name, a comment or brief description field, an origin (the conceptual origin of the information object), and an era (the time frame of the concept) to be defined. These fields may in turn be used to define temporal relationships such as order and equivalence (refer to

Secs. 3.4 and 3.5), and are referred to as the HLPC's set of properties. The HLPC also contains a list of related LLCCs and HLPCs that are user defined. The HLPC frame schematic is detailed in Fig. 2.

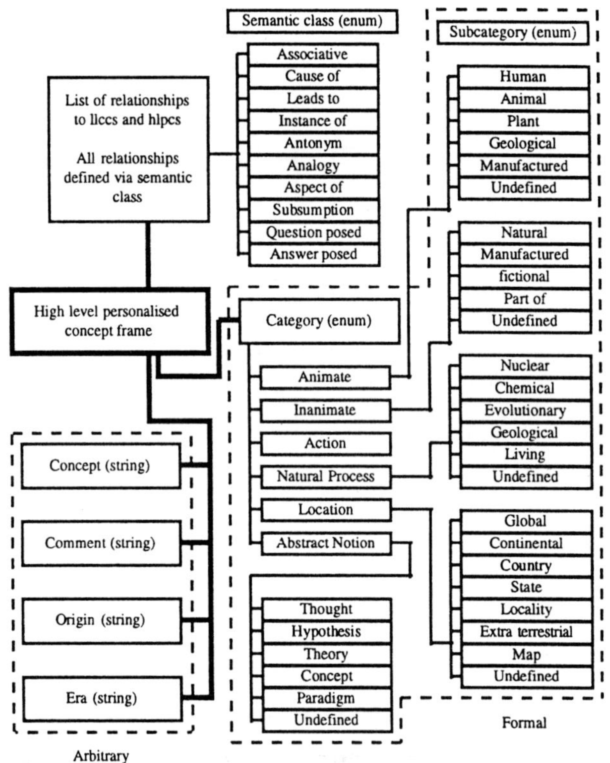


Fig. 2. Schematic of HLPC frame.

More formally, let **P** be the set of properties, **C** the set of categories, **S** the set of subcategories, **H** the set of HLPCs, **L** the set of LLCCs, **Rel** the set of relations, and $\mathbf{N} \subseteq (\mathbf{H} \cup \mathbf{L})$.

A HLPC ($h \in \mathbf{H}$) is defined as the following list:

$$[p_1, p_2, p_3, p_4, Cat, Subcat, Links]$$
where $p_i \in \mathbf{P}$
$Cat \in \mathbf{C}$
$Subcat \in \mathbf{S}$,

and,

$$Links \text{ is a list of connections: } ((r_1, n_1), (r_2, n_2), \cdots, (r_k, n_k)),$$
$$\text{where } r_i \in \mathbf{Rel} \text{ and } n_i \in (\mathbf{N} - h) \quad . \qquad (1)$$

The corresponding conceptual map $CM$ consisting of elements of the set $\mathbf{N}$, can now be defined as a graph:

$$CM = (A, B, \theta) \quad \text{where } A \subseteq \mathbf{N}, \text{ and } B \subseteq \mathbf{Rel} \ , \tag{2}$$

and $\theta$ is defined as a set of triples:

$$\theta = (n_i, r_i, n_j) \quad \text{where } n_i, n_j \in A, \text{ and } r_i \in B \ . \tag{3}$$

Table 1. Category table.

| Category type | Node list |
|---|---|
| $C_1$ | $n_1, n_2, \cdots, n_k$ |
| $C_2$ | $n_1, n_2, \cdots, n_k$ |
| $C_3$ | $n_1, n_2, \cdots, n_k$ |
| . | |
| . | |
| $C_k$ | $n_1, n_2, \cdots, n_k$ |

### 3.4. Concept Similarity

One of the most fundamental relationships between concepts is that of similarity. Whether we choose to delve into the complexities of analogy, such as encountered in story telling, or just consider simple, shared characteristics of objects (such as color and shape), similarity must be part of any conceptual representation.

Nodes that are related via a shared property or shared relationship with a specific node, can be thought of as belonging to the same equivalence class. For example, all synonyms of a given concept are an equivalence class, and all causes of an event also form an equivalence class. A given concept may have many characteristics, and it may also be "similar" to other concepts on the basis of different characteristics. Therefore, the representation must allow similarity to be defined between concepts.

Equivalence (or similarity) is another type of relation. However, we introduce a distinction between equivalence and order to facilitate a more efficient access for the user. Whereas order is represented as links, equivalence would require $n!$ links for a class of size $n$, and hence members of an equivalence class are not explicitly connected.

A similarity that is established between two or more concepts is represented as a similarity node, where a list of all similar LLCCs and HLPCs is maintained. A table of all similarity nodes established by a user is also maintained (Table 2). The operations allowed on equivalence classes are as follows:

> **Members (label):** Given the label of an equivalence, list all concepts that are members of this class.

**Equivalence classes (concept):** Given a concept (LLCC or HLPC), return all equivalence classes that it belongs to.

**Attributes (label):** List the characteristic function of the equivalence class.

The characteristic function requires a textual annotation as to what is its intended purpose and what are its properties. A concept may belong to an unlimited number of equivalence classes, and an equivalence class may have an arbitrary number of names. A similarity is a special type of concept defined as follows:

$$label \in L$$
$$membership\_test \in Functions$$

where $L$ is a set of labels (character strings chosen by a user) and *Functions* is a set of boolean functions that take one argument (an LLCC or HLPC concept) and return true or false depending on whether the given concept satisfies the similarity criteria.

Table 2. Similarity table.

| Similarity rule | Node list |
|---|---|
| $S_1$ | $n_1, n_2, \ldots, n_k$ |
| $S_2$ | $n_1, n_2, \ldots, n_k$ |
| $S_3$ | $n_1, n_2, \ldots, n_k$ |
| . | |
| . | |
| $S_k$ | $n_1, n_2, \ldots, n_k$ |

## 3.5. Order On Concepts

Some of the built in relationships, such as analogy, subsumption and antonym, (refer to Sec. 3.6) can be viewed as standard equivalence classes or partial orders. The purpose of predefined relations is to allow (potentially novice) users to easily and quickly build representations. Depending on the number of concepts to be related to each other and on the intended use of attributes of relationships, the user may take advantage of benefits specific to either the equivalence classes or order. For example, a set of causes of some event may be modeled as an equivalence class, if each cause offers a potential alternative. However, if all of the "causes" co-exist and they may in turn be "caused" by something else, then an order may be more suitable as a representation.

At no time is the user limited to the built-in relations. The user may add and redefine their own set of relations and equivalence classes.

Whereas similarity allows users to demarcate conceptual groups, concepts may also be ordered according to some comparative function. For example, temporal precedence can be modeled as a linear order. Any property $p$ can be used to impose an order relation on a set of elements. We restrict the set of elements to define to $\{<,=\}$. Imposing order using a property $P$ defines a subgraph $S$ of the following form:

$$\begin{aligned} &\text{Let } S_o = \mathbf{Rel} \cup \{<,=\} \\ &S = (x, y, z) \qquad \text{where } x \in \mathbf{N}, y \in S_o \ , \\ &\text{and } z \text{ is a triple } (n_i, r_i, n_j) \qquad \text{where } n_i, n_j \in \mathbf{N}, \text{ and } r_i \in S_o \ . \end{aligned} \tag{4}$$

For example, based on $P$ = time, two nodes can be ordered as being $\{<,=\}$ in terms of $P$. This assumes that the same frame of reference for determining $P$ is maintained for the entire structure for a user. Therefore, a list of properties and their meaning is maintained for each user (Table 3).

Table 3. Order table.

| Order property | Node list |
|---|---|
| $P_1$ | $n_1, n_2, \ldots, n_k$ |
| $P_2$ | $n_1, n_2, \ldots, n_k$ |
| $P_3$ | $n_1, n_2, \ldots, n_k$ |
| . | |
| . | |
| $P_k$ | $n_1, n_2, \ldots, n_k$ |

Some concepts cannot easily be tested for *less than* and *equality*. Each of these tests may require a specific function to be associated with the definition of the order. This function would accept two arguments and return an approximate result to indicate equal, less than, greater than, or incomparable as possible outcomes.

The function, as well as the order represented by the function, can have various properties such as transitivity, reflexivity, symmetry, etc.

### 3.6. Built-in Relationships

To provide a means of grouping and classifying concepts, UMART has 10 built-in semantic relationships that define links between nodes: {Associative, Subsumption, Instance of, Analogy, Antonym, Aspect of, Cause of, Leads to, Question posed, Answer offered}. A relation between two nodes is defined as $mRn$ where $m \in \mathbf{H}$, $R \in \mathbf{Rel}$, and $n \in \mathbf{N}$, then relationships between $m$ and $n$ are interpreted thus:

1. Subsumption – Represents a strict subset relation between concepts.
2. Instance of – To define a specific element of a set, or instance of an object.
3. Analogy – To indicate similarity and interchangeability between concepts.
4. Antonym – To indicate an opposite concept.
5. Aspect of – To define properties of a concept.
6. Cause of – To define relations of cause and effect.
7. Leads to – To define a dependency on the presence of pre-conditions without implying the cause and effect relationship.

8. Question posed – A chunk of knowledge raises an issue but does not indicate the complete fact (e.g., "Mark taught at a local school" poses the question "What did Mark teach?").
9. Question answered – A matching answer that solves "Question posed".
10. Associative – Default relation for cases of similarity other than the above definitions.

### 3.7. Using the Representation

Associative relationships between two nodes are symmetrical, transitive and reflexive in nature and are provided as a default link type when a user links two concepts without specifying the relation. They are analogous to the type of link provided in most hypermedia systems. In a brute force information retrieval query, all associative nodes can be reached and any connected information can be returned to the user.

When navigating a knowledge representation in UMART, any link can be treated as an associative link, where the user can move around in a representation by means of selecting a link from a displayed list of links with a pointing device.

As stated in Sec. 3.3, HLPCs can be grouped via general semantic classes by means of categories and related sub-categories. This provides a means for keyword querying, and provides one method for grouping information objects. Other fields defined in HLPCs (and to a lesser extent LLCCs), in addition to providing a means of querying a representation by using keywords, also allow order relations to be imposed. Semantic relations between knowledge objects provide a means of querying the representation in ways not available when only associative and category properties are utilized. The following structures are used to provide group and order characteristics:

CT – category table (refer to Table 1), contains an ordered list of tuples, where each tuple has the following structure:

$$\{Category_{id}, (n_1, n_2, \cdots, n_{jk})\} \; . \tag{5}$$

OT – order table (refer to Table 3), contains an ordered list of tuples, where each tuple has the following structure:

$$\{Order_{id}, ((n_{11}, n_{12}), (n_{21}, n_{22}), \cdots, (n_{km}, n_{km+1}))\} \tag{6}$$

where each $(n_{ij}, n_{ik})$ represents two nodes related by $Order_{id}$.

There are several fundamental aspects to creating and using the representation. These aspects are discussed below. In the algorithms the following symbols are used:

"+" – add an element to a set.

"−" – remove an element from a set.

$\downarrow$ – project an element from a tuple.

$\oplus_j$ – e.g., $A \oplus_j (b_1, b_2, \cdots, b_n)$: get the $j$th element of $A$ and replace by $(b_1, b_2, \cdots, b_n)$.

1. Define a new HLPC ($h$)
   To define a new concept, we must allow the user to create the structure defined by (1) and update the category table ($CT$) incrementally as new HLPCs are created:

   $New(h_i)$ /* Create new HLPC */
   $\mathbf{H}' = \mathbf{H} \cup \{h_i\}$ /* Update HLPC set */
   $(n_1, n_2, \cdots, n_k) = CT \downarrow c_j$ /* Project $j$th element of $CT$ */
   $CT' = CT \oplus_j (n_1, n_2, \cdots, n_k, h_i)$ /* Update CT */

2. Modify components of a HLPC ($h_i$)
   Modification to a HLPC can be performed by either a change to its property fields, or a change to its list of connections. The function projects out a property indicated by $p_{id}$ of $h_i$ and replaces its value with *new-val*. Thus:

   $$h_i' = h_i \ \oplus_{p_{id}} \ new\text{-}val \ . \tag{7}$$

3. Define a new similarity
   Similarity lists are defined by the user and are based on some property $P$ that makes them similar. They are stored in a similarity table (refer to Table 2). A similarity list $S$ is defined as:

   $$S = ((s_p, n_1), (s_p, n_2), \cdots, (s_p, n_k)) \tag{8}$$

   where $s_p$ is a property a similarity is based on, and $n_i \in \mathbf{N}$.
4. Query based on similarity
   This is done by a table look-up performed on the similarity table (Table 2).
5. Define a new order
   Order is imposed between two nodes $n_i$ and $n_j$ using $\{<, =\}$ by associating property $P$ with $\{<\}$ for total orders, and $\{<, =\}$ for partial orders. Defining an order requires:

   (a) Given $OT$, and $new(order_i)$ ,
   (b) $OT' = OT \cup \{Order_i, ((n_{11}, n_{12}), (n_{21}, n_{22}), \ldots, (n_{km}, n_{km+1}))\}$
   where $((n_{11}, n_{12}), (n_{21}, n_{22}), \cdots, (n_{km}, n_{km+1}))$ is the list of paths between nodes related by the new order.

6. Query on conceptual map
   Given a HLPC $n_i$, and an ordered list of links, find a path in the conceptual map (originating from $n_i$), such that labels of the links in the path match the given list of links, i.e., given a query $Q$ where $Q = (ql_1, ql_2, \cdots, ql_j)$, and $ql_i$ is a link that connects two nodes.

Let the current node be $n_c$.

$n_c = n_i$.

$result = []$.

Repeat

Current link $(ql_i) = head(Q)$.

$L = \text{retrieve\_list}(n_c)$ /* $L = ((l_1, n_1), (l_2, n_2), \cdots (l_k, n_k))$ */

If $(\{(l_j, n_j) \in L \mid (l_j = ql_i) \wedge (n_j = qn_i)\} \neq 0)$

$n_c = qn_i$.

$result = result + [qn_i]$.

$Q = Q - (ql_i)$.

Else

$Q = NULL$.

Until $Q$ = NULL.

$return(result)$.

This facilitates a direct match for a path, and returns a list of nodes connected by the path.

## 4. IMPLEMENTATION AND PRELIMINARY RESULTS

### 4.1. UMART Interface

The UMART interface (refer to Fig. 3) allows users to build conceptual maps by creating LLCCs and HLPCs to represent desired data. Fragments of the conceptual map can be created or loaded into the interface, where they can be edited, and connected with each other via a set of provided semantic relations. The current UMART implementation runs on the Silicon Graphics platform under X-windows.

The user is presented with a set of lists: a list of LLCCs, a list of HLPCs, and the list of a set of nodes that are connected to the currently selected HLPC in the HLPC list. To edit properties of any list node or linked node, they must be: (1) loaded into the interface, and (2) selected. Newly created HLPCs have no defined category or subcategory and the user can set these properties via the pull-down menus *Category* and *Sub Category*.

Manual navigation of a conceptual map is achieved by selecting HLPCs in either the HLPC list or the current links list. A navigation screen is then activated, and further navigation is facilitated by selecting objects in this screen. The pathway through the map can then be navigated by selecting new nodes, or linear go-forward and go-back functions can be applied. When an LLCC is selected the user is presented with the properties of the node, and may activate the low level concept if desired. LLCCs are always leaf nodes in the representation as they cannot contain links to other nodes. Multiple LLCC nodes can be displayed simultaneously.

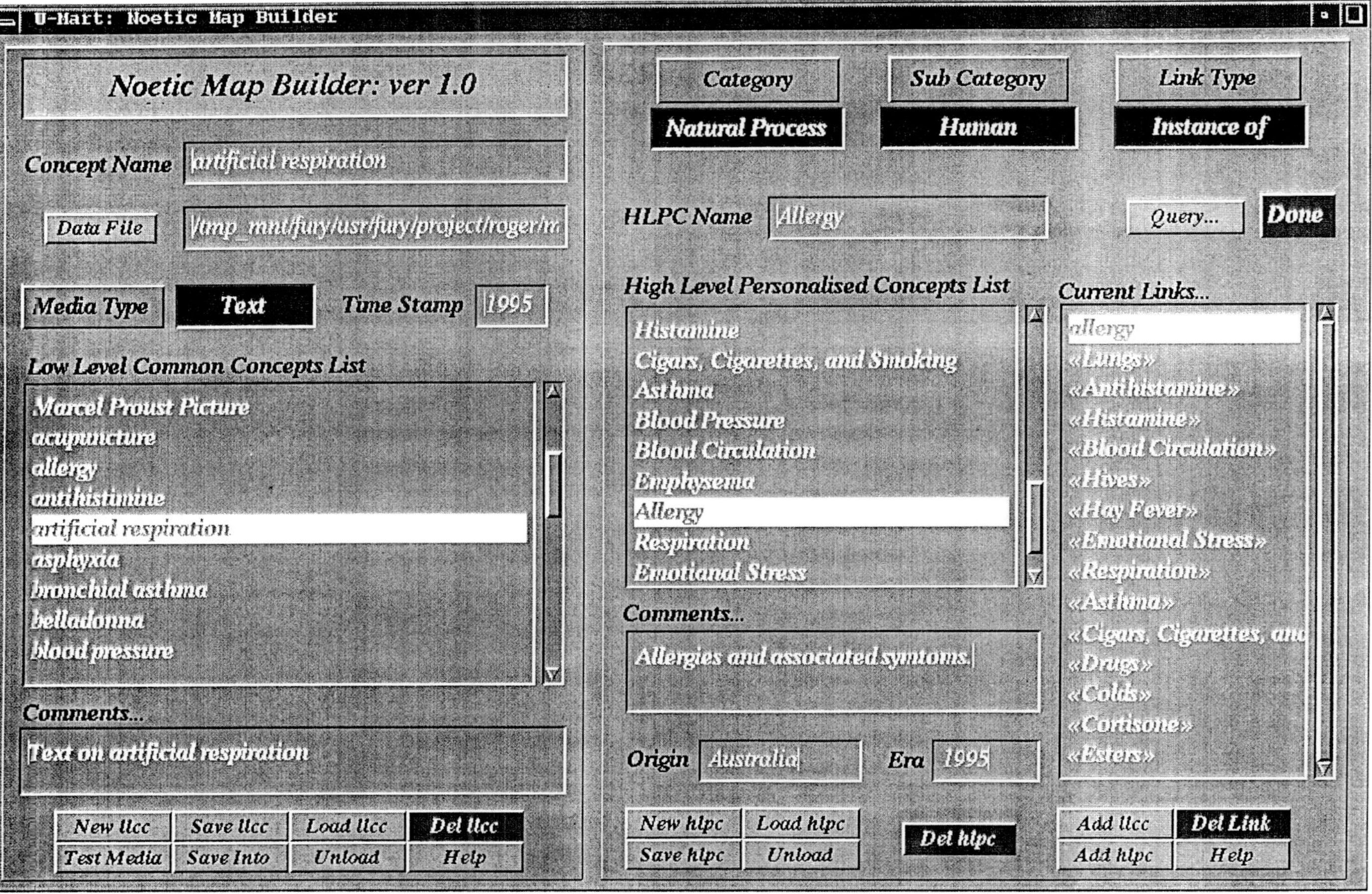


Fig. 3. UMART interface.

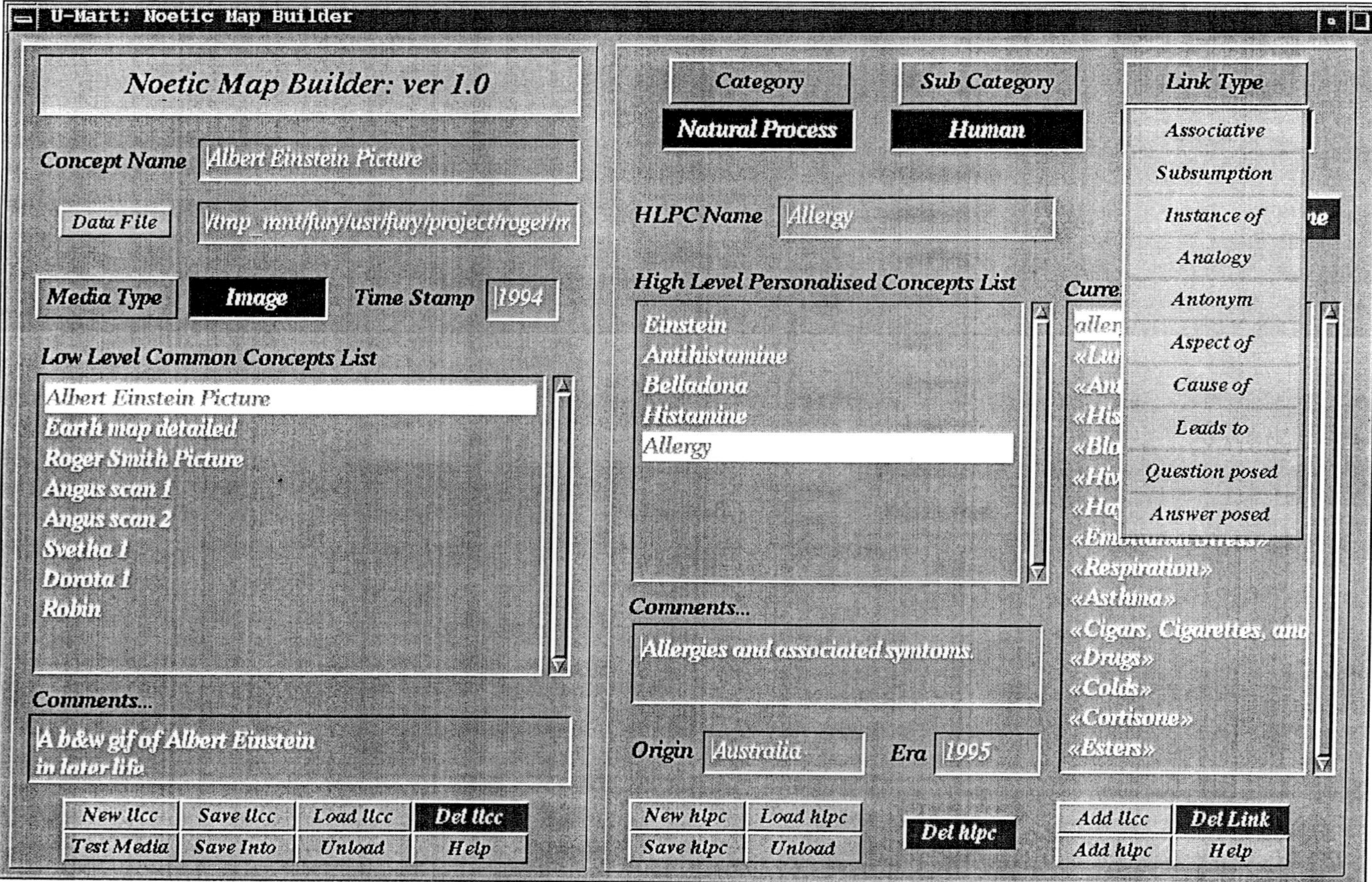


Fig. 4. Selection of semantic relation via pull-down menu.

To connect LLCCs to a currently selected HLPC, the user first loads, creates or selects an LLCC from the LLCC list, then selects the *Add llcc* button. The HLPC's list of connected nodes is then updated to include the new node. To add a HLPC as a connected node to another HLPC's list of connected nodes, the parent HLPC is first selected, then selecting the *Add hlpc* button presents to the user a list of all other HLPCs currently loaded into the interface. The desired HLPC is then selected, and the parent HLPC's connection list is updated. Other functions that the interface provides include deleting nodes and links from a conceptual map, and querying the map. By default, nodes are connected by an associative relation, but the user may change the relation by highlighting the connected node and selecting a new semantic relation from the *Link Type* menu (refer to Fig. 4).

### 4.2. Example — Asthma Information System

#### 4.2.1. Data gathering

Knowledge objects related to the topic of asthma were gathered from various sources. Thirty-six objects were gathered, and knowledge representations were then built using both HTML and UMART. This resulted in thirty-seven HTML pages (including an index of related information). The corresponding UMART conceptual map nodes totaled sixty-eight (thirty-one of these were HLPCs and the other thirty-seven were LLCCs). The HLPC and LLCC representations that made up the conceptual map are shown in Figs. 5 and 6. The aims of the comparison were to gauge how hard a conceptual map was to build (of a specific domain of knowledge) utilizing the two types of representations, and to test the effectiveness of queries using the semantic knowledge represented in the relations between information objects.

#### 4.2.2. Building representations

The HTML documents were set up using a text editor to create each page. In the case of text media objects, the files were imported into their respective pages, then re-formatted into HTML syntax to provide links to other pages. Non-text media was imported into the representation by setting up separate pages that encapsulated the picture via HTML's "IMG SRC" link, so that the HTML pages containing such links could be referenced as other pages in the representation. This provided a structure analogous to an LLCC frame.

Wherever possible, existing text was used as mark-up points for links to other pages. If the mark-up word appeared multiple times in the text, then it was used to highlight a link to the relevant page each time it appeared. An index page of all HTMLs was created and each page was provided with a link to that page. Extra links were added to pages where the original content of the imported text was lacking, to provide links with relationships other than associative. This was analogous to (or at least partly resembled) HPLC nodes. Pages that clustered information objects (i.e., groups of objects not able to be clustered by using the content of the imported text) could have been set up also, but this was not implemented due to the amount of time needed to create them.

| | High level personal concept (HLPC) | | Links to other HLPCs and LLCCs |
|---|---|---|---|
| 1 | Acupuncture | (Action) | Ant(18) C(23,24) I(59) |
| 2 | Artificial respiration | (Action) | L(3,25,28) A(11) C(23) I(32) |
| 3 | Asphyxia | (Action) | L(2) A(11) C(23,26) Ant(28) I(33) |
| 4 | Fight or flight | (Action) | A(17) L(19,24,29) I(34) |
| 5 | Medicinces & cures for asthma | (Action) | Ant(6) I(1,2,14,15,16,17,18,20) |
| 6 | Causes of asthma | (Action) | Ant(5) C(21,22,27,29,30,31) |
| 7 | Colds | (Animate) | L(14) C(23,27,31) I(37) |
| 8 | Diaphragm | (Animate) | A(11) I(38) |
| 9 | Theodore Roosevelt | (Animate) | Ana(13) As(23) I(36,39) |
| 10 | Marcel Proust | (Animate) | Ana(13) As(23) I(40,68) |
| 11 | Lungs | (Animate) | S(8) A(22,23,28) I(41,43) As(64) |
| 12 | Greg Louganis | (Animate) | Ana(13) As(23) I(42,53) |
| 13 | Famous asthmatics | (Animate) | Ana(9,10,12) |
| 14 | Anithistamine | (Inanimate) | C(7,27,31) Ant(21) I(44) |
| 15 | Belladonna | (Inanimate) | A(5) I(55) |
| 16 | Caffeine | (Inanimate) | A(5,11,24) I(46) |
| 17 | Cortisone | (Inanimate) | A(5,24) I(47) |
| 18 | Drugs | (Inanimate) | Ant(1) A(23,25,27,28) I(48) |
| 19 | Epinephrine | (Inanimate) | C(4,24,29) A(11,23,25) I(49) |
| 20 | Esters | (Inanimate) | A(5,24) I(50) |
| 21 | Histamine | (Inanimate) | Ant(14) L(23,27) I(51) |
| 22 | Smoking | (Inanimate) | L(3,23,24,26,27) A(6,11,28) C(29) I(52) |
| 23 | Asthma | (Natural process) | L(5) C(6) A(11,13,28) S(60,63) |
| 24 | Blood pressure | (Natural process) | C(4,22,29) A(11,27,28) C(22,29) As(25,35) I(54) |
| 25 | Blood circulation | (Natural process) | A(11,28) S(35,55) C(24) |
| 26 | Emphysema | (Natural process) | L(3) A11,28) I(56) C(22,23) |
| 27 | Allergy | (Natural process) | L(7,18) A(11,17,20,25,28) I(14,30,31,32) C(21,22,23,29) |
| 28 | Respiration | (Natural process) | S(2,65) Ant(3,8) As(11) A(25) I(58,63) |
| 29 | Stress | (Natural process) | C(4) L(18,22,23,24,27,30) A(28) I(66) |
| 30 | Hives | (Natural process) | L(14,23) C(21,29) A(27) I(67) |
| 31 | Hay fever | (Natural process) | L(14) C(21) A(23,27,30) I(61) |

| Link Legend | |
|---|---|
| A | (Associative) |
| C | (Cause of) |
| L | (Leads to) |
| I | (Instance of) |
| Ant | (Antonym) |
| Ana | (Analogy) |
| As | (Aspect of) |
| S | (Subsumption) |

Fig. 5. Table view of asthma conceptual map showing HLPCs.

As described in Sec. 4.1, the UMART interface allows users to build conceptual maps using a GUI. There was also no need to modify existing information objects in order to place them in a representation. An LLCC was created for each object,

| Low level common concept (LLCC) | | |
|---|---|---|
| 32 | Artificial respiration | (t) |
| 33 | Asphyxia | (t) |
| 34 | Fight or flight | (m) |
| 35 | Human circulatory | (v) |
| 36 | Theodore Roosevelt | (i) |
| 37 | Colds | (t) |
| 38 | Diaphragm | (t) |
| 39 | Theodore Roosevelt | (t) |
| 40 | Marcel Proust | (t) |
| 41 | Lungs | (t) |
| 42 | Greg Louganis | (t) |
| 43 | Human lungs | (i) |
| 44 | Anithistamine | (t) |
| 55 | Belladonna | (t) |
| 46 | Caffeine | (t) |
| 47 | Cortisone | (t) |
| 48 | Drugs | (t) |
| 49 | Epinephrine | (t) |
| 50 | Esters | (t) |
| 51 | Histamine | (t) |
| 52 | Smoking | (t) |
| 53 | Greg Louganis | (i) |
| 54 | Blood pressure | (t) |
| 55 | Blood circulation | (t) |
| 56 | Emphysema | (t) |
| 57 | Allergy | (t) |
| 58 | Human respiration | (v) |
| 59 | Acupuncture | (t) |
| 60 | Bronchial asthma | (t) |
| 61 | Hay fever | (t) |
| 63 | Human respiration | (t) |
| 63 | Asthma | (m) |
| 64 | Alveoli | (i) |
| 65 | Respiration lower life | (m) |
| 66 | Stress | (t) |
| 67 | Hives | (t) |
| 68 | Marcel Proust | (i) |

| Legend: Media type | |
|---|---|
| (t) | Text |
| (i) | Image |
| (m) | HTML |
| (v) | Video |

Fig. 6. Table view of asthma LLCC nodes.

and each LLCC's property list was set with the relevant information. To set up the HLPCs, general concepts were created first such as: "Asthma", "Symptoms of asthma", "Treatment of asthma", "Causes of asthma", etc., then other HLPCs were created and linked to each other as desired. The property lists of HLPCs were filled as they were created. Links were added both at the time of creation, and after considering the form of a given concept. In all, 171 semantically defined links were used to build the conceptual map. HLPCs were also created to add value to the representation by constructing concepts that could be defined only after clustering several LLCCs and HLPCs to provide enough "weight" for the new concept.

For example, the concept of "Treatment of asthma" was not defined by any particular low level concept. Rather, this concept was created because there was a sufficient number of low level concepts detailing specific instances or aspects of treatment that allowed a meta-concept about asthma treatment to be created. As stated above, this also could have been simulated using HTML, but it would have been too time consuming.

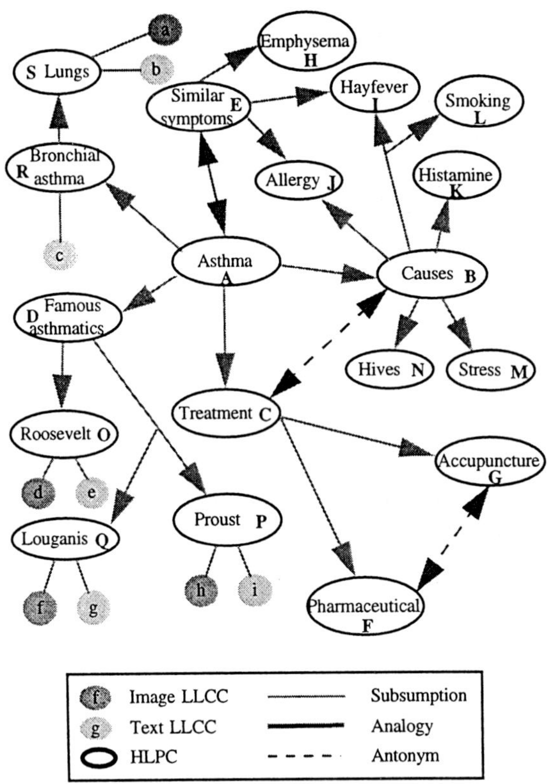


Fig. 7. Fragment of asthma conceptual map.

## 4.3. Queries Using Semantic Relationships

To demonstrate the types of queries that can be performed via the UMART's structures, it is necessary to take note of the fragment of the conceptual map shown in Fig. 7. The basic querying function *find* is defined thus:

**find**$(media\_type, start\_node, relation, depth)$, where:
$media\_type$ is a property of $l$, and $l \in \mathbf{L}$
$start\_node \in \mathbf{H}$
$relation \in \mathbf{Rel}$, and
$depth$ is the maximum length of any path from $start\_node$.

Specifying *media_type* allows specific types of LLCCs to be targeted. The field allows any node (or set of nodes) to be returned when no specific media type is specified. *Start_node* specifies the node in the graph to begin searching from. If no node is specified, *start_node* defaults to the current node. The *relation* field allows the user to specify the type of edges to follow. Relations have different properties such as transitivity and symmetry, and these dictate the type of search strategy applied. For example, subsumption relationships are transitive (i.e., $aTb \wedge bTc \rightarrow aTc$) and this allows nodes to be "chained together" in a search for subsumed nodes. Antonyms are not transitive, but are symmetrical (i.e., $aAb \iff bAa$), meaning that only pairs of nodes connected via an antonym relation can be returned with total accuracy (there may, however, be instances of the antonym relation that are transitive). Analogies arc both transitive and symmetrical, so transitivity provides the basis for the search strategy (in that chains of nodes can be searched), and symmetry allows any nodes found to be grouped as a similar set (not just pairs). The *depth* field constrains the search by not traveling more than the specified number of edges from the start node along any particular path.

A sample of queries that can be performed on the conceptual map fragment (refer to Fig. 7) are discussed below:

1. **find**(*, A, subsumption, 2) $\Rightarrow B(I, J, K, L, M, N), C(F, G), D(O, P, Q), R(S, c)$.
   Interpretation: Find all nodes that are connected to the node $A$ by a subsumption relation. Travel no more than 2 nodes from $A$. The query returns parent nodes and their children that are linked by subsumption relations.
2. **find**(*, *, antonym, *) $\Rightarrow (B, C), (F, G)$.
   Interpretation: Find all pairs of nodes that are connected via the antonym relation.
3. **find**(text, A, subsumption, 3) $\Rightarrow (b, c, e, g, i)$.
   Interpretation: Find all LLCCs with a text property, that are subsumed under $A$, to a depth of three nodes from $A$.
4. **find**(*, A, analogy, *) $\Rightarrow (E)$.
   Interpretation: Find all nodes that are analogies of $A$, to any number of nodes in a path. This query will follow paths of nodes related by analogies until a link that is not an analogy is found.
5. **find**(*, F, antonym, u/d) $\Rightarrow (G)$.
   Interpretation: Find nodes that are marked as "opposite" to $F$. This cannot be transitive and therefore the search is limited to a depth of one node.

## 5. CONCLUSION

In this work, we have introduced the UMART, and defined its associated structures. The types of queries that are possible using these structures have also been defined. We have outlined related work that UMART builds on, and a discussion of how UMART's representations, and the methods for building and querying representations, differ from other hypermedia systems (in particular HTML documents) has been presented.

One of UMART's fundamental aims is to provide tools and mechanisms for the sharing of knowledge between various users, whereby the LLCCs need never be duplicated, and the high level structures can be shared and augmented by other users. The conceptual maps built by individual users will be a method of adding value to the information stored in LLCCs. Information becomes *value added* because every user's conceptual map that is related to a non-redundant information object will be slightly different.

Due to natural limitations imposed by the fact that each user has the freedom to create arbitrary structures on top of LLCCs, we cannot assume that the structures will bear any similarity or will be able to be merged to create a single global map. Instead, we envisage tools for copying sections of other user's structures that can then be incorporated into one's own conceptual map. Any knowledge can be broadly divided into static concepts, and active relations, where static concepts can be thought of as domain knowledge and relations represent properties of concepts that affect or are related to other concepts. What makes knowledge a higher-level notion than information is the relationship between information objects — value-added information. The user imposed structure is that added value.

Work thus far has provided the means of creating structures (conceptual maps) that are allowing us to test ideas about information retrieval, by building useful representations that can be analyzed and operated on. It is hoped that the UMART project will contribute towards finding solutions that will be required as the demand for improved data management increases.

## REFERENCES

1. T. J. M. Bench-Capon, *Knowledge Representation: An Approach to Artificial Intelligence*, Academic Press, London, 1990.
2. T. Doszkocs, "A large semantic network for associative searching", in *5th Int. Conf. on New Information Technology*, ed., C. C. Chen, 1992.
3. A. Fountain, W. Hall, I. Heath and H. Davis, "Microcosm: An open model with dynamic linking", in *Hypertext: Concepts, Systems and Applications, Proc. of the European Conf. on Hypertext*, eds., A. Rizk, N. Strietz, and J. Andre, INRIA, France, Nov. 1990, pp. 298–311.
4. M. Joyce, "Siren shapes: Exploratory and constructive hypertexts", in *Academic Computing*, 1988, pp. 10–14, pp. 37–42.
5. C. L. Langston and A. C. Graesser, "Question asking during learning with a point and query interface", in *Proc. of the Fourteenth Annual Conf. of the Cognitive Science Society*, July–August, 1992, pp. 921–926.
6. D. B. Lenat and R. V. Guha, "Strongly semantic information retrieval", in *AAAI-94 Workshop Program — Indexing and Reuse in Multimedia Systems, Twelfth National Conf. on Artificial Intelligence*, eds., C. Baudin, M. Davis, S. Kedar, and D. M. Russell, Seattle, Washington, 1994, pp. 58–68.
7. G. A. Miller, R. Beckwith, C. Fellbaum, D. Gross and K. Miller, "Five papers on WordNet (TM)", in *Int. J. of Lexicography* **3**, 4 (1993).
8. M. Minsky, "A framework for representing knowledge", *The Psychology of Computer Vision*, ed., P. H. Winston, McGraw-Hill, New York, 1975, pp. 211–277.
9. M. Minsky, *The Society Of Mind*, Simon and Schuster, New York, 1988.
10. R. E. Osgood, *The Conceptual Indexing Of Conversational Hypertext*, Northwestern University Technical Report #52, Evanston, Illinois, 1994.
11. M. R. Quillian, "Semantic memory", in *Semantic Information Processing*, ed., Marvin Minsky, MIT Press, Cambridge, 1968, pp. 216–270.

12. D. Mac Randal, "Semantic networks", in *Approaches To Knowledge Representation*, eds., G. A. Ringland and D. A. Bruce, Research Studies Press Ltd., Somerset, 1989, pp. 45–79.
13. R. C. Schank, *Conceptual Dependency, A Theory for Natural Language Understanding*, Cognitive Psychology 3, 1972.
14. R. C. Schank and R. C. Rieobeck, *Inside Computer Understanding: Five Programs Plus Minialire*, Lawrence Erlbaum & Associates, 1981.
15. R. W. Smith, "Representing and manipulating user-specific knowledge in a semantic net, to aid in the treatment of Aphasia victims", Honours Thesis, Curtin University Of Technology, 1994.
16. L. Snyder, "Reconceptualizing literacy and hypertext", *English In Australia*, April 1995, pp. 27–34.
17. P. H. Winston, "Language understanding", in *Artificial Intelligence*, Addison-Wesley Publishing Company, Massachusetts, 1984, pp. 291–334.
18. P. H. Winston, "Learning structural descriptions from examples", in *The Psychology of Computer Vision*, ed., P. H. Winston, McGraw-Hill, New York, 1975, pp. 157–209.

---

**Roger W. Smith** is a Computer Science Masters student currently studying under the supervision of Prof. Svetha Venkatesh and Dr. Dorota Kieronska at Curtin University of Technology (Perth, Western Australia).

His research is in the area of knowledge representation in a multimedia environment

*Photograph of R. W. Smith is not available.*

**Dorota Kieronska** obtained her B.Sc. and Ph.D. in computer science from University of Western Australia in 1986 and 1990, respectively. She is a senior lecturer in the Department of Computer Science at Curtin University of Technology.

Her research interests include knowledge indexing and representation for multimedia, spatial reasoning and parallel algorithms.

*Photograph of D. Kieronska is not available.*

**Svetha Venkatesh** holds a Bachelor of Engineering from Roorkee University and a Masters of Technology degree from the Indian Institute of Technology in India. She received her Ph.D. from the University of Western Australia in Perth.

She is currently an associate professor at the School of Computing in Curtin University, Perth. She has worked in the areas of active vision, object recognition systems, biological based vision systems, and is currently working on the application of computer vision to image and video database indexing and retrieval.

She is the co-director of the MARVIN group at Curtin University. She is a Senior Member of the IEEE, and was the President of the Australia Pattern Recognition Society in 1991. She is the author of about 80 papers, and is the co-author of the book *From Living Eyes to Seeing Machines* to be published in 1996.

*Photograph of S. Venkatesh is not available.*